IMAGINE
NATION

IMAGINE NATION

The American Counterculture of the 1960s and '70s

Edited by
Peter Braunstein and
Michael William Doyle

ROUTLEDGE   NEW YORK • LONDON
2002

Published in 2002 by
Routledge
711 Third Avenue,
New York, NY 10017

Published in Great Britain by
Routledge
2 Park Square, Milton Park,
Abingdon, Oxon, OX14 4RN

Routledge is an imprint of the Taylor & Francis Group.

Transferred to Digital Printing 2009

Library of Congress Cataloging-in-Publishing Data

Imagine nation : the American counterculture of the 1960s and '70s / edited by Peter
Braunstein & Michael William Doyle.
    p. cm.
Includes bibliographical references and index.
ISBN 0–415–93039–1 — 0–415–93040–5 (pbk.)
    1. Counterculture—United States—History—20th century. 2. United States—History—
1961–1969. 3. United States—Intellectual life—20th century. 4. United States—Social
conditions—1960–1980. 5. Nineteen sixties. 6. Nineteen seventies. 7. Radicalism—United
States—History—20th century. 9. Popular culture—United States—History—20th century.
I. Braunstein, Peter. II. Doyle, Michael William, 1953–

E839.4.I46 2001
306'.0973'0904—dc21   2001019648

Publisher's Note
The publisher has gone to great lengths to ensure the quality of this reprint
but points out that some imperfections in the original may be apparent.

Acknowledgments

The gestation of this project witnessed a whole set of obstacles, setbacks, and quirky or menacing characters that would not have been out of place in your average Sixties flashback. Over the past four years we were confronted by faux Hopi curses; the "possessive memory" of certain veterans of the era who took umbrage at anyone outside their ranks writing "their" history; photographers who sold us vintage photos for the volume, but insisted we meet them at 11 p.m. in Washington Square Park and bring cash; and peer reviewers who treated us like a neo-Stalinist cell that had fatally deviated from the party line. The fact that we still managed to deliver this baby is due in large part to the help we received from various other quarters.

We would like to acknowledge and thank the following individuals and organizations for their generous assistance in making *Imagine Nation* a reality, and just generally helping us keep The Man at bay, including Eleanor Johnson and Gwendolyn Doyle; master strategist and contributor Debra Michals for her advice, insight, and endless moral support; James and Alice Doyle; Angèle Braunstein; Kevin Brooks; Eric Noble; William J. Rorabaugh; David Farber, who was the first noted scholar to sign on; Luisa Passerini of the European University Institute; Andrius Balukas; Susan Ware for giving us advice about publishers (even though we still chose the wrong one, initially). We also would like to salute Beth Bailey, David James, Lauren Onkey, Doug Rossinow, Jeff

Hale, Robert McRuer, Timothy Miller, Phil Deloria, and Andy Kirk, for their patience through revisions and the editing process.

At the Ball State University Department of History we would like to thank Chair John Barber; clerical staff Denise Hile, Stephanie Lantz, and Susan Blair; and student assistants Corrie Cook, Julie Martelli, and Ginger Rezy. At New York University, kudos are in order for Marilyn B. Young, Carl Prince, Robin D.G. Kelley, and Dave Reimers. Elsewhere in New York, the anthology as a whole benefited from discussions with Richard Goldstein of the *Village Voice*.

At Routledge, we are especially grateful to editors Brendan O'Malley, Dave McBride, and Tom Wang, editorial assistants Stefanie Forster and Catherine Fredenburgh, Publishing Director Karen Wolny, and a special thanks to Jon Herder for his cover design.

For helping us locate and gather some rare and incredible photos, we owe a debt of gratitude to Ralph Elder and Janis Olsen, Photography Services Coordinator, at the Center for American History, University of Texas at Austin; Jennifer Thom, Western History Collection, Denver Public Library; Kathy Lavelle, Archive Photos; Michael Alexander, San Francisco Beautiful; Kristin Eshelman, Kansas Collection, Spencer Research Library, University of Kansas at Lawrence; Rob Paulette; and Kim Klausner at the GLBT Historical Society of Northern California.

Finally, we would like to honor Julie Christie for serving as iconographic inspiration during the long course of the project.

Contents

Foreword

Marilyn B. Young

One knows an era is definitively over when its iconic films are shown as late-late movies. One night, I channel-surfed into the middle of *Easy Rider*. There was a fat Dennis Hopper and an anorexic Peter Fonda low-riding and looking for America. When I tuned in they had just arrived at an example of that period's social formation, the commune. Women cooked, cleaned, fucked; children gamboled; everyone was high. As urbanites scattered seed to the wind, apparently in an effort to plant a crop, the commune's guru spoke earnestly of the land and its fruits. A sensible Hopper asks the guru if it rains much there in the high desert and observes that in the circumstances they are unlikely "to make it." "They'll make it," Fonda insists, his eyes shining, though whether with dope or a vision of the future it is impossible to say. Shortly thereafter a cherubic-looking Jack Nicholson joins the heroes and together all three ride the limitless highways of America on their way to that festival of life and death, Mardi Gras in New Orleans. Over a campfire discussion en route, Nicholson is praised as a "dude." "Dude?" he says in surprise. "What's he mean, 'dude,' dude ranch?" "No, no," Fonda replies. "Dude means, um, nice guy. Dude means a regular sort of person."

A bit later, after an unpleasant encounter with some rednecks in a small town diner, Nicholson shakes his head in despair: "You know, this used to be a hell of a good country. I can't understand what's going on." What's going on, we next learn, is that Americans are jealous and fearful of the freedom represented by Hopper, Nicholson, and Fonda. It's hard to be free, one of them says, when you are bought and sold in the marketplace. Which seems, of course, true as well of Fonda and Hopper, with their drug money tightly rolled inside the gas tank of Fonda's motorcycle. Ultimately the rednecks kill all three of them, though not before Fonda rises to self-criticism: "We blew it," he tells Hopper as they muse upon the meaning of Nicholson's death. Hopper disagrees, but it's clear the film agrees with Fonda.

Thirty odd years later, *Easy Rider* isn't the countercultural document it appeared to be at the time but a soft sermon on the lost virtues of individualism. It doesn't counter American culture so much as give it a kiss on both cheeks. For conservative critics and commentators, indeed, the meaning of the Sixties lies almost entirely in its legacy of individualism and consumerism, which they deplore. In the name of individual freedom, they argue, public authority has been delegitimized in almost all arenas of social life with a consequent weakening of democratic institutions. The antibourgeois utopian movements of the 1960s destroyed themselves through excess and violence, only to be born again in the 1970s in individualistic liberation movements. So Peter Fonda rides again: it was all about freedom and instead of blowing it, he and Hopper have won.

In this analysis of the period, the civil rights, welfare rights, antiwar, feminist, and New Left movements appear ancillary. The burden of that long decade (by some accounts beginning with the Beats in the mid-1950s and ending with the 1950s redux presidency of Ronald Reagan) is entirely cultural rather than political. The rejection of the political culture of the nuclear family, corporate capitalism, and military aggression, expressed through an embrace of sex, drugs, and rock and roll, turned out not to be nearly as corrosive as antibourgeois youth thought or wished. The counterculture, not so threatening after all, won.

The sharp line such an analysis draws between culture and politics misses the point of the period altogether. An interpretation of the Sixties that understands the counterculture as entirely about individualism and consumerism and the 1960s themselves as embodied by the counterculture is about marketing, nostalgia, and current politics; it is not about history. The culturalist approach to the 1960s began with the movie *The Big Chill*, whose subtitle might have been "How the Easy Riders Escaped Death, Married, and Gave a Big Party for All Their Friends." At the same time, a number of Sixties radicals began to have doubts about the politics of the period. This has been especially true since 1989, when the United States was said to have "won" the fifty-year-long Cold War. If few went as far as conservatives who saw the

Vietnam War as a battle lost on the way to total victory, there was a pervasive sense that overall the politics of the period had been as excessive as its cultural manifestations. The problem with this analysis is that it underestimates the widespread disaffection people felt, *at the time*, from America and all its works.

The Sixties were centrally about the recognition, on the part of an ever-growing number of Americans, that the country in which they thought they lived—peaceful, generous, honorable—did not exist and never had. As the violence of the war expanded and government lies about its history were exposed, people withdrew the automatic trust and confidence that mark the legitimacy of public authority. The withdrawal was both contemporary and retrospective, as the whole of the national epic and its ethos came into question. The destruction of a small Southeast Asian country by the most powerful military machine in the world, which unfolded daily in the press and on TV screens, never felt ordinary. Rather, it assumed nightmare proportions, requiring an ever-greater need to protest and somehow bring it to an end.

In this effort, politics and culture came together. Traveling around the country to participate in various antiwar activities, I can remember the sense of surprise, arriving after dark in Cairo, Illinois, a place as distant from the familiar as a foreign country, at finding that I felt instantly at home: the same outrage, the same dope, the same music, the same struggle. The community of protest that was established in those years, however temporary, was nevertheless real.

The powerful anti-military consensus of the postwar period had a name: the Vietnam syndrome, which can be defined as a serious lack of blood lust on the part of the public (as opposed to secretaries of state, the Joint Chiefs of Staff, or many elected representatives). Presidents who wished to send troops into combat had to mount campaigns to persuade people that such action was necessary. Public expressions of disapproval over the use of force paused when soldiers were actually deployed, but that did not lessen their impact on politicians and policymakers. Recently, reliance on air power and the substitution of human rights as a motive for the use of force rather than anticommunism has fractured that consensus. But its power is not quite spent, and of all the legacies of the Sixties, it remains strong.

However, there is no equivalent to the Vietnam syndrome that expresses the long-term domestic residue of the 1960s. If *Easy Rider* was instantly iconic, its success marveled over, its themes imitated, the exploits and arguments of its stars the stuff of legend,[1] a movie that in my view deserves iconic status, the Coen brothers' *The Big Lebowski*, has been largely ignored or panned. The film is a slightly crazed encyclopedia of Americana over the past half century. It is a parody of *The Big Sleep* and indeed of all *film noir*, from the original model to Quentin Tarantino's faux parodies. In its irreverence toward just about all post–World War II sacred symbols, the movie counters not only contemporary American culture but the history that produced that culture.

The Big Lebowski brings together the Korean and the Vietnam Wars, reminding the country that post–World War II America did not move in a straight line from the Good War to the evil that lurks in the jungles of Southeast Asia. The two eras, of Korea and Vietnam, are each personified by a man named Jeff Lebowski. The Korean Lebowski is a rich and successful Korean War veteran, paralyzed by a "Chinaman's bullet." The Vietnam-era Lebowski is the druggy unemployed author of the *original* Port Huron statement answering only to the name Dude, whose closest friend is a Vietnam veteran in a state of permanent rage. The Dude is not one of the easy riders alive and well in L.A. He is ironic about himself, his friends, the world, his fantasy life, and the dope he smokes. He lives in the United States, but he doesn't seem to need or want to cherish it. The Dude has only one major value (and virtue): loyalty to his difficult friends.

Mark Lilla, a political scientist and commentator, has observed that we all recognize "a before and an after [the Sixties], and we are all still groping for the meaning of what happened in between."[2] One clue to what happened in between is what happened after: not *Easy Rider II* but *The Big Lebowski.* The enduring legacy of the Sixties may lie in filmmakers like the Coen brothers, who recognize the passage of historical time without indulging in nostalgia and flaunt a lack of sentimentality that leaves no room for the sentimentality of rugged individualism.

The Dude abides, the cowboy narrator of *The Big Lebowski* reassures us. If he wrote or edited books, it would be a collection of essays like this one that combines serious historical research, moral integrity, and a full measure of irreverent curiosity.

Notes

1. See, for example, Peter Biskind's *Easy Riders, Raging Bulls: How the Sex-Drugs-and-Rock 'n'-Roll Generation Saved Hollywood* (New York: Simon & Schuster, 1998).

2. Mark Lilla, "A Tale of Two Reactions," *New York Review of Books,* 14 May 1998, 4.

Historicizing the American Counterculture of the 1960s and '70s

Peter Braunstein and Michael William Doyle

"The American people are turning sullen," preaches Diana Christensen, the hyperkinetic TV programming executive in the 1975 high-concept film *Network*. "They've been clobbered on all sides by Vietnam, Watergate, the inflation, the depression. They've turned off, shot up, and they've fucked themselves limp and nothing helps. The American people want somebody to articulate their rage for them. . . . I want angry shows. I don't want conventional programming, I want counterculture, I want anti-establishment." Diana and her colleagues end up recruiting a radical left-wing terrorist group called the Ecumenical Liberation Army (obviously parodying the Symbionese Liberation Army) for a weekly TV show called the "Mao Tse-Tung Hour," which opens with live footage of bombings, bank robberies, and assassinations. While her concept clearly anticipates "reality television" of the 1990s, Diana's speech bears scrutiny for its use of the term "counterculture." Groups like the SLA, if one wanted to split hairs, really fall into the category of terroristic cadres like the Red Brigades, the last gasp of the 1970s ultra-left. Strictly speaking, they were more interested in fomenting a political revolution than a cultural one. But by the 1970s, the "counterculture"—a term popularized in 1968 by Theodore Roszak—was well on its way to becoming a term referring to all 1960s-era political, social, or cultural dissent, encompassing any action from smoking pot at a rock concert to offing a cop.[1]

This casual inflation of the term "counterculture" into a nebula of signifiers comprehending bongs, protest demonstrations, ashrams, and social
nudity rears its head at seemingly any Sixties retrospective. In a 1997 E!
Television special on Playboy Playmates of the 1960s, two former playmates
discussed the history of the era, one remarking that during the Sixties "a generation of young people rebelled against the old guard, expanded their minds,
and lived outside the norms of society." "In other words," her fellow playmate
rejoindered, "they partied, got stoned, and stopped bathing."[2]

Her joke sounds similar to California governor Ronald Reagan's 1967
description of a hippie as someone "who dresses like Tarzan, has hair like Jane,
and smells like Cheetah."[3] In fact, the problem with terms like "the hippies"
or "the counterculture," once they become decontextualized, dehistoricized,
and converted into assumptive categories, is that they can easily fall into the
hands of the wrong people. In 1995, Speaker of the House Newt Gingrich
recast "counterculture" into a pejorative term when he pointed to "a long pattern of counterculture belief that had contributed to a thirty-year pattern of
social and moral decay."[4] The *New York Times* came to the defense of this
counterculture-turned-bogeyman, crediting "it" with producing "a renewal of
the Thoreauvian ideal of the clear, defiant voice of the dissenting citizen."[5] But
couldn't the *Times* have also credited the Civil Rights movement, which predated the counterculture, with that accomplishment? Indeed, during this mid-
'90s skirmish in the culture wars, it became clear that there were as many
definitions of the term "counterculture" as there were utopian fantasies during
the actual counterculture. Theodore Roszak, for his part, despaired of the neo-
conservative demonization of the term, lamenting that "the word 'counterculture' is often defined as little more than an adolescent outburst."[6] But that's
the inexorable fate of easy terms like "counterculture" or, for that matter,
"Generation X": they inevitably lose their original historical mooring, become
shorthand references, then shortcuts to thinking, and finally Pepsi commercial
soundbites.

The journey of the word "counterculture" from the jargon-clotted
precincts of sociology into wider public awareness begins, curiously enough, at
the dawn of the 1960s through a scholarly article by J. Milton Yinger. His
research was at the time anchored in the previous decade's preoccupation with
the psychological dimensions of social deviance (reflected outside academe by
such pop cultural productions as *The Wild One* (1954), *Rebel Without a Cause*
and *Blackboard Jungle* (1955), *West Side Story* (1957), and the like).[7] Yinger
proposed the term "contraculture" to distinguish it as a sociological phenomenon from the more familiar category "subculture," which he defined as a neu-
tral subset of a larger society, as, for example, racial, ethnic, or religious groups.

A subculture generates those characteristics that are considered normative primarily through an internally directed process of socialization and interaction. By contrast, Yinger argued, a contraculture represents a full-fledged oppositional movement with a distinctively separate set of norms and values that are produced dialectically out of a sharply delineated conflict with the dominant society. Unlike subcultures, a contraculture aspires to transform values and mores of its host culture. If it is successful (think of the early Christian church in its Roman catacomb phase), it *becomes* the dominant culture. It may even stimulate the development of a new adversarial movement that seeks to supplant its system of values.

Yinger, it should be noted, acknowledged that his term "contraculture" was derived from the sociologist Talcott Parsons's earlier coinage of "counterculture." (Parsons had featured it in passing in a discussion of the ideology of subcultures in his 1951 book *The Social System*.) When Roszak revived the original term in his best-selling volume *The Making of a Counter Culture* near the end of the 1960s, it entered public discourse as an exclusive signifier for the Sixties version of cultural radicalism, *the* paradigmatic Counterculture.[8] And that in turn compromised its utility for analyzing other previous or subsequent manifestations of this sociological phenomenon. It's analogous to reserving the term "cult" solely for denominating the Branch Davidian movement, or "subculture" for the acolytes of Goth.

Historians of the 1960s have been complicit in this restrictive assignation of the term "counterculture." In any number of tomes published since the mid-1980s, the counterculture is accorded the requisite chapter wherein cultural revolt is extracted from (and then reinserted within) the rest of 1960s history. What has emerged is a canonical, Iliad-like narrative, wherein the counterculture is reduced to easy-to-follow "big moments" that typically include: (1) Albert Hofmann tottering on his bicycle in 1943 after having concocted, and inadvertently ingested, LSD for the first time in his Sandoz laboratory; (2) the Beats—represented as a kind of bohemian Rat Pack—tearing it up during Ginsberg's "epochal," overhyped recitation of *Howl* at San Francisco's Six Gallery; (3) Jim Morrison naming his L.A. rock band after Aldous Huxley's allusion to William Blake's epigram "If the doors of perception were cleansed"; (4) Ken Kesey and the Merry Pranksters tripping on acid, rediscovering America, this time from west to east, aboard their "magic bus," *Further;* (5) Leary chanting "Turn on, tune in, drop out," sampled onto the Beatles' "A Day in the Life"; (6) the flowers, the music, the vision that was (but in actuality, wasn't) the Summer of Love in San Francisco, 1967. This stroboscopic light show will then draw to an abrupt close with the mandatory montage of the counterculture's "dark side"—someone shooting up speed or having a bad trip, the Manson Family murders, and finally the Altamont concert-debacle—all ritualistically invoked as mutually-reinforcing tombstones.[9]

The Sixties counterculture in the United States didn't come out of nowhere: it appeared gradually as a ripening of popular discontent over America's shrill postwar triumphalism. It was a fruit that had been assiduously cultivated throughout the 1950s in the many scattered patches of bohemia across the land, and across the Atlantic. The Beats were the first named set of cultural dissidents to be associated with this critique. And although their numbers never approached the status of a true "Beat Generation," as commentators often referred to them, their vigorous denunciation of cold war militarism, anticommunist demagoguery, racial segregation, social regimentation, and rampant, near-orgiastic consumerism articulated most of the themes that adherents of the 1960s counterculture would echo and amplify.

During the longest and most robust economic expansion in our nation's history to that point, there were early signs that all was not well in America. An undeclared war to contain communism in the Korean peninsula ground to an inconclusive truce, while the mania to expose and purge "card-carrying" communists and their "fellow traveler" sympathizers at home undermined the very civil liberties that made up the foundation of our self-described liberal democracy. When the U.S. Supreme Court struck down "separate but equal" treatment of racial minorities in the 1954 *Brown* decision, a burgeoning movement led by African Americans to dismantle the legal edifice Jim Crow had built was confronted by a virulent backlash. White racists seemed determined to beat, burn, and bomb their opponents into submission "with all deliberate speed." Elected officials and law enforcement authorities initially did little to stop the carnage; that is, when they weren't themselves complicit in the repression. By the time the landmark Civil Rights and Voting Rights Acts had been signed into law, the smoldering resentment of impoverished urban minorities over institutionalized inequality erupted into flame and spread like riotous wildfire to nearly every major urban ghetto. Literally hundreds of violent "civil disorders" convulsed American cities from coast to coast between 1964 and 1968. Square miles of inner-city devastation that were left in their wake resembled the carpet-bombed capitals of Europe and Asia of twenty years earlier. In the aftermath, those not killed, driven off, or incarcerated saw their circumstances worsen as the multiple pathologies of addictive drugs, STDs, spiraling rates of teen pregnancies, and homelessness descended.

This metropolitan apocalypse had an ironic counterpart in what American policymakers were attempting to do to Vietnam—"bomb them back into the Stone Age," in the memorable phrase of Barry Goldwater's 1964 running mate

General Curtis LeMay. The motivations were complex. There was the oft-cited fear that unstable regimes throughout Southeast Asia would topple as easily as a standing stack of dominoes if communist expansion wasn't contained. Or the unspoken desire for enlarging an American empire where the French had been forced to dismantle their colonial grasp on Indochina. Or the high-octane machismo of presidents from Eisenhower to Nixon who would not permit themselves to be guilty of "losing" the region as Truman's State Department had putatively "lost China." In the summer of 1964, on the pretext that a pair of American warships had been attacked at sea by the North Vietnamese (at night and during a storm, no less), Congress passed the Gulf of Tonkin Resolution. It authorized President Lyndon Johnson as commander in chief "to take all necessary measures to repel any armed attack against the forces of the United States." LBJ took that blank check and bet the farm on guns and butter. By the next summer, with conscription augmenting enlistments, the number of American troops in South Vietnam had escalated to 125,000, with no end in sight. At first, scores, then hundreds, and soon thousands of young men returned home in body bags.

Elaine Tyler May and others have persuasively documented how the cold war's geopolitical strategy of containment was accompanied by a domestic theater of operations. There were of course the well-publicized "witch hunts" for enemies of the state presumed to be lurking in our midst.[10] This thinking gained institutional status under the aegis of the House Un-American Activities Committee, whose very name, typical of the era, asserted with Manichean certainty that there was but one way to be a true American; all others would be subject to investigation and prosecution. But there was also a carefully coordinated campaign to reassert patriarchy by pressuring middle-class women to quit the workplace, marry, bear and care full-time for their brood, all while being confined to suburban tract homes arrayed like so many nuclear family reactors. The American higher education system geared up to perpetuate the new technocracy by educating young citizens, particularly white middle-class males, for compliantly assuming their rightful place in the corporate hierarchy. Those who had their doubts, who looked wistfully for other ladders of life to climb, were ridiculed, persecuted, or psychoanalyzed into conformity. But, importantly, occasional cris de coeur—*The Invisible Man* (1952), *The Man in the Grey Flannel Suit* (1956), *The Feminine Mystique* (1963)—did manage to insinuate themselves into public discourse, questioning these arrangements.

It was a hard sell, considering the veritable cornucopia of consumer goods that seemed to materialize and dematerialize just out of reach, as if through some untunable frequency. Our world has since become so permeated with the shimmering chimera of status symbols—signs of things as well as real objects like cars, appliances, clothing, toiletries, jewelry, foodstuffs, and so on—that it is difficult to imagine a time when images of such items weren't quite so ubiquitous, before the trickle had become the flood we strive to navigate in a vain attempt to satisfy most wants and some needs. One's identity increasingly became the sum of one's inventory: to be was to buy, and that meant cash. The "rat race" was run around a cache of cash all the livelong day. To give up this pursuit of the American dream was to go down the social stratum. The Great Society promised those already at the bottom a limited share of the bounty as entitlement. Getting and spending were no longer considered activities performed primarily to sustain life; they became synonymous with social life itself, its raison d'être.

Affluence for some, the unsubstantial prospect of sufficiency for the rest, muted outrage over yet another undeclared war in yet another corner of the world remote to most people's awareness, racial bigotry, sexual double standards, political paranoia, utopian expectations, "God is dead," "Better dead than red," "Our country right or wrong," "Love it or leave it"—these and other factors and slogans defined the conditions of the time when a demographic tremor rippled and American culture heaved in unexpected directions. The counterculture, as one manifestation of this "Youthquake" came to be called, was just as inchoate, diffuse, and palpable as any trembler.

The term "counterculture" falsely reifies what should never properly be construed as a social movement. It was an inherently unstable collection of attitudes, tendencies, postures, gestures, "lifestyles," ideals, visions, hedonistic pleasures, moralisms, negations, and affirmations. These roles were played by people who defined themselves first by what they were not, and then, only after having cleared that essential ground of identity, began to conceive anew what they were. What they were was what they might become—more a process than a product, and thus more a direction or a motion than a movement. For the sake of taxonomy, those who were subsumed belatedly by others under the label of counterculture generally understood the crisis that befell not just the American nation, but evidently all the industrialized West, as emanating from our common *culture*; the *state* was erected on the platform of culture, not vice versa as a vulgar Marxist might argue.

In this cosmology, if one wanted to effect long-lasting social change, politics was understood to be epiphenomenal. The lever instead would need to be positioned so as to shift the culture, and the culture would be moved one person at a time. If and when enough people had transformed themselves, the result would be like magnetizing a piece of iron: its energy becomes concentrated when the polarity of a sufficient quantity of individual molecules is realigned. The dominant culture could hardly help but be changed when thousands, perhaps millions of people formerly in its thrall incrementally realigned their values and actions to contradistinguish themselves from it.

It may be useful to think historically of the Sixties counterculture in the United States as divisible into two major phases. The first was the white youth-dominated, highly optimistic, even utopian counterculture of the "Flower Children" period. Starting points may differ, but this phase took off roughly when the Beatles launched their first tour in 1964, reached its zenith of visibility in 1967–68, and then gradually but inexorably returned to earth following Nixon's 1968 election to the presidency. In this initial phase, the counterculture contained many paradoxes, foremost among them its status as a youth-based movement whose primary spokesmen (Leary, Ginsberg, Snyder) were considerably older than its core constituency. Another vexing issue is whether "hippies" and "the counterculture" are essentially synonyms. Since the term "hippies" was used unproblematically at the time primarily by the mainstream news media, it may be safer to consider the "hippies" as an ideological charade adopted temporarily by some "counterculturists," but then dropped by 1968–69, after which the term persisted as an assumptive signifier to designate a look, a fashion, an attitude, or a lifestyle.

The utopian orientation of the first phase of the counterculture owed greatly to the full-employment prosperity of the era and the optimistic economic prognostications it engendered. The sustained peacetime boom in turn prompted expectations of an imminent postscarcity society, based on the optimistic view that the United States was reaching a stage of automation, industrial development, agricultural productivity, and economic growth in which the need to work for a living might soon be radically diminished, if not eliminated altogether. The end of work would herald the onset of a vast leisure society in which human pursuits, liberated from the drudgery of alienating, soul-slaying labor, might be redirected to self-actualization involving the cultivation of each individual's creative talents. The implications of this orientation were far-reaching: not only would the work/play dichotomy be erased, but so would the distinction, on a certain level, between childhood and adulthood, given that adults could be considered for all practical purposes simply damaged children with jobs.

Postscarcity thinking wasn't the loopy fantasy of sci-fi writers; the anticipation of a millennial society characterized by surplus leisure time was widespread. President Lyndon Johnson in a 1964 address observed that "in the past we fought to eliminate scarcity. In the future we will also have to learn the wise use of abundance."[11] Alan Watts, a Beat Generation writer widely recognized as a 1960s counterculture elder, predicted "a huge leisure society—where they're going to reverse taxation and PAY people for the work the machines do for them,"[12] while the Yippies called for "[a] society which works toward and actively promotes the concept of 'full unemployment' under the slogan 'Let the machines do it.'"[13] Much of the current historical debate over how cozy the relationship was between capitalism and the counterculture fails to adequately factor in the pervasiveness of these postscarcity assumptions at the time. Many of those comprehended by the term "hippies" in the mid-to-late 1960s felt that it would be easier to transcend capitalism than destroy it. Time was on their side, they maintained, because the coming leisure society would likely erode most of the strictures associated with capitalism.

Of course, the postscarcity orientation of many so-called hippies betrayed the white middle-class constituency of the counterculture. College-educated beneficiaries of the "Affluent Society," counterculture luminaries like Abbie Hoffman and Jerry Rubin could garner media attention with such actions as burning dollar bills. But only white Americans who unthinkingly took material comfort and security for granted would engage in such symbolic actions. Meanwhile, the privileged status of white hippies placed them at odds with their inner-city neighbors in the two largest hippie urban meccas, San Francisco's Haight-Ashbury and New York City's East Village. The hippies' adoption of virtual poverty as part of their outsider, Christ charade was often regarded as cruel mockery by the black, Hispanic, and immigrant residents of these neighborhoods, who dreamed of attaining entry into the very material world the hippie children had casually—and provisionally—repudiated. As a result, tempers flared in the various hippie "fantasy ghettos" as voluntary poverty met its hereditary other. As one black resident of New York's East Village put it, "the hippies really bug us, because we know they can come down here and play their games for a while and then escape. And we can't, man."[14]

The years 1969–70 marked the descent of the utopian phase of the counterculture, along with its race-based assumptions of material plenitude. The economic downturn that began in the very early 1970s, combined with Nixon's election to office on a "law and order," anticounterculture platform, dealt Sixties utopians a double dose of harsh reality. The political system was real and hostile, and it wouldn't be eclipsed or rendered irrelevant by a beneficent, liberating economy. The counterculture fragmented into a number of cultural liberation movements during the 1970s that were different in tone and constituency. Expectations ebbed that American society could be radically altered, whether by politics, revolution, or alchemy, while at the same time "practical liberation" on the level of lifestyle became the countercultural mode.

Even by prolonging the counterculture into the 1970s via the "two-phases" schema posited here, there is still one outstanding, and possibly irremediable, problem associated with historicizing the counterculture. Scholars of the 1960s seem contractually obligated to assess the counterculture using an epistemology that most of its proponents had rejected. The countercultural mode reveled in tangents, metaphors, unresolved contradictions, conscious ruptures of logic and reason; it was expressly anti-linear, anti-teleological, rooted in the present, disdainful of thought processes that were circumscribed by causation and consequence. Countercultural knowledge can't be accurately represented by a straight line, or even the squiggly line; a more evocative figure would be the matrix, or perhaps the concentric circle. Yet by disciplinary convention, historical accounts are linear, chronological, and teleological. One can't help wondering what a truly countercultural historiography of 1960s cultural radicalism would look like. Perhaps the present volume, by presenting a mix of synthetic and speculative essays on this amorphous, multifaceted, and inherently fascinating phenomenon called the counterculture, can serve as a portal through which the next perspicacious wave of interpretation may be glimpsed.

NOTES

1. Theodore Roszak, *The Making of a Counter Culture: Reflections on the Technocratic Society and Its Youthful Opposition* (Berkeley: University of California Press, 1995 [1969]). Roszak's book was a revised and expanded version of a four-part article he published in *The Nation* in March–April 1968, beginning with the March 25 issue.

2. Quoted in "E! Playmates of the '60s," television special on E! Entertainment Network, 1997.

3. Reagan quoted in Don McNeill, "Parents and Runaways: Writing a New Contract," *Village Voice*, 14 December 1967, 1, 21–22, 24–27 at 21.

4. Newt Gingrich quoted in Frank Rich, "Gingrich Family Values," *New York Times*, 14 May 1995, sec. 4, p. 15.

5. "In Praise of the Counterculture," *New York Times*, 11 December 1994, sec. 4, p. 14. This editorial only appeared in the late final edition of the day's paper.

6. Theodore Roszak, "The Misunderstood Movement," *New York Times*, 3 December 1994, A23.

7. For but one example of this research, a collection spanning the 1950s and early '60s, see Howard S. Becker, *Outsiders: Studies in the Sociology of Deviance* (New York: Free Press, 1963).

8. J. Milton Yinger, "Contraculture and Subculture," *American Sociological Review* 25, no. 4 (October 1960): 625–35. This article constitutes the first sustained discussion of "contraculture" in the literature. When Theodore Roszak's term "counter culture" later gained currency in social science and popular discourse, Yinger gracefully yielded his own neologism to it (although rendering it a compound word in the process, as have most others). In his book *Countercultures: The Promise and Peril of a World Turned Upside Down* (New York: Free Press, 1982), 3, Yinger acknowledged Talcott Parsons as having first used the term "counter-culture" in his study *The Social System* (New York: Free Press, 1951), 522.

9. While acknowledging that "[i]t is now a cliché that the Woodstock Nation died on the Altamont drag strip," David Chalmers nonetheless concludes his narrative chapter on the coun-

terculture with just this summary statement. See Chalmers, *And the Crooked Places Made Straight: The Struggle for Social Change in the Sixties* (Baltimore and London: Johns Hopkins University Press, 1991), 99–100.

10. Elaine Tyler May, *Homeward Bound : American Families in the Cold War Era* (New York: Basic Books, 1988); Daniel Horowitz, *Betty Friedan and the Making of* The Feminine Mystique*: The American Left, the Cold War, and Modern Feminism* (Amherst : University of Massachusetts Press, 1998).

11. This quote by President Johnson is taken from his 6 June 1964 speech to the International Ladies Garment Workers' Union. The whole of his remarks may be found in the article "Text of President's Talk Here," *New York Times*, 7 June 1964, sec. 1, p. 77.

12. Alan Watts, quoted in "Changes," popularly known as the "Houseboat Summit" of February 1967, *San Francisco Oracle*, 21 March 1967, 10ff.

13. "Free" (pseud. Abbie Hoffman), *Revolution for the Hell of It* (New York: Dial Press, 1968), 167.

14. Quoted in Richard Goldstein, "Love: A Groovy Thing While He Lasted," *Village Voice*, 19 October 1967, 43.

Section One
Deconditioning

Introduction

"Free your mind, and the rest will follow." Whether identifiable as a New Age truism or the lyrics to a hit by *En Vogue*, this slogan percolated through the counterculture of the 1960s. In their collective attempt to overturn or transcend dominant American values, cultural revolutionaries ranging from Timothy Leary to Robin Morgan believed that the key to societal transformation lay first and foremost in personal transformation. To rid oneself of the drives that produced aggression, authoritarianism, sexism, racism, intolerance, and sexual repression, counterculturists sought to disinherit pernicious social conditioning through a process alternately dubbed "deschooling," "reimprinting," or "deconditioning." Regardless of the name, the modus operandi was the same: take all the programming you received from your parents, schools, the mass media, and other tainted authority systems and jettison it as the first step toward developing a higher consciousness.

As David Farber explains in his essay "The Intoxicated State/Illegal Nation: Drugs in the Sixties Counterculture," high-test hallucinogens like LSD or mellow mood-altering substances like marijuana soon became the deconditioning tools of choice for a large segment of the counterculture. But just as drug use didn't necessarily or consistently raise the consciousness of everyone who popped, dropped, or inhaled, neither did all cultural dissidents seek liberation from oppressive societal norms through ingesting psychedelics. Debra Michals, in her essay "From 'Consciousness Expansion' to 'Consciousness Raising': Feminism and the Countercultural Politics of the Self," traces the path by which "CR" emerged as the primary deconditioning vehicle for the Women's Liberation movement, a means of identifying and countering the sexism women endured in the male-dominated counterculture and the larger society.

One

The Intoxicated State/Illegal Nation
Drugs in the Sixties Counterculture

David Farber

"Them first kicks are a killer, Jim."
—*Mezz Mezzrow*[1]

Among the cognoscenti in the history-of-the-1960s business, the current fashion has been to denude the so-called Sixties counterculture of its peacock feathers and to piece it well inside the puzzle of the (ever) burgeoning consumer culture of the twentieth century. Thomas Frank argues in his dazzling book *The Conquest of Cool* that "the counterculture may be more accurately understood as a stage in the development of the values of the American middle class, a colorful installment in the twentieth century drama of consumer subjectivity."[2] I've made similar claims in my own work, referencing the Big Business guru of the 1950s, Ernest Dichter, who told corporate executives: "One of the basic problems of prosperity, then, is to demonstrate that the hedonistic approach to . . . life is a moral and not an immoral one."[3] Party hearty, dude, says the ad man to the hippie.

Characterizing the Sixties-era counterculture as nothing more or less than an exotic variant of twentieth-century Americans' hunt for consumption without limits is not just a *post hoc* argument, reflective of the now endemic mass global commercialization of "youth lifestyles." During the 1960s, radical politicos from Tom Hayden to Michael Harrington bemoaned the hippies' lack of political vision and dismissed the counterculture as a way station for middle-class white youths between prosperous suburban childhood and prosperous corporate adulthood.[4] In this version of the Sixties counterculture a paragraph or two narrating the Jefferson Airplane's easy back-and-forth between their roles as rock sirens extolling the wonders of the psychedelic experience in "White Rabbit" and as celebrity pitchmen for "White Levi Jeans" becomes a sneering sort of "enough said."[5]

No doubt what *some* have called the counterculture was just a lifestyle up for sale.[6] And, no doubt, even that most daring of countercultural consumer choices, the purchase of illegal drugs, fits—albeit, uneasily—into a picture of a commodifying nation nervously playing around with the boundaries of supermarket sweepstakes: Well, dear, we can buy Hustler at the Rexall, Smirnoff at the Walgreens, Snoop Dog at the Kmart, a Walther at the Big Five, SuperLotto at the Giant, nipple rings at The Alley, and Marlboros at the Safeway, but I say let's make sure they never sell (fill in the blank). And yet, I will argue in the next few pages, reducing the Sixties counterculture to its commodified components, to its relatively indifferent politics and its separate peace with the free market, is to miss the point.

The illegal drugs of choice in the 1960s complicate the reductive exercise. In the '60s, white middle-class youths restocked the medicine chest. In particular, they added marijuana and LSD. What some of them took and why some of them took what they did challenged the meaning most Americans— with the law on their side—had uneasily attached to the intoxicated state. The difference between legally medicated, legally intoxicated, and illegally high *did* sometimes signify a new cultural orientation, even a cultural rebellion, in the United States both because some of the young white middle-class drug users insisted that it did and because legal and legally designated authorities *ensured* that it did. The way some people used some drugs in the Sixties era facilitated their purposeful exit from the rules and regulations that made up the culture they had been poised to inhabit.

The difficulty in separating countercultural aspirations from youth culture commodifications begins with the plausibility of individual will in the overdetermined, structurally hegemonic capitalist universe of the late-twentieth-century United States.[7] In the encapsulating base of market production and consumer-driven lifestyles, the boasts of pot-smoking, acid-dropping heads that they really meant it and that they had something else in mind might seem a minor eddy in the tide of history that was soon enough brought back into the main current of the river of time. But if we consider culture not as a simple bruiting of relations of production but as an active arena in which categories of meaning are produced, tested, and renegotiated, then some actors in the life drama summed up as the Sixties counterculture have earned a re-hearing.

The anthropologist Marshall Sahlins has argued that "culture is . . . a gamble played with nature."[8] He means—to stretch and update the remark a bit—that old ways and means sometimes do and sometimes don't work acceptably in new situations. William Sewell, in his essay "A Theory of Structure," clarifies this line of thought by arguing for "the polysemy of resources." He explains: "Any array of resources is capable of being interpreted in varying ways and, therefore, of empowering different actors and teaching different schema. . . . Agency, to put it differently, is the actor's capacity to reinterpret and mobilize an array of resources in terms of cultural [schemata] other than those that initially constituted the array."[9]

In this essay, I will explore how some people used LSD (also commonly known as acid) as a "resource" that enabled them to hunt out, recombine, and produce cultural schemata that changed their trajectory on the social map of space and time. I have left out the broad middle ground of LSD users who found their trips personally useful if not broadly life-altering. I have used this essay to tell the tale not of LSD use in general but of LSD use as an agent in the production of cultural reorientation. As a result, I have retold a kind of canonical tale of the struggle to place LSD use in a suitable social frame: medicine, sacrament, "hard kick," or illegal narcotic. My central purpose, herein, is to show how some took the medicine/illegal narcotic and used it as a sacrament/hard kick. Their story compels our attention, I think, because it reminds us of the power not just of structure but of agency; not just of the spectacle but of the human spectacular.

To begin this compressed and selective narrative of getting high in the Sixties, I first offer a critical context: drug use was endemic in the United States by the mid-1960s, well before any Summer of Love. Americans lived in a society in which powerful substances were metabolized to change mental processes and bodily functions. To put it bluntly, by the early 1960s, Americans had officially decided that consciousness-changing drugs worked and that they should be massively deployed to change people's consciousness. Americans accepted an intoxicated state as either medically or recreationally necessary—at least for some Americans, some of the time. With very little challenge, doctors—with psychiatrists in the catbird seat—ran the heavy end of this enterprise. In 1965, doctors wrote 123 million prescriptions for tranquilizers and 24 million prescriptions for amphetamines.

Overwhelmingly, these drugs were taken by people considered normal functioning citizens. Doctors prescribed "uppers" and "downers" to help everyday people cope with their everyday duties. Of course, many citizens abused these drugs in a manner not recommended by their physicians. In 1965, some three thousand Americans died from overdoses of their legally prescribed drugs (for a popular account of this problem, read the 1966 bestseller *Valley of the Dolls*).[10] Even more ubiquitous, though by the mid-1960s not recommended by doctors, was the use of tobacco. In 1960, roughly 80 percent of men between eighteen and sixty-four used tobacco, most of them by smoking cigarettes, which was the most powerful means of introducing the user to tobacco's dangerous addictive agent, nicotine.[11] Alcoholic beverages, to say the least, were equally commonplace. As the U.S. Brewers Foundation celebrated in the "conservative" 1950s: "In this friendly, freedom-loving land of ours—Beer belongs . . . Enjoy It!"[12]

Whether mellowed out on Valium, hyped up on speed, socially drunk, or gently buzzed on nicotine, Americans in the 1960s had seemingly accepted the intoxicated state as part and parcel of the American way of life. I stress this somewhat obvious point because some politicians, historically ignorant pundits, and loads of contemporary youths seem to forget/not know/walk around this truth for a variety of reasons ranging from the mendacious to the ideological to the ignorant. It is how and why certain kinds of people use certain kinds of drugs that makes the 1960s "the Sixties."[13] Given this larger history of medical or recreational intoxication, this short history aims to recuperate the intention early proponents of LSD use brought to their drug taking. Their intentionality, in turn, helped to frame the meaning LSD use had both for those who followed them and for those who fought their claims that acid visions had specific beneficial utility for individuals and society.

While no single factor figured the emergence of claims of an altered consciousness in the 1960s, LSD played a fundamental role. LSD was supposed to be just another profit-producing tool in this American pharmaceutical cornucopia, another means by which doctor's patient would get well on a fee-for-service basis. But LSD would not remain so confined. Instead, LSD tripped the light fantastic on the sidewalks of New York . . . and most every other burg on the planet.

D-Lysergic acid diethylamide was first used by the Swiss chemist Albert Hofmann at Sandoz Pharmaceuticals in Basle, Switzerland, on August 19, 1943. He was not trying to "turn on" a new generation; he was hoping to find a profitable analeptic that might, perhaps, cure migraines. Hofmann dosed himself with his synthetic drug and discovered that it did little for headaches but much for his head. He hallucinated. Sandoz had a problem: headache medicines had a clear market, but what was the market for a hallucinogenic drug? Since they had no clear answer, Sandoz executives gambled on Say's

Law, the economic principle that holds that supply will create demand. Sandoz began shipping LSD to America's exploding population of psychiatrists and clinical psychologists and hoped they'd find some use for it.[14]

Here another framing context in this wayward story of cultural change and rebellion needs to be summarized. Only after World War II did "mental health" and mental health practitioners become a fully legitimated, well-funded enterprise in the United States. The mental health business's takeoff point can be dated precisely. In 1946 Congress passed, and President Truman signed, the Mental Health Act, which, among other things, created the National Institute of Mental Health. In large part due to the solid perform-ance of a small coterie of psychologically trained experts during World War II (their duties ranged from testing military inductees to patching together psy-chiatric battle casualties), both military and political elites had come to believe that psychiatry and the behavioral sciences should play a critical role in the liminal world of national security.[15] In part due to federal funding, psychiatry boomed in post–World War II America. In 1940 only three thousand psychi-atrists practiced in the United States; by 1956 over fifteen thousand were in business. Part of this scientizing of humans' internal mental processes included medicating expanding populations of the mentally unhealthy. By the mid-1950s brand-name drugs such as Thorazine had become proven tools in the fight against mental illness and mental instability. A multitude of other pharmaceuticals were being tested for their utility in promoting a more pro-ductive, healthy citizenry. LSD was one of those drugs.[16]

As legend and the historical record have it, one of the humans involved in government-funded research was a young writer named Ken Kesey. Kesey had volunteered for the study (as he later recounted: "I mean the first acid I took was Sandoz, given me by the federal government in a series of experi-ments . . . what now, Uncle? Don't give me that anti-American drug field bull-shit: you turned me on . . . And it was beautiful").[17] Another of the early government-sponsored researchers into the properties of LSD was the Harvard University scientist Timothy Leary. A horde of other credentialed types, ranging from Hollywood therapists to CIA spooks, had also hooked into LSD research by the cusp of the 1950s and the 1960s.

By the early 1960s, mass media accounts praised LSD as a cure for psy-chological problems. Cary Grant told his fans that LSD administered under the supervision of his psychiatrist had helped him learn to love women more fully and truly. In 1963, *My Self and I* was published and widely reviewed; in it, the author, Constance Newland, detailed how LSD cured her frigidity.[18] California psychiatrists were parceling LSD out to writers, artists, actors, and movie directors to combat various creative blocks. Therapists were recommending it to one another as a means of self-inducing an extreme mental state akin to psychosis. The experience would enable doctors to better understand the emotions of their disturbed patients. LSD inventor, Albert Hofmann, had explained that the "creation of new remedies is the goal of a pharmaceutical chemist's research activity."[19] Seemingly, problems were being discovered for which LSD was a suitable remedy, and LSD was on its way to being another pharmaceutical in the doctor's kit bag. But the drug did not stay in the bag.[20]

Why and how LSD became party favor, sacrament, and mind blower of the masses is not an easy story to tell quickly. Albert Hofmann states the obvious when he confesses: "It was obvious that a substance with such fantastic effects on mental perception and on the experience of the outer and inner world would also arouse interest outside medical science. . . . I had expected curiosity and interest on the part of artists outside of medicine—performers, painters, and writers—but not among people in general."[21] LSD's breakout from the discourse and practice of "medical science" to alternative frames of meaning and use first occurred in the very realms to which LSD was narrowly prescribed: mental health test sites.

Dr. Timothy Leary played a critical role in the unleashing and reconceptualizing of LSD. And while Leary participated in the historical casting of his own comic persona—to the extent that by the late 1960s he came across as more of a huckster than a visionary—what he chose to do was extraordinary.[22] By 1960, Leary had moved away from the academic expertise in personality testing that had brought him a Harvard professorship, pursuing instead a relatively scientific investigation into the effects of mind-altering drugs—a research agenda that had begun in behavioral science circles in the immediate post–World War II years on both sides of the Atlantic. In early 1961, a young British writer named Michael Hollingshead, who'd been informed by Aldous Huxley of Leary's research into the personality-altering effects of psilocybin (a synthetic form of the psychotropic agent found in "magic mushrooms"), introduced LSD to the Harvard academic. Hollingshead possessed a gram of Sandoz LSD, Lot number H-00047. Sandoz had sent him the perfectly legal product after he wrote the company on the letterhead of a New York City hospital requesting a supply for "a series of bone-marrow experiments."[23]

Leary took LSD and came quickly to believe that the drug was not just another pharmaceutical product. And he was in a socially authorized, credentialed position to make his personal feelings matter both to elite and mass audiences. Leary would spend most of the 1960s as an "LSD prophet." His efforts to promote LSD use helped to frame the drug in the 1960s not as just another recreational intoxicant but as a psychedelic sacrament that would lead individuals to a higher consciousness.

Dr. Leary and his fellow researchers at the Harvard Psychedelic Research Project began to publicize their LSD trips. In a 1962 *Bulletin of the Atomic Scientists* they noted that LSD "may produce dramatic changes in personality leading to unprecedented peace, sanity, and happiness." In a 1963 *Harvard Review* article entitled "The Politics of Consciousness Expansion," Leary (and his colleague Richard Alpert) argued: "The social situation in respect to consciousness-expanding drugs is very similar to that faced sixty years ago by those crackpot visionaries who were playing around with the horseless carriage. Of course, the automobile is external child's play as compared to the unleashing of cortical energy, but the social dilemma is similar."[24] Leary's evocation of a "social dilemma" reveals the professor's knowledge of his predicament: What exactly is LSD for? Should it just be unleashed upon the people as the auto was? Who should control the new technology of the mind that Leary believed LSD presented? What would/could/should LSD do?

Leary believed that LSD allowed individuals to test their realities. LSD allowed individuals to explore the inner workings of their minds. LSD-induced visions developed people's spiritual capacities. Leary's studies showed, he believed, that LSD rearranged the "imprinting process" and allowed new "imprints to be made." LSD, in other words, through its reality-bending properties, challenged people to rethink social norms and life patterns. In a 1961 experiment with prisoners at the Concord State Prison in Massachusetts, Leary claimed to have shown that convicts, under proper guidance—and the guidance, Leary believed, was crucially important—had used psychedelics to stop the mental "game" that made them criminals.[25] LSD, Professor Leary decided, allowed people to rethink what they had become and reinvent themselves according to a deeper, truer, drug-produced set of understandings. From 1961 onward, Leary would promote, in increasingly dramatic ways, the power of the LSD trip to change individual lives and, by extension, society. Despite Leary's prison experiments, he was not primarily concerned with those deemed mentally ill, sociopathic, or at least neurotic, by themselves or by credentialed authorities. Instead, Leary's circle understood LSD as a life-enhancing, spiritual-inclining tool. Productive, happy people should use LSD to evolve.

Leary and his associates proselytized for LSD as an agent of spiritual growth. To best achieve that growth, they experimented, controlling for what Leary called "set" and "setting." Their investigations into how best to structure an individual's LSD experience led them to a variety of esoterica. They searched out past masters of the spiritual quest, turning "Eastward" for guidance in using visionary experiences. In particular, they came to believe that the *Tibetan Book of the Dead* offered a remarkable guide to the LSD experience;

its authors seemed to be working with the same visions that structured the LSD experience. In addition, inspired by the sacramental use of peyote by certain North American Indians, Leary and his associates attempted to ritualize the taking of LSD.

All of these efforts pointed LSD use away from the behaviorists' emphasis on clinical control and rational remediation and toward a far more pointed search for spiritual awareness. These nonscientific efforts and the Harvard group's increasing lack of interest in maintaining rigid control over the distribution of LSD resulted in the dismissal of Leary and the removal of the Psychedelic Research Project from Harvard. What Leary was doing—as Harvard's administrators proved with a vengeance—was not behavioral science, was not academically appropriate, and was not the business of America's premier university. Leary's use of LSD to explore inner space as a means to promote spiritual growth did not fit established cultural parameters.

Leary had begun by taking a product invented by Sandoz Pharmaceuticals to make a profit. He had experimented with it as a credentialed behavioral scientist under the auspices of Harvard University. By 1963, he was somewhere else: out of a job, out of Harvard, and searching for a new set of categories to fit the LSD experience within, be it secular spirituality, inner space, expanding consciousness, or "renewal by the discovery of new mysteries." He and a growing circle of fellow believers set up headquarters at Millbrook, a mansion in upstate New York. Leary later said: "On this space colony we were attempting to create a new organism and a new dedication to life as art."[26] The institutional administrators that had credentialed, employed, and legitimated Leary's investigations into the human predicament had cast him out. His game no longer fit their story.

Across the continent, at roughly the same time (as the canonical story of hallucinogenic history goes), another band of intrepid trippers explored what LSD was for. The writer Ken Kesey and his compatriots, the self-styled "Merry Pranksters," also believed that LSD—or, as they called it, acid— should not be restricted to doctor's prescription for those deemed neurotic or be locked away as a pharmaceutical awaiting the discovery of an applicable illness. Unlike Leary's Harvard crowd, the Pranksters took acid not so much to explore inner space as to re-negotiate social space. Whereas the Leary circle of adepts believed that "set and setting" should be carefully controlled to create an individual LSD experience pointed toward maximum inner exploration, the Pranksters insisted on "freaking freely." They went out adventuring, seeing what the world looked like while tripping and—critically—what they could do in that world to make it comply or at least be complicitous with their acid vision.

Allen Ginsberg protesting against the criminalization of marijuana use, Women's House of Detention, New York City, March 1964. The Beat poet personified a quintessential Sixties notion that political dissent was the best expression of the American pursuit of happiness. Copyright © Benedict J. Fernandez.

Most famously, their collective incursions took two forms. In 1964, the Pranksters painted a school bus in Day-Glo splashes, tricked it out with an elaborate sound system, named it *Further*, and traveled from California to New York for the World's Fair, making multiple stops to and fro. In Arizona they used *Further*'s array of electronics to blast passing pedestrians with their acid vision of the presidential election: "A vote for Barry is a vote for fun."[27] They goofed on the crowds, they reveled in not being them. They were the selves they discovered while tripping, archetypal adventurers rolling into whatever came next: "Mountain Girl," "Intrepid Traveler," "Chief." The acid ventilated the pretensions of the established order, held it up as just another game that nobody had to play if they found something better to do. Acid seemed to give them something better to do.

In 1966, the Pranksters began a series of "Acid Tests" in the Bay area: public LSD parties. The Grateful Dead (first known as the Warlocks) was the house band. LSD was parceled out freely. The Grateful Dead's Jerry Garcia described the scene as "thousands of people all helplessly stoned, all finding themselves in a roomful of people, none of whom any of them were afraid of. It was magic, far out, beautiful magic."[28] The Acid Tests were far from the Leary-inspired, carefully guided and structured, individual and contemplative LSD experiences aimed at inner truths. At the tests—and at Kesey's compound at La Honda, California—costumes, electronic feedback devices, Day-Glo paint, film loops, and strobe lights were all geared toward maximizing psychic, sensual input, loading up the mind and pushing tripsters toward a vast collective experience that roared toward the unknown. The Acid Tests pointed toward the creation of enclaves, social spaces in which visionaries played out new collective games. Instead of individuals competing for resources in a socially prescribed marketplace and then retreating into private households to consume goods with a tiny set of loved ones, the Pranksters took their acid visions as a sign of the immensely entertaining, challenging, and occasionally enlightening free spaces people could create if they cared to.

By the middle 1960s, a host of acid advocates worked at the local and regional level. In the middle of the country, the Detroit-area rock and roll promoter and writer John Sinclair spoke to the melding of visions acid luminaries like Kesey, Leary, and his spiritual strivers were producing among those carefully tuned into the drug scene. Sinclair preached that LSD made youth's most visible cultural creation—rock music—more than just another form of commercial entertainment, that LSD made Vietnam War–era youth culture more than just another adolescent stage. LSD, he argued, moved young people:

... from alienation to the total embrace of humankind. . . . The music was what gave us our energy and our drive, but it took the magic sacramental acid to give us the ideology which could direct that energy. Marijuana, which had come to us directly from black people and black musicians, in particular, had given us a start in this direction, but LSD opened the road into the future as wide as the sky and we were soaring! Acid blasted all the negativism and fear out of our bodies and gave us a vision we needed to go ahead, the rainbow vision which showed us how all people could live together in harmony and peace just as we were beginning to live with each other like that. . . . LSD brought everything into focus for the first time in our mixed-up lives. . . . [U]ntil we started eating all that acid we couldn't figure out what was happening—we knew things were all wrong the way they were but we didn't know how they could be different, which meant we really didn't know which way to move. LSD cleared all that up. . . .[29]

For Sinclair and the rest of his cohort who would form the White Panther Party in 1968, their acid visions turned them from anomie and isolation to a belief in the possibility of a communal youth consciousness. Acid was a tool, they believed, in achieving a group identity, a new collective social presence that could change society. For Sinclair's group, dropping acid pointed them toward political struggle.

In San Francisco, a horde of visionaries traveling from different origin points coalesced uneasily around the hard kick LSD provided. In 1966, Stephen Gaskin, who'd been teaching English at San Francisco State, began talking out loud, before increasingly large audiences, about the meaning of his acid visions and the collective wisdom he thought they offered: "We have a kind of funny thing in this culture because you can take a psychedelic, and then you can experience satori, probably, you know, if your Karma's not too bad you can probably just get kicked right into it for awhile, whether you notice it or recognize it or not. It may not even be the part of the trip you enjoy the most." Gaskin mused about a common acid experience:

I started slipping into myself. . . . Then I was looking from over a view of a little creek that was very bright yellow, running down over the rocks. I looked at it, and there were bubbles in it. And suddenly I was one of the bubbles on the creek, running down this little golden river. I bounced around a few times, and then I popped. My bubble popped, and then I was indistinguishably a part of the river."

Dow Chemical's contemporary advertising slogan was appropriated (*detournement*) by a popular poster in the late 1960s and early '70s, one extolling the ecstatic potentialities of LSD. Copyright © Kansas Collection, Spencer Research Library, University of Kansas.

For Gaskin, acid pointed toward a lived experience of collective harmony. Acid supplied that vision; realizing it would be up to the visionaries. Acid was, again, only a means for creating a better vision by which to live.[30]

Allen Cohen, who co-founded the first underground psychedelic newspaper in 1966, the *San Francisco Oracle*, saw the role of LSD similarly. He described LSD as "the rocket engine of most of the social or creative tendencies that were emerging in the 1960s. It sped up change by opening a direct pathway to the creative and mystical insights that visionaries, artists and saints have sought and experienced and communicated through the ages. . . ." The availability of LSD, Cohen believed, meant that "The rebellion, insight and visionary experiences of the artists of the 50s would now come wholesale to anyone who wanted or needed to get out on the edges of the only frontier left in America—their own mind and their own senses."[31]

Cohen used his acid visions to push for a collective enterprise, a social beacon of what could be if given the right cultural orientation. He and others so attuned began "a rainbow newspaper," a multicolored trip sheet expressive of the "cosmic consciousness" LSD proffered. The *Oracle* became a sounding board for acid visions. It explored Eastern religions, American Indian rituals, and the artistic sensibilities of the mind blown. With the acid faith that nothing that was had to be, the *Oracle* promoted a deliberately naive investigation of the premises of pre-industrial and non-industrial cultures. What if, the *Oracle*'s writers and artists pondered, those pre-industrial or non-industrial cultures had it right? What if key aspects of American culture, like the materialist striving for individual status, was a tragic wrong turn?

The Haight-Ashbury district of San Francisco became a critical nexus for this acid possibility, in part because of its decades-old bohemian trajectory, in part because acid was more easily available there than anywhere else in the world (due to the efforts of the underground acid chemist Augustus Owsley Stanley III and his compatriots). In 1965, Ron Thelin, the son of the man who managed the Woolworth's on Haight Street, dropped a sugar cube dosed with "Owsley" acid. In January 1966, he opened up the Psychedelic Shop at 1535 Haight. He and his brother stocked "everything an acidhead might be interested in"—incense, esoteric books, Indian paisley prints, brass bells, dope pipes, posters, bamboo flutes—anything that moved the eye or touched the ear or tickled the body in an unexpected way. It was a "head shop."[32] Other acid-driven enterprises ensued. The district became a place to try out the reality-bending trips acid offered.

In that district, the Diggers, better than anyone else, played with acid possibilities. The Diggers were loosely self-defined "Life-Actors." Most of the original crew had met as members of the San Francisco Mime Troupe and had decided in 1966 to take their theater into the everyday acts of their collective enterprises. Acid, of course, was not the only fuel driving Digger energies. The men and women in San Francisco who went by the name Diggers from 1966 to 1968 took off from multiple points of view. But conceptually what united them was, in the words of Digger co-founder Peter Coyote, "the competition to 'de-school' yourself, to continually transcend limits when you discover them." A prime tool in that process was drugs. The Diggers, like all of the people referenced here, by no means restricted themselves to acid. In search of "hard kicks"—the means to shatter the day-in and day-out from which they meant to diverge—some shot heroin and speed. The inner circle prided themselves on being edge-walkers unafraid of using whatever tools were necessary to de-link themselves from cold war structures and the commercial marketplace.[33]

The Diggers used spectacle and pageantry to turn the streets of the Haight-Ashbury into a steady play on the possibility of concrete imagination. Working from a garage they called the Free Frame of Reference they gave away food they had scavenged from produce markets, butchers, and other sources to the young runaways (and anybody else who wanted it) who had begun to crowd the psychedelic Haight. They gave out the food at the Fell Street Panhandle of Golden Gate Park: "It's free because it's yours," they explained. For a time those who wanted the food passed through an orange thirteen-foot-square Frame of Reference. Emmett Grogan, a key instigator, explained: "When the Free Food arrived, it would be placed on one side of the frame and the hungry would be made to walk through it to get at the stew and whatever else was being shared on the other side, changing their frame of reference as they did."[34] The frame was an acid flash mnemonic, a way to remember that their ways did not have to be your ways.

As LSD use rippled through the United States and Europe, authorities worried. The Swiss pharmaceutical giant Sandoz, which had been the sole commercial supplier of LSD, decided to pull the plug in 1965. In an official letter released August 23, 1965, Sandoz stated: "All the evidence . . . carried out in the Sandoz research laboratories pointed to the important role this substance could play in neurological research and in psychiatry . . . [but] cases of LSD abuse have occurred. . . . The flood of requests for LSD . . . has now become uncontrollable."[35] While a Czech lab would later take up commercial production for research authorized by various government bodies, LSD users became almost completely dependent on so-called underground chemists and dealers. As a result, "pure" LSD became essentially unavailable; "street" LSD often deliberately contained speed—some producers believed this was a useful aid in tripping—or impurities accidentally introduced in the underground production facilities.[36] The massive turn from pharmaceutical to underground

LSD was compounded by state and federal government officials' decisions to make LSD possession and distribution illegal.

Three major congressional hearings were held on LSD in 1966.[37] The hearings were driven by the increasing unauthorized use of LSD and the spectacular mass media coverage that use produced. The mass media began covering LSD use with a vengeance in early 1966. The expanded coverage was due, in large part, to doctors' reports of LSD-induced psychiatric breakdowns. As *Time* magazine reported in March 1966, "The disease is striking in beach side beatnik pads and in the dormitories of expensive prep schools; it has grown into an alarming problem at UCLA and on the UC campus at Berkeley." The federal Food and Drug Administration contributed to the media attention by briefing reporters on LSD-induced breakdowns and violent episodes. Local police departments followed the FDA lead and told local reporters of similar incidents they had investigated. The Los Angeles police described such incidents as two young men chewing tree bark under the influence of LSD; a man screaming "I love you! I love you!" while kneeling in the Pacific Ocean; and two teenagers having sex in the hall of an apartment building while yelling "god" and "life" very loudly. The behavior was clearly not normal, but the LAPD had arrested only four youths for LSD-related incidents in the first four months of 1966.

While violent behavior was, in fact, extremely rare among LSD users, sober-minded researchers by 1966 had accumulated enough data to argue that LSD use was clearly risky. About two percent of LSD users had severe psychological or emotional reactions, and of that group about one-third suffered a psychotic break. These figures suggested that about seven out of one thousand people would experience some kind of mental breakdown from LSD use. In fact, most people who suffered severe adverse effects from LSD experimentation had histories of severe psychological problems. But none of the early advocates of LSD use would have been surprised by the researchers' statistics. They were aware that LSD, so to speak, played for keeps. That was a piece of the adventure. The problem, of course, was: How many American teenagers knew the price they might pay for their trip?

The congressional committees deciding the legal status of LSD heard a great deal of testimony about the dangers of the drug. Not unlike the hearings that produced federal criminalization of marijuana in the 1930s, much of what Congress heard involved highly sensationalized stories of drug-induced violence. But some testimony spoke to a more profound concern about the unsupervised, wide-open use of LSD and about its effect on young people's cultural values. Dr. Stanley Cohen testified that his research into LSD use left him deeply troubled: "We have seen something which in a way is most alarming, more alarming than death in a way. And that is the loss of all cultural values, the loss of feeling of right and wrong, of good and bad. These people lead a valueless life, without motivation, without ambition . . . they are decultured, lost to society, lost to themselves."[38] Cohen asserted that most people who used LSD did not gain radical new insights into their own lives or society. They just became unproductive, amoral citizens, lost in empty dreams that led nowhere. National and local authorities overwhelmingly agreed that LSD use was dangerous both to individuals and to society. LSD was made illegal in 1966; possession and distribution were criminalized. LSD advocates' claim that acid opened the mind's eye to new possibilities was deemed delusional, or an outcome not worth the risks, by those who had the power to arrest and jail people.

The onslaught against LSD resulted in a counterattack by the nation's best-known advocate, Dr. Timothy Leary. Leary had been ambivalent for several years about the utility of LSD among unsupervised, spiritually disinclined individuals. He and his Millbrook colleagues were suspicious of the Merry Pranksters' promiscuous distribution of LSD. But in the face of the mass media, congressional, and legal attacks on LSD, Leary launched into LSD promotion. He met with the reigning mass media expert of the times, Marshall McLuhan, and brainstormed. McLuhan, according to Leary, suggested the following: "You must use the most current tactics for arousing consumer interest. Associate LSD with all the good things that the brain can produce—beauty, fun, philosophic wonder, religious revelation, increased intelligence and mystical romance." As spokesman, McLuhan continued, Leary must always smile when photographed, "never appear angry and radiate courage." Leary understood the risk: "I was pushed from scientific detachment and scholarly retirement into public opposition to the policies of the ruling regime." Soon after, Leary came up with an advertising slogan: "Turn On, Tune In, Drop Out," by which he meant, "Activate your neural and genetic equipment . . . interact harmoniously with the world around you . . . [pursue] an active, selective and graceful process of detachment from involuntary or unconscious commitments." Leary also saw, quickly enough, that "the press took it to mean 'get stoned and abandon all constructive activity.'"[39] Many among the LSD-attuned scene were dismayed by Leary's huckstering, even if they understood why he was doing it. His use of a 1966 *Playboy* magazine interview to promote LSD use by claiming, among other absurdities, that women stoned on LSD might well have hundreds of orgasms during a single sexual encounter further distressed and angered LSD compatriots.[40]

Taken together with the mass media attention and the government's decisions to criminalize LSD, Leary's promotions indicated that the meanings attached to LSD use were multiplying and were hotly contested. Federal and state authorities had weighed in. "Medical science" was fighting for re-control. Learyites, Keseyites, Diggers, White Panthers, and other acid visionaries were no longer speaking to small circles of fellow travelers. Increasingly, a curious mass was hearing the LSD conversation refracted and spread through the mass media. Underground chemists were making acid, and street dealers were selling it around the country. LSD, as a cultural artifact, was in play. Its possible uses/abuses were by no means restricted to Leary's spiritual discourse, Kesey's notion of intrepid tripping, the Diggers' pursuit of hard kicks, or the musings of underground newspapers like the *Oracle* that promoted acid as an entryway to a new collective youth culture.

As the number of LSD users and the drug's cultural manifestations multiplied, some individuals struggled to build lives attuned to their acid visions. In the midst of nineteenth-century industrialization, Karl Marx had argued that consciousness emerged out of material conditions at the point of production (i.e., at the workplace). By the mid-twentieth century, LSD advocates—in sync with a host of ad men and corporate marketers—had turned that thought on its head. Consciousness, they would argue, came at the point of consumption. But those most committed to turning their acid dreams into ongoing lives—not the majority of users—understood that the Marxian focus on production was dead-on. Even if the origin point for their cultural departure was not built from some factory floor epiphany, they understood that the reproduction of their acid-based identity would take more than staying high. They had to figure out how to live the vision acid proffered, and that took effort built on the material plane.

The Haight-Ashbury, Chicago's Old Town, blocks of Manhattan's Lower East Side, and chunks of Atlanta's 14th Street were all laboratories in that process. Many of the more committed residents of those districts helped keep the experiment up and running by selling illegal drugs. By becoming drug dealers these advocates of alternative consciousness took another step toward breaking free of the rules and constraints demanded by what was then called "straight" society. Staking out a few blocks of core cities, and smuggling or producing and then selling dope, gave them the economic means to pursue their new way of life even as it contributed to the reproduction of their new drug-driven cultural scene. But by the late 1960s, that point of production and reproduction was breaking apart.

Two forces were at work. The first was the increasing police attention the highly visible and, by 1966, criminalized "freak" culture attracted. By the late 1960s, Kesey, Leary, Sinclair, and thousands of lesser known hallucinogenic drug advocates were caught in the criminal justice system or under constant police threat. In Chicago, for example, the staff of the pro-acid underground newspaper the SEED endured regular police surveillance and harassment. The Diggers had to watch city building inspectors bust apart their wooden Frame of Reference and use the pieces to board up their headquarters in the Haight-Ashbury. These experiences were unpleasantly normal for most visible advocates of the drug culture.

The criminalization of LSD (and the earlier criminalization of marijuana) emphasized—in an often misleading way—the divide between the world of the stoned and the world of the drunk. By making everyone who was stoned a part of an "illegal nation," the "Intoxicated State" seemed to define all drug users as a part of a counterculture, whether they used their stoned state simply to watch TV and giggle or to figure out how to live a completely new life as far outside the boundaries of the State and commercial marketplace as they could get. Government authorities, supported by most Americans, saw illegal drug use as a dangerous practice. Parents worried about the physical and mental health of their children and feared that drug use would turn their children away from parental authority and productive lives. Many parents and authorities worried that the use of obviously less dangerous drugs, like marijuana, would lead to the use of clearly more dangerous drugs, like heroin. Parents worried, too, that their children's use of illegal drugs might result in their arrest and incarceration. Many antidrug advocates made little effort to differentiate between the illegal drugs and cared even less as to why people used the illegal drugs they did. To drop LSD after 1966 and, even more so, to produce or to sell it was to risk jail.

Criminalization made LSD use both more dangerous (impure "street" acid/jail time) and more a clear sign of cultural rebellion. Just by using LSD or even marijuana, an individual was declaring himself or herself an opponent of the status quo willing to go to jail in pursuit of a favorite form of altered consciousness. Society had declared that everyone who dropped acid was a criminal. It didn't matter, by this legally binding definition, if one's acid experience caused one, while in a sober state, to somehow counter American culture or to somehow adopt an altered consciousness as a result of one's drug experience. The very act of dropping acid, authorities and most parents said, was in and of itself a verification that one was a member of something called "the counterculture." As those who counted themselves—or got counted as— a part of the "psychedelic revolution" grew in number, the meaning and practice of the "counterculture" in the United States became ever more diffuse.

Jerry Rubin, a leading Berkeley antiwar activist in the mid-1960s, saw the potential political meaning of the turn toward illegal drug use in the late 1960s by young people. Talking about the criminalization of marijuana use (and marijuana was the mildest and most popular of the illegal highs sought in the Sixties era), Rubin wrote: "Grass shows us that our lives, not our consciousness, are at stake. As pot-heads we came face to face with the real world of cops, jails, courts, trials, undercover narcs, paranoia and the war with our parents. An entire generation of flower-smokers has been turned into criminals. . . . Grass teaches us disrespect for the law and the courts."[41] Rubin, a decent political tactician, was trying to increase his radical constituency by enfolding anyone who'd taken a toke into his cause. He and another "turned-on" political radical, Abbie Hoffman, teamed up in 1968 to form the Yippies in an attempt to bring drug-using "hippies" into the political movements of the era. The Yippies and the State, strange bedfellows, were claiming/making a counterculture, so to speak, out of a great many people who were, in effect, no more radical than speakeasy patrons in the 1920s or underage nicotine addicts in the 1990s.

In addition to the problems posed by criminalization of psychedelics, many of the youths who flocked to the hip enclaves, whether as long-term runaways or short-time "day-trippers," were ill prepared for spiritual exploration or cultural creation. Some were just clueless kids caught in a mass-mediated fad. It looked like fun but, as many found out, it was not. In early 1967 the San Francisco Diggers attacked the Learyite LSD/counterculture promotions that lured the unwary to a life for which they were not ready. In a broadside titled "Uncle Tim'$ Children," the Diggers wrote:

> Pretty little 16-year-old middle-class chick comes to the Haight to
> see what it's all about & gets picked up by a 17–year-old street
> dealer who spends all day shooting her full of speed again & again,
> then feeds her 3000 mikes [of acid] and raffles off her temporarily
> unemployed body for the biggest Haight Street gang bang since the
> night before last. The politics & ethics of ecstasy. . . . Tune in, turn
> on, drop dead? One wonders.[42]

So-called hippie enclaves throughout the United States attracted a great many hard cases interested above all in taking advantage of those who believed that "turning on" indicated a wholehearted commitment to collective harmony, a.k.a. peace and love. As one self-described "hippie drug dealer" admitted in an underground newspaper, "Dealers on the whole you know, uh, are . . . pretty, uh, unreasonable, uh, dishonest . . . thieves."[43] Ed Sanders, a member of the rock group The Fugs, poet, and skeptical cofounder of the Yippies, put it most provocatively: the counterculture is a "valley of plump rabbits surrounded by wounded coyotes."[44] Charles Manson was not the only "acid fascist" trolling the turbulent waters in which too many turned-on youths floundered.[45]

Drug use, including acid, did not automatically redirect users anywhere in particular. Acid was a powerful substance that could shatter minds, provoke ecstatic visions, facilitate profound insights. But LSD did not, in and of itself, make people rebel just as working on a shop floor did not make everyone dream of joining a labor union. LSD, as well as other consciousness-altering tools, did enable some users to map a new consciousness, a new set of cultural coordinates. It was not the getting high, per se, that mattered to this relatively small group of explorers—though the euphoria and the grand inner adventure their high provided them were critical to the kick that propelled many to imagine new life possibilities. It was the sense and sensibility that altered consciousness provided, often channeled by the collective or group-oriented drug-taking process itself, that encouraged some drug users to seek realities of their own making.

By fall 1967, many of the more dedicated explorers began leaving the hip enclaves in which they had first played out the dramas of their acid consciousness. For the more capable and dedicated these places had become overrun with too many ill-equipped kids who were not able to turn their visions—often derivative visions structured by mass-mediated versions of "hippie"—into workable realities. The Diggers, in league with fellow travelers, literally celebrated "The Death of Hippie" on October 6, 1967 when they paraded down the streets of the Haight with a makeshift coffin full of beads, bangles, flowers, and hair which they burned on a funeral pyre. They left the city and began looking for more controllable enclaves. The Diggers set up a series of communes in northern California. Others moved to Vermont, Colorado, New Mexico, Hawaii. . . . . Stephen Gaskin led hundreds of San Francisco hippies to a rural area of Tennessee where they worked hard to build the Farm. In 1968, original Merry Prankster veteran Stewart Brand coordinated an effort that produced *The Whole Earth Catalog*, a compendium of practical and theoretical information for people who wanted to set up rural communes or otherwise take part in the back-to-the-land movement. Rather than preaching the utility of such early tools as acid and grass, the *Catalog* detailed where to get the next generation of equipment—geodesic domes, farm implements, how-to-guides—that would turn acid visions into lived environments. "If we're gods, we might as well get good at it," Brand half-joked.[46]

By the late 1960s—and thereafter—getting high could result in jail time but did not necessarily mean you believed in peace and love. The Illegal Nation of drug takers was populated by a citizenry without one overarching higher purpose. Exotic drug use and such encoded accoutrements of the acid flash as tie-dyed clothes, strobe lights, and psychedelic posters had made their way into the great American shopping mall. Youth culture and the counterculture blurred on network television shows and major label record promotions. Timothy Leary and the Grateful Dead became iconic representations of just another variant of celebrityhood. The structures of the marketplace did consume much of the sublime, raw visions of alternative realities that LSD had flashed inside the minds of individuals. (Another essay could and should explain that just because the marketplace, in some ways, was able to consume aspects of the LSD experience does not mean that nothing significant happened, post-Sixties, as a result of that hegemonic incorporation, to that process we call the market or to us in our social roles as consumers and producers of that market; consider a close reading of Ben and Jerry, *Outside* magazine, the Santa Fe Flea market, and yesterday's pot luck at the Zen Center.)

Acid (and other hallucinogenics), as hard kick, as producer of visions, was no small instrumentality. People, then, used it to rethink who they were and what they wanted. Some people dropped acid (or ingested psilocybin mushrooms or peyote), and their lives changed forever. A subset of those people acted on their visions of another way, a more collective way in which simple living facilitated spiritual searching. Many attempted to live off the land; scorning materialism, they sought a simple life more attuned to the natural world. Some grew marijuana, many took up craft and artisanal work. They are still out there, well into a third generation, coming together by the tens of thousands once a year at the Rainbow Gatherings. These counterculturists meant it. So did many others who lived outside the law and social custom and then reassimilated into mainstream society.[47] The hallucinogenic age, while tamed in some respects, has survived and mutated and reproduced. The absurdly self-important solipsism of the hallucinogenic experience is revealed in the torpid narcissism of much of the behavior associated with New Age spiritual adherents. Then, too, the reality-shattering possibilities of the acid flash glimmers in social spaces crafted by people who still know that visions matter. LSD, some of its users might note, erases the boundaries between inner processes and external settings, between the contrived line dividing culture and counterculture.

ACKNOWLEDGMENTS
Special thanks for critical readings offered by Beth Bailey, Diana Robin, Virginia Scharff, Peter Braunstein, and Michael Doyle.

NOTES
1. Mezz Mezzrow and Bernard Wolfe, *Really the Blues* (New York: Citadel Underground, 1990), 73. *Really the Blues* was first published in 1946. Mezzrow, of course, was the marijuana-peddling, jazz-playing hipster, born white in Chicago in 1899, who opted to become, in all ways possible, a black man. He was no day-tripper.

2. Thomas Frank, *The Conquest of Cool* (Chicago: University of Chicago Press, 1997), 29. For a recent celebration of the market utility of "alternative" cultures see Janine Lopiano-Misdon and Joanna de Luca, *Street Trends: How Today's Alternative Youth Cultures Are Creating Tomorrow's Mainstream Markets* (New York: Harper Business, 1998). The authors are corporate consultants who sell their knowledge of what's happening among urban youth to the highest bidders.

3. David Farber, *The Age of Great Dreams* (New York: Hill and Wang, 1994), 16.

4. David Farber, *Chicago '68* (Chicago: University of Chicago Press, 1988). Chapters 2, 3, and 7, address the suspicion and even contempt with which many Old and New Leftists viewed countercultural tendencies and adherents.

5. The politics of labeling the counterculture as just another free market variation are fairly straightforward. If "countercultural" hedonism is, at base, capitalistic behavior engendered by consumer desire, it puts conservatives in an awkward position. Maybe the market—not liberals—produces some unpleasant outcomes the market cannot rectify. Drug laws, of course, interfere with the free market demand for certain substances; if such drug laws are acceptable why are not other interferences in the free market? Staunch economic conservatives, such as Milton Friedman, accept this logic and argue for the repeal of drug laws.

6. Who among us is not acquainted with a "Deadhead," who subsequent to the Grateful Dead's demise in 1995 has turned to alternative groups such as Phish? I have a young relative, a business student interested in real estate development, who considers himself a "Deadhead." His position informs this essay as do reports from Wall Street, on the day of Jerry Garcia's death, that many traders were in mourning, noting that Jerry was, like them, a "risk taker." Consider the editorial by Micah Morrison, "Jerry Garcia: A True Original," published in the *Wall Street Journal*, 17 August 1995, on the editorial page.

7. One of the few academic historians to write about the rise of drug use in the United States, John Burnham, lumps most drug users together and argues that, really, they all were just irresponsible hedonists after a dumb, dangerous kind of fun. His picture of drug users is heavy on portraits of losers—not unlike discussing the use of alcoholic beverages in the United States by honing in on skid row. Burnham is right to show how badly many have used drugs, but his enfolding of the counterculture within a portrait of American drug abuse is like locking Jefferson into a portrait of slaveholding; John Burnham, *Bad Habits* (New York: New York University, 1993), chap. 5.

8. Marshall Sahlins, *Islands of History* (Chicago: University of Chicago Press, 1985), ix.

9. William Sewell, "A Theory of Structure: Duality, Agency and Transformation," *American Journal of Sociology* 98 (1992), no. 1: 18–19.

10. The drug statistics come from Jay Stevens, *Storming Heaven: LSD and the American Dream* (New York: Harper and Row, 1988), 306. Valley of the Dolls was Sixties slang for addiction to prescription drugs; for more, see Jacqueline Susann, *Valley of the Dolls* (New York: Random House, 1966).

11. The statistic is provided by Burnham, *Bad Habits*, 102.

12. Ibid., 74. See also W. J. Rorabaugh, *The Alcoholic Republic: An American Tradition* (New York: Oxford University Press, 1979).

13. In the 1960s, too, people on both sides of the illegal drug debate tended to act as if the question was whether or not drug use was good or healthy. People talked about "straights" versus people who got "stoned." In the 1960s, "straight" meant someone who did not use illegal drugs (and looked the part, i.e, for a man, short hair, neat and bland appearance). This false dichotomy made it then, and now, harder to understand why certain substances that affected mind and body, such as tobacco and alcoholic beverages, were legal and widespread and others, like marijuana and LSD, were illegal.

14. The story of LSD, especially from Sandoz to Owsley and as experienced by acid luminaries, is best told by Jay Stevens in *Storming Heaven*. Besides its being a page-turner, Stevens has written a masterpiece in the history of culture and technology. The best autobiographical

account of LSD use is by the early zealot Michael Hollingshead, *The Man Who Turned On the World* (New York: Abelard-Schum, Ltd., 1974 [© 1973]), available at http://www.psychedeliclibrary.org/hollings.htm.

15. Ellen Herman, *The Romance of American Psychology* (Berkeley: University of California Press, 1995). Herman brilliantly explores the therapeutic turn in American history.

16. I am leaving out a critical part of the story. The CIA and the United States Army also heavily subsidized LSD experiments into the 1950s. While this sounds like a paranoid conspiracy theory, it is simply true. LSD seemed to have potential uses as a truth serum, or possibly a means of driving enemies crazy. See John Marks, *The Search for the Manchurian Candidate: The CIA and Mind Control* (New York: Times Books, 1979) and Martin Lee and Bruce Shlain, *Acid Dreams: The CIA, LSD, and the Sixties Rebellion* (New York: Grove Press, 1985).

17. Quoted in Bruce Eisner, "LSD Purity—Cleanliness Is Next to Godliness," *High Times*, #17 January 1977. A slightly different version of this line appears in Ken Kesey, "Dope," in *Kesey's Garage Sale* (New York: Viking, 1973), 191.

18. Albert Hofmann relates LSD success stories such as these in *LSD—My Problem Child* (New York: McGraw-Hill, 1980), chap. 5; unpaginated on the web at http://www.psychedeliclibrary.org/ho115.htm.

19. Ibid., chap. 5.

20. An invaluable treatment of LSD as psychological tool is given by Stanislav Grof, *LSD Psychotherapy* (Alameda, Calif.: Hunter House, 1994).

21. Hofmann, *LSD*, chap. 5.

22. Leary's celebrity role in America by the late 1960s made him seem to most a kind of charlatan—a butt of Johnny Carson and other late-night comedians. Leary's lecture tours in the 1980s, where he was sometimes paired with Watergate burglar and right-wing talk show host G. Gordon Liddy, solidified the crackpot image. Intriguingly, by the end of the twentieth century, his persona was being reorganized on the Internet where his writings and deeds are celebrated on numerous sites. For a perceptive account of Leary's social roles see Stevens, *Storming Heaven*, 166–70.

23. Hollingshead, *The Man Who Turned On the World*, 7–8.

24. Both articles are excerpted in Hollingshead, 40–41 and 59–63, respectively.

25. Timothy Leary, *Flashbacks: A Personal and Cultural History of the Era; an Autobiography* (Los Angeles: Jeremy P. Tarcher, 1983), chap. 11, "Prisoners to Prophets."

26. For one version of this story see http://www.leary.com/Biography/Millbrook/millbrook.html. This is a page from Leary's own website devised before his death on May 31, 1996. The site has several key documents from his Harvard and Millbrook days.

27. From a Prankster recollection of the road trip: Gurney Norman, interview by Ron Grele, September 1986, 44–47, Columbia Oral History Project Research Office, Columbia University, New York. A classic account of the Pranksters is by Tom Wolfe, *The Electric Kool-Aid Acid Test* (New York: Bantam, 1968).

28. Stevens, *Storming Heaven*, 249.

29. John Sinclair, *Guitar Army* (New York: Douglas Books, 1972), 22–23.

30. The quotes and other material come from a copyrighted piece titled "The Farm," by Albert Bates, found on the Internet via the home page of the Farm, the Gaskin-led community in Summertown, Tennessee: http:www.thefarm.org/lifestyle/miller.html.

31. Allen Cohen, "The San Francisco Oracle: A Brief History," in *San Francisco Oracle Facsimile Edition: The Psychedelic Newspaper of the Haight-Ashbury, 1966–1968*, ed. Allen Cohen, xxiv (Berkeley, Calif.: Regent Press, 1991). Also on the Net at http://www.rockument.com/webora.html —"Additional Notes on the S.F. Oracle: For the *Haight-Ashbury in The Sixties* CD-ROM," 4.

32. For an empathic portrait of Ron Thelin see Peter Coyote's *Sleeping Where I Fall* (Washington, D.C.: Counterpoint Press, 1998), 133–36; also available on the Internet in the incomparable Digger Archives overseen by Eric Noble; Peter Coyote, "Ron Thelin and the Red

House," http://www.diggers.org/freefall/redhouse.html. For the Psychedelic Store see the rich portrait by Charles Perry, *The Haight-Ashbury* (New York: Vintage, 1985), 76.

33. The quote is from Peter Coyote, interviewed by Etan Ben-Ami, Mill Valley, Calif., 12 January 1989, 8; the Digger Archives: http://www.diggers.org/oralhistory/peter_interview.html.

34. Described by Grogan in his autobiography, which tells Grogan's truths as he felt they needed to be known; Emmett Grogan, *Ringolevio* (Boston: Little, Brown, 1972), 250. Grogan's essential work was reprinted in the much-missed Citadel Underground series.

35. Hofmann, *LSD—My Problem Child*, chap. 5 (unpaginated on the web).

36. Eisner, "LSD Purity—Cleanliness Is next to Godliness," *High Times*, #17 January 1977.

37. The debate and decisions leading to the criminalization of LSD are compellingly narrated by Jay Stevens in *Storming Heaven*; read it for a fuller, richer treatment of the criminalization process. This section is based on Steven's chap. 21, "Psychotic Reaction." While sympathetic to LSD use, the book is extremely well researched and documented.

38. Taken directly from a passage quoted by Stevens, 279. Sidney Cohen was a behavioral scientist who had been running clinical studies of LSD use; see Cohen, *The Beyond Within* (New York: Athenaeum, 1965).

39. All quotes are from the Leary website: http://leary.com/Biography/Cheerleader/cheerleader.html.

40. "Playboy Interview: Timothy Leary," *Playboy*, Sept. 1966, 100. For a good example of the disgust with which some viewed Leary's promotions see Grogan, *Ringolevio*, 268.

41. Jerry Rubin, *Do It!* (New York: Ballantine, 1970), 100.

42. A broadside issued by ComCo, mainly the work of Chester Anderson in loose partnership with the Diggers, "Uncle Tim'$ Children," CC030: Uncle Tim's Children, Digger Archives, http://www.diggers.org/bibscans/cc030a_m.gif.

43. "Alice?" *Vortex* (Lawrence, Kansas), 4–17 February 1970, 5–6.

44. Quoted in Terry Anderson, *The Movement and The Sixties: Protest in America from Greensboro to Wounded Knee* (New York: Oxford University Press, 1995), 286.

45. See the classic David Felton, *Mindfuckers: A Source Book on the Rise of Acid Fascism in America, Including Material on Charles Manson, Mel Lyman, Victor Baranco and Their Followers* (San Francisco: Straight Arrow Books, 1972).

46. Farber, *The Age of Great Dreams*, 188.

47. While working on this piece I spoke to fifteen people from both the "Sixties generation" and those born in the late 1950s to mid-1970s about their acid experiences. Only two of them—both of them older—had participated in rural communal living driven, in part, by their LSD experiences. All, however, stressed that their LSD experiences were important and changed their lives at least in some small way. One more thing: somebody should write a book about the race/class/gender meanings and practice of drug use. My story has focused mainly on the white men (of different socioeconomic backgrounds) who did their best to direct LSD use toward hard kicks and sacramental use. Writing a good social history of illegal drug production and use in America is extremely difficult, as I have learned the hard way. Those who live outside the law are almost never honest.

Two

From "Consciousness Expansion" to "Consciousness Raising"

Feminism and the Countercultural Politics of the Self

Debra Michals

On an August evening in 1968 in an apartment in New York City, a dozen or
so women huddled together watching a feminist experimental film called
Schmearguntz.[1] Part of a weekly "rap" session for the year-old women's liberation group New York Radical Women (NYRW), the art film sparked an
intense and emotional discussion. Members of the group were most disturbed
by the images of Miss America that flashed across the screen, as they recalled
their own struggles with body image from adolescence into adulthood.[2]
Personal memories of growing up in the shadow of the pageants intertwined
with social critique, and before the reel wound down, it became clear to all
present that the commodification of beauty was the hallmark of male privilege
and women's oppression.[3] They saw a connection between organized pageants
in macrocosm and the ways in which, in microcosm, girls, and later women,
learned to internalize messages linking female social value with the individual's approximation to the Miss America ideal of beauty and congeniality. In
the months since many of these women had broken with civil rights, New
Left, and other groups, they searched for an appropriate first political activity.[4] Now it was right in front of them: they would picket the upcoming Miss
America Pageant in Atlantic City, New Jersey.[5]

With just a few weeks to go before the pageant, members of NYRW sent
out a call to action that brought over 100 protesters from many of the nascent

women's liberation groups around the country.[6] Borrowing from the guerrilla street theater techniques that were the hallmark of the counterculture, these young women crowned a sheep "Miss America"—paralleling a similar action by the Yippies who months earlier had nominated a pig for president[7]—and threw girdles and other symbols of sexist oppression into a "freedom trash can."[8] They waved banners and handed out leaflets headed with such phrases as "Miss America Sells It." To invert sexual inequality, organizers refused to speak to male reporters and would be interviewed by female journalists only. News cameras nonetheless captured every minute of the demonstration, and, to date, it stands as the pivotal moment—a sort of "Day One"[9]—for the burgeoning women's liberation movement. While organizers and participants came away with different interpretations of the protest itself, they agreed that it was a success if for no other reason than it introduced the nation to this younger, more radical arm of the women's movement, one that unlike the National Organization for Women would not settle for a few reformist crumbs from the establishment table.[10] Rather, as NYRW and other groups made clear from the start, they wanted an all-out revolution in gender roles and relations.[11]

The August "rap session" and the now famous demonstration it inspired illustrate a vital link between feminist strategies for changing society and those proffered by the so-called counterculture. Aside from direct replication of street theater, at the core of the similarity is the very organizing technique—consciousness raising—that led to the pageant protest in the first place. The 1960s were awash with countercultural strategies for social revolution, many of which built upon varying notions of "consciousness" as the key to overhauling society. For these groups, consciousness referred to adopting a new perception, becoming aware of the ways in which the existing patriarchal, capitalistic order co-opted the individual's core human existence and identity.[12] Coming to consciousness was about unraveling the lessons learned from birth—the very socialization process—so that the individual could see how the system operated to mold one's social self, and in doing so, envision alternatives. As Charles Reich described in *The Greening of America* (1970), "today's emerging consciousness seeks a new knowledge of what it means to be human ... in order that man can once more become a creative force, renewing and creating his own life and thus giving life back to his society."[13] In lieu of unquestioningly playing the social roles that were expected in terms of work, goals, and interpersonal relations—entering "role prison"[14]—consciousness would facilitate a "new way of life [that] makes both possible and necessary a culture that is nonartificial and nonalienated, a form of community in which love, respect, and a mutual search for wisdom replace the competition and separation of the past, and a liberation of each individual in which he is

Recognized as a pivotal moment in the history of the women's movement, the 1968 protest at the Miss America pageant in Atlantic City, N.J. was actually the result of consciousness raising. Women meeting in New York to talk about the aspects of public culture that exploited and held women back ultimately settled on the pageant as a vivid example. The mission of the protest: to show how pageants objectified women, reducing them to the same process of grading cattle used at state fairs, valuing beauty over brains, and dividing women rather than uniting them. Many of the placards and banners were made at CR meetings both in New York and nationwide, proving that from speaking did indeed come action. Henry Crossman/TimePix.

enabled to grow toward the highest possibilities of the human spirit."[15] As Reich added with countercultural zeal, "This means a 'new head'—a new way of living—a new man" or woman.[16]

Grappling for a way to build a coalition of women, some radical feminists expanded on these philosophies to develop what came to be known as CR. Put simply, consciousness raising referred to the notion that by coming together weekly in small groups to discuss their individual female experiences, women would not only end their isolation but would also learn that what they assumed to be their personal problems had broader social implications.[17] In short, by talking about everything from beauty and work to sex and marriage, participants would uncover a collective female oppression, which, proponents believed, would ultimately lead women to join together in rebelling against the status quo.[18] The line drawn by CR was from self-discovery to social discovery, from self-actualization to social change.

The genesis of CR was an early NYRW meeting in 1967, when Anne Forer told the group that before they took political action, they needed to "raise their consciousness."[19] Kathie Sarachild, Carol Hanisch, and other members were intrigued by the expression and began to explore ways to bring this articulation to life. "I've only begun thinking about women as an oppressed group," Forer explained, "and each day, I'm still learning more about it—my consciousness gets higher."[20] Ultimately Sarachild and her cohorts at NYRW developed a detailed program for CR, but it was Forer who ignited the spark. Sarachild ultimately coined the phrase "consciousness raising," and she and Hanisch knew from their experiences as civil rights workers the potency of that movement's strategy of "speaking truth to power."[21] Other influences no doubt included the politics of "speaking pains to recall pains" from the Chinese Revolution,[22] the rising popularity of psychotherapy encounter groups, and the increasing awareness of the hippie emphasis on "consciousness expansion." After all, in the burgeoning media culture of the 1960s, new trends, lifestyles, and philosophies were rapidly circulated and popularized in the mainstream press,[23] while an expanding underground press proliferated countercultural ideas and politics. Terms like "consciousness" could be, and were, subsumed into the public vocabulary virtually overnight. In addition, many of the anti-establishment groups of that era, while remaining distinct, undoubtedly knew intimate details about each other's credos because their paths crossed at several key '60s events, such as the 1967 Be-In, which brought drug culture enthusiasts together with the New Left; the 1968 Democratic Convention, which convened Yippies, New Left, and women's liberationists; and the many antiwar demonstrations of the era, which united all of these groups in an effort to stop the fighting in Vietnam.[24] For the upstart women's groups of 1968 forging their own brand of consciousness, the pageant protest proved a test case for CR, to see if talking could lead both to movement building and, more importantly, to political activism.

To date, the history of radical feminism and that of the counterculture have been treated as separate. They are typically portrayed as distinct groups traveling through the same space and time on parallel paths that converged every so often at antiwar and other demonstrations. In part, this has been because scholars have defined the counterculture in the narrowest terms to refer strictly to hippies and advocates of the drug culture, and few, if any of the women who later became feminists were direct participants in the hippie experiment. But this narrow definition belies the importance of understanding not only the expansive and varying aspects of the counterculture but, more importantly, the interconnectedness of all these groups. It also denies the existence of a feminist counterculture, and in so doing negates the impact of women and women's movements on the social and cultural revolution of the 1960s and 1970s. While few feminists had been hippies, the trajectory that the new women's movement took, its experience with the mainstreaming of its core ideas and strategies, and most of all, its emphasis on a politics of the conscious self overlap greatly with those of traditionally defined counterculture groups. Therefore, for the purposes of this discussion, the term "counterculture" will be used to refer to any entity, large or small, that sought to transform the existing political, economic, and cultural models and replace them with its own, often utopian, vision of a "new society."

Moreover, the term "social revolution" should be understood as a process of altering the existing culture and actualizing this new vision. Unlike traditional or even New Left terminology, it is important to understand that for the counterculture, revolution centered on changing *culture* and not on immediately replacing existing political systems or institutions. That would come later, and was seen as the natural by-product of a countercultural revolution, but hardly the point of origin. Instead, as Reich described, "The new consciousness is in the process of revolutionizing the structure of our society. It does not accomplish this by direct political means, but by changing culture and the quality of individual lives, which in turn change politics and ultimately structure."[25] Even the moniker "women's liberation" smacked of a desire for an alternative society in which women would be free and equal rather than a model based on a specific political structure. Virtually all groups of the era used the word "liberation" on some level, to describe the process of freeing the individual from "automatic acceptance of the imperatives of society" as well as the steps toward "building his own philosophy and values, his own life-style, and his own culture from a new beginning."[26] Seeing connections between women's and other groups brings the entire history of the 1960s and '70s counterculture into sharper relief and helps explain why the experiment was ultimately short-lived.

Through CR, a feminist counterculture—or at a minimum, the sense of a feminist countercultural ideology—emerges. Most radical feminists had experience with CR, and while some embraced the tool more wholeheartedly than others, it was nonetheless radical feminism's vehicle for attaining a new society. Because the term "radical" in contemporary discourse negatively connotes a militarist or extremist position, the fact that women's liberationists had given *themselves* this label has slipped through the cracks of history.[27] But the term "radical" connects neatly with the CR agenda. As Kathie Sarachild pointed out, "The dictionary definition says radical means root. . . . And that is what we meant by calling ourselves radicals. We were interested in getting to the roots of the problems in society. You might say we wanted to pull up weeds in the garden by their roots, not just pick off the leaves at the top to make things look good momentarily."[28] CR was the device for getting to the root of social ills as they pertained to women, and as such became the necessary first step toward building a new order. As Robin Morgan explained, "Sexism is the root oppression, the one which, until and unless we *up*root it, will continue to put forth the branches of racism, class hatred, ageism, competition, ecological disaster and economic exploitation."[29]

CR worked by enabling the individual within a group setting to uncover her authentic self, the person—or the essence of the person—beneath the programming that dictated what a woman "should" be and the socially sanctioned roles available to her.[30] Participants would take their new awareness home with them after each session and ideally begin to fuse their fresh vision onto their old lives. Over the course of weeks, they would start to see connections between their own personal dissatisfactions and those of other women, and through these links begin to envision possibilities for reinventing society. Another vital component, of course, was repetition. No one came to consciousness necessarily after just one session, though one visit could provoke initial enlightenment. But with continuous participation in a group over the course of weeks or months, the process of listening and disclosing could have a powerful and long-term transformative effect. As Sarachild explained, "Going to the sources, the historic roots, to the work that sets the program in motion is one of the ways to fight this process (of socialization)."[31]

Like other members of the so-called new generation, CR feminists saw a vast gulf between the possibilities and realities of women's lives. The 1960s may well have been the most affluent decade in American history, offering the promise of a better world and a bright future to its youth. But juxtaposed with this era of opportunity, security, and technology was "a threat to that promise posed by everything from neon ugliness and boring jobs to the Vietnam War and the shadow of nuclear holocaust."[32] While on the one hand, the younger generation situated itself optimistically at the dawn of a new era—in terms of educational opportunities and the promise of greater leisure offered by new technology—it also saw such hopes threatened by the Vietnam War and a lack of innovation in job prospects at home. Taken together, the younger generation increasingly felt betrayed, and it is this betrayal that provided the fuel for the social and cultural revolution of the 1960s.[33] As Reich argued:

> To them, the discrepancy between what could be and what is, is
> overwhelming; perhaps the greatest single fact of their existence. . . .
> They feel the betrayal in excruciatingly personal terms. Between
> them and the rich possibilities of life there intervenes a piercing
> insecurity—not the personal insecurity their parents knew, but a
> cosmic insecurity. Will the nation be torn apart by riots or war?
> Will their lives be cut short by death or injury in Vietnam? Will
> the impersonal machinery of the state—schools, careers, institu-
> tions—overwhelm them?[34]

For women, the betrayal took a distinct form. As NYRW and later Redstockings member Ellen Willis explained in 1969, despite the era of prosperity and the legal gains since Betty Friedan published *The Feminine Mystique* in 1963, women still incurred traditional obstacles in every aspect of their lives. State laws requiring a married woman to "perform domestic services, have sexual relations on demand" and live with her husband wherever he says remained on the books. Restaurants, bars, and other public accommodations could legally refuse to admit a woman without a male escort or exclude her altogether.[35] The number of female college entrants may have increased, but education maintained its masculinist bias in terms of the canon and course requirements. Willis noted that "Graduate schools discriminate in their admissions and financial aid policies on the grounds that it is a risk to train women who are going to have children and drop out."[36] Even if a woman managed to get through graduate school, continued job discrimination awaited her at the other end. Looking back on the era, Ann Snitow recalled being part of a generation of women who were told during their college days that they could do anything, but after graduation found themselves blocked from the career and lifestyle opportunities open to their male classmates.[37] Consequently, for feminists, consciousness raising would come to explain how the betrayal occurred, why it continued, and what it would take to change the picture and women's destiny. "This is a revolution in consciousness, rising expectations, and the actions which reflect that organic process," explained Morgan in 1968.[38]

"The personal is political" has become the single identifying mantra of second-wave feminism, but it has more direct links to the CR politics of the self than is typically recognized. Since its first utterance in the late 1960s, the phrase underscored the recognition that the boundaries between private/personal life and public/political life are artificial. Instead, all aspects of one's existence, including the most private of choices, have direct political links and consequences for each individual. But this tells only part of the story. "The personal is political" reflected a deeper notion that the individual, and one's private life, is the point of origin for all subsequent political action or social change. This was a powerful concept: the idea that acceptance of the status quo or the creation of an alternative system began and ended with the individual's recognition of her complicity in the larger society. In effect, implicit in "the personal is political" is the belief that awareness of the individual self can lead to the creation of a cosmic or collective self—a body of women together—that in turn would fuel the social revolution necessary to radically alter society. The individual's self awareness, then, was a vital springboard for movement building. And indeed, practitioners remember their experiences with CR as compatible with this trajectory. Reflecting on her initial foray into CR, the author Susan Brownmiller wrote, "My solitary efforts to forge my own destiny were fragments of women's shared, hidden history, links to past and future generations, pieces of the puzzle called sexual oppression. The simple technique of consciousness raising had brought my submerged truths to the surface, where I learned I wasn't alone."[39]

From the start, proponents of CR believed it would take the individual outside herself to the broader society. Though it was not articulated in quite this language, feminists believed in the possibility of a fusion of individual selves into a collective self through the experience of CR, and that this would be transformative in ways vital to igniting political activism and social change. CR gave each woman the ability "to see," to understand the processes and institutions that predated, yet governed, their lives and sense of self. Morgan described CR as having "a ripple effect" on the feminist revolution, starting "from each individual woman gaining self-respect and yes, power, over her own body and soul first, then within her family, on her block, in her town, state and so on out from the center, overlapping with similar changes other women are experiencing, the circles rippling more widely and inclusively as they go."[40] For CR feminists—and not all radical feminists were CR enthusiasts—it was this ripple effect that would enable CR to fuse each renewed, authentic individual self and create a group consciousness, an awareness of shared oppression as women that, would, in turn, effect change. In essence,

CR feminists redefined prevailing notions of the "self" beyond a static concept to a more evolutionary one: the idea that once you became aware of your individual self and relationship to society, you could create a cosmic self with those around you. Therein lay the potential to revolutionize society because, CR advocates believed, once the individual understood the problem, she would want to take action. Morgan described the process as "[t]he nascent rage everywhere budding into energy and organization and determination, the faces the voices the meetings and partings and indelible encounters where consciousness meets consciousness and the connections are electric. . . ."[41]

While feminists politicized the notion of consciousness, this focus on the conscious self was hardly new. Psychedelic self-exploration through LSD and other drugs began as early as the 1950s but gained momentum with the hippies in the mid-1960s. Calling it "consciousness expansion," advocates of LSD such as Timothy Leary and Ken Kesey believed that mind-expanding drugs provided a direct route to the true self. Much like CR, Kesey, for example, saw LSD as a "deconditioning agent," a "mind detergent"[42] that would literally wash away years—and perhaps generations—of social programming.[43] Because of the way the drug operated on the user's psyche, LSD advocates believed it would take them beneath the surface, back past the norms and behaviors society ordained as acceptable, to the root of their own, pre-programmed humanity. Unlike education or political activism, LSD worked quickly, and proponents regarded it as "the most effective means of short-circuiting the mental straightjacket that society imposes on its members."[44] As Aldous Huxley, author of *Brave New World* and avid LSD enthusiast saw it, if the "doors of perception" were "suddenly thrust open by a chemical substance such as mescaline or LSD, then the world would appear in an entirely new light."[45] Ultimately, such heightened consciousness would lead the user to see that his or her original priorities were wrong, that the quest for the rewards of capitalism had led them astray.

Consciousness expansion through LSD, and later its non-drug substitute Transcendental Meditation, concentrated on changing the individual self first before even beginning to attack social ills. In fact, Leary's classic credo, "Turn On, Tune In, Drop Out," was a directive for individuals to take themselves *out* of the social and political orbit in order to repair their psyches. As the LSD guru Michael Hollingshead described the transformative effects of LSD, "The reality on which I had consciously based my personality had dissolved into maya, a hallucinatory facade."[46] On the scale of social revolution, and despite their individual differences, Learyites and Keseyites envisioned mass use of the drug—"fixing" each broken individual one by one—as the first step toward a better society. Toward that end, Kesey popularized the "Electric Kool-Aid Acid Tests" in the mid-1960s offering the drug free of charge to all who thought they could "pass" the test.[47] Captain Alfred M. Hubbard, noted as the first to "emphasize LSD's potential as a visionary or transcendental drug," was nicknamed the "Johnny Appleseed of LSD" because he saw it as his life's vocation to "turn on as many men and women as possible."[48]

The question of whether to perfect the self or society first had plagued many counterculture groups and proved a dividing line between the New Left and the hippies. While individual members of the New Left experimented with LSD, they did so with none of the visionary implications of the Learyites or Keseyites. In fact, the New Left considered it socially irresponsible to focus on oneself when the real task was to benefit all mankind by ridding the country of the existing political and economic system.[49] Leary and Kesey had equally harsh critiques for the New Left emphasis on political structure. At an antiwar demonstration in Berkeley in 1965, Kesey was disgusted to see the crowd display the same anger and aggression that he believed led the nation into Vietnam in the first place, which confirmed his belief that political activism would have little impact on cleaning up society without enlightening the masses first. In a heartfelt diatribe, he told the protesters that they weren't going to change man's propensity for war with signs and slogans. "Do you want to know how to stop the war?" he yelled to the demonstrators. "Just turn your backs on it, fuck it!"[50] For Leary, the focus on changing "our heads" before even attempting to engage in political change or social revolution was an article of faith. As Martin Lee and Bruce Shlain note in *Acid Dreams: The CIA, LSD and the Sixties Rebellion*, Leary "dismissed any action that did not emanate from an expanded consciousness as 'robot behavior.'" Describing the New Left as "young men with menopausal minds," Leary urged, "Don't vote. Don't politic. Don't petition. You can't do *anything* about America politically."[51]

Ultimately, though, LSD created a new dilemma, that of consciousness expansion without a politics. After all, once the individual saw the world anew, what then? Millenarian hopes that acid could transform the world—like Paul McCartney's famous 1967 statement that if world leaders tried the drug once they would be ready to "banish war, poverty, and famine"[52]—faltered when it came to specifics on *how* to attain such results. In fact, there were no practical suggestions at the time for transmuting the LSD experience into an active political vehicle for building a better society. Similarly, there was immense resistance within the drug culture to structural organization. Leary believed in the possibilities of human evolution, but he didn't think an organized movement could lead people to a higher state of being. One thing was certain: many LSD advocates by the late 1960s were seeking the next level of consciousness expansion, one that would move them beyond regular drug use. Eastern religions and Transcendental Meditation stepped into the void, providing a holistic manner for reconnecting with the lessons offered by a drug trip, or enabling new converts to become "more aware of their own consciousness" without taking LSD.[53] Like LSD and, later CR, TM made bold promises about its impact on the user, especially about its ability to help people get to the source of their own creativity, a vital force for reshaping their world.[54]

Before, during, and long after meditation came into vogue, the encounter group movement was offering its own recipe for expanded consciousness. Beginning in 1946 with the psychologist Carl Rogers, these groups helped returning World War II servicemen cope with readjustment and wartime trauma by talking out their feelings with others who had had similar experiences and with a psychologist or psychiatrist facilitating the exchange.[55] Though seen as part of traditional psychotherapy at the outset, encounter groups evolved dramatically in the hands of organizations such as Esalen Institute in California, which merged group dynamics with existential philosophy. The "encounter" bypassed the individual self, not by requiring participants to learn or share with the group but by teaching them to "grasp [sic] the being of the other person."[56] Marathon sessions—sometimes lasting as long as forty-eight hours—came to be seen as celebrations of the inner self and its connection to humanity rather than treatment for mental disorders. Through the encounter group movement, psychotherapy took on a positive connotation as self-exploration, self-actualization, and a tool for both "sensory awareness" and "community."[57]

While encounter groups afforded human connections, they had none of the political underpinnings that CR would proffer. No doubt, many women who later became feminists participated in encounter groups or psychotherapy, though it is difficult to measure the full impact or the number of women involved in either. A few openly discussed the encounter phenomenon during the developmental phases of CR, noting the similarities between the exercise of sharing and the goal of personal growth. Some were critical; others were quick to point out the benefits of CR over psychotherapy. "'After years of psychoanalysis in which my doctor kept telling me my problem was that I wouldn't accept—quote—*my female role,*' said [sic] a married woman with two children who held [sic] a master's degree in philosophy, 'the small group was a revelation to me.'"[58]

Ultimately, though, encounter/group therapy would prove the thorn in the side of CR advocates. Betty Friedan derided the practice in its early days "as so much 'navel gazing.'"[59] Joan Didion saw it as the descent of the movement from sociopolitical reform to "a litany of trivia."[60] Kathy McAfee and Myrna Wood described their disdain for CR in 1969 this way: "More often than not these groups never get beyond the level of therapy sessions; rather than aiding the political development of women and building a revolutionary

Bettye Lane photo of a consciousness raising session in New York, 1970. Small group meetings became a staple of the women's movement in the late 1960s and 1970s, serving as a vehicle for building theory around women's shared experiences of gender acculturation. Often the first step toward political action, women would come together in urban apartments and suburban living rooms to explore the scope and limitations of being female in America.

women's movement, they often encourage escape from political struggle."[61] Some of the trouble no doubt came from the psychology profession's close and public scrutiny of consciousness raising. CR as a phenomenon was studied extensively by practitioners and scholars throughout the 1970s, many of whom began to employ the technique as part of a new genre of feminist psychotherapy.[62] But astute psychotherapists such as Barbara Kirsh not only noted but hoped to learn from the differences: "The individual is the unit of change in psychotherapy. In contrast, the goal of the consciousness-raising groups is to change the social structure and culture through the individual."[63]

Still, the negative image of CR as a "personal change mechanism"[64] prevailed, partly due to media stereotypes and the fact that some of the small groups focused more on issues of well-being and far less on social change. Pam Allen hailed her San Francisco group in 1970 as a "testament to our collective thinking and to our growth as individuals through experiencing the group process."[65] While driven by the politics of women's liberation, Allen's group saw itself as being in the formative stages of the movement, seeking to develop an ideology through a combination of CR and study programs focusing on

Debra Michals

historical and theoretical materials. Political activism was anticipated, but far down the road and not as a direct result of CR sessions themselves. Instead, she emphasized the psychological benefits of CR for the women who took part.[66] Another organization, the Women's Action Alliance of New York, veered even farther away from political activism when it described CR as "a place where we can be free, where we can be honest, where we can explore our hopes, successes and failures."[67] In fact, by its very nature, there was a built-in tension in consciousness raising "between individual empowerment and collective action, between an identity based reflexivity and a goal directed strategy, between a self-transformative knowledge and a strategic power."[68] Meanwhile, male members of the New Left, threatened perhaps by this "barely emerging politics of *revolutionary feminism*," denigrated both women's liberation and more important CR. As Robin Morgan noted in 1970, "The technique attracted a lot of ridicule from men; it seems that when the Chinese used such a technique, 'Speak Pains to Recall Pains,' it was right-on revolutionary, but when women used it, it was 'group therapy' or a 'hen party.'"[69] CR was described by its detractors as "bitch sessions," which feminists reclaimed when they retorted, "Bitch, Sisters, Bitch" in posters and other literature.[70]

The CR used by NYRW and later Redstockings, while having many external similarities to group therapy—such as earnest rap sessions—was marked instead by its political genesis and agenda. CR sessions weren't about helping women as individuals deal with their problems or *feel better*; rather, they were designed to illustrate the constants (systemic) between each individual's discontent or frustration. Indeed, much of the early, groundbreaking written work of radical feminism came from these very CR sessions. According to Susan Brownmiller, almost half of the now famous *Notes from the First Year of Women's Liberation* published in 1968 "consisted of transcribed material from consciousness raising sessions and speeches."[71] Nonetheless, criticisms from other feminists over both the similarities to therapy and, more importantly, the unknown link to activism and social change kept CR advocates on the defensive. In her legendary essay, "The Personal Is Political," Carol Hanisch launched a counterattack, noting, "Therapy assumes someone is sick and that there is a cure, e.g., a personal solution. . . . We need to change objective conditions, not adjust to them. Therapy is adjusting to your bad personal alternatives." CR, on the other hand, was by its very nature not only analytical but "a form of political action. . . . It is at this point a political action to tell it like it is, to say what I really believe about my life and not what I've always been told to say."[72] While Hanisch agreed that CR had therapeutic benefits, she described this as "political therapy" because it freed women from "self-blame" for their discontents.[73] Allen made similar statements about her San Francisco

CR group: "The total group process is not therapy because we try to find the social causes for our experiences and the possible programs for changing these. But the therapeutic experience of momentarily relieving the individual of all responsibility for her situation does occur and is necessary if women are to be free to act."[74] For CR advocates, the technique's significance stemmed from its ability to uncover the sources of women's problems—or, as it was termed at the time, "women's oppression"—and forge links between disparate classes or races of women who would unify through their shared experience of "womanhood." As Sarachild explained, "The importance of listening to a woman's feelings was collectively to analyze the situation of women, not to analyze *her*."[75]

Concerns about CR's therapy-like nature also fueled existing tensions within NYRW. By no means the only source of discord, debates about CR proved to be the final straw that led to NYRW's dissolution.[76] Ironically, the troubles began after the Miss America pageant protest, when publicity about the women's movement sent scores of women flooding to—and overwhelming—NYRW meetings and CR sessions. As many as a hundred women would show up, far more than the dozen that made for a good session.[77] In addition, the protest itself divided NYRW on how next to proceed: Should the focus be on more CR, or on abandoning CR and moving toward activism? Some, like Hanisch and Sarachild, felt that CR had only scratched the surface of its activist potential with the pageant protest; others, such as Robin Morgan and Peggy Dobbins, thought CR had gone as far as it could and believed the pageant protest revealed that the age of activism had arrived.[78] Rosalyn Baxandall recalled several splits in the group, with each going off to address specific issues like cooperative child care or employing different strategies for social change.[79] They were not alone. Other women's groups across the country were making similar decisions about privileging the activist agenda over CR, including the West Side Group in Chicago that Amy Kesselman, Heather Booth, Vivian Rothstein, and Noami Weisstein had joined.[80] For many of these women, CR's emphasis on the personal and political, while a great recruiting tool, did not in and of itself reveal any clear strategies for social change.[81] Many women believed CR merely led to more CR.[82]

Consequently, NYRW split into several groups in 1968 and 1969, at first under the NYRW umbrella and later functioning separately. On the one end was Redstockings, founded by Ellen Willis and Shulamith Firestone as "an action group based on a militantly independent, radical feminist consciousness."[83] At the other end was WITCH (for Women's International Terrorist Conspiracy from Hell, although it often gave varying explanations for the acronym),[84] founded by Morgan, Dobbins, and others to expose capitalism—and not men, per se—as the real enemy of American women. The moniker was as much an acronym as core symbolism: "It's an awareness that witches and gypsies were the original guerrillas and resistance fighters against oppression—particularly the oppression of women—down through the ages," declared an early WITCH document. "Witches have always been women who dared to be: groovy, courageous, aggressive, independent, sexually liberated, revolutionary."[85] Where Redstockings made CR the centerpiece of its revolutionary agenda, WITCH abandoned the rap sessions to focus on Yippie-style "zap actions" using street theater techniques to further dramatize women's oppression theatrically. Morgan herself had been a Yippie and was familiar with its formula for exposing systemic problems—not by talking or by politically seeking alternatives, but through biting dramatizations.

WITCH got its start on Halloween 1968, when organizers outfitted in full witch costume descended on Wall Street to put a hex on the financial district, labeling it the vertex of corporate America and its oppression of women.[86] The group focused on the class struggle between rich and poor—rather than between men and women, an emphasis it later deemed an oversight—and "demanded an audience with Satan, our superior, at the Stock Exchange."[87] Members of the group took jobs at Travelers Insurance Company and AT&T to expose sexism in the workforce by thwarting unfair and ridiculous company policies. The women at Travelers were fired "for such infractions of office rules as wearing slacks to work."[88] The WITCH typists at the telephone company lost their jobs for insubordination, and others were "smoked out and dismissed for being 'overqualified'" before they could stir up trouble there.[89] In February 1969, WITCH took on a Bridal Fair at Madison Square Garden, wearing black veils and singing "Here come the slaves/off to their graves" to show the ways in which marriage keeps women down. Prior to the event, they also posted stickers around New York City that stated, "Confront the Whore-makers." Though the stickers were meant as an indictment of the Bridal Fair organizers for encouraging women to enter the slave state of marriage, attendees thought they were being compared to prostitutes.[90]

WITCH's outrageous theatrics drew sharp criticism across the movement and within the group itself. The drama often upstaged the political message or offended the very women it hoped to reach. Lost was the joyous, affirmative side of the group that defined itself as "an all-woman Everything. It's theater, revolution, magic, terror, joy, garlic, flowers, spells."[91] Visible to anyone who cared to look was WITCH's fierce anger and absent-minded insensitivity. Even Morgan admitted that demanding to meet with Satan was "an ignorant *faux pas* which now makes me cringe: the members of the Old Religion (witches) never worshipped Satan. . . . We were dumb with style."[92] Following criticism that its disruption of the Bridal Fair was largely anti-woman, WITCH organizers backed away from guerrilla theater as its primary strategy, recognizing that they had much to learn about the motivations behind their activism before embarking on an activist agenda.

Instead, WITCH members found their way back to CR after a short time, though adopting the strategy on their own terms. "At this point," Judith Duffett, an original member, told Susan Brownmiller for a *New York Times* article in 1970, "you could say that WITCH is just another small group in Women's Liberation. We're concerned with consciousness raising and developing an ideology through collective thinking. We don't do the freaky, hippie stuff anymore."[93] Morgan put it more severely, saying the group had ceased to identify "with the confrontative tactics of the male Left and stylistically with the clownish proto-anarchism of such groups as the Yippies. . . . Having not raised our consciousness very far out of our combat boots, we didn't know what we were doing, or why."[94]

For Redstockings, the appeal of CR was overpowering. Sarachild pushed the CR agenda, and like Leary's embrace of LSD, her commitment to this technique took on a religious fervor. Along with the influence of Marxism on her thinking, Sarachild and others advocated that women's stories, revelations, and insights collectively become the theory on which activism would be built, rather than slotting women's lives into existing theoretical frameworks. Testimony from women themselves on the forces that acted upon them—whether they felt free to choose the single life over marriage, the kind of work they wanted to do—would over time create a new theoretical framework from which to act.[95] "New Knowledge is the source of consciousness raising's strength and power," wrote Sarachild. "The idea was to take our own feelings and experiences more seriously than any theories which did not reflect the actual experience and feelings and necessities of women."[96]

Next, and probably most controversially, through CR Redstockings developed its "pro-woman line." Women, the argument followed, were not to blame for their own oppression—that happened at the hands of men through the enforcement power of patriarchal institutions. As such, women could not be complicitous in any manner in their destiny, whether they collaborated with the system or remained victims of it. At the same time, Redstockings rejected the notion of women as dupes. Instead, in its position paper (or "manifesto," to use the leftist lingo of the era) Redstockings argued, "Women's submission is not the result of brainwashing, stupidity or mental illness but of continual daily pressure from men."[97] Men were to blame for women's problems, and literally anything women did to survive under the pressure of patriarchy was seen as understandable within this framework.

Equally contentious was the fact that CR, in Sarachild's hands, increasingly focused on awakening "class consciousness" in women and building a movement around women's shared oppression.[98] At the core, the strategy was essentialist but pragmatic, arguably, for the purpose of initial movement building. Simply put, this approach stressed a belief in the similarity of women's experience under sexist oppression that transcended racial, class, ethnic, educational, and virtually any other differences between them individually. In her program for feminist consciousness raising and in the Redstockings Manifesto, Sarachild insisted that the predominantly white middle-class women who made up the group must "identify with all women. We define our best interest as that of the poorest, most brutally exploited woman." And as if one could accomplish such transcendence and sisterhood with the wave of a magic wand, she averred, "We repudiate all economic, racial, educational or status privileges that divide us from other women. We are determined to recognize and eliminate any prejudices we may hold against other women."[99] While the idea of such unity was wonderfully idealistic, in reality women's vast differences regularly manifested themselves as a natural part of the CR process. After all, self-exploration involved addressing every aspect of identity formation. Some members believed that an honest examination of such differences might have had a greater effect on creating sisterhood than avoiding the subject ultimately did. The claim that privileged white women and underprivileged women of other races or classes knew the same kind of oppression was, in hindsight, not only preposterous but insulting. In addition, such negation of differences meant repression rather than openness in CR sessions, and it often created discord among women within the groups.[100] Nonetheless, by universalizing women's experience through the discursive creation of them as a class, radical feminists could claim that "they were the legitimate agents of revolutionary change."[101]

For Sarachild and many other members of Redstockings, this three-part formula was the key to guaranteeing that CR ultimately led to action. In this context, social revolution was understood as a process that takes place over an extended period of time—it could be months, maybe years, before results manifested themselves. For Sarachild, it was important that women take their time to learn and grow with CR and not feel pressured that action must necessarily result from everything they discussed. Rather, a dialectical relationship would be produced by CR in which discussions could influence an activist agenda and activism could influence CR.[102] Sarachild insisted CR would lead to action, noting that it would begin "when our experience is finally verified and clarified. . . . Learning the truth can lead to all kinds of action, and this action will lead to further truths."[103]

Unquestionably, CR was the engine that drove the women's movement from disjointed liberal-versus-radical factions to a major movement, although not everyone at the time understood the mechanism that made it happen.[104] In studies and dissertations appearing both during and after CR's heyday, psychologists, ethnographers, and other academics dissected the CR process to figure out just how it exacted its magic on the self. In essence, they explained that CR worked through the ongoing process of "storying" or storytelling. "Culture members construct and hold together a shared view of the world through the stories they tell and don't tell each other," noted Joan Bromberg in a 1982 study of the links between the narrative process of CR and social action.[105] According to Bromberg, the telling and retelling of personal struggles in a group context could have the cumulative effect over time of creating a new narrative—one that eventually leads to activism. Stories, in effect, "monitor and shape learning processes" and, over time, alter the previous understanding of the world in ways that demand a change in the status quo.[106] "The exchange of personal experience stories becomes the pivot on which the healing wheel turns. . . . by facilitating the transfer of meaning from one to another." In the course of this exchange, all aspects of an individual's personal narrative—past, present, and future—are reconstructed. The woman comes to reflect on the past or present anew, and in turn, this reconstructs her relationship to, and view of, the future.[107] Out of this "storying" comes first a new self-identity and next a new social identity: "In effect, they enact (construct) the kind of social world they want to experience by talking about what they don't want to occur in relations with others."[108]

The very use of the term "consciousness," some of the studies pointed out, implied group identity rather than merely individual self-awareness.[109] Deborah Gerson, in a psychology dissertation, described the transformative effects of CR this way: "The women's liberation movement happened when women collectively looked at their personal troubles and named them out loud, called them political and tried to struggle against them: worked together to change the conditions of women's lives: the praxis from pain."[110] She described the process as four steps: "(1) collective construction (2) mobilization of shared and compared experience, making visible the invisible (3) commitment to the frame of 'women's oppression' and (4) elaboration and illustration of the claim that the 'personal is political.'"[111] Other studies likewise saw the shift from self to cosmic identity occurring in four stages that also account for the revolutionary bent of radical second-wave feminism. Stages in this case flowed from "self-realization of a new identity" through the initial experience of constructing and reconsidering a personal narrative through CR to the second stage of "group identity through polarization" based on a sense of difference between the individual and those outside the group. The third step—the construction of "new values for the group"—naturally followed. The final stage came when CR participants who wanted to build a new world order related their vision to that of other active revolutionary groups.[112]

Debra Michals

Indeed, CR's "speaking pains" proved to be a direct link to political action. Aside from the pageant protest, CR inspired the growth of women's centers and rape crisis centers across the country, as well as the development of feminist publishing. Women's writing, be it manifestos or full-length tomes, could be a kind of written CR, an exposition of rising awareness about institutionalized oppression.[113] Shulamith Firestone was roused to write her renowned feminist work, *The Dialectic of Sex*, as a direct result of the new awareness that came from her CR experiences. Susan Brownmiller, too, credited her CR enlightenment as inspiration for her classic *Against Our Will: Men, Women and Rape*. CR techniques led to the repeal of New York state anti-abortion laws in 1969. Legislative hearings called fourteen men and a nun to testify on the matter, enraging feminists like Sarachild who disrupted the hearing with demands for "*real* experts." In response, Redstockings held its own "hearings" in the form of speak-outs where three hundred real women met to listen and exchange abortion stories. Gloria Steinem to this day describes this mass CR session as her conversion experience to feminism, where for the first time she learned her private pain was not just her own.[114]

At a 1970 CR session of New York Radical Feminists and Media Women, a discussion about women's representation and opportunities in publishing fueled a take-over of the offices of *Ladies' Home Journal*. The group wanted to take on the magazine for its degrading images of women only as housewives, its emphasis on trite articles like "Can This Marriage Be Saved?" and the fact that this so-called women's magazine was run largely by men. As a result, up to three hundred women staged an eleven hour sit-in at *Ladies' Home Journal*, taking over editor in chief John Mack Carter's office and the *Journal*'s test kitchen, demanding "Carter's resignation, an all-female staff, free day-care centers for employee children, elimination of ads that degrade or exploit women, of the focus on a lifestyle in which there is no alternative to marriage and the family, of articles tied to advertising, of back-to-the-home romance and fiction and. . . . one issue of the magazine edited entirely by members of the women's liberation movement." In the end, they won control of an eight-page insert in an upcoming issue with a $10,000 fee for the writers, as well as media coverage on ABC and "thoughtful, almost *respectful* pieces on the movement" in major national magazines such as *Newsweek* and the *Atlantic Monthly*.[115]

But the protest at *Ladies' Home Journal* marked a turning point for CR as a revolutionary strategy. The publication of the feminist insert in the August 1970 issue included an article explaining what CR was and why it was important, along with instructions on how to conduct a CR session. Envisioned as a way of turning the female masses on to CR—much as Leary and Kesey had fantasies of turning the straight world on to LSD—such public dissemination, in fact, ultimately helped dilute CR of its radicalism. With the distance of more than two decades, it's clear that much of the original, edgy language was reworked to make the practice and its consequent activism more clearly understandable to the *Journal's* suburban middle America readership. "Sisterhood is a warm feeling!" the writer noted, explaining that through CR, "we see that 'personal problems' shared by so many others—not being able to get out of the house enough, becoming exhausted from taking care of the children all day, perhaps feeling trapped—are really *political problems*."[116] Mainstreaming also brought with it a whole new set of dilemmas. Like the hippies, feminists learned quickly that once the message is distributed, the messenger can no longer control its reception—what people do with it or how they reinvent it for their own ends. Ironically, the more exposure CR received in the mass media, the more watered-down its power became. Instead of building a core base of followers who shared in the goals of revolution, CR's newer groups never got past the female-bonding stages to engage in political activism.

CR was all but dead as a revolutionary force by 1973, though it continued to exist as an organizing tool that brought women together well into the early 1980s. But by the early 1970s, "touchy-feely" self-help groups were embracing the technique as a way to bridge communication gaps between generations, the sexes, or within a family. Gone was CR's radical core, the idea that women and only women should come together in these groups, that they formed a kind of secret circle where truths would be uncovered. Instead, books such as *The New Way to Become the Person You'd Like to Be: The Complete Guide to Consciousness Raising* (1973) told readers that CR was "an effort to increase personal functioning and potential."[117] The advice to readers was on "learning to express feelings. . . . needs and wants."[118] In essence, CR was being proposed to help readers better *adapt* to the dominant culture. Most of all, it stressed mixed sex groups— the very antithesis of CR's original philosophy. "CR helps both men and women see themselves reflected as equals," the authors wrote. "The destiny of woman does not have to be, as Freud said, 'determined through beauty, charm, and sweetness,' so that she is incapable of any 'higher human tasks' than caring for a home and children. Nor does the destiny of man have to be that of the strong, silent breadwinner. Either may secretly yearn for other roles—which makes neither unnatural. So CR is a human thing, not only a 'woman thing.'"[119] Toward that end, mainstream CR featured "open groups" composed of married or single men and women of all ages, including children. Its new adherents provided guidelines for forming groups, with discussion topics listed by sex and age, all designed with a therapy-like agenda of enlightening participants about other people's viewpoints and leading them to the zenith of their own capabilities.[120] Men's groups also sprung up around the country, sometimes promoted with the androgynous images of David Bowie or Mick Jagger.[121] In 1973, even the U.S. government had something to say about the meaning and role of consciousness raising to women's groups in a research report on the women's movement.[122]

Similarly, another 1973 entrée in CR discourse watered down the activist agenda into volunteerism and philanthropy. Using rather hip yet deflated feminist language, *The Not So Helpless Female: How to Change the World Even if You Never Thought You Could, A Step-by-Step Guide to Social Action*, advocated small groups as a means of helping participants "break out of the cage" of their sex roles and lives, so that they may "learn to talk to each other as human beings, to cope with fear, to view problems not just abstractly, but in living terms."[123] What did Tish Sommers, the book's author, think CR would ultimately lead to? Not social revolution or even cultural change as advocated by radical feminists, but rather personal triumphs and the courage to speak one's mind. Case in point: "When paying bills, a woman encloses a note: 'I would like to see more women and persons from minority races in policy-making positions.' . . . Fed up with parties at which people segregate themselves by sex, a wife wears a Women's Liberation button to such gatherings. Conversation becomes livelier, with both sexes participating. . . . A pair of pantyhose that develops a premature run is returned with a letter to the manufacturer and a carbon copy to Virginia Knauer, the President's Advisor on Consumer Affairs."[124] Stripped of its radicalism by popularizers, CR was here reduced to the trappings of the homemade encounter group.

NOW had originally shied away from such overtly radical strategies, but by 1972 it not only called CR its own but became the major vehicle for distributing information on how to conduct a CR session.[125] In part, the shift was pragmatic: as more women joined its ranks, NOW hoped to use small CR groups to bring new members up-to-speed quickly on its activist agenda.[126] In the process, however, NOW changed the mantra from "The personal is political" to "*From* the personal *to* the political in recognition of the fact that women's personal lives are shaped by our sexist society."[127] The distinction, while seemingly minor, contributed to the final erosion of consciousness raising's power to create a cosmic and politicized self. The reinvented phrase inverted the radical notion of personal life as the site of all politics and instead shifted the focus away from the political milieu *back* onto the private realm. Consequently, at best, this linguistic turn replaced the radical feminist notion of reorienting one's vision to create a new society with liberal feminism's emphasis on reforming existing institutions. That said, even in NOW's hands CR touched—and changed—more women's lives in the 1970s and facilitated the rise of a mass women's movement, simply by encouraging women to talk about their daily injustices and find solace with others. As Charlotte Bunch described in 1970, CR held such power for individuals and the movement because it gave "public visibility and common analysis to an uneasiness and hostility that many women feel, but that had been confined until now to the personal sphere and thereby dismissed."[128] At a CR reunion in the mid 1980s, participant-observer Anita Shreve talked to women who saw it as a powerful force of unity and awareness, a kind of "Glory Days" of sisterhood for women—before women went back off into the divided land of individual self-interest that was the careerism of the 1980s.[129]

Along with mainstreaming, part of what killed CR's activist potential was the shift from politics to cultural feminism, a transition that linguistically and in actuality put radical feminism on the same path as the broader counterculture. Driven in part by frustration with both CR and the lengthy process that lay ahead in overhauling American traditions and institutions, radical feminists began to turn from CR-as-activist strategy toward privatization of their politics. They realized that radical revolution, despite initial pyrotechnics, was a long and winding road, with no guarantee that the end would ever be reached. Revolutionaries across all segments of the counterculture were not necessarily willing to end up like Moses, laboring yet never seeing the promised land in their lifetimes. Slowly, cultural feminism—the notion that women could "build a culture, a space, uncontaminated by patriarchy"—began to replace radical feminism.[130] In essence, these women wanted to withdraw and concentrate on living lifestyles that reflected their political values and unity with other women while striving for women's equality in the existing system.

Granted, the seeds of such a shift were present from the start of radical feminism, which like other contemporary movements stressed cultural change as a prerequisite for political change. But opting out of social change movements in favor of lifestyle or cultural concerns did not enable these women to "do their own thing" outside the system. It simply created the illusion of "dropping out" all the while remaining "in," a dilemma every countercultural group from the hippies to the New Left ultimately faced. After all, starting a feminist credit union, cooperative business, or commune might take those involved out of mainstream corporate culture in an immediate sense, but they still relied on the market system and operated within the broader economy. While living by one's principles could prove more rewarding on an individual level, it also undermined the sense of collectivism and the alternative society that CR proffered.

In the end, CR raised not only the consciousness of the women who participated, but ultimately that of the nation and other countercultural movements. The term had so infused the broader society that before the 1960s were over, Secretary of State Henry Kissinger referred to a diplomatic meeting as "consciousness raising." Radical feminists raised America's consciousness by

daring to speak the unspeakable, by bringing to light the discriminatory practices embedded in the culture and the ways they disempowered and ultimately
hurt women. In terms of the history of the counterculture more broadly conceived, without the creation of a feminist counterculture through CR, these
groups would have continued to replicate the sexist politics both of the larger
culture and of the countercultural organizations themselves. From the sexual
revolution to the hippies and the New Left, women's place prior to CR varied
little from the so-called straight to hip worlds. The CR politics of the self held
a magnifying glass up to the masculinist assumptions of the counterculture, its
equating of sexual freedom with men's access to women's bodies. CR entered
this and other debates of the era, altering discourse to include female models
of sexual pleasure, gender roles, and rights.

Arguably, CR truly was one of the last great revolutionary forms. It alone,
unlike its predecessors and certainly anything that has come along since, had
the potential to change society by changing minds first. Younger generations
today, coming of age in an overly expressive media culture, cannot begin to
understand the transformative meaning and power that speaking out had for
radical feminists in the 1960s and 1970s. In fact, in the late 1990s, women in
their twenties and thirties were instead coming together in groups inspired
not by their shared womanhood but by nostalgia for their lost girlhood. In
New York, the birthplace of CR, women in 1999 were forming "beauty par-
lor nights," where they swapped makeup and relationship tips. Similar "girl
talk" gatherings emerged nationwide, including over thirty-five Ya-Ya groups
inspired by Rebecca Wells's best-selling novel *The Divine Secrets of the Ya-Ya
Sisterhood.* "It's an educated return to those girlie gatherings of our adolescence," said one organizer of women's slumber parties.[131] By 1999, this
watered-down incarnation of the term "consciousness raising" was so much a
part of the popular parlance that Nancy Evans, founder of the Internet
women's website iVillage, could proclaim that "the Internet is the new consciousness-raising group." Evans's personal agenda as the architect of a highly
successful women's online network aside, her likening of the Internet to a
modern CR group was completely devoid of the radical politics of its second-
wave feminist predecessor. Instead, she compared this "new consciousness
raising" to women's social networks of days gone by, an analogy that in itself
speaks volumes. "Like a river where women washed clothes and swapped stories, or a backyard fence where they shared wisdom about raising kids and saving marriages, it [the Internet] has become a gathering place where we can
help each other. It's a support group, networking tool, and information source,
all rolled into one," Evans wrote in *Working Woman* magazine.[132] At the dawn
of the twenty-first century, at precisely the moment when a new generation

embraces the diminutive moniker "girls," CR has devolved into female bonding—with none of the political implications and zeal so central to its inherent power. Without question, the re-emergence of women's groups in the late '90s speaks to the importance of relationships with other women and a hunger for the female bonds lost as women retreated into private lives in the 1980s. And perhaps this is ground zero—a starting point of unity that may one day lead to a more political agenda—though on the surface it holds no such promise. By articulating their dissatisfaction out loud to other women, 1960s and '70s CR advocates learned first that they were not alone, second that their feelings were valid, third that they were linked to a sociopolitical system. From words came realization, from realization came a desire to change the world.

NOTES

1. Carol Hanisch, "Bra-Burner: The 1968 Miss America Protest," in *Frankly Feminist* (New York: Truthteller Publications, 1997), 78. Carol Hanisch, "What Can Be Learned: A Critique of the Miss America Protest," *Redstockings: First Literature List and a Sampling of Its Materials,* 27 November 1968, 9–11. Alice Echols, *Daring to Be Bad: Radical Feminism in America, 1967–1975* (Minneapolis: University of Minnesota Press, 1989), 93.

2. Hanisch, "What Can Be Learned: A Critique of the Miss America Protest," *Redstockings: First Literature List and a Sampling of Its Materials,* from the Archives Distribution Project, Gainesville, Fla., 9–11.

3. The term "oppression" was everywhere in vogue among student, left, and counterculture activists. Feminists similarly used this language to emphasize the limitations they felt imposed upon their lives and their ability to achieve self-determination. Though it sounds dated by today's standards, this linguistic emphasis was crucial for 1960s and 1970s radical feminists as part of a larger agenda to strike down institutions that kept women down and construct a new society that would lead toward individual self-actualization.

4. Rosalyn Baxandall and Linda Gordon, eds., *Dear Sisters: Dispatches from the Women's Liberation Movement* (New York: Basic Books, 2000), 67–77. The editors note the connections between Civil Rights activism and the emerging women's movement in their introduction to the section on "New Organizational Forms," which includes documents describing CR written by the former Civil Rights activist Pamela Parker Allen and members of Gainesville Women's Liberation in 1969 and 1970, respectively.

5. The story of the pageant protest is retold in many women's movement histories, both during the heyday of second-wave feminism and more recently. Most note that the idea originated with Carol Hanisch. See Rachel Blau DuPlessis and Ann Snitow, eds., *The Feminist Memoir Project: Voices From Women's Liberation* (New York: Three Rivers Press, 1998), 10. Echols, *Daring to Be Bad,* 93.

6. Echols, *Daring to Be Bad,* 93.

7. Ibid.

8. As an aside, the pageant protest is also the moment that spurred the myth of bra burning, since feminists did throw symbols of women's oppression—girdles, cosmetics, and yes, even bras—into a freedom trash can. And while no bras were ever burned, the debate remains over whether the organizers intended to spark a flame. Echols, 94.

9. DuPlessis and Snitow, *The Feminist Memoir Project,* 10, 21.

10. Kathie Sarachild, "The Power of History," in *Feminist Revolution* (New York: Random House, 1975), 13–33. Hanisch, "What Can Be Learned . . ."

11. Ellen Willis, "What Ever Happened to Women? Nothing—That's the Trouble,"

Mademoiselle, September 1969, 150. A little more on goals of radicals. Shulamith Firestone, *The Dialectic of Sex: The Case for Feminist Revolution* (New York: Bantam Books, 1970). Marlene Dixon, "Why Women's Liberation," in *Liberation Now! Writings from the Women's Liberation Movement* (New York: Dell, 1971), 9–25. Margaret Bentson, "The Political Economy of Women's Liberation," in *Liberation Now!*, 139–44.

12. William Chafe, *Women and Equality: Changing Patterns in American Culture* (New York: Oxford University Press, 1977), 103.

13. Charles Reich, *The Greening of America*, (New York: Random House, 1970), 139–40.

14. Ibid.

15. Reich, *The Greening of America*, 19.

16. Ibid., 5–6.

17. Feminists compiled instructions on holding CR groups as early as 1968, insisting that groups be no larger than twelve so that everyone would have a chance to talk. Other rules stressed a non-judgmental and non-directive approach. Chafe, *Women and Equality*, 97–98, 103. "Protective Rules for Consciousness Raising," *Redstockings*, 45. Kathie Sarachild, "A Program for Consciousness Raising," in *Feminist Revolution*, 202–03. Pamela Parker Allen, "The Small Group Process (1969)," in Baxandall and Gordon, eds., *Dear Sister*, 67–69.

18. Sarachild, "Consciousness Raising: A Radical Weapon," in *Feminist Revolution*, 144. Susan Brownmiller, "Sisterhood Is Powerful," *New York Times*, 3 March 1970, 27.

19. Sarachild, "Consciousness Raising."

20. Ibid.

21. Ruth Rosen, *The World Split Open: How the Modern Women's Movement Changed America* (New York: Viking, 2000), 196–198. Susan Brownmiller sees a strong connection between Women's Liberation and other groups of the era. She writes: "Women's Liberation, in name and spirit, sprang from the radical ferment of the civil rights, antiwar, and counterculture movements." See Brownmiller, *In Our Time: Memoir of a Revolution* (New York: Dial Press), 7.

22. Echols, *Daring to Be Bad*, 84.

23. Media textbooks note the increasing prevalence of television and print news sources throughout the 1960s. Edwin Emery et al., *Introduction to Mass Communication, 2d ed.* (New York: Dodd, Mead, 1968), 66, 116–117.

24. Martin A. Lee and Bruce Shlain, *Acid Dreams: The CIA, LSD and the Sixties Rebellion* (New York: Grove Press, 1985), 159–63, 174–75, 214–224, 233–23; Echols, *Daring to Be Bad*, 25, 55, 58, 85.

25. Reich, *The Greening of America*, 19.

26. Ibid., 225.

27. Sarachild, "Consciousness Raising," 144.

28. Ibid.

29. Robin Morgan, *Going Too Far: The Personal Chronicle of a Feminist* (New York: Vintage Books, 1968), 9.

30. Kathleen A. Loughlin, *Women's Perceptions of Transformative Learning Experiences within Consciousness Raising* (San Francisco: Mellon University Press, 1993), 155–219.

31. Sarachild, "Consciousness Raising," 147. Edith Hoshino Altbach, "Notes on a Movement," in *From Feminism to Liberation*, ed. Edith Hoshino Altbach (Cambridge, Mass.: Schenkman, 1971), 8. Even radicals who had other problems with the split between women's liberation and left politics saw the value of CR in its ability to enable an individual to recognize her own oppression as part of a broader class oppression. See Marlene Dixon, "Women's Liberation and the Cultural Revoltion," *Radical America*, February 1970, 23

32. Reich, *The Greening of America*, p. 218.

33. Ibid., 218, 220, 229.

34. Ibid., 220–21.

35. Willis, "What Ever Happened to Women?" 150, 206–07.

36. Ibid., 207.

37. Conversation with Ann Snitow, editor of *The Feminist Memoir Project*, May 1998. Marcia Cohen, *The Sisterhood: The True Story of the Women Who Changed the World* (New York: Simon & Schuster, 1988), 185. The betrayal women felt is recounted in numerous other sources, among them: Shulamith Firestone, *The Dialectic of Sex*, 30; Sarah Evans, *Personal Politics: The Roots of Women's Liberation in the Civil Rights Movement and the New Left* (New York: Vintage Books, 1979), 21; Caroline Bird, *Born Female: The High Cost of Keeping Women Down* (New York: Pocket Books, 1968), 40–60.

38. Morgan, *Going Too Far*, 9.

39. Brownmiller, *In Our Time*, 7.

40. Morgan, *Going Too Far*, 9.

41. Ibid., 158.

42. Peter Braunstein, (M.A. thesis, New York University, 1992) "Graduating Acid: The Evolution of the Haight-Ashbury Counterculture," 3.

43. Lee and Shlain, *Acid Dreams*, 121.

44. Ibid., xvi.

45. Ibid., 47.

46. Ibid., 83.

47. Ibid., 125.

48. Ibid., 44.

49. Ibid., 127.

50. Ibid., 134.

51. Ibid., 166.

52. Charles Perry, *The Haight-Ashbury: A History* (New York: Rolling Stone Press, 1984) 207–08.

53. Aaron E. Klein and Cynthia Klein, *Mind Trips: The Story of Consciousness-Raising Movements* (New York: Doubleday, 1979), 6–9.

54. Ibid., 45.

55. Ibid., 12–13.

56. Walter Bromberg, *From Shaman to Psychotherapist: A History of the Treatment of Mental Illness* (Chicago: Regnery, 1975), 278–79.

57. Ibid., 284–87. Max Rosenbaum, Martin Lakin, and Howard B. Roback, "Psychotherapy in Groups," in *History of Psychotherapy: A Century of Change*, ed. Donald Freeheim (Washington, D.C. American Psychological Association, 1992), 704.

58. Brownmiller, "Sisterhood Is Powerful," 134.

59. Echols, *Daring to Be Bad*, 87

60. Joan Didion, as cited in Sheila Ruth, "A Serious Look at Consciousness-Raising," *Social Theory and Practice* 2, no. 3, (spring 1973): 290.

61. Kathy McAfee and Myrna Wood, "Bread & Roses," in *From Feminism to Liberation*, ed. Edith Hoshino Altbach (Cambridge, Mass.: Schenkman, 1971), 22.

62. See Barbara Kirsh, "Consciousness-Raising Groups as Therapy for Women," in *Women in Psychotherapy: New Therapies for a Changing Society*, ed. Violet Franks and Vasanti Burtle (New York: Brunner/Mazel, 1974), 326–354. The entire collection is useful for this purpose. James W. Chesebro, John F. Cragan, and Patricia McCullogh, "The Small Group Technique of the Radical Revolutionary: A Synthetic Study of Consciousness Raising," *Speech Monographs* 40, (June 1973): 136–46. Cary Cherniss, "Personality and Ideology: A Personological Study of Women's Liberation," *Psychiatry*, May 1972, 109–25. Claire M. Brody, ed., *Women's Therapy Groups: Paradigms for Feminist Treatment* (New York: Springer, 1987).

63. Kirsh, 326.

64. Ibid.

65. Pamela Allen, *Free Space: A Perspective on the Small Group in Women's Liberation* (New York: Times Change Press, 1970), 11.

66. Ibid., 39–44, 49. Echols, *Daring to Be Bad*, 88.

67. Women's Action Alliance, *Consciousness Raising Guidelines*, (New York, 1973), 2.

68. Deborah Ann Gerson, "Practice from Pain: Building a Women's Movement through Consciousness Raising" (Ph.D. diss. in sociology), University of California, Berkeley, 1996), 6.

69. Robin Morgan, "Introduction," in *Sisterhood Is Powerful: An Anthology of Writings from the Women's Liberation Movement* (New York: Random House, 1970), xxiii. Robin Morgan, *Saturday's Child: A Memoir* (New York: Norton, 2000), 255.

70. Sarachild, "Consciousness Raising," 146.

71. Brownmiller, *In Our Time*, 26, 44.

72. Hanisch, "The Personal Is Political," in *Feminist Revolution*, 204.

73. Ibid.

74. Allen, *Free Space*, 30–31.

75. Sarachild, "Consciousness Raising," 148.

76. Echols aptly demonstrates the pressures on NYRW due to tensions from the outset between feminists who wanted to focus only on women's issues and New Left politicos who wanted to address broader social ills. See *Daring to Be Bad*, 51–101.

77. Ibid., 99.

78. Echols, *Daring to Be Bad*, 96–97. Brownmiller, "Sisterhood is Powerful," 27, 134.

79. Brownmiller, *In Our Time*, 23.

80. Amy Kesselman, with Heather Booth, Vivian Rothstein, and Naomi Weisstein, "Our Gang of Four: Friendship and Women's Liberation," in DuPlessis and Snitow, *The Feminist Memoir Project*, 40.

81. Steven M. Buechler, *Women's Movements in the United States: Woman Suffrage, Equal Rights and Beyond* (New Brunswick, N.J.: Rutgers University Press, 1990), 73.

82. Echols, *Daring to Be Bad*, 114.

83. Ellen Willis, "Up from Radicalism: A Feminist Journal," *US*, 1969.

84. The meaning of the acronym WITCH was often changed to suit the theme of a given demonstration. Among its interpretations: Women Interested in Toppling Consumption Holidays, for a Mother's Day protest; Women's Independent Taxpayers, Consumers and Homemakers; Women Inspired to Commit Herstory; in "WITCH Historical Documents," reprinted in *Sisterhood Is Powerful*, 550–51, 539.

85. Ibid., 539.

86. Ibid., 538. Echols, *Daring to Be Bad*, 97. Brownmiller, "Sisterhood Is Powerful," 132.

87. Morgan, *Going Too Far*, 73.

88. Brownmiller, "Sisterhood Is Powerful," 132.

89. Ibid., 132.

90. Echols, *Daring to Be Bad*, 97.

91. "WITCH," in *Sisterhood Is Powerful*, 539.

92. Morgan, *Going Too Far*, 72.

93. Brownmiller, "Sisterhood Is Powerful", 132.

94. Morgan, *Going Too Far*, 72.

95. Echols, *Daring to Be Bad*, 84.

96. Sarachild, "Consciousness Raising," 148.

97. "Redstockings Manifesto," *Redstockings: First Literature List and a Sampling of Its Materials*, available through the Archives Distribution Project, Gainesville, Fla., 7.

98. Sarachild, "A Program for Feminist Consciousness-Raising," in *Feminist Revolution*, 202.

99. Ibid., 203. "Redstockings Manifesto," 8.

100. Several of the essays in *The Feminist Memoir Project* directly address the repressed side of CR.

101. Echols, *Daring to Be Bad*, 91.

102. Kathie Sarachild, "Going for What We Really Want," in *Feminist Revolution*, 159.

103. Ibid., 149.

104. Susan Brownmiller discusses the impact of consciousness raising on the individual and

the collective group(s) of women who banded together to form the women's liberation movement in her memoir. See Brownmiller, *In Our Time*, 5–7, 26, 44.

105. Joan Berlin Bromberg, "Storying and Changing: An Ethnography of Speaking in Consciousness Raising" (Ph.D. diss. in folklore and folklife, University of Pennsylvania, 1982), 2.

106. Ibid., 5.

107. Ibid., 9, 26.

108. Ibid., 308.

109. Carol Ann Reichenthal, *Feminism: Consciousness Raising and Psychology* (Ph.D. diss. in clinical psychology, State University of New York at Buffalo, 1975), 9–10.

110. Gerson, *Practice from Pain*, xxv.

111. Ibid., 88.

112. Chesebro et al., "The Small Group," 139, 141–143.

113. Note on the extent of feminist publishing—Know Inc, Solanis, and so on. Roxanne Dunbar, "Outlaw Woman: Chapters from a Feminist Memoir in Progress," in DuPlessis and Snitow, *The Feminist Memoir Project*, 98.

114. Echols, *Daring to Be Bad*, 140–42. Cohen, *The Sisterhood*, 225. Sarachild, "The Power of History," in *Feminist Revolution*, 20–21.

115. Brownmiller, *In Our Time*, 83–92. Cohen, *The Sisterhood*, 184–86, 189–94.

116. "How to Start Your Own Consciousness-Raising Group," *Ladies Home Journal*, August 1970, 71.

117. Jane Sorensen, OTR, and Edythe Cudlipp, *The New Way to Become the Person You'd Like to Be: The Complete Guide to Consciousness Raising* (New York: McKay 1973), 5.

118. Ibid., 6.

119. Ibid., 7.

120. Carol Hanisch, "The Liberal Takeover of Women's Liberation," in *Feminist Revolution*, 166. Jan Moore, "The Changing Face of Consciousness Raising," *her-self*, April 1972, 12.

121. Cohen, *The Sisterhood*, 312.

122. Helen Shaffer, "Women's Consciousness Raising" in *Editorial Research Reports on the Women's Movement* (Washington, D.C.: Congressional Quarterly, 1973).

123. Tish Sommers, *The Not-So-Helpless Female: How to Change the World Even if You Never Thought You Could, A Step-by-Step Guide to Social Action* (New York: McKay, 1973), 12.

124. Ibid., 26–27.

125. Brownmiller outlines the problems with the mainstreaming of CR, both within NOW and in the hands of the newly established *Ms.* magazine in 1972. See Brownmiller, *In Our Time*, 79, 233.

126. Rosen, *The World Split Open*, 87.

127. Harriet M. Perl, coordinator, NOW National Task Force on C-R, "Letter to Ms," *Ms.*, November 1977, 12. The letter was in response to an article in a previous issue. See Sally Arnold, "Consciousness Raising: Truth and Consequences," *Ms.*, July 1977, 101–104, 108. Sarachild, "The Power of History," 17.

128. Charlotte Bunch, "A Broom of One's Own: Notes on the Women's Liberation Program," in *Passionate Politics: Feminist Theory in Action*, ed. Charlotte Bunch, (New York: St. Martin's Press, 1987), 28.

129. Anita Shreve, *Women Together, Women Alone: The Legacy of the Consciousness-Raising Movement* (New York: Viking Press, 1989).

130. Echols, *Daring to Be Bad*, 245.

131. Rachel Lehmann-Haupt, "In Women's Groups, Back to 'Girl Talk,'" *New York Times*, 11 April 1999, 1, 8.

132. Nancy Evans, "The New Consciousness Raising," *Working Woman*, October 1999, 24–26.

Section Two
Cultural Politics

Introduction

It was commonplace in the 1960s for observers to distinguish between "political" movements like the New Left, which sought structural renovations in the nation's political system, and "apolitical" movements like the hippies that rejected what passed for political activism, focusing its energies instead on transforming American culture. This distinction was often sustained by Sixties radicals themselves, with New Leftists charging hippies with derailing the youth rebellion onto the track of passivity by answering the siren song of drugs and sitar music. Counterculture gurus like Timothy Leary shot back by labeling politicos "young men with menopausal minds." What this rhetorical saber-rattling eclipses is the fact that the cultural revolution of the 1960s and '70s generated an array of innovative, often highly successful fusions of "politics" and "culture." Whether in the form of co-ops, "guerrilla theater," or revolutionary rock bands, the American counterculture produced a virtual encyclopedia of cultural politics. So successful and resounding were these countercultural initiatives that today most Americans, from Jesse Helms to the Wu-Tang Clan, accept "the culture is political" as an article of faith.

Michael William Doyle, in his essay "Staging the Revolution: Guerrilla Theater as a Countercultural Practice, 1965–68," traces the history of the artist-anarchist collective that single-handedly reset the parameters for cultural politics: the San Francisco Diggers. A group of aspiring theater people turned political "life-actors," the Diggers acted out a form of prefigurative politics—living the revolution as if it had already been won. In doing so they fused utopianism with (literally) bread-and-butter practical considerations. Doug Rossinow argues in "'The Revolution is About Our Lives': The New Left's Counterculture" that New Leftists were indeed affected by the culturalist orientation of Sixties revolt, and in their quest for sexual liberation, authenticity, and a less repressed way of living pursued many of the same objectives as their "hippie" cousins. Finally, Jeff Hale in his essay "The White Panthers 'Total Assault on the Culture'" tells the story of Midwestern counterculture rebel John Sinclair, who proselytized his revolutionary faith of sex, drugs, and "fucking in the streets" through management of the boisterous and controversial rock band the MC5. Ultimately culminating in the now-legendary "political organization" known as the White Panthers, Sinclair's trajectory—apart from constituting a checklist of Sixties radical postures—reveals the extent to which the Nixon administration, like Sinclair, made little distinction between politics and culture.

Three

Staging the Revolution

Guerrilla Theater as a Countercultural Practice, 1965-68

Michael William Doyle

One sunny afternoon in August 1965, R. G. Davis, founder of the San Francisco Mime Troupe (SFMT), staged a spectacle of politics and art in a public park. On this day, their fourth summer of presenting free commedia dell'arte performances throughout the Bay Area, the Mime Troupe was going ahead with plans to perform their latest play, Giordano Bruno's *Il Candelaio*, in Lafayette Park in defiance of the San Francisco Park and Recreation Commission. Two days earlier commission members had declared the premier show to be "obscene, indecent, and offensive" due to its "suggestive . . . words and gestures" and therefore had revoked the Mime Troupe's permit for future park performances. Davis and the American Civil Liberties Union responded by denouncing what they considered to be a blatant attempt to censor the Troupe and violate their right to free speech. "We'll see you in the park and we'll see you in court," Davis brazenly promised.

The controversy was simultaneously a farce about civil authorities policing public morality and a publicity stunt in one act crafted out of Davis's principled chutzpah and Bill Graham's promotional savvy. (Graham, who worked for a heavy equipment manufacturer in his previous job, had recently been hired as the Mime Troupe's business manager.) A small crowd of free-speech proponents and curious onlookers turned out to see the show. When one of the commissioners tried to prevent the troupe from erecting its stage, Davis maneuvered in front of the milling audience and announced: "Ladieeeees and Gentlemen, *Il Troupo di Mimo di* San Francisco presents for your enjoyment this afternoon . . . AN ARREST!!!" And with these words he flung himself into the upraised arms of the police. "The job of the artist in politics is to take leaps the politicos never take," Davis afterward wryly observed.[1]

This brief drama in Lafayette Park was little noted outside the region, but it helped set a wave in motion that would soon hit the country like a riptide. The forms of political activism and the content of avant-garde theater in the United States converged in the mid-1960s. Artists, particularly those who worked in the theater, used the stage to bring au courant controversies and sweeping social commentaries to the fore of public awareness. Political protesters, meanwhile, began increasingly to adopt dramatic forms as a means of expressing their collective dissent from a society they saw as morally bankrupt, racist, militaristic, and culturally stultifying. Together these two developments contributed a distinctive sensibility to Sixties cultural politics; the interaction of New Left politics and avant-garde performance fused to produce the nation's first counterculture to be called by that name.[2] How this came to pass can be cogently grasped by tracing the evolution of "guerrilla theater" as a countercultural practice through its three principal phases.

Guerrilla theater was first articulated in 1965 in a manifesto fitfully produced by R. G. Davis, founding director (six years earlier) of the San Francisco Mime Troupe. By exhorting his theatrical ensemble to become a Marxian cadre, or at the very least a catalyst for social change, Davis committed the Mime Troupe to serve as a movement vanguard in the nascent cultural revolution. This was the formula: they would continue to broaden their audience by performing in new spaces, such as public parks. Their plays would be nothing if not topical, suffused with radical content, and enlivened by biting satire and repartee improvised to suit the occasion. Funding was to be primarily by free will offerings; no admission fees would be charged. Largely through the Mime Troupe's efforts, widely disseminated by means of national tours, the staging of improvisatory, didactic skits in public spaces became a staple of antiwar, women's liberation, and other social movement protests.[3]

Guerrilla theater grew directly out of Davis's rediscovery of commedia dell'arte, in which he became interested after studying modern dance and mime during the 1950s. A sixteenth-century Italian popular theatrical form, commedia is known for its stock characters in grotesque masks who improvise much of their dialogue while playing close to type. Commedia performers customarily make sport of human foibles and universal complaints while burlesquing the most socially or politically prominent members of a given community. Reviving this comedic form was a stroke of genius on Davis's part. It recuperated the carnivalesque—that fecund bawdiness that Bakhtin delineated in Rabelais—and transposed it to a modern American setting.[4] Furthermore, it furnished the Mime Troupe with an earthy, subversive art form that was tailored for itinerant players who found their audiences in the streets and marketplaces. Commedia troupes adapted their skits to local issues, supported themselves by passing the hat and therefore were not beholden to wealthy benefactors, and were able to quickly disperse and slip out of town when the magistrates took offense and came calling.

In May 1962, Davis and the company produced their first commedia— *The Dowry*—in the parks of San Francisco. The signal importance of this initiative is that it took serious theater out of the playhouses and resituated it out of doors, where it might again attract a diversely popular following. In the parks performers could mount plays that were fresh and challenging before new audiences who might not otherwise go to see theater on a regular basis. The Mime Troupe may well have been the first artistic company in a generation to establish or perhaps reclaim the public parks as a performance venue.[5] As such they prepared a site for countercultural entertainment and festivity that would soon be thronged with outdoor rock concerts and be-ins, culminating at the end of the decade with Woodstock and People's Park.

Davis's leftward lurch accelerated in the early 1960s when he met and became friends with political activists Saul Landau and Nina Serrano. Before moving to San Francisco in 1961 from Madison, Wisconsin, the married couple had been instrumental in founding the influential journal *Studies on the Left*. Their mutual interests in theater had led to their involvement in staging the celebrated Anti-Military Balls at the University of Wisconsin in 1959 and 1960. The highlights of these events were elaborate, irreverent skits that satirized the contemporary national political scene from an overtly socialist perspective.[6] Shortly after meeting Ronnie Davis, Serrano and Landau became his artistic collaborators.[7] Landau wrote scenarios and lyrics for a couple of plays, while Serrano codirected *Tartuffe* in the commedia style for performance in the parks. Through them Davis was introduced to Robert Scheer who was then working as a clerk in Lawrence Ferlinghetti's City Lights Book Shop. Davis's political perspective was thoroughly radicalized through his association with these three individuals.[8]

By mid-decade the Mime Troupe's commitment to radical theater culminated in an artistic statement that Davis drafted and read to the company in May 1965. Christened "guerrilla theater" by actor-playwright Peter Berg, Davis's manifesto took its cue from Che Guevara:

The guerrilla fighter needs full help from the people. . . . From the very beginning he has the intention of destroying an unjust order and therefore an intention . . . to replace the old with something new.

Davis glossed this quotation to contend that the guerrilla cadre provided a model worth emulating by their theatrical ensemble. Both were small, highly disciplined groups who were motivated by a righteous cause to do battle against enormous odds. Journalistic reports by Landau and Scheer, based on their recent visits to Cuba, may well have brought home to Davis the powerful example of a revolutionary cadre movement that was successful in overthrowing a corrupt regime.[9]

Davis's essay indicted American *society* (but curiously not the *state*) for having allowed the political establishment to vigorously pursue such foreign policy fiascos as the Bay of Pigs invasion and the Vietnam War. His response to this deplorable state of affairs was to mobilize the American theater as an instrument of far-reaching social and political change. He proposed that the Mime Troupe and other like-minded theaters adopt a three-pronged program: to "teach, direct toward change, [and] be an example of change." Accomplishing the first objective would require actors to educate themselves so that they would have something to teach. The second point openly accepted Brecht's insistence that all art served political purposes, whether implicitly or explicitly. Davis wanted his fellow troupers to declare themselves against "the system" and then devote themselves to its wholesale transformation. (Just a few weeks earlier, the Students for a Democratic Society activist Paul Potter had delivered his much-discussed "Name That System" speech in Washington, D.C., before the largest peace demonstration in U.S. history.)[10]

This task was to be accomplished by fulfilling Davis's third objective: the company should "exemplify change as a group" by installing "morality at its core" and establishing cooperative relationships or a coalition with like-minded organizations. Here he recommended that radical theaters take up Che's example, which for all its martial trappings was essentially how the traditional commedia troupes had operated: "[B]ecome equipped to pack up and move quickly when you're outnumbered. Never engage the enemy head on. Choose your fighting ground; don't be forced into battle over the wrong issues."[11]

Guerrilla theater was not intended to be a call to arms, but a *cultural* revolt aimed at replacing discredited American values and norms.[12] As Davis phrased it, "There is a vision in this theater, and . . . it is to continue . . . presenting moral plays and to confront hypocrisy in the society."[13] What stands out from Davis's intentions in 1965 is his desire to mobilize a corps of politi-cized artists to act as the vanguard of an American cultural revolution.

And so by mid-decade, as the civil rights, free speech, and antiwar move-ments ripened into the Movement, Davis was leading the Mime Troupe into the van of New Left activism. He, Landau, and Serrano originated the idea for what would become known as the Mime Troupe's most controversial play from that era: *A Minstrel Show, or: Civil Rights in a Cracker Barrel*, a produc-tion quite unlike other irreverently political revues of the day. It was to polit-ical theater what Lenny Bruce was to stand-up comedy, an exercise in wringing the rude truth from the day's news, while straddling the fine line between mere "bad taste" and the flagrantly lewd. Alternately subtitled *Jim Crow a Go-Go*, the show consisted of a series of skits performed by a racially integrated cast, all but the white, straight-man "Interlocuter" appearing in blackface. The self-designated "darkies" were costumed in blue and ivory satin suits and white cotton gloves and topped off with short-haired wigs like jet-black scouring pads. Audiences found it perplexingly difficult to discern the true racial identity of the six masqued performers, a predicament that ren-dered the actors' raucous banter all the more unsettling. Mime Troupe veteran Peter Coyote attributes the show's critical success to its offering "a rare cul-tural epiphany perfectly in synch with the historical moment." A *Minstrel Show* appeared at a time, he surmises, "when the Civil Rights movement and the emerging black consciousness fused with a social upheaval in the nation's youth to make society appear suddenly permeable and open to both self-inves-tigation and change."[14]

Davis hoped to hone the radical edge of this production by means of form as well as content. To this end he solicited members of the local civil rights activist community to audition for parts, conjecturing that if he could locate several men who possessed both a progressive political sensibility and a meas-ure of native talent, they would be able to polish their acting skills in rehearsal. Experience in civil rights advocacy, he maintained, would be indispensable to carrying out the task Davis and his collaborators had set out for the show: exposing the deep-seated nature of prejudice in contemporary society. The American minstrel show format would be redeployed in a way that subverted the racist stereotypes that had permeated the traditional traveling mode of entertainment. It would parallel what the Mime Troupe had done with com-media: adapt a popular theatrical form to explore a series of wide-ranging, contentious topics, in this case selected from more than a century of American racial discourse.

No subject was to be considered off-limits: interracial sexual relation-ships, myths of African-American male potency, and class conflicts within the black community were each dramatized and critiqued. The ghettoization of the past as represented by "Nego [*sic*] History Month" was lampooned without mercy (Crispus Attucks, the first African American to die in the Revolutionary War, gets shot by Redcoats while pushing a broom). In another skit, the irony of black soldiers killing "yellow men" in Vietnam by orders of a white imperialist command is put across with the austere didacticism of Bertolt Brecht. Institutional racism, naive integrationism, police brutality, craven Uncle Toms, supercilious white liberals, and arrogant black militants—all received their jocund due. In order to ensure that the play's satirical barbs hit their many intended targets, staff members of the local Student Nonviolent Coordinating Committee and Congress of Racial Equality organizations were invited along with the cast to critique the play while it was still in development.[15] A *Minstrel Show* attracted national attention for the Mime Troupe when they produced it on their first cross-country tour in 1966. The comedian and civil rights activist Dick Gregory sponsored its performance at Town Hall in New York, which garnered an enthusiastic review from no less than the *New York Times*.[16]

Around this same time Davis sought other ways to strengthen ties between the avant-garde and the Bay Area radical movement. The Mime Troupe made their rented studio in the Mission District available for use by the New School, a project coordinated by Landau and Paul Jacobs as the first of the "free universities" to spring up in the wake of the free speech movement. Davis was one of its board members and cotaught a course on art and politics during its summer session in 1964.[17] When the troupe relocated to a downtown loft on Howard Street the next summer, they furnished SDS with an office. Still later, they shared their facilities with San Francisco Newsreel, a radical filmmaking collective. This mingling of artists and political activists facilitated by the Mime Troupe ensured that culture and politics would not be as bifurcated in the Bay Area as it may have been elsewhere.

Davis clarified and extended his guerrilla theater idea twice more in essays published before the decade's end. The next installment, written in late 1967, embraced an eclectic Marxism glimpsed through the prism of the Summer of Love. In it he located the source of American ills not in corporate liberalism, as *Studies on the Left* and SDS had, but in the very system of private property. To counteract this "disease" of creeping materialism he advocated "dropping out" of bourgeois society and devising in its stead an alternative "life-style that replaces most, if not all, middle-class capitalistic assumptions." Davis was sparse on the details—as with his plays, he preferred the dramatic gesture to the searching soliloquy. He did explain that this lifestyle must itself constitute

Comedian and social activist Dick Gregory lent political credibility to the Mime Troupe's subversion of the 19th-century minstrel show form by recasting it as "guerrilla theater." Their subsequent performances helped garner the racially integrated ensemble an Obie (Off-Broadway) award from the *Village Voice* "for uniting theatre and revolution and grooving in the parks." Reproduced from R.G. Davis, *The San Francisco Mime Troupe: The First Ten Years* (Palo Alto, Cal.: Ramparts Press, 1975), 48.

a "moral force" that would work within one's community of origin (reckoned not by geography, necessarily, but by one's class, racial, and/or ethnic background). Its purpose was to criticize "prevailing conditions . . . expressing what you (as a community) all know but no one is saying . . . truth that may be shocking and honesty that is vulgar to the aesthete."[18] Speaking truth to power, just as Quaker activists had been urging, would before long become standard practice among those operating within the framework of identity politics.

The serious purpose behind Davis's proposal was elaborated in a third essay he published the next year. There he noted that guerrilla theater as he had formulated it in 1965 had subsequently "become a catch-all for non-professional theater groups," because of a fundamental misinterpretation by these would-be imitators. He now took care to distinguish his original idea, "which describe[d] activity on the *cultural* front in the USA" [emphasis mine], from that of "armed revolutionary action." Despite obvious differences, he argued, the two did have this much in common: "The cultural revolutionary, just as the armed guerrilla, must want and be capable of taking power." Power will be seized, he averred, by radicals who operate simultaneously on three fronts: ideological (e.g., performing for audiences of the unconverted, undermining their "bourgeois mentality"), economic (ending exploitation and consumerism by organizing not-for-profit alternative cultural institutions), and physical (here, while his meaning was unspecified, he encouraged disciplined collective action aimed at destroying both individualism and elitism).

The article was to be his longest think piece on the subject, yet it is vexingly vague about what it would mean for cultural revolutionaries to actually seize power. One must infer from certain textual clues that America's "corporate liberalism" and "imperialism"—its dream of global domination—(he finally did employ these terms) would both be smashed and that some sort of socialism would be adopted in the postrevolutionary society. But all we can be sure about Davis's intentions at this point is that he recognized the politicized artist as the vanguard of the cultural revolution. "This is our society," he intoned, uttering the last lines of the Mime Troupe's recent antiwar play *L' Amant Miltaire*; "if we don't like it[,] it's our duty to change it; if we can't change it, we must destroy it." Perhaps then, perhaps only then a vision of what exactly to replace it with would emerge. Davis's nihilistic bombast forecast the direction that at least some members of the ultraleft would head in the months and years ahead.[19]

Guerrilla theater's second phase began in fall 1966 when a number of Mime Troupe members, some twenty in all, broke away from the company to found

Michael William Doyle

a freewheeling anarchist collective they called the Diggers.[20] Just as Ronny Davis had turned to the past for inspiration in reviving popular theatrical forms such as commedia dell'arte and the minstrel show, so too did the Diggers. Their name derived from a seventeenth-century group of English millenarians who, in the aftermath of the English Civil War, quixotically resisted the enclosure of the commons. Envisioning the establishment of a cooperative commonwealth, these displaced peasants and artisans practiced what they preached, sharing their food and possessions among themselves as well as with those who were even more destitute. "And let the common people, that say the earth is *ours*, not *mine*," Gerrard Winstanley, their most eloquent spokesman, beseeched all who would listen, "let them labor together, and eat bread together upon the commons, mountains, and hills." But when the Diggers dared to dig up, fertilize, and plant their crops on the common of St. George's Hill, a barren heath near Surrey, they were decisively put down and scattered by the combined forces of the lords, freeholders, and soldiers from Cromwell's New Model Army.[21]

The Diggers of San Francisco seem not to have made a detailed study of their English forebears, probably because they were less interested in them as an explicit model than as an inspiration. What appealed to them about the earlier group was that they had emerged spontaneously from within the ranks of the oppressed. What the two groups shared was a vision of the total transformation of social and economic relations, a dedication to bringing about the New Jerusalem by peaceable means, a reliance on pamphlets and direct appeals to spread their message, and, perhaps most important, a belief that exemplary actions were the key to realizing their ambitious goals. And like their namesakes, the Haight-Ashbury Diggers were seeded with inspired writers who produced tracts filled with prose that was overtly political and verged occasionally on the ecstatic. Both groups managed to exert a measure of influence that was disproportionate to their small number; both proved ultimately to be short-lived.

Most of the founding core of the later Diggers had had no professional training or even much experience in drama before they joined the Mime Troupe. Davis announced in his original guerrilla theater essay that he wanted to work with people from outside of theater. He hoped that this would bring in fresh perspectives from other disciplines, just as he himself had done by importing techniques derived from modern dance and mime.[22] That Davis succeeded in his object may be seen in the variety of artistic talent represented by those Mime Troupe members who left to form the Diggers. They included writers (Berg, Coyote, Grogan, Kent Minault, Billy Murcott), dancers (Judy Goldhaft, Jane Lapiner), painters, sculptors (Roberto La Morticella), filmmakers, musicians, printmakers (Karl Rosenberg), among others.[23] Significantly, by being relatively unschooled in dramatic theory and technique beyond what they had absorbed in the SFMT, the Diggers felt no compunction to strictly observe theatrical convention. Instead of attaining artistic critical success or even raising the political consciousness of popular audiences, the Diggers strove to dramatize the hip counterculture as a "social fact." Utopia—the "good place" that in Thomas More's coinage is "no place"— would be played out daily in the Haight.

To this end, the Diggers borrowed from the Mime Troupe the ensemble form, as well as the aggressive improvisational style, the itinerant outlaw posture, and the satirical social critique mode of commedia dell'arte. They also appropriated Davis's dramatic form of guerrilla theater and gave it a new twist. Where he had taken theater out of its traditional setting to stage it in the parks, the Diggers took theater into the streets. In the process they attempted to remove all boundaries between art and life, between spectator and performer, and between public and private. The resulting technique, which they referred to as "life-acting," punned on the dual meaning of the verb "to act," combining the direct action of anarchism with theatrical role playing. The Diggers' principal project was to enact "Free," a comprehensive utopian program that would function as a working model of an alternative society.

For the Diggers the word "free" was as much an imperative as it was an adjective. The object was to place it before any noun or gerund that designated a fundamental need, service, or institution, and then try to imagine how such a thing might be realized.[24] Thus "free press" evolved a new connotation from First Amendment guarantee to an "instant news" service that disseminated free broadsides in the Haight on a daily basis. Free transportation suggested the obligation to pick up hitchhikers and for a time called into existence a small fleet of vans, trucks, and buses that shuttled people around town and across the bay to Berkeley. Bill Fritsch thought up the free bank and stashed a wad of donated cash in his hat from which to make no-interest "loans." He even kept a ledger to keep track of where it all went.[25]

The project of "Free" all started in early October 1966 with free food dished out in Golden Gate Park every day at 4 P.M. Next it was manifested in the free store, which parodied capitalism even while redistributing the cornucopian bounty of that system's surplus. The free store's first name was the Free Frame of Reference, which derived from the tall yellow picture frame that the Diggers would have people step through before being served their daily stew and bread. The frame represented what was possible when people changed their conceptual paradigm for apprehending reality. As such the Diggers stood squarely on the side of the hippies in their ongoing philosophical debate with the politicos: if one wanted to change the world, it was necessary first to change one's consciousness or point of view.

Added to these various free services were others that gradually took shape between 1966 and 1968: free housing in communal crash pads and outlying farms, free legal services, and a free medical clinic. For entertainment there were occasional free film screenings and of course free dance concerts by local bands of growing renown such as the Jefferson Airplane, the Grateful Dead, Big Brother and the Holding Company, and Country Joe and the Fish. By the winter of 1967–68, there was even a Digger-sponsored initiative supported by prominent members of the Bay Area clergy to provide "free churches" by allowing their sanctuaries to remain open to worshipers around the clock. Taken together, these institutions, practices, and services constituted what, by the end of the Summer of Love, the Diggers were calling the Free City network.

The sources of support for the Free City activities were various. Labor for Digger projects was furnished almost entirely by volunteers. The story of the Haight was the sizable number of idle youths who had come to explore the hippie lifestyle, and it was this population that the Diggers attempted to mobilize. Demographically those who chose to work with the Diggers were in their teens and twenties, primarily white, from middle- and working-class backgrounds, and many were at least partially college-educated. Along with these advantages, they had time on their hands; some could depend upon financial assistance from their families of origin. Rock bands and promoters were probably the single largest financial donors (e.g., the Grateful Dead's communal dwelling housed the Haight-Ashbury Legal Organization, which they funded to provide free legal assistance). In addition, at least up until the middle of 1967, certain community-minded dealers of psychedelic drugs made cash contributions. And whether because of guilt, coercion, or altruism, some members of the Haight Independent Proprietors association tithed to the Diggers from the profits they realized on their retail sales (primarily to tourists who had come to gape at the hippies).

The Diggers would be unimaginable without their having been able to draw upon the vaunted affluence of a postscarcity society. Surplus goods were more easily available during the economic boom of the mid-1960s, which followed a long period of postwar prosperity. California's share of defense spending was huge; consequently unemployment was minimal and more discretionary spending was possible. Ironically, the Bay Area in particular benefited from being the point of departure and reentry for troops involved in prosecuting the Vietnam war. Then, too, there was the money being pumped into the city by Great Society programs, some of which undoubtedly trickled down to the Diggers.

Other factors which facilitated the Free City network include the relatively low cost of living in San Francisco at the time; for example, large apartments and storefronts were quite plentiful and could be leased at reasonable rates.[26] Communal living helped further reduce expenses for individuals by the pooling of resources, enabling members to subsist on a meager income. Finally, the city's Mediterranean climate was relatively mild compared with much of the rest of the country, thereby keeping expenditures for heating and cooling to a minimum, as well as negating the need for extensive seasonal wardrobes. All of these factors were conducive to incubating the Diggers' utopian project.

When beneficence and windfalls failed to deliver essential items, the Diggers hustled; they were not above resorting to theft or intimidation to obtain food, for instance. The principle of "Free" authorized, even valorized "liberating" goods from uncooperative suppliers for the benefit of the "New Community."[27] It wasn't so much that the Diggers believed the ends justified the means, as that the means and the ends were for all practical purposes identical. Those who thought otherwise would be in Rousseauvian terms forced to be free.[28]

The Diggers understood from the outset that their project involved "acting," but it wasn't exactly theater—even by Ronny Davis's iconoclastic standards. To their mind, if one strongly objected to capitalism, then one simply abolished the system of private property along with the controlling assumptions of a money-based economy. In its place the Diggers pushed the concept of "everything free," another notion that combined two commonly understood meanings of the word: costing nothing and liberated from social conventions. Freedom or liberty, they maintained, is one of the genetic codes in the American body politic. By the middle 1960s, in the wake of the Civil Rights movement's legislative victories, "freedom now" acquired a new, transpolitical/psychological cast that was conveyed by the term "liberation." The Diggers' notion of "free" drew on this free-floating cultural striving for total emancipation. But their particular practice of "free" was also inspired by the Mime Troupe's approach to producing theater in the parks: free public performances to be covered by free-will donations.

The guerrilla theater of the Diggers was manifested in its most spectacular form in street theater "events" they staged in public places at irregular intervals of approximately every few weeks. The purpose of these avant-garde happenings varied from attacking the creeping commodification of the counterculture, as in the "Death of Money, Birth of the Haight" (17 December 1966), to the widely noted and similarly named "Death of Hippy, Birth of the Free Man" (6 October 1967). Held to ceremonially mark the end of the Summer of Love, the "Death of Hippy" event mounted a radical critique of the mass media's role in framing and defaming the counterculture via sensationalistic news coverage. Each event was unique. To impart a sense of what one involved, here is how the "Full Moon Public Celebration" of Halloween 1966 was structured.

On the southwest corner of the intersection of Haight and Ashbury Streets, the symbolic heart of what some in the community were calling "Psychedelphia," the Diggers set up their thirteen-foot-tall yellow "Frame of Reference." Two giant puppets, on loan from the Mime Troupe and resembling Robert Scheer and the Berkeley congressman, Jeffrey Cohelan,[29] performed a skit entitled "Any Fool on the Street." The puppets were maneuvered back and forth through the frame, as their puppeteers improvised an argument in character about which side was "inside" and which "outside." All the while the eight-foot-high puppets encouraged bystanders to follow their lead and pass through the frame as a way of "changing their frame of reference." Meanwhile, other Diggers distributed smaller versions of the frame made out of yellow-painted laths six inches square attached to a neck strap. These were meant to be worn not as talismans for warding off baleful influences but as reminders that one's point of view (and hence waking consciousness) was mutable. Effecting changes in objective reality, the Diggers maintained, had to be preceded by altering people's perspective on the assumed fixity of the status quo. Renegotiating those underexamined assumptions might well produce new and more imaginative ways of organizing social relations.

Next, participants were guided in playing a game called "Intersection" that involved people crossing those streets in a way that traced as many different kinds of polygons as possible. The intended effect was to impede vehicular traffic on Haight Street as a way of deterring the growing stream of tourists who had come to gawk at the hippies. One problem, however, was that as groups like the Diggers acquired a reputation for creating spectacles in the Haight, such doings inevitably attracted curiosity seekers from outside the neighborhood. From the Diggers' standpoint, anyone was welcome to join in their events, but mere spectators were actively discouraged. And they and the other hip residents of the district reserved a special animosity toward the nonstop, bumper-to-bumper carloads of people who had come to stare at them through rolled-up windows and locked doors.

Within an hour (at around 6 P.M.) a crowd of some 600 pedestrians had gathered to partake in the Digger activities. Not long afterward the police

The cadre of artist-anarchists known as the Diggers dropped out of the San Francisco Mime Troupe exactly one year before this picture was taken at perhaps their best known event, the "Death of Hippy, Son of Mass Media" mock funeral in the Haight-Ashbury district, 6 Oct. 1967. Their revision of the guerrilla theater concept fused dramatic acting with direct-action anarchism. The only stage they played was the streets, where spectators unwittingly became actors improvising an event around the theme "create the condition you describe." © Popperfoto/Archive Photos.

arrived in several squad cars and a paddy wagon to disperse the crowd. In a priceless moment of unscripted theater of the absurd, police officers began a series of verbal exchanges with the puppets! A journalist on hand captured the ensuing dialogue:

> *Police*: "We warn you that if you don't remove yourselves from the
>   area you'll be arrested for blocking a public thoroughfare."
> *Puppet*: "Who is the public?"
> *Police*: "I couldn't care less; I'll take you in. Now get a move on."
> *Puppet*: "I declare myself public—I am a public. The streets are
>   public—the streets are free."

The altercation, it should come as no surprise, resulted in the arrest of five of the Diggers—Grogan, Berg, La Morticella, Minault, and Brooks Butcher—along with another member of the crowd who objected to the police's action by insisting that "These are our streets." As the arrestees were being driven away, the crowd began chanting "Frame-up! Frame-up!" to which the arrested men responded from within the van, "Pub-lic! Pub-lic!" As many as 200 people remained on the scene afterward in defiance of police orders. They resumed the Intersection game and, after one of the Diggers set up a phonograph and started playing music, began to dance in the street. The officers may well have attributed the night's outlandish public behavior to the effects of a "blue moon" on All Hallows' Eve. To the Diggers it was a demonstration of their power to confound the authorities and stake their claim on the urban turf.

As the author of the guerrilla theater idea, R. G. Davis was sharply critical of the Diggers, as he would soon also be of the Yippies. He rejected what the Diggers were doing as being neither serious nor effective. Nor to his mind did it qualify as a legitimate type of political theater. (This he distinguished from merely acting theatrically in public.) Davis defined himself and the Mime Troupe first and foremost as theater *professionals* who were dedicated to the transformation of society through the practice of their art.[30] For the Diggers' part all theater involved the willful suspension of disbelief by those who participated in it. Their play on guerrilla theater attempted to extend that suspension of disbelief, act out alternatives to bourgeois "consensus reality" in its liminal space, demonstrate that these alternatives were possible, and thereby convince others to join them in enacting the Free City into existence. Stripped to its bare essentials, today's fantasy might well furnish a description of tomorrow's reality. And in this belief, they situated themselves squarely in the American utopian tradition.

The third phase of guerrilla theater is exemplified by the Yippies, who emerged in New York in early 1968 through the efforts of Jerry Rubin, Abbie Hoffman, Jim Fouratt, and Paul Krassner, among numerous others. Another loosely bounded collective, they intended their felicitously named Youth International Party to mobilize a mass demonstration of antiwar activists, Black Power advocates, and disaffiliated hippies in Chicago that August at the Democratic Convention. The Yippies turned guerrilla theater away from a kind of premodern reliance on face-to-face contact with a popular audience, as it was practiced by the Mime Troupe. But they also moved it away from its more modern adaptation by the Diggers, who had attempted to obliterate the distinction between art and life, and between actor and audience. By contrast, the Yippies' version of guerrilla theater, which Hoffman designated as "media-freaking," was to commit absurdist, gratuitous acts that were carefully crafted to obtain maximum publicity. As Hoffman explained it, "The trick to manipulating the media is to get them to promote an event before it happens. . . . In other words, . . . get them to make an advertisement for . . . revolution—the same way you would advertise soap."[31]

In the months prior to the founding of the Yippies, in fact, throughout 1967, several members of the group had put themselves forward publicly as the de facto East Coast branch of the Diggers. The Haight-Ashbury Diggers, more than any other group during the past year and a half, had served as the New Yorkers' inspiration.[32] The Diggers had instructed them in the art of guerrilla theater, had given them a vocabulary for expressing direct-action politics, and had improvised scenarios the latter group drew upon in their own efforts to enact the counterculture.

Besides freely adapting scenarios that had been scripted largely by their Haight-Ashbury counterparts, the New York Diggers occasionally improvised some novel ones of their own. For examples of the former, they began serving free food to hippies in Tompkins Square Park, organized a "communications company" to freely distribute mimeographed broadsides that were often reprints of the Digger Papers, and even opened a free store. They borrowed the San Francisco Diggers' guerrilla theater technique of "milling-in" (i.e., the Intersection game) as it had been improvised on Halloween night 1966 in response to the vehicular traffic congestion on Haight Street. On the first Saturday night of August 1967, Jim Fouratt and other New Yorker Diggers summoned hippies to block traffic on St. Mark's Place between Second and Third Avenues. Their object was to convince the city to convert that block, the heart of the Lower East Side's hip community, into a pedestrian mall. They carried cardboard replicas of traffic signs, so that in place of the usual protest demands, their placards read "Stop," "Yield," and "No Parking." Throngs of hippies laid claim to the street in equally inventive ways, some of them through the expression of mystical exuberance by chanting and dancing "the Hare Krishna hora." The police were present in force, but did nothing to halt the activities because of a prior arrangement between them and Fouratt. Securing the officers' restraint came with a price, though. Fouratt had to agree to keep the demonstration brief—no more than fifteen minutes.[33]

Later that same month the New York Diggers created their most memorable spectacle that represented a decisive break with the San Francisco group's practice of guerrilla theater. It was planned and executed by Hoffman, Fouratt, and several others including Jerry Rubin, who had just moved to town from Berkeley a few days earlier. The group arranged for a tour of the New York Stock Exchange (NYSE) under the auspices of ESSO (the East Side Service Organization, a hip social services agency; the fact that this acronym

Several of the founding core of the Haight-Ashbury Diggers hailed from New York, and their efforts to stimulate guerrilla theater activity in the Lower East Side during the "Summer of Love" inspired a group who for a time referred to themselves as the New York Diggers. Taking their cues from their San Francisco counterparts, Abbie and Anita Hoffman, Jim Fouratt, Paul Krassner, and others organized a Free Store at 264 East 10th Street, where this photo was taken on opening day, 22 September 1967. By year's end, the collective would proclaim a new name for themselves—Yippies! © Fred W. McDarrah.

was better known as the name of a giant oil corporation is probably what gained them entrée to the NYSE). Once they had been escorted into the visitors' gallery above the trading pit, they produced fistfuls of dollar bills and flung them from the balcony onto the floor below. All bidding stopped as traders impulsively switched from their usual frantic mode to an atavistic frenzy, scrambling to grab what they could from the shower of cash. Then they began to berate the Diggers, perhaps in part because they realized how this interruption had manipulated them to reveal the fine line between greed and self-interest that runs through the heart of finance capitalism.[34]

This event was pivotal for the New York Diggers. It retained elements of borrowing from the Haight-Ashbury group. Fouratt, for instance, explained their action as signifying "the death of money." Hoffman, who had registered for the tour under the West Coast Digger alias "George Metesky," set fire to a five-dollar bill afterward outside the Exchange, just as Emmett Grogan had done famously earlier in the year.[35] But the New York group also introduced some new elements into the neoteric art of guerrilla theater. The choice of setting was far from their accustomed habitat: the very capitol of capital. It was also presented for the edification of two audiences. The primary one consisted of the traders themselves, who were unwittingly manipulated into acting in a kind of latter-day morality play; the secondary one was not present. Hoffman intended to reach the latter audience via the print media by tipping off reporters to the Diggers' plans in advance. The Haight-Ashbury Diggers would denounce such a tactic as a mere publicity stunt, not permissible under the rules of engagement of their version of guerrilla theater because it created spectators instead of engaged actors. Furthermore, the Stock Exchange event was not meant to ritually constitute a countercultural community in place, nor to extend or defend its boundaries, as most of the San Francisco Diggers' events were designed to do. The New Yorkers' action instead preached to the unconverted about a cultural revolution that would not stay confined to the psychedelic ghettos. As the first Digger spectacle to involve both Rubin and Hoffman, it also indicated the types of activities that Yippies would soon be undertaking.[36]

During the second week of September the New York Diggers staged another innovative guerrilla theater event, which they called "Black Flower Day," at the Consolidated Edison building on Irving Place. It began by their placing a wreath of daffodils dyed with black ink on the ledge above the lobby entrance, and then handing out similarly stained wreaths to passersby. They also strung up a large banner on the building that declared "BREATHING IS BAD FOR YOUR HEALTH." Next they fanned into the lobby a sizable pile of soot they had dumped on the sidewalk, and danced around—one of them clad in a clown suit—throwing soot in the air. As the police arrived, the Diggers hurriedly lit a couple of smoke bombs and fled the scene. Don McNeill, a *Village Voice* journalist who wrote the article on which this account is based, remarked that "the Digger drama [was] improvised with the idea that a handful of soot down an executive's neck might be more effective than a pile of petitions begging for cleaner air."[37] This event furnishes another example of how the New York Diggers were not merely being derivative of their Haight-Ashbury counterparts. By focusing attention on the effects of pollution on the natural and urban environment they skillfully adapted the technique of guerrilla theater to articulate an ecological critique before it had become a popular cause.

Around this time, members of the Haight-Ashbury Diggers began to strenuously object to the use of the name Diggers by the New York collective. It would seem that they were ideologically disposed to share everything freely with anyone—except their good name. The objection in this case, however, was directed specifically toward Abbie Hoffman and Jerry Rubin for cultivating their images as countercultural leaders or spokesmen. They also took offense at the New Yorkers' penchant for publicizing their zany activities in the mass media. The San Francisco group insisted that their East Coast namesakes disassociate themselves from the Digger movement. As a result, by the end of the year the name "Yippie!" was devised, along with a new organizational framework for the New York group; it had the virtue of being free of any contested associations and also marked a shift in the focus of operations from the local to the national scene.[38]

By the summer of 1968 this tension between the Diggers and the Yippies exposed an irreconcilable conflict between two of the most prominent tendencies within countercultural activism. For the utopia-tinged vision of the Yippies' Festival of Life had its roots at least partly in the Free City project of the Diggers. On the other hand, the "Festival of Blood" (as a Chicago Yippie organizer was to presciently call it a week before demonstrators clashed violently with police) was scripted in concert with what I maintain was the Yippies' deliberate misprisioning of the Diggers' approach to guerrilla theater. Interestingly, the Yippies' version would resemble in its praxis the more militant theoretical formulation by R. G. Davis.[39]

The Yippies' proclaimed raison d'être was to create a new national organization whose goals were, first, to politicize members of the hippie counterculture generally; and, second, to bring them together with other Movement activists and curious uncommitted young people at a "youth festival" to be held concurrently at the Chicago Democratic Convention in late August 1968. Initially, at least according to Jerry Rubin's announcement of Yippie plans for the festival in mid-February 1968, the gathering was to represent a new direction for the antiwar movement. Instead of being designed to shift activists from "protest to resistance" against the state, as the National Mobilization Against the War in Vietnam had represented its October 1967 march on the Pentagon, it would mark a turn from protest to a frontal assault on American culture. The charge, however, would be led by a most unconventional brigade. Nonviolent hip youths would come to Grant Park, near the convention center, and recreate their incipient "alternate lifestyle" in all its variegated splendor, much as though they were a living exhibit of Plains Indians on stockaded display at the 1893 World's Columbian Exposition. An audience of millions would visit the Yippie "Do-In" with the news media's unwitting compliance. Television and print journalists from around the world could be counted on to troll for colorful feature stories to augment the endless speeches and procedural vote taking of the four-day political convention.

In February 1968 Rubin wrote his friend Allen Cohen, editor of the *San Francisco Oracle* underground newspaper, that he wanted to recreate the communitas of the Haight-Ashbury's "Human Be-In" through what would soon be designated as the Festival of Life:

> [O]ur idea is to create a cultural, living alternative to the Convention. It could be the largest gathering of young people ever: in the middle of the country at the end of the summer. . . . We want all the rock bands, all the underground papers, all the free spirits, all the theater groups—all the energies that have contributed to the new youth culture—all the tribes—to come to Chicago and for six days we will live together in the park, sharing, learning, free food, free music, a regeneration of spirit and energy. In a sense, it is like creating a SF-Berkeley spirit for a brief period in the Midwest . . . thereby breaking people out of their isolation and spreading the revolution. . . . The existence of the Convention at the same time gives us a stage, a platform, an opportunity to do our own thing, to go beyond protest into creative cultural alternative.[40]

Rubin elaborated on this notion not long afterward in an interview in the *Chicago Seed*:

> In Chicago in August, every media [outlet] in the world is going to be here . . . , and we're going to be the news and everything we do is going to be sent out to living rooms from India to the Soviet Union to every small town in America. It is a real opportunity to make clear the two Americas. . . . At the same time we're *confronting* them, we're offering our alternative and it's not just a narrow, political alternative, it's an alternative way of life.[41]

The operative term in this statement is "confronting," for Rubin and Hoffman clearly understood that their Festival of Life would likely provoke a violent backlash by Mayor Richard Daley's minions of law and order.[42] And as expected Mayor Daley relished his role in this scenario, playing a cat-and-mouse game with the various protest organizations that attempted to secure permits for holding demonstrations outside the convention and for sleeping outdoors in the parks. Ultimately no permits were granted, thus ensuring a confrontation. To meet this contingency, Daley coolly marshaled his forces into place: 11,500 policemen, 5,600 Illinois National Guardsmen, 1,000 federal agents, plus a reserve of 7,500 U.S. Army troops stationed at Fort Hood, Texas, who were specially trained in riot control and could be summoned to Chicago on a moment's notice should their services be required. The 10,000 or so protesters who eventually did show up readily grasped their predicament. When the pitched battles inevitably erupted, their only recourse was to chant to the news cameras: "The whole world is watching!" in the vain hope that the cops would be chastened by this presumed collective gaze and desist.[43]

By the summer of 1968, then, one can discern the divergence of two tendencies among cultural radicals on the left. The first is the Yippie project of organizing a media spectacle ostensibly for the purpose of promoting the counterculture. The New York-based organizers, however, had an ulterior motive: to intentionally trigger a violent reaction so as to, in Rubin's words, "put people through tremendous, radicalizing changes." Their objective, he added, was to stimulate a "massive white revolutionary movement which, working in . . . cooperation with the rebellions in the black communities, could seriously disrupt this country, and thus be an internal catalyst for a breakdown of the American ability to fight guerrillas overseas."[44]

A second tendency, already fading from the scene by this time, was represented by the San Francisco Diggers' experiment in fashioning a communitarian utopia by means of guerrilla theater that performed a new set of social relations within distinct geographical boundaries. It was the New West's answer to the City upon a Hill. During their twenty-one-month tenure, the Diggers in effect improvised a play whose plot concerned how one community could be transformed root and branch into an alternative to the rest of American society. What the Yippies took from the Digger version of guerrilla theater was an appreciation of its spectacular component and its weirdly appealing absurdity; they appreciated as well its potential value for garnering publicity. These aspects they blended with the rhetoric of an artistic insurgency as initially formulated by R. G. Davis.

The Diggers' civil rites were intended symbolically to constitute a small-scale "new community" out of the otherwise anomic mass of their urban milieu.[45] Where the Mime Troupe had dramatized their radical politics in the parks, and the Diggers had enacted theirs in the streets, the Yippies projected a kind of postmodern critique of and challenge to Lyndon Johnson's Great Society designed to play on the stages of the mass media. But instead of galvanizing a groundswell of support for their cause, as they had hoped, the Yippies' mass-mediated countercultural revolt culminated in a bloody "police riot" in real time, one that ultimately lost in the ratings. To paraphrase Gil Scott-Heron, the revolution would not be televised.[46]

Notes

1. Harry Johanesen, "Park Show Canceled; 'Offensive,'" *San Francisco Examiner* [*Exam.*], 5 August 1965, 1, 16; Donald Warman, "Cops Upstage Mimers in the Park," *San Francisco Chronicle* [*Chron.*], 8 August 1965, 1A, 2B; Michael Fallon, "Park Mime Star Arrested; Banned Show Goes On," *Exam.*, 8 August 1965, 1B; Ralph J. Gleason, "On the Town" column, "Maybe

We're Really in Trouble," *Chron.*, 9 August 1965, 47. Davis's account is in his memoir, *The San Francisco Mime Troupe: The First Ten Years* [*The SFMT*] (Palo Alto, Calif.: Ramparts Press, 1975), 65–69. The second quote by Davis is taken from the transcript of a panel discussion in *Radical Theater Festival, San Francisco State College, September 1968* (San Francisco: San Francisco Mime Troupe [SFMT], 1969), 30. Davis's arrest was recorded in the 1966 documentary film *Have You Heard of the San Francisco Mime Troupe?* by Donald Lenzer and Fred Wardenburg, a copy of which may be found in the Visual Materials collections of the Wisconsin Historical Society Archives, Madison [WHS].

2. In the best theoretical study of the Sixties counterculture, Julie Stephens characterizes the product of this interaction as constituting an "anti-disciplinary politics." In her formulation, the term connotes "a language of protest which rejected hierarchy and leadership, strategy and planning, bureaucratic organization and political parties and was distinguished from the New Left by its ridiculing of political commitment, sacrifice, seriousness, and coherence." Stephens, *Anti-Disciplinary Politics: Sixties Radicalism and Postmodernism* (Cambridge: Cambridge University Press, 1998), 4.

3. Davis has ruefully acknowledged that the Mime Troupe inadvertently "germinated all sorts of mutants" who were inspired by his 1965 "guerrilla theater" manifesto, namely the Diggers, the Yippies, and a phenomenal number of agitprop street theater groups. *The SFMT*, 125. I discuss the first two collectives in this essay, but, due to space limitations, not the proliferation of guerrilla theater ensembles. This last phenomenon has been examined at length in Henry Lesnick, ed., *Guerrilla Street Theater* (New York: Bard/Avon, 1973); Karen Taylor Malpede, ed., *People's Theatre in Amerika* (New York: Drama Book Specialists, 1973); James Schevill, *Break Out! In Search of New Theatrical Environments* (Chicago: Swallow Press, 1973); and John Weisman, *Guerrilla Theater: Scenarios for Revolution* (Garden City, N.Y.: Anchor Books, 1973). A short but useful discussion of the variety, aims, and dramaturgy of such groups that acknowledges their ultimate debt to Davis's seminal ideas may be found in Richard Schechner, "Guerrilla Theatre: May 1970," *The Drama Review* 14, no. 3 [T47] (1970): 163–68. The role of radical theater groups during the era, one which contrasts them with their counterparts of the 1930s, is concisely given in Dan Georgakas, "Political Theater of 1960s–1980s," in *Encyclopedia of the American Left*, 2d ed., ed. Mari Jo Buhle et al. (New York: Oxford University Press, 1998), 614–16.

4. Mikhail Bakhtin, *Rabelais and His World*, trans. Helene Iswolsky (Cambridge, Mass.: MIT Press [1968]).

5. Journalist Michael Goodman confirmed that "the Mime Troupe was involved with a great deal of what came to be known as the counter-culture . . . [including] the move into the parks. . . ." See his article, "The Story Theater, the Mime Troupe, and a Political Rap with R.G. Davis," *City* magazine [San Francisco], (29 May–11 June 1974), 29. Davis himself observed that when the Mime Troupe started performing in the parks in 1962 they were "unique." But six years later, he noted, "there are rock bands in the street and puppet plays and all kinds of things. . . . We do stimulate that kind of alternative." Davis, *The SFMT*, 100; and excerpt from a panel discussion in *Radical Theatre Festival* (San Francisco: San Francisco Mime Troupe, 1968), 34. Also in this last source, Peter Schumann, the founding director of Bread and Puppet Theatre, states that when his company began staging plays in the streets of New York late in 1963, "it was new to New Yorkers. They hadn't seen that since the twenties" (34).

6. See the short memoirs by Serrano, "A Madison Bohemian," (67–84), and Landau, "From the Labor Youth League to the Cuban Revolution," (107–12) in *History and the New Left: Madison, Wisconsin, 1950–1970*, ed. Paul Buhle (Philadelphia: Temple University Press, 1970). Lee Baxandall's account, "New York Meets Oshkosh," (127–33), also discusses the Anti-Military Balls; a script for "The Boy Scouts in Cuba," one of the skits he co-authored, is included in the book's appendix, (285–89). These early countercultural events bear investigating as examples of politically tinged participatory theater. They were still being staged later in the

decade: Davis mentions giving a Mime Troupe performance at an antimilitary ball at Oregon State University in 1967. See *The SFMT*, 112.

7. This is a mark of the high esteem in which he held them. Judy Goldhaft, who was an early member of the Mime Troupe, recalled that you couldn't exactly "join the company at this time. [Davis] had to want to work with you" (author's interview with Judy Goldhaft, San Francisco, 5 February 1993).

8. Author's interview with R. G. Davis, San Francisco, 2 February 1993. The other source of Davis's education in radical politics was the New School (West). Here for example, is an account of one of his political epiphanies: "The New School brought me into contact with the minds of the Bay Area.... On April 22, 1964 we heard an indictment of the system and its objectives. The new Left became concrete, my head buzzed for 20 minutes.... Current political insight is astounding." Untitled document written by Davis concerning his activities in the year 1964, 2–3, located in the SFMT archives, box 2, Peter J. Shields Library Special Collections Department, University of California at Davis [PJSL].

9. Davis, "Guerrilla Theater," originally published in the *Tulane Drama Review*, summer 1966, and reprinted in *The SFMT*, 149–53. On p. 70 he states that when he read the first draft of this essay to the Mime Troupe in May 1965, member Peter Berg suggested he title it "Guerrilla Theater." The quotation by Che Guevara may be found in his book *Guerrilla Warfare*, trans. J. P. Morray (New York: Vintage/Random House, 1969 [1961]), 4, 32.

10. The text of Paul Potter's speech was first published in the *National Guardian*, 29 April 1965; an abridged version is in *The New Left: A Documentary History*, ed. Massimo Teodori (Indianapolis and New York: Bobbs Merrill, 1969), 246–48.

11. Davis, *The SFMT*, 150.

12. This is the sine qua non countercultural project as defined by sociologist J. Milton Yinger in his study *Countercultures: The Promise and Peril of a World Turned Upside Down* (New York: Free Press, 1982). In his formulation a counterculture consists of any group, past or present, that devises not only an ideology but an ethos and a set of practices counterpoised to those of the dominant society of which it is a part, and then sustains them through a relationship of calculated (though, typically, low-intensity) conflict with that society.

13. Davis, "Guerrilla Theater," in *The SFMT*, 150.

14. Coyote, *Sleeping Where I Fall; A Chronicle* (Washington, D.C.: Counterpoint Press, 1998), 39, 41.

15. Davis, *The SFMT*, 57. See the undated comments (but circa June 1965) directed to Davis from a writer identified only as "Terry," who was a staff member of the Student Nonviolent Coordinating Committee of California; and also the correspondence of the SNCC field secretary Mike Miller from circa summer 1966 in the R. G. Davis papers, box 5, folder 6, WHS. Miller's letter refers to the Mime Troupe as "very good friends of the movement [in the Bay Area]—kind of the movement's artistic arm." It is addressed to SNCC offices across the country, notifying them that the SFMT is available to do local fund-raising benefits. The Troupe has continued to the present in offering this kind of material aid to progressive organizations.

16. Richard F. Shepard, "Mr. Interlocutor, Updated, Arrives; 'Minstrel Show' from Coast Slashes at Racial Hypocrisy," *New York Times*, 22 October 1966, sec. 1, p. 36.

17. See the spring 1964 New School prospectus in the SFMT archives, box 2, PJSL. The list of summer 1964 course offerings is in the R. G. Davis papers, box 1, folder 2, WHS. Davis encouraged the members of his company to take classes at the New School so that it would help them better to "comprehend the political[,] psychological and social problems of a play." He also looked to it as a potential source for recruiting actors and adding to the Mime Troupe's audience base. See his notes for a company meeting dated 27 July [1964] in the Davis papers, box 4, folder 3, WHS. On the origins of the New School, see Kirkpatrick Sale, *SDS* (New York: Vintage Books, 1973), 265, 267.

18. Davis, "Guerrilla Theater: 1967," originally published in the Boston-based underground newspaper *Avatar* (1967) and reprinted in *The SFMT*, 154–55. Davis's rejection of bourgeois society has a familiar avant-garde ring to it. Looking back from 1975, he acknowledged as much: "The Mime Troupe moved from . . . an avant-garde period . . . to outdoor popular theater . . . and then onto radical politics, often preceding the political awareness of its audience. . . . When we were moving from the avant-garde to a radical political stance, we retained the progressive spirit of the avant-garde" (Davis, "Politics, Art, and the San Francisco Mime Troupe," *Theatre Quarterly* 5, no. 18 [June–Aug. 1975]: 26). As an ideological analysis, the views he expressed in his second guerrilla theater essay were being assimilated by the nascent counterculture in 1967. Cf. Ralph Larken and Daniel Foss: "The youth movement was not merely against racism, the war or school administrations, but against the *totality of bourgeois relations* [emphasis theirs]. It is easy to forget that many took drugs . . . to experience a reality that superseded and opposed bourgeois reality." In Ralph Larkin and Daniel Foss, "Lexicon of Folk-Etymology," 360–377 at 360. In *The Sixties without Apology*, ed. Sonya Sayres et al. (Minneapolis: University of Minnesota Press, 1981), 360.

19. Davis, "Cultural Revolution USA/1968," originally published in *Counter Culture*, ed. Joseph Berke (London: Peter Owen, Ltd., 1969), and reprinted in *The SFMT*, 156–64. Cf. Davis's incendiary rhetoric with that of H. Rap Brown (later known as Jamil Abdullah Al Amin) in a speech delivered in Cambridge, Md., on 24 July 1967: "Black folks built America, and if America don't come around, we're going to burn America down." Transcript of "The Cambridge Speech," Page Collection of H. Rap Brown Materials, Accession no. MSA SC 2548, Maryland State Archives Special Collections.

20. Peter Berg interview in Ron Chepesiuk, *Sixties Radicals, Then and Now: Candid Conversations with Those Who Shaped the Era* (Jefferson, N.C.: McFarland, 1995), 118–32 at 128.

21. Marie Louise Berneri, "Utopias of the English Revolution: Winstanley, *The Law of Freedom*," in her book *Journey through Utopia* (London: Routledge & Kegan Paul, 1950), 143–73; quote taken from Winstanley's text appears on p. 149. The complete document may be found in his *The Works of Gerrard Winstanley*, ed. George H. Sabine (Ithaca, N.Y.: Cornell University Press, 1941), 501–604.

22. Davis, the "Handbook" section of his essay "Guerrilla Theater: 1965," in *The SFMT*: "Start with people, not actors. Find performers who have something unique and exciting about them when they are on stage. . . . Liberate the larger personalities and spirits" (151). "Amateurs can be used if you cast wisely. . . . Ask a painter to do a backdrop or a sculptor to make a prop. . . . If you need . . . new material, find writers, politicos, poets to adapt material for your group. . . . The group must attract many different types of people" (152).

23. Davis seems to have respected the *theatrical* talents of only a few of these. The rest he put down hard in 1975. In a pointed remark about "the street hoods . . . without skills who should not have been in the company" (apparently referring to Diggers who had left the Mime Troupe between 1966–1968), he archly dismissed them thus: "They left . . . to work elsewhere, not in art but in craft" (Davis, *The SFMT*, 125).

24. Author interviews with Peter Berg and Judy Goldhaft, 24 November 1992, Ithaca, N.Y., and 5 February 1993, San Francisco.

25. Interview with Jane Lapiner and David Simpson, 27 and 28 February 1994, Petrolia, Calif.

26. During the Summer of Love, an apartment in the Haight could be leased for $90 and a three-story, eleven-room house for as little as $210. Stephen A. O. Golden, "What Is a Hippie? A Hippie Tells," *New York Times*, 22 August 1967, sec. 1, p. 26.

27. "New Community" was a term used by Haight-Ashbury hippies and avant-gardists to proclaim their collective identity in situ beginning about 1966. The adjective signified both their status as newcomers to the neighborhood and their conceit that what they were attempt-

ing was without precedent. The noun was as much aspirational as descriptive: theirs was at that time very much a community in the process of coalescing. In retrospect the term was self-representative of only the first phase of the Haight-Ashbury counterculture; one does not encounter it in the historical record after the Summer of Love. By that time, of course, the sense of novelty had passed, but also the notion of a hip community in the Haight was regarded as an established if contested reality. [Clint Reilly], "Editorial: The New Community," *Middle Class Standard* 1, no. 1 (16 July 1967): 1. A copy of this newsletter is filed in the San Francisco Hippies collection, box 2, folder "Middle Class Standard," San Francisco Public Library Special Collections Department (SFPL). The earliest appearance of the term that I have located is in the Communication Company broadsheet titled "Press Release 1/24/67," filed in the New Left collection, box 32, folder: "Digger Papers—1967," Hoover Institution on War, Revolution and Peace, Stanford University [HIWRP]. See also David E. Smith and John Luce, "The New Community," part II of *Love Needs Care: A History of San Francisco's Haight-Ashbury Free Medical Clinic and Its Pioneer Role in Treating Drug-Abuse Problems* (Boston: Little, Brown, 1971), 73–148; and Charles Perry, *The Haight-Ashbury: A History* (New York: Rolling Stone/Random House, 1984), 131.

28. Chester Anderson, a self-identified Digger and cofounder of the Communication Company, used this phrase ("Force them to be free") in an untitled broadsheet, the first line of which is "Every time somebody has turned on a whole crowd of people at once, by surprise [. . .]," dated 28 January 1967. Here the context is different but its intention remains arrogantly coercive. He urges his fellow acid heads to commit "psychedelic rape"; that is, surreptitiously introduce nonusers to LSD without their foreknowledge or consent out of the misbegotten certainty that it will promote "social evolution," and even "save the world." Filed in the Social Protest collection, carton 6, folder 10, Bancroft Library, University of California at Berkeley [BANC]. This same approach had already been taken by the Merry Pranksters in their "acid test" happenings beginning in fall 1965. See Tom Wolfe, *The Electric Kool-Aid Acid Test* (New York: Bantam Books, 1968), especially 241–53.

29. In the 1966 primary election, Scheer had come close to wresting away the Democratic Party nomination from Cohelan. William J. Rorabaugh, *Berkeley at War: The 1960s* (New York: Oxford University Press, 1989), 99–104. Scheer was an antiwar activist and journalist for *Ramparts* who was also a close associate of the SFMT director, R. G. Davis. The puppets had been made by the sculptor Robert La Morticella (a Digger who was arrested in this "public celebration") for the SFMT skit "Congressman Jeffrey Learns of Robert Scheer," which was performed on the UC-Berkeley campus during the fall of 1966.

30. Davis was reinforced in his meritocratic attitudes on this score by Saul Landau. In a note Davis made of a conversation that Landau had had with him on 19 April 1965 (around the time that he was drafting the guerrilla theater essay), he paraphrased Landau as saying: "We are dealing with amateurs [in the Mime Troupe] who do not act as professionals, . . . [who] have that attitude about theater that . . . smacks of the unconcerned. . . . Amateurism is death to the growing theatre." Typescript document by Davis titled "1965 Notes/Letters," in PJSL San Francisco Mime Troupe Archives, box 2.

31. Reverend Thomas King Forcade, "Abbie Hoffman on Media," in *The Underground Reader*, ed. Mel Howard and Thomas King Forcade (New York: New American Library, 1972), 68–72 at 69. This interview was recorded in Ann Arbor, Mich., in July 1969, and was originally published in the Vancouver, B.C., underground newspaper *The Georgia Straight.*

32. The evidence for this claim may be examined in my Ph.D. thesis, "The Haight-Ashbury Diggers and the Cultural Politics of Utopia, 1965–1968," (Cornell University, 1997), chap. 7: "Free City Limits: New York as an Example of Countercultural Diffusion." Other authors, while acknowledging the Haight-Ashbury Diggers' impact on Abbie Hoffman in particular, have instead stressed multiple sources of influence on the New York scene, not privileging any single source. See especially Marty Jezer, *Abbie Hoffman, American Rebel* (New Brunswick, N.J.:

Rutgers University Press, 1992); Jack Hoffman and Daniel Simon, *Run, Run, Run: The Lives of Abbie Hoffman* (New York: G. P. Putnam's Sons, 1994); Jonah Raskin, *For the Hell of It: The Life and Times of Abbie Hoffman* (Berkeley: University of California Press, 1996), Larry Sloman, *Steal This Dream: Abbie Hoffman and the Countercultural Revolution in America* (New York: Doubleday, 1998), as well as Hoffman's own memoir *Soon to Be a Major Motion Picture* (New York: G. P. Putnam's Sons, 1980).

33. Howard Smith, "Scenes" column, *Village Voice*, 3 August 1967, 11; ibid, 10 August 1967, 7; photos by Fred W. McDarrah and captions, 1, 25.

34. Marty Jezer, *Abbie Hoffman*, 111–12.

35. Leticia Kent, "Evangelizing Wall Street: Square Sales & Odd Lots," *Village Voice*, 31 August 1967, 3; John Kifner, "Hippies Shower $1 Bills on Stock Exchange Floor," *New York Times*, 25 August 1967, sec. 1, p. 23, accompanied by a photo of group members tossing the money from the gallery (Abbie Hoffman is plainly visible in this picture). See also the untitled account by the pseudonymous "George Washington" [journalist Marty Jezer, who also observed the event], in *WIN* magazine 3, no. 15 (15 September 1967): 9–10, and Jezer's later account in *Abbie Hoffman*, 111–12. Hoffman's version is in his book *Revolution for the Hell of It* (New York: Dial Press, 1968), 32–33, where the event is misdated 20 May 1967. Setting fire to dollar bills was another practice popularly associated with the Haight-Ashbury Diggers. George P. Metesky (occasionally the Diggers misspelled it Metevsky) was dubbed the "Mad Bomber" by the New York press when in the 1950s he conducted a seven-year bombing campaign throughout the city primarily aimed at the interests of Consolidated Edison. Metesky was most frequently used as a pseudonym by the Haight-Ashbury Digger and Brooklyn native Emmett Grogan as part of the collective's commitment to anonymity. It may seem a bizarre choice of identity for him to have assumed except when one considers the great fascination that outlaws and antiheroes in general held for mass culture audiences in the 1960s. Furthermore, invoking the specter of the "Mad Bomber" was a way of indulging in symbolic violence for the Diggers, who, while they could be militant in their rhetoric, were for the most part nonviolent in practice. It may also have been intended as a witty send-up of the stereotypical anarchist bomb thrower sensationalized in the propaganda of the various Red Scares since the Bolshevik Revolution. This last possibility emerges from Grogan's own criticism of the historical Metesky as ineffectual in fomenting positive social change. See Grogan, *Ringolevio; A Life Played for Keeps* (Boston: Little, Brown, 1972), 399.

36. The Yippies' activities and theory of the mass media are reprised in Hoffman's *Revolution* and Jerry Rubin's *Do It! Scenarios of the Revolution* (New York: Simon & Schuster, 1970). The best secondary sources are Jezer, *Abbie Hoffman*, and David Farber, *Chicago '68* (Chicago: University of Chicago Press, 1988).

37. Don McNeill, "Turning the City into a Theatre; The Hippie in New York," *Village Voice*, 14 September 1967, 9, 26–27.

38. I document the tension between the two groups in "Free City Limits" cited in note 32.

39. The term "Festival of Blood" was coined by the *Chicago Seed* editor Abe Peck, whom Jerry Rubin had recruited to be the key local organizer of the festival. Peck broke with the Yippies in the weeks before the convention, justifying his decision in the editorials "An Open Letter on Yippie," *Chicago Seed* 2, no. 11 ([n.d., but ca. late July–early August 1968]): 2, 23; and "A Week in Our Lives: The Great Media Backfire, *Seed* 2, no. 12 ([n.d., but ca. mid-to-late August 1968]): n.p. For a somewhat different conceptualization of the "two festivals," see Jezer, *Abbie Hoffman*, 125–27, 147. Jezer portrays Rubin as supporting active confrontation and Hoffman as preferring something closer to a celebratory be-in. These two key organizers, however, did not allow their differences to derail the goal of realizing a Yippie festival at the convention.

40. SFPL Archives, San Francisco Hippies collection, box 1, folder: "S.F. Hippies. Letters. Jerry Rubin to Allen Cohen."

41. Interview with Jerry Rubin by the editor Abe Peck, "The Yippees [*sic*] in Chicago," *Chicago Seed* 2, no. 3 ([n.d., but ca. 1–15 March 1968]): 8–9, emphasis added. As a result of his meeting with Rubin, Peck agreed to serve as one of Yippie's Chicago-based organizers for the Festival of Life. He discusses his growing unease with the rhetoric of violent confrontation propounded by the Yippie founders in his memoir-history *Uncovering the Sixties: The Life and Times of the Underground Press* (New York: Citadel Press, 1991), 99–119.

42. Rubin admitted as much some years later when reflecting on the convention: "We were not just innocent people who were victimized by the police. We came to plan a confrontation" (quoted in Alan Greenblatt, "Winds of War Blew through Chicago," *Congressional Quarterly* supplement, 54, no. 33 [17 August 1996]: 23–24). As early as November 1967, Rubin had boasted that "We can force Johnson to bring the 82nd Airborne and 100,000 more troops to Chicago next August to protect the Democratic National Convention" (Rubin, "We Are Going to Light the Fuse to the Bomb," *Village Voice,* 16 November 1967, 7).

43. Farber, *Chicago '68*; Todd Gitlin, *"The Whole World Is Watching!" Mass Media in the Making and Unmaking of the New Left* (Berkeley: University of California Press, 1980).

44. Rubin, "We Are Going to Light the Fuse to the Bomb," 7.

45. My interpretation of the function served by these Digger events is informed by A. P. Cohen, *The Symbolic Construction of Community* (New York: Tavistock Publications and Ellis Horwood, in association with Methuen, 1985), and Benedict Anderson, *Imagined Communities: Reflections on the Origin and Spread of Nationalism,* rev. ed. (London and New York: Verso, 1991).

46. Gil Scott-Heron's protorap poem "The Revolution Will Not Be Televised" was first released on his album *Small Talk at 125th & Lenox* (New York: Flying Dutchman, 1970), no. FD 10131. The album's lyrics were also published in book form by World Publishing Co.

"The Revolution Is about Our Lives"

The New Left's Counterculture

Doug Rossinow

"The revolution is about our lives." By 1968, this slogan had gained wide popularity within the white left of the United States. As a concise expression of the New Left's spirit, this slogan was to American radicals what "All power to the imagination!" was to their opposite numbers in France.[1] The New Left was a political movement that rose to prominence in the United States, and elsewhere in the world, on and around college and university campuses in the 1960s. Almost all those who identified with this movement were white college students and recent college graduates. The American New Left demanded direct democracy and a dilution of elite power in the United States, as well as a change in America's role in the world. However, the New Left's attraction to cultural rebellion was perhaps as controversial in the late 1960s as any discrete political stance that this movement took, and when young political radicals said "The revolution is about our lives," they fused their desire for individual empowerment with their dissident cultural politics.

To American New Leftists, it always seemed self-evident that their politics should be relevant to their personal lives. Starting in the early 1960s, when the radical sociologist C. Wright Mills urged radicals to link "personal troubles" to "public issues," young leftists believed in "the personal is political" as a general principle.[2] But they also gradually came to assert that specifically *their* personal lives—the lives of white college-educated youth—were central to the revolutionary project they saw under way in America. This was the double meaning of "The revolution is about our lives"; the emphasis might be on either *lives* or *our*.

These beliefs about personal politics are on fullest display in the New Left's countercultural activities. Clearly, this aspect of the New Left took inspiration from the hippie counterculture of the 1960s and 1970s, a movement that attained coherent shape around 1965 in the Haight-Ashbury neighborhood of San Francisco (among other locales) and soon after took the imagination of the nation's youth by storm. At the same time, leftists and hippies each responded to the larger historical circumstances that the two youth movements shared. The New Left developed a complex stance toward the hippie counterculture, one marked by ambivalence and confusion, but also by self-consciousness and strategic thought.[3] Young political radicals held a sympathetic if critical view of the hippies' cultural revolt against mainstream America. Most significantly, New Leftists concluded that the growth of the New Left, which drew on a social constituency similar to that of the hippies, was rooted in cultural discontent.

In the late 1960s, New Left radicals chose to pursue their own countercultural activities as a means of attracting and maintaining members and as a way of fomenting social change in America. We can think of these activities as constituting a second counterculture, separate from the one built by the hippies, or we may view them as forming the left wing of a larger white youth counterculture. In either formulation, these leftist cultural activities were somewhat different and remained separate from hippie undertakings; the New Left cultural activities carried a sharper political edge. An examination of these activities and the ideas that helped shape them sheds considerable light on New Left radicals' views about culture, politics, and ultimately, themselves. Their cultural gambit also tells us a good deal, more generally, about the links between efforts at cultural and political change in the twentieth-century United States. The New Left's attempt to synthesize cultural and political aspirations in a search for hegemony has strongly influenced American dissenters since the 1960s, and the fate of this attempt goes far toward explaining the state of American political radicalism in the post–New Left era.

Students for a Democratic Society (SDS) broke apart in a factional schism in 1969, primarily over disagreements about which social group would lead the political revolution that, by this time, the New Left favored. But behind these disagreements stood differences over how to view the hippie counterculture. Marxists said that only the industrial working class could make the revolution and often urged a "Worker-Student Alliance." Many, most prominently the adherents of the Weatherman faction in SDS, felt that only people of color, both in the United States and in the Third World, could overthrow U.S. imperialism and capitalism, and that the most that young, white, college-educated SDS radicals could hope to do was act as junior partners in a revolutionary alliance with African Americans, Vietnamese, and other nonwhite peoples. Yet perhaps the most popular position within SDS, one whose advocates did not cohere as an organized faction, was based on the notion that the New Left's main constituency—again, young white college students and graduates—could act as a revolutionary force on their own.[4]

Those who took this last position embraced the idea that "the revolution is about our lives," and also viewed the hippie counterculture more sympathetically than did the other factions. Such leftists felt sure that in the final analysis, they were fighting "for the sake of the freedoms for which the hippies fight." To them, the "revolt against personal repression, against dominance and exploitation felt by individuals in their own lives," was really "what 'the revolution' is all about."[5] Others on the left, Marxist radicals most of all, shared with many political liberals a disdain for the counterculture, viewing it as so much middle-class escapism that both estranged the working class from any potential worker-student alliance and siphoned energy away from pressing political tasks. Marxist activists, whether Maoists or Trotskyists, sported a straight-laced personal style and appearance, leaving the long hair, mustaches, sandals, and other accoutrements of the counterculture to other left-wing elements. They attempted to enforce a cultural conservatism among their ranks, sometimes expelling members for having extramarital affairs, for instance, and frowning on the use of marijuana. Perhaps as much as anything else, this personal conservatism and hostility toward the counterculture excited among many New Left radicals a deep and lasting disgust for the Marxist groups. Thus, differences over how to view the hippie movement played a crucial, if sometimes unnoticed, role in the breakup of SDS.

It was no accident that sympathy for the counterculture and a belief that white college-educated youth were a revolutionary force went hand in hand in the New Left. In the second half of the 1960s, New Left radicals came to believe that cultural activism was their most certain path to creating significant political change in the United States. Two convictions were planted deep in their consciousness: that culture mattered politically ("it's the end of people's belief in a way of life that brings revolution," expressed one underground journalist in a characteristic statement); and that they could shape the culture.[6] Growing up in the 1950s and coming to adulthood in the 1960s in an increasingly youth-oriented consumer culture, the children of the "affluent society" believed in their hearts that they themselves formed the leading edge of that culture. They were critical of the hippie counterculture as a force for political change, so they sought to create their own, politically radical counterculture. By doing so, they aspired to break through to their numerous peers: first the baby boomers, then all of American society might move to their beat.

In 1967, Larry Freudiger, a New Leftist in Austin, Texas—a place where the cultural path of New Left radicalism was blazed as thoroughly as anywhere—could barely contain his excitement at his discovery that there existed a veritable horde of "pleasure-oriented" youth in California just waiting to be influenced by cultural role models. And who were the models to which postscarcity youth were drawn? Blue-collar workers? African Americans (as "hip" white Americans, like Norman Mailer, long had said)? No, Freudiger revealed to his comrades. The coming "white revolution" was looking to a different group for leadership: "Us, baby—*us*." If the New Left could rise to this challenge and provide cultural leadership to white youth, he felt, "inevitable victory" lay ahead.[7]

Since the 1960s, it has seemed obvious to many that American leftists should display a strong sympathy for cultural dissent and that they should even participate in alternative or bohemian lifestyles. However, this is an association that, a few decades ago, might have seemed surprising. The New Left moved the American tradition of radical politics toward a revivified cultural orientation. Was a cultural approach to political change the logical course for the New Left to take, as radicals like Freudiger felt, or was it improbable? The historical record, and specifically the history of American dissent, offers ample support for either view. Americans of a conservative outlook long have associated the political left with "free love" and other (by their lights) socially corrosive tendencies, viewing political radicals as the enemies of "traditional" family life. Either through anarchist or statist means, traditionalists have consistently warned, leftists—should they ever come to power—would dissolve the familiar personal bonds of obligation and affection that so many hold dear.[8] Such fears may have seemed foolish in 1950 or 1960, even to many Americans with little sympathy for the left. Yet by the early 1970s, the New Left had given this long-lived association between political radicalism and cultural revolt a new lease on life; in fact, the New Left revived the very idea of a "cultural left."

Amid these traditionalist scare tactics there lay a grain of historical truth, although it remained unseen to most Americans during the mid-twentieth century. From the Gilded Age until the 1920s, the American left was a highly heterogeneous force, "a loose community of revolt," a "refreshing and lively . . . movement," in the judgment of Irving Howe and Lewis Coser.[9] The socialist movement of the Progressive Era mainly comprised workers, many of them

"New Immigrants," all of whom looked forward to a new society whose rationality and equity would afford stability to families then buffeted by the forces of urban, industrial capitalism. Left-wing farmers, mainly native-born, likewise combined radical political and economic doctrines with traditional aspirations.

Yet the American left of this time also harbored cultural visionaries who have consistently received attention from historians out of all proportion to their numbers. This bohemian "lyrical left" criticized familiar sex roles and family arrangements, helping by the 1910s to produce the first cohort of activists to call themselves "feminists." The lyrical left extolled what it viewed as the spontaneity and authenticity of children and people of color, in contrast to the dull, seemingly repressed culture of white bourgeois adulthood. Christopher Lasch called these rebels the "new radicals," and to them, he said, "the cultural revolution seemed as important as the social revolution."[10] The lyrical left looked not to a preservation of traditional family life and community but to a wholly new society and culture, one that would be freer and more authentic, composed of voluntary communities and liberated selves. Ultimately, it was this side of the American left-wing tradition that the New Left of the 1960s would renew, even if unwittingly.

Between the lyrical left and the New Left lay the Communist-led "Old Left" that dominated American radicalism from the 1920s to the 1950s. The place of cultural revolt in the Old Left is a complicated matter. On the one hand, there was a cosmopolitan, bohemian tendency among the revolutionaries of the Depression era that featured radical theater productions, interracial friendships, and even an unconventional sex life based on the preexisting radical critique of marriage as a bourgeois institution modeled on property relations. On the other hand, especially during the Popular Front years of the late 1930s and throughout World War II, the left manifested a cultural conservatism that was both sincere and strategic. This change complemented the increasingly centrist political stance of the Communist Party USA (CP) between 1935 and 1945, a period when the CP joined the Democratic Party's liberal coalition. Sentimental, nationalistic populism was important to the Old Left's acceptance into the mainstream of American life during these years; it also expressed the genuine patriotic and assimilationist feelings of the CP's membership, which was strongly first-generation. When the CP turned sharply left after World War II, preaching class warfare once again (and hemorrhaging members in the process), it no longer celebrated the nationalist tradition of the United States so easily, but neither did it turn to a countercultural orientation. The American left suffered through the doldrums of the 1950s, the era of McCarthy and McCarran, an embattled, ineffectual, and increasingly small political force. Its cultural tenor was ambiguous: an alternative, exile nationalism, critical of society but not straying too far from the cultural centrist fold.

It was in this senescent Old Left atmosphere—characterized by Weavers records and the speeches and music of Paul Robeson, by CP youth camps, by militant support for trade unions and civil rights, and by quieter sympathy for the Soviet Union—that the earliest New Left activists were nurtured. By the late 1950s these young people were entirely alienated from the Soviet Union yet still opposed to the cold war. They, like others dissatisfied with the state of American politics, wanted to strike out on their own, leading a New Left untainted by accusations of un-American sympathies.[11] In an echo of the Popular Front, the estranged "red-diaper babies" from CP backgrounds came together with the children of New Deal liberals (a far larger constituency), and by 1960 these young people had formed Students for a Democratic Society as their instrument.[12]

The Old Left, in its decline, may have exerted a stronger *cultural* influence on the early New Left than it did on the new movement's political positions. The highly politicized folk music of the early 1960s, as practiced by artists like Bob Dylan and Peter, Paul and Mary, owed much to the Old Left's dissident subculture in its visions of interracial harmony and moral outrage over racism and the arms race. However, the folk scene, by this time, had expanded well beyond the Old Left's orbit. The cultural milieu of the coffee-houses, with their acoustic music and paperback volumes of Camus and Kerouac, proved attractive to idealistic, restless young people of diverse backgrounds and temperaments. For example, it appealed to Brad Blanton, a young wanderer from rural Virginia with militant liberal politics and an experimental attitude toward life in general, and also to Todd Gitlin, the child of middle-class New York City Roosevelt Democrats who became SDS president in the 1963–64 school year. Though from different backgrounds, Gitlin shared with Blanton an affinity for the dissident white youth culture of the early 1960s, defined by folk music, existentialist philosophy, and Beat literature. While some of Blanton's friends became involved in SDS, he never became part of the New Left.[13] It is instructive to note how far the folk-Beat subculture's appeal stretched. The political elasticity of this youth culture was merely a small taste of things to come.

What is most striking about this cultural dissidence in retrospect is how timid it seems in comparison to the counterculture of a mere five or seven years later. A well-known group photograph of the SDS National Council from late 1963 illustrates this point. The young people in the picture have their right hands raised in clenched fists even as they smile, in a half-mock-ing gesture of defiance; they were anything but bomb throwers. They look very conventional indeed, dressed like almost any group of young Americans from the time might have been. The dresses and skirts, their short-sleeved collared shirts, horn-rimmed eyeglasses, and neat hair make the group look like an overgrown high school yearbook committee. The gestures of stylistic dissent are few: one woman, Sarah Murphy, wears pants; Tom Hayden, seeming to smirk, has his shirt untucked.[14]

These people saw no need to wear their radicalism on their sleeves, so to speak. They believed in a transparent politics, marked by honesty and true community; this was basic to their political ideal of "participatory democracy." Yet they did not believe in a transparency made physical, in surface or aesthetic manifestations of their beliefs and values. Perhaps nothing would change more drastically in the American culture of radicalism during the next ten years than this. By 1970, it would become an article of faith among young American rebels of all kinds that one could indeed judge a book by its cover.

Were these SDS activists of 1963 truly the rebels who answered the call of Camus and Kerouac? Many, including Gitlin, have cited the Beats in particular as pioneers of the 1960s counterculture. Yet despite his attraction to the romanticism of the Beats, Gitlin conveyed more sympathy for the anticommunist liberal James Wechsler than for Jack Kerouac when narrating a 1958 confrontation between these two men.[15] This is emblematic of the New Left's early ambivalence regarding the white youth counterculture emerging in 1960s America. The earnest political radicals felt a connection to the alienation expressed by the counterculture, and were far from immune to the allure of the cultural alternatives fashioned by the Beats, and then the hippies. They felt sure that in this sense of kinship with the counterculture, the New Left marked an improvement over the Old Left. Malvina Reynolds, whose song "Little Boxes" became an anthem of disdain directed at post–World War II suburbia and its culture of affluent conformity, claimed that in past decades "there was an inhuman quality about radicals." She echoed the familiar charge that the Old Left had ignored the personal in favor of the political, in both its economic program and its authoritarian organization. Reynolds played to the young radicals, telling them that they were better than their predecessors; clearly, they agreed.[16] Despite the links between the different generations of radicals, members of the New Left defined their movement to some extent against the example of the Old Left, feeling that they had reached a new level of understanding about human needs and motivations.

Yet New Left radicals also viewed cultural rebellions like those of the Beats and the hippies as basically misguided and irrelevant to the important processes of change occurring in the United States, which were political. As late as the summer of 1966, Jeff Shero Nightbyrd, then national vice president of SDS, declared that the New Left "must deal with questions of power rather than act out our generation's alienation."[17] In this sense, the New Left, past mid-decade, held fast to what had become the conventional distinction between culture and politics. About this, enthusiasts of cultural rebellion commonly agreed. Ken Kesey, leader of the "Merry Pranksters" and one of the most prominent countercultural agitators of the 1960s, made his rejection of politics plain. In 1965, with protest against the Vietnam War rapidly mounting, Kesey appeared at an antiwar protest in Berkeley and shocked the event's organizers by urging the assembled to "turn your backs and say . . . Fuck it" in order to dissent from the war. Rejecting political protest, he said politics was "what *they* do." Few there could have wondered for long who *they* were. *They* were the squares.[18] In Kesey's terms, the 1963 picture of the SDS National Council told the whole story: the political radicals *were* squares, certainly through 1965. Gitlin testified that even as late as 1967, "I doubt whether a single one of the Old Guard [those who had begun SDS] had sampled the mystery drug LSD. Most were leery even of marijuana."[19]

No place in America provided a better testing ground for the New Left's cultural approach to political change in the late 1960s than did Austin, Texas. "What can I tell you about Austin?" asked one wit in 1972. "This town, this community is so organic people will turn to compost before your very eyes."[20] By the 1970s, Austin had acquired a reputation as a hip enclave in a part of the country that was very conservative, both politically and culturally. Austin is home to a large public university, the University of Texas (UT), and for many years has maintained the cosmopolitan cultural complexion of many large university towns while also bearing rather distinctive local features. It long has been a musical center, helping give birth in the 1970s to a hybrid of country-and-western music and rock and roll that was dubbed "progressive country," or "cosmic cowboy," music. In the 1970s Austin teemed with cooperative enterprises, from natural food "co-ops" to "free schools," virtually all owned and operated by young college-educated people who had been touched by the era's counterculture. According to one activist, in the 1960s Austin became a "major transit center" for psychedelic wholesalers and retailers who brought marijuana and hallucinogenic mushrooms across the Mexican border (peyote, generally legal in the United States until 1966, was grown in central Texas itself).[21]

In the late 1960s and 1970s, it was difficult for anyone in Austin who was young and other than staunchly conservative to remain insulated from these phenomena, and Austin New Left radicals were no exceptions to this rule. As noted earlier, the young leftists had misgivings about the politics of the counterculture; Jeff Nightbyrd, who criticized the tendency toward "acting out" one's alienation, was the early leader of the SDS chapter formed in Austin in the fall of 1963 and later became vice president of national SDS. Nonetheless, Austin New Leftists participated in countercultural activities enthusiastically. SDS-UT activist Mariann Wizard, who first got "turned on" to marijuana by a folksinger at the local Methodist Student Center, issued a sweeping summation of late-'60s Austin: "Basically, everybody turned on; basically everybody smoked; very few people did not smoke dope." Thorne Dreyer, another local SDS activist and the leading light of the *Rag*, the "underground" newspaper that New Leftists started in Austin in the fall of 1966, claimed that "Austin's a very funny scene . . . .There aren't the real ideological-philosophical splits between politicos and hippies that exist [in] many places. We probably have the most political hippies and the most hip politicos around."[22] He exaggerated, since there were indeed ideological differences between the Austin leftists and the hippies over how best to foment social change. But then again, Austin radicals liked to proclaim their distinctiveness whenever this was remotely plausible. Still, the conviviality between leftists and hippies in Austin and their sense that they had something important in common were observed with notable frequency.

One thing they shared was an array of enemies. Conservatives in an environment like Texas often neglected to distinguish between leftists and hippies, in part because SDS activists in Austin began to take on hippie attire and personal style in the mid-1960s. Police forces and vigilantes harassed both groups. Larry Freudiger was one of the first male SDS activists in town to grow his hair long, and he was one of the first to get beaten up for it. Conservative citizens frequently called male hippies "queers"; some Austin police, after arresting two hippies on one occasion, called them "anti-social queers" and then, for good measure, inquired why these young American men were "dressin' up like a bunch of niggers." Dreyer remarked on a vivid feeling of "us against THEM" in Texas. New Leftists and hippies felt that perhaps conservative Texans were onto something in associating the two dissident groups so closely, and on a more tactical level, the two groups typically thought that they should hang together, lest they hang separately.[23]

Despite the differences between the hippies and the Texas political radicals, from the viewpoint of the national SDS old guard it was the Texas New Left's relative closeness to the counterculture that stood out. The SDS-UT group first appeared at national SDS meetings in force in 1965 and quickly became identified as the advance guard of two emerging phenomena within the 1960s left: the legion of young people without left-wing backgrounds, many of them from the Midwest or the South, who came streaming into what had previously been a small movement; and a pronounced countercultural influence. Political doctrine seemed to coincide with cultural style. The Texas radicals were dubbed "anarchistic"; to the old guard, their attitudes toward both lifestyle and political organization boded instability.[24]

The Austin leftists were not unhappy to be called anarchists, associating this label with liberation and antiauthoritarianism. Although they were not doctrinal anarchists, they saw a marked looseness of organization—indeed, a minimum of ongoing, centralized bureaucracy—as the real meaning of participatory democracy. Several of them descended upon the SDS national office in Chicago in the summer of 1965, determined to institute this understanding of the New Left's political beliefs within the national organization. According to all accounts, this initiative went badly. But the SDS-UT group continued to advocate vocally within the New Left for a decentralized vision of how a national left ought to operate.[25] This decentralist orientation was associated on all sides with an openness to the hippie counterculture. This counterculture, it was widely assumed, was sharply opposed to the kind of personal discipline and organizational structure required of traditional political movements. The New Left's old guard had wanted to lead a very new kind of political movement, but at mid-decade, the new wave of people in SDS upped the ante, casting the old guard as traditionalists.

After their failure to make the SDS national office run the way they wished, the Austin group retreated to central Texas in fall 1965, and their subsequent reflection on their Chicago experience led them to articulate their cultural politics more explicitly than ever before. Judy Schiffer Perez of SDS-UT said she had felt "totally alienated" by the way national SDS operated. Treated like an office worker in Chicago, her labor exploited, like any worker's, for the benefit of an organization, she and many of her closest comrades believed that people should never be subordinated to the needs of organizations—not in the future society and not in the New Left. New Leftists were quick to charge both contemporary society and the CP with this type of bureaucratic repression. (Perez, interestingly enough, may have been the only red-diaper baby in SDS-UT at that time.) Robert Pardun, Perez's common-law husband, moved from this personal experience to social analysis and political strategy. He agreed that what separated the New Left from the Old was what he called the New Left's commitment to "social radicalism." This meant a kind of radicalism that extended into one's everyday life, that affected all of one's personal interactions. It was different from the Old Left's "political radicalism," which was limited to one's positions on specific questions of public policy and societal organization. One might be a political radical while still behaving in an authoritarian fashion. "Social radicalism" was what was best in the New Left, according to Pardun.[26]

Disagreeing with those who thought that social radicalism might get in the way of political effectiveness, Pardun argued that New Left radicals had to embrace, not resist, social radicalism if they wished to take advantage of their strategic opportunities. He speculated that young people like themselves came to the left for the same reason they came to the counterculture: they wanted to be "real individuals" and were tired of being the "game-players of society."[27] They wanted authenticity, which was the opposite of alienation— exactly the malady that Perez reported suffering in Chicago. They wanted a different and more "real" way of life than the dominant culture offered them. They wanted social radicalism. In a sense, Pardun's argument of 1965 was that the New Left had to embrace its own identity as a counterculture if it truly desired political success.

Like the hippie movement, which began to spread out of its early enclaves at mid-decade, leftists like Pardun reached the conclusion that the desire for a qualitatively better way of life underlay the youth rebellions of the era. The New Left's cultural side was influenced, in the late 1960s, by the hippie counterculture, whose pervasiveness came to dwarf the cultural activities of the New Left. Yet Pardun and other leftists articulated this cultural analysis early enough that, it seems clear, members of the New Left and the hippie movement reached some of the same conclusions independently. Pardun's analysis proved prescient, for when the organized factions within national SDS rejected social radicalism after 1968 in order to precipitate a revolution by more confrontational means, they found themselves abandoned by the bulk of the New Left's members. To most of the membership, the factions seemed like "game-players."

Although one would not know it to look at the national office of SDS, social radicalism was indeed the path that the New Left trod in the late 1960s and early 1970s in localities all over the country, nowhere more forcefully than in Austin. Avant-gardism displaced vanguardism in the young radicals' self-image. Instead of aiming to seize state power, as many earlier left-wing movements all around the world had done, the New Left would seek to establish cultural hegemony. New Left radicals were determined to make inroads among their social peers. They felt they understood the deeply personal needs and aspirations within white middle-class America that had given birth to both the New Left and the counterculture, and they felt they could design a new kind of left that would appeal to the youth of this dominant social group. The New Left's cultural politics ended by influencing this target constituency to a considerable degree, while ultimately revealing the limits of this culturally oriented program.

The New Left's attraction to cultural politics stemmed not only from circumstances and recreational interests but from a foundation of ideas. A brief summary of these ideas will clarify the New Left's approach to cultural agitation. The most basic of these concepts were *alienation* and *authenticity*. Alienation meant estrangement or separation. While, in the leftist view, alienation from the political system might be a desirable phenomenon, the type of alienation on which the New Left focused, and that it consistently bemoaned, was an inner or personal one.

This inner alienation, New Left radicals believed, was endemic among youth—certainly white middle-class youth—in the midcentury United States. Those of a religious bent might have said that those suffering from personal alienation were estranged from God. More commonly, New Leftists asserted that their peers were alienated within themselves, cut off from certain parts of their potential as human beings and from their better, truer, more complete selves. The leftists also felt that many Americans were estranged from one another, that they lacked the experience of true community. Leftists of the 1960s traced alienation ultimately to social and political arrangements (instead of viewing alienation as an autonomous cultural or spiritual problem, as religious thinkers might). A just society, they believed, would allow all people to achieve authenticity, and their efforts at achieving personal integration and community were directed to this end.

New Left radicals talked a great deal about becoming "authentic," but they also used other terms to evoke their quest for authenticity. Most commonly, they said they wished to be "real" and "natural." The tropes of the artificial versus the natural, the real versus the unreal, the living versus the dead, love versus hatred, and the whole versus the fragmented were deployed again and again as variations on the radical quest for an end to alienation. Mariann Wizard summed up the young radicals' goals, saying that their society had bequeathed to them "a culture of unhappiness and misery, and a culture that promulgates death and conformity. And we want a culture that's open and alive . . . where love is able to happen."[28] Drawing on the religious language of love and life, influenced by the Civil Rights movement's concept of the "beloved community," the New Left developed a humanistic ideal of the complete personality and the authentic society. The social ideal on which New Leftists ultimately fixed was not so much a socialist government or economy as a natural culture, one characterized by spontaneity, love, and community. They always maintained their commitments to justice and democracy and to confronting the existing political system; the prominence of these commitments, after all, was what separated them from the hippies and underpinned their criticism of the hippie counterculture. But the struggle to plant the seeds of a whole and

Doug Rossinow

natural culture gradually became the leading New Left strategy, at the grass-roots level, for building a new society.

As noted earlier, New Left radicals recognized that they shared with the hippies a conviction that American society had moved beyond economic scarcity, and that this post-scarcity order ought to allow for a newly human and natural culture. Ironically, technology and modern organization paved the way for a return to the most basic of instincts, instincts supposedly repressed since time immemorial. Already, the "affluent society" of cold war America had given birth to a counterculture that, in some precincts at least, was hostile to industrial-era technology and organization. In Herbert Marcuse, the exiled German "critical theorist" and renegade Freudian then teaching in the United States, the New Left found an elder who lent intellectual heft to the idea of a post-scarcity politics. Contrary to orthodox Freudianism, Marcuse argued that the instinctual repression human beings habitually practiced was not really necessary in order to keep them from tearing each other to pieces. Repression was required only so long as there was too little in the way of tangible resources to go around. But thanks to modern industry and government policy, this was no longer the case, so Americans and the inhabitants of other wealthy societies were simply engaging in "surplus repression."[29]

This surplus repression worked to the clear advantage of those who ruled the existing undemocratic and inequitable system. Psychically repressed citizens would remain out of touch with their true needs and desires, which, if everyone pursued them, would overwhelm the resources of wealth and power monopolized by social elites. Instead, the theory went, human needs for freedom and community were diverted into an insatiable hunger for consumer goods, for the slick, shiny packages of cold war America (prizes that Marcuseans would view as objects of inauthentic desire). To the extent that surplus repression was not surplus—that is, to the extent that it was really necessary—this was the result of an unfair political and economic system that kept some people walled off in an enforced scarcity and powerlessness. If existing resources were easily accessible, repression could at least be considerably lessened. Marcuse lent philosophical expression to ideas that circulated widely among young American dissidents, both political and cultural, in the 1960s. Allen Ginsberg (undoubtedly a more widely read author) stated the radical view more concisely in 1967 when he casually remarked that "man's basic nature is that he's a pretty decent fellow when there's enough to go around."[30] Though saddled with a rather big qualifier, this view reflected a tremendous faith in the goodness of human beings. To be cooperative and loving, in the view of both New Leftists and hippies, was to be natural. All the evil they saw around them they interpreted as perversion, as the twisted actions of people who had been torn from their true paths by malign social and cultural forces.

Ginsberg made this remark on a visit to Austin, and the New Left radicals who interviewed him while he was in town shared his viewpoint. In the previous year, they had resolved to "act like we'd act if the Revolution [had] already come," as one activist put it.[31] Again, New Left radicals thought this was now possible specifically because they lived in the "affluent society." Now that the groundwork for universal comfort had been laid, Americans could ascend to a politics of joy, not of accumulation. Furthermore, post-scarcity politics—which was inevitably a cultural politics—was a calculated political strategy on the part of these young activists. Especially in a conservative locale like Texas, making a political appeal through cultural means might prove less incendiary than a traditional leftist organizing effort. While the harassment visited upon hippies, and upon leftists who looked like hippies, casts doubt on the viability of this strategy, it was an idea nonetheless widely held among New Leftists in the South and the Midwest. The radicals might appeal directly to the deep personal longings of their peers by preaching the doctrine of liberation, thereby avoiding traditional left-wing rhetoric and the prejudice against it that circulated even within their potential audience.

In the fall of 1966, SDS-UT announced that it would step up its antiwar activism in the coming school year. But the radicals also declared their intention to delve more deeply into cultural politics. That fall they initiated the *Rag*, preceded by only a handful of other underground newspapers in the 1960s (and most of them either in New York or California), which would become the most important left-wing institution in Austin, especially after 1968. The *Rag* sported a combination of radical political analysis and cultural advocacy; according to Abe Peck, the leading historian of the 1960s underground press, "the *Rag* was the first independent undergrounder to represent, even in a small way, the participatory democracy, community organizing, and synthesis of politics and culture that the New Left of the midsixties was trying to develop."[32]

At this time the SDS chapter also initiated a festival it called "Gentle Thursday," a free-form afternoon of fun and games on the university's grassy west mall, as a means of attracting attention to itself and its cultural vision. This idea spread, proving popular among SDS activists at public universities in conservative areas. SDS chapters in Colorado, Iowa, Kentucky, Missouri, and New Mexico all initiated their own versions of the campus Be-In.[33]

In the New Left's cultural politics, showing that one knew how to have a good time was politically meaningful. Activities like Gentle Thursday allowed radicals to put their picture of a post-scarcity society on display and to draw in young people who were alienated but not politicized. Over time,

Austin New Leftists brought more explicit political content into these celebrations; for instance, in spring 1967 Gentle Thursday was part of a week-long series of political and cultural events, "Flipped-out Week," whose highlight was a speech by the Student Nonviolent Coordinating Committee (SNCC) chairman, Stokely Carmichael, militant advocate of "Black Power." The radicals were working to construct their own, left-wing counterculture.

Gary Thiher, another leader of the SDS-UT group, asserted with considerable bravado that Gentle Thursday was one battle in a cultural "revolution." It was a matter, said Thorne Dreyer, of making "open warfare against all that is dull and inhuman." Was "dullness" the great evil that the New Left heroically opposed? Perhaps this does not seem like a grand moral cause. However, the link Dreyer drew between dullness and "inhumanity" brought him back to the realm of the serious. The New Left's cultural politics yoked the ecstatic search for "real life" that the lyrical left had embraced to the earnest humanism typical of cold war idealists. Thiher described what life would look like after the cultural revolution was completed: it would be more "organic," more "spontaneous," and more "human." He suggested that becoming more natural or organic and less emotionally repressed would qualify one as truly human. People thus would become "real individuals." Dreyer declared, "The bureaucratic system cannot survive if people are people."[34] The New Left's cultural politics aimed at the restoration of a lost humanity, or the fulfillment of a potential never realized. To many today, as for some observers in the 1960s, the young radicals who cast the struggle for a better society as a battle between dullness and spontaneity may seem frivolous or confused. The "warfare against all that is dull and inhuman" has become a cliché of our culture, with the struggle joined by advertisers as easily as by socialists.[35] However, the young people of the New Left believed, with an almost painful sincerity, that social and political concerns were at stake in this battle. They were without irony on the subject. In this conviction, which flowed directly from their quest for authenticity, they were returning to a submerged tradition of the American left—even if they did not know it.

Between 1966 and 1973, the Austin New Leftists ventured far down the cultural avenue toward social transformation. Although they continued their political protest activities in these years, with many of the young radicals moving further to the left in their outspoken criticism of capitalism, war, and imperialism, cultural politics gradually became their chief means of pursuing revolutionary ends. A brief examination of two areas of their activism during these years gives a fuller sense of their cultural vision, and of the possibilities and boundaries of their cultural politics.

"Gentle Thursday" gathering on the campus of the University of Texas, April 1968, where political radicals mingled with members of the nascent counterculture. Austin's New Left had emerged over the preceding decade largely out of a group of Christian social activists who initially were affiliated with the University YMCA/YWCA. Ritual footwashing recalled Christ's bathing of his disciples' feet during the Passover feast that came to be known as the Last Supper. By such symbolic gestures during these festive occasions each spring, the political and cultural wings of the movement fashioned themselves into an alternative community. At the same time, the image provides a telling representation of the power dynamic within the New Left/counterculture that led many women to defect from its ranks. The Center for American History, The University of Texas at Austin, CN10760.

To coincide with the national Spring Mobilization Against the War in Vietnam, the Austin chapter of Students for a Democratic Society organized "Flipped Out Week" on the University of Texas campus, 10–16 April 1967. However, mixing antiwar teach-ins and marches with free outdoor rock concerts and poetry readings proved too much for the UT administration. Referring to an SDS flier promoting the week's events, three administrators issued an official statement objecting to "certain activities [that] could not be sanctioned by the University. For example—kissing, mellow yellow, en masse, and 'all over campus.'" The Center for American History, The University of Texas at Austin, CN10759.

The first of these areas is sex. In the late 1960s the idea of "free love" found much sympathy on the left. What this actually meant, in practice, is a matter of some dispute. Greg Calvert, national secretary of SDS in 1966–67, moved from Chicago to Austin in 1968 and found his new southwestern home especially liberated when it came to such matters. Calvert was bisexual, and Austin was the first place in America he had lived that did not seem "sexually uptight." However, Judy Perez struck a different note when she recalled that individuals in the Austin New Left circle might be pressured by their peers about their so-called hang-ups if they maintained conventional attitudes about sexual relations. Paul Pipkin, another SDS-UT activist, reported frankly, "I did get laid a lot in Austin. . . . Y'know, people traded off partners an awful lot." Lori Hansel, who arrived in Austin in the late 1960s and became an active leftist for many years, stated that radicals there "were into, on the one hand having monogamous relationships and at the same time sleeping with everyone they could get their hands on." Echoing a viewpoint expressed by other female radicals, she added, "And I think that was true of both men and women." The tradition of left-wing bohemianism, evidently, was alive and well in central Texas.[36]

The New Left's apparent determination to question conventional sexual mores, and perhaps even gender roles, helped revive the old conservative charge that the left was the enemy of the American family. Some who view the New Left sympathetically agree that, in fact, the sexual politics of 1960s radicalism dissented from, and even posed a threat to, the dominant social order.[37] But ironically, the New Left's sexual politics was less radical than many of this movement's admirers and enemies have been willing to acknowledge.

New Left radicals seemed not to see how much ground they shared with liberals on these matters. The radicals viewed themselves as among the leaders in a "sexual revolution," a revolt against sexual "myths that deprive humans of joy."[38] However, they were involved in a process that was more an evolution than a revolution, part of a long-term liberalization of the rules governing sexual interaction among the young that had been under way since the time of the lyrical left.[39] New Leftists viewed sexual experience as one area of human potential that certainly should not be closed off. Many liberals, like Betty Friedan, also embraced the idea of human potential, influenced by humanistic psychology; they thought that since the material foundation in a "hierarchy of needs" had been laid for many Americans, higher levels of aesthetic and cultural satisfaction now demanded construction.[40] Very important differences separated liberal and radical viewpoints on sex. Radicals felt that at least some familiar sexual mores ought to be abandoned in the pursuit of a natural society, while liberals thought that these rules should be relaxed, not entirely discarded. Liberals stressed the importance of individual choice in these matters, while radicals emphasized the value of experimentation. Still, for all the distance between liberals and liberationists, both parties expressed their sexual agendas in the language of individual human potential and growth.

To complicate matters even further, New Left sexual politics had a deeply conservative aspect as well. While liberals like Friedan worked to erode familiar sex-role differences, bringing women the same opportunities in public (and private) life that men enjoyed, the New Left's sexual agenda for most of this movement's existence included neither gender equality nor androgyny. Not until the last years of the New Left, between 1968 and 1973, did radical women (and some men) move the New Left toward feminism. A recognition of this fact undermines the view that the New Left pursued a revolutionary cultural and sexual politics.

For most of its existence as a movement, the New Left's sexual politics was dominated by a search for authentic masculinity on the part of the male radicals. For them, this was a crucial part of the quest for authenticity. From the beginning, the New Left had embraced male heroes like C. Wright Mills and Fidel Castro, men who were admired not only for their political ideals and activities but also for their macho air of derring-do. The swagger of these icons promised a way out of the cultural malaise engulfing most Americans.[41] Although New Left men ventured a radical social analysis that helped explain their longings for feelings of personal empowerment, autonomy, and "naturalness," the ways in which their yearnings sometimes were manifested linked them to men whose heroes were Hugh Hefner and James Bond, not Mills and Castro. The New Left, at least during the period when it was dominated by SDS, also was dominated by men, and men were able to define the movement's agenda. Consequently, in their quest for sexual authenticity they often cast women in the role of sexual helpmeets, albeit newly uninhibited ones.

Throughout the 1960s and into the 1970s, New Left radicals made a distinction between authentic and inauthentic sexuality, claiming that inauthentic sexuality was the norm in mainstream American culture. This allowed them simultaneously to criticize the dominant culture for "puritanism" and for prurience. The sex that "[m]odern, liberal, corporate America" used "to sell almost anything you can think of," as Gary Thiher put it, was fake sex.[42] It was what a Marcusean would call "repressive desublimation," a kind of libidinal release that stopped short of true liberation and in fact worked to stabilize the existing cultural system.[43] Exactly how to tell real sexuality from the phony kind, New Left radicals could never easily say. To paraphrase Justice Potter Stewart, they felt they knew repressive desublimation when they saw it. Barbara Ehrenreich's description of the hippie counterculture's aims also fits the New Left: both movements sought to do "an end run around the commodities . . . to the true desire: real sex, not the chromium sublimation of sex; real ecstasy, not just smoke."[44] Yet left-wing radicals found it difficult to reach consensus on which forms of stimulation were "real" and which were "chromium," as evidenced by recurring disagreements over the respectability of pornography. Eventually, the rise of a feminist left would make clear that sexual authenticity and political empowerment might not be the same thing, even if they sometimes went hand in hand.

While the New Left's sexual politics was (and remains) the most emotionally charged sector of the movement's cultural initiative, the same tortured distinction between authentic and alienated culture arose across the board, extending to relatively mundane, but crucially important, undertakings such as the cooperatives, or "co-ops." These were the multifarious small-scale enterprises that mushroomed across the American landscape after 1968, organized by both hippies and leftists, offering goods and services ranging from farm produce to automotive repair to primary education. While New Leftists and hippies celebrated the value of individual revolt against the stultifying forms of contemporary social life, whether corporations or "multiversities," they sought social authenticity in small organizations of their own creation.

The co-op movement flourished around the country and produced some of the most tangible and enduring accomplishments of this era's counterculture. At first, the co-ops were valued for their immediate benefit, as venues where young people could avoid the alienation generated by the capitalist economy both on the level of production (in the Marxist analysis) and consumption (in the neo-Marxist view). But soon, these "counterinstitutions" also came to be viewed as "ways of settling down for the long haul," in Gitlin's words. Political radicals, undoubtedly influenced by hippie co-op efforts (given that leftists and hippies worked together in many co-ops), started to build their own co-ops in earnest after 1968, viewing this activity as part of a long-term political strategy. While French New Leftists envisioned a "long march through the institutions" that already existed in their country, American New Leftists marched to the beat of a different drummer and typically sought to build their own institutions. To leftists who soured on the insurrectionary politics of the late 1960s and felt that a long-term strategy was required to transform American society, co-ops acquired a vital significance.[45]

Many co-ops started and folded quickly, and leftists imprinted their own list of choices on the ever-changing menu of hip co-ops in Austin during the late 1960s and early 1970s. The first leftist co-ops in town were the *Rag* and the Critical University (CU), which was initiated in 1965 as one of the numerous "free universities" organized by New Leftists alongside colleges and universities around the country. The free universities were designed to offer classes in areas deemed off-limits by the existing educational system and strove to establish a nonauthoritarian learning environment. The Austin CU offered classes on topics such as racism, ecology, and women—subjects that in the coming decades would be warmly embraced by the educational mainstream.[46]

Other co-ops were even more explicit in their leftist bent. The Armadillo Press was a cooperatively owned and operated printshop whose activist worker-owners organized themselves as a local of the Industrial Workers of the World (IWW) in 1969. In doing so, they fulfilled a dearly held New Left dream by actually becoming Wobblies, those contemporaries of the lyrical left who became icons of decentralist radicalism for the rebels of the 1960s. (Subsequently, the women at the press took over the shop, renaming it Red River Women's Press; in addition to the local feminist materials it produced, the press won the contract to print the national IWW constitution.) The staff at Armadillo aligned the IWW with Robert Pardun's "social radicalism." In their political statement prospectus, these new Wobblies proclaimed their objectives: "a fundamental change in personal values and in personal and group relations" in addition to the establishment of a socialist economy. They voiced their "distrust" of "those who speak only of economic and political transformation and not of the liberation of persons."[47] Here was the late New Left ideal of "libertarian socialism," as it often was (and still is) termed, which combines collective enterprise with personal liberation. The most concrete expression and vehicles of this creed were left-wing co-ops such as the Armadillo Press.

After the initial stage of unrestrained enthusiasm about co-op organization, a debate emerged in the early 1970s over the political effectiveness of these counterinstitutions. On the one hand, radicals like Alice Embree, one of the early SDS activists in Austin, continued to view the co-ops as one piece of a long-term leftist revolutionary strategy. In 1972 she urged radicals to organize "cells, cadres, affinity groups," and co-ops. Did co-ops really belong on this list, which sounded like a recipe for an underground struggle? Some wondered whether they did. Although virtually no one on the left dared to condemn institution-building per se, some radicals worried that co-ops held the potential to disperse and privatize left-wing activism. Others simply drew a distinction between good and bad co-ops: some were "radical" while others were merely "liberal" (this was bad), some were highly individualistic while others were collectivist.[48] The criteria for separating authentically oppositional co-ops from non-radical ones were, unfortunately, difficult to specify.

Authentic or inauthentic, politically disruptive or irrelevant, the New Left's countercultural practices were consistent with the historical logic and social background of this radical movement. As much as any aspect of the New Left, the cultural turn that occurred in this movement's later years would have a profound influence on left-wing thought and practice in the United States in the decades after the New Left's demise in the early 1970s. The New Left ended with the dictum that "culture counts," and this truism is about as far as leftist thought has traveled in the United States since the New Left went the way of the Old. Today's strategic impasse was reached many years ago, as New Left radicals moved from a conviction that their cultural politics could be revolutionary to an inability to discern exactly what their cultural activities counted for. It perhaps makes little sense to blame the New Left for taking a turn into a confusing cultural politics, since this politics was merely the vehicle that expressed the New Left's deepest sense of itself. Only in the late 1960s did New Leftists find the words to say, and the theory to announce proudly, "The revolution is about our lives"; but they had felt this intrinsically cultural belief in their bones from their movement's inception. In this sense it seems inevitable that the New Left turned toward cultural politics. Even if it had not, its politics still would have expressed New Leftists' conviction that their lives lay at the center of historic change in America and the world.

This is not to say that the New Left's cultural politics accomplished nothing good or significant. It accomplished quite a bit—at least for some. It simply did not succeed in transforming American society. The New Left's counterculture helped make consumption and education less alienating for middle-class Americans. It offered sex and sociability to many. It worked to delegitimize violence and racism among the white middle class in particular. These are notable changes, and they took hold primarily in university towns and in certain neighborhoods of metropolitan areas around the United States. What the New Left's cultural politics did not achieve was cultural hegemony over the United States.[49] Far from taking over the culture, and thence the politics, of the entire society, the New Left reformed the culture of white middle-class America. (The theory of cultural hegemony, as formulated by the Italian Leninist Antonio Gramsci, was hardly compatible with the libertarian means of cultural advocacy on which the New Left fixed. The American right of the 1970s and 1980s hewed more closely to a Gramscian strategy than did the left, with impressive results.)[50] The New Left's counterculture produced results that were neither negligible nor revolutionary. Like so many other radical political movements in the American past, the New Left helped to reform, and thus perhaps in the long run to strengthen, the way of life it had opposed. The New Left focused on the problems in the lives of middle-class youth, the main source of this movement's membership. By ameliorating these problems, certainly a commendable achievement in itself, the New Left's focus on "our lives," ironically, drained some of the urgency from the movement's program of social transformation. With some success, the young leftists helped treat the cultural symptoms of what they had claimed was a systemic social and political disease.

The New Left revived the spirit of left-wing bohemianism in American life and, in so doing, raised anew questions about two linkages that the New Left, like the lyrical left, assumed were real. One was the linkage between cultural and political change. Since the time of the *Port Huron Statement* (1962), activists on the left and the right in the United States have agreed that "values" are the foundation of political life and the biggest prize of all in political struggle; in this sense, we are all Gramscians now. Perhaps the tactics of cultural politics help determine how effectual it is; on the other hand, perhaps cultural agitation cannot, no matter how intelligently conceived, lead directly to political power or social transformation. This is not a question that the New Left answered decisively. Instead, the matter was left tantalizingly unresolved.

The second linkage is the association of the search for authenticity with the familiar left-wing goals of social justice and democracy. The New Left's sexual politics in particular makes clear that a quest for authenticity need not also be a search for equality. The New Left bundled together authenticity, radical democracy, and social justice, believing that these goals would be achieved together or not at all. During the decades immediately after World War II, the search for authenticity was widely associated with the political left, and in part for this reason, those in search of authenticity tended toward dissident politics (if they were politically interested at all); the association was somewhat self-fulfilling. Yet the yearning to be a "real individual," the desire for unmediated access to "real life," the attraction to the spontaneous and the seemingly natural, could all be found, in later years as in earlier ones, across the political spectrum. In the 1990s, the search for authenticity sometimes was taken as evidence of left-wing sympathies, but those who make such inferences, on the assumption that the old association still holds, are destined for disillusionment. Nonetheless, in some precincts of our society, the romance of culture and politics, of authenticity and justice, lives on. It continues, very often, in the minds of those who live their own lives as private revolutions. Hegemons of personal realms, they are freed from the prison of alienation and, despite all their rhetoric of dissent, at home in the world and at peace with themselves.

NOTES

1. Paul Buhle, "The Eclipse of the New Left: Some Notes," *Radical America* 6 (July-August 1972): 4–5, and James O'Brien, "Beyond Reminiscence: The New Left in History," *Radical America* 6 (July–August 1972): 29, both note the widespread use of this phrase.

2. See C. Wright Mills, "The Big City: Personal Troubles and Public Issues," in *Power, Politics and People: The Collected Essays of C. Wright Mills*, ed. Irving Louis Horowitz, (New York: Oxford University Press, 1963), 395–402. This was the first publication of a speech transmitted over the Canadian Broadcasting Company in 1959.

3. See Doug Rossinow, *The Politics of Authenticity: Liberalism, Christianity, and the New Left in America* (New York: Columbia University Press, 1998), 247–55, for a more detailed discussion of the New Left's stance toward the hippie counterculture.

4. The Progressive Labor Party (PL) advocated the Worker-Student Alliance. The Revolutionary Youth Movement (RYM), which subsequently split in two, with RYM I becoming Weatherman, emphasized the overthrow of imperialism by people of color. "New working-class theory" was the strain of thought most closely identified with the view that college-educated youth composed a revolutionary force in the United States. For ample coverage of factionalism in late SDS see Kirkpatrick Sale, *SDS* (New York: Random House, 1973),

and Irwin Unger, *The Movement: A History of the American New Left, 1959–1972* (New York: Harper & Row, 1974). Neither book, however, gives adequate attention to the last of the three positions outlined above.

5. Sandy Carmichael, "Mother's Grits Texas Traveling Troupe," *Rag*, 22 August 1968.

6. "Teen Queen—The American Dream," *Rag*, 14 November 1966.

7. Larry Freudiger, "Grassroots Sociology: A Weekly Discussion of the American Social Revolution and the Reactions against It: The White Revolution," *Rag*, 30 January 1967; Norman Mailer, *The White Negro* (San Francisco: City Lights Books, 1957).

8. For a recent iteration of this anxiety see Irving Kristol, "Countercultures," *Commentary* 98 (December 1994): 35–39. For background on the "countersubversive" tradition in America see Michael P. Rogin, *Ronald Reagan, the Movie, and Other Episodes in Political Demonology* (Berkeley and Los Angeles: University of California Press, 1987), 44–80, 236–71.

9. Irving Howe and Lewis Coser, *The American Communist Party: A Critical History (1919–1957)* (Boston: Beacon Press, 1957), 1, 4. In light of the enmity that developed in the 1960s between older social democrats like Howe and the New Left, it is ironic that Howe and Coser's brief sketch of the pre-Communist U.S. left and the contrast they draw between this "lively" movement and the Communist Party are similar to a common New Left view of the American radical past.

10. Christopher Lasch, *The New Radicalism in America, 1889–1963: The Intellectual as a Social Type* (New York: Knopf, 1986), 286.

11. See Stanley Aronowitz, "When the New Left Was New," in *The 60s without Apology*, ed. Sohnya Sayres et al., (Minneapolis: University of Minnesota Press, 1984), 21.

12. SDS began as the Student League for Industrial Democracy (SLID), the student affiliate of the League for Industrial Democracy (LID), a labor-funded, social democratic think tank. The well-known 1962 Port Huron Conference, where SDS ratified its most famous statement of purposes, occurred at a United Auto Workers (UAW) camp in Michigan. Al Haber was the most important individual in the formation of SDS; his father, an economist, had been a highly placed policy adviser to Democratic administrations in Washington in the 1930s and 1940s. James Miller, *"Democracy Is in the Streets": From Port Huron to the Siege of Chicago* (New York: Simon & Schuster, 1987), 23–24.

13. Brad Blanton, interview with author, 14 April 1993; Todd Gitlin, *The Sixties: Years of Hope, Days of Rage* (New York: Bantam, 1987), 66–77.

14. The photograph is reproduced in Miller, *"Democracy Is in the Streets,"* between 208 and 209.

15 Gitlin, *The Sixties*, 54–56.

16. "Malvina Reynolds," *Rag*, 11 November 1968. Reynolds herself was an older California-based leftist, one sufficiently broad-minded to criticize her own generation of radicals.

17. Jeff Shero, "The SDS phenomenon," *New Left Notes*, 29 July 1966.

18. Tom Wolfe, *The Electric Kool-Aid Acid Test* (New York: Bantam, 1968), 200.

19. Gitlin, *The Sixties*, 225.

20. Dave, "one comment . . . ," *Rag*, 21 February 1972.

21. Mariann Wizard, interview with author, 8 July 1992.

22. Wizard interview; Dreyer quoted in Abe Peck, *Uncovering the Sixties: The Life and Times of the Underground Press* (New York: Pantheon, 1984), 59.

23. Robert Pardun, interview with author, 27 August 1993; Anthony Howe, "I would suggest that the situation of Texas hippies vis-à-vis their physical well-being could rightly be termed very dangerous, or Paranoia," *Rag*, 2 January 1967; Jeff Shero, "Dallas Police Jail Banana Users," *Rag*, 27 March 1967; Dreyer quoted in Peck, *Uncovering the Sixties*, 59.

24. Gregory N. Calvert, "Democracy and Rebirth: The New Left and Its Legacy" (Ph.D. thesis, University of California at Santa Cruz, 1989), 497; Sale, *SDS*, 113.

25. Miller, *"Democracy Is in the Streets,"* 241–54, 256; Sale, *SDS*, 223–35. Jeffrey Shero, "The S.D.S. National Office: Bureaucracy, Democracy and Decentralization" (paper prepared for a

national SDS meeting held in December 1965, Students for a Democratic Society Papers, Wisconsin Historical Society Archives, Madison; available in Library of Congress, Washington, D.C.; hence SDS Papers, reel 20, 3:3.

26. Judy Pardun, "Alienation and the N.O.," *SDS Bulletin* 4, no. 2 (n.d.); Judy Schiffer Perez, interview with author, 27 August 1993; "Statement by Bob Pardun," SDS-UT retreat working papers, n.d., SDS Papers, Locality File, 1964–68—Texas, reel 25, 3:62. At this time Judy Perez used Robert Pardun's name.

27. "Statement by Bob Pardun."

28. Wizard interview.

29. Herbert Marcuse, *Eros and Civilization: A Philosophical Inquiry into Freud* (Boston: Beacon Press, 1955), first brought Marcuse's ideas to fairly widespread attention in the United States; Herbert Marcuse, *One-Dimensional Man: Studies in the Ideology of Advanced Industrial Society* (Boston: Beacon Press, 1964), was pessimistic about the possibilities for political change; Herbert Marcuse, *An Essay on Liberation* (Boston: Beacon Press, 1969), was optimistic. See Paul Robinson, *The Freudian Left: Wilhelm Reich, Geza Roheim, Herbert Marcuse* (New York: Harper & Row, 1969), 202–08; Richard King, *The Party of Eros: Radical Social Thought and the Realm of Freedom* (Chapel Hill: University of North Carolina Press, 1972), 128–31; and Wilfred M. McClay, *The Masterless: Self and Society in Modern America* (Chapel Hill: University of North Carolina Press, 1994), 272–75, for accessible discussions.

30. "The King of May Comes to Austin: The Rag Interviews Allen Ginsberg," *Rag*, 24 April 1967.

31. Quoted in Glenn W. Jones, "Gentle Thursday: Revolutionary Pastoralism in Austin, Texas, 1966–1969" (master's thesis, University of Texas at Austin, 1988), 52. Sociologists call this "prefigurative politics": the effort by social visionaries to act out the ideal society toward which they are working. See Wini Breines, *Community and Organization in the New Left, 1962–1968: The Great Refusal* (South Hadley, Mass.: J. F. Bergin, 1982).

32. Peck, *Uncovering the Sixties*, 58. Peck may have exaggerated here, but he understood the ideals that those who participated in the *Rag* typically held dear and worked ever harder to honor.

33. Sale, *SDS*, 327.

34. Gary Thiher, "Gentle Thursday as Revolution," *Rag*, 24 April 1967; Thorne Dreyer, "Flipped-out Week," *Rag*, 10 April 1967.

35. Thomas Frank, *The Conquest of Cool: Business Culture, Counterculture, and the Rise of Hip Consumerism* (Chicago: University of Chicago Press, 1997), quickly has become an authoritative statement of disdain for the subversive power of "hip" in recent American life. It carefully avoids endorsing the retro-left stance that this analysis might seem to imply; articles by Frank and others in the journal *The Baffler*, however, throw caution to the wind.

36. Greg Calvert, interview with author, 20 March 1995; Perez interview; Paul Pipkin, Linda Pipkin, and Joe Ebbecke, interview with author, 4 July 1992; Lori Hansel, interview with author, 2 July 1992.

37. See the discussion in Alice Echols, "'We Gotta Get out of This Place': Notes toward a Remapping of the Sixties," *Socialist Review* 22, no. 2 (April–June 1992): 9–22. Echols contends (12) that the New Left drew on "counterhegemonic constructions of masculinity," and appears sympathetic to a similar view of the New Left's sexual politics.

38. Jeff Shero, "Changing Sex Mores Pose Questions," *Daily Texan* [UT student newspaper], 5 December 1963.

39. See Beth Bailey, "Sexual Revolution(s)," in *The Sixties: From Memory to History*, ed. David Farber (Chapel Hill: University of North Carolina Press, 1994), 235–62, and Beth Bailey, *From Front Porch to Back Seat: Courtship in Twentieth-Century America* (Baltimore: Johns Hopkins University Press, 1988).

40. Betty Friedan, *The Feminine Mystique* (New York: Dell, 1963), 299–325. On humanistic psychology see Carl Rogers, *On Becoming a Person: A Therapists's View of Psychotherapy* (Boston:

Houghton Mifflin, 1961), and Barbara Ehrenreich, *The Hearts of Men: American Dreams and the Flight from Commitment* (Garden City, N.Y.: Doubleday/Anchor, 1983), 88–98.

41. For a detailed discussion of this matter see Van Gosse, *Where the Boys Are: Cuba, Cold War America, and the Making of a New Left* (London: Verso, 1994).

42. Gary Thiher, "Desolation Row," *Rag*, 16 April 1969.

43. Marcuse, *One-Dimensional Man*, 56–83.

44. Ehrenreich, *Hearts of Men*, 113.

45. Gitlin, *The Sixties*, 429.

46. "Your Mistake," *Rag*, 15 September 1969; "Critical University," *Rag*, 21 October 1969.

47. "The Armadillo Press Political Statement Prospectus," *Rag*, 14 August 1969.

48. Alice Embree, letter, *Rag*, 1 May 1972; Robert B., "more on community," *Rag*, 9 November 1970; suzi and mike, "Revolution for the Life of It!" *Rag*, 26 October 1970.

49. Jackson Lears, "A Matter of Taste: Corporate Cultural Hegemony in a Mass-Consumption Society," in *Recasting America: Culture and Politics in the Age of Cold War*, ed. Lary May (Chicago: University of Chicago Press, 1989), 38–57, links the New Left to a broader humanistic "drive toward counterhegemony" (53) in the 1950s and 1960s. Barbara Epstein, *Political Protest and Cultural Revolution: Nonviolent Direct Action in the 1970s and 1980s* (Berkeley and Los Angeles: University of California Press, 1991), discusses the New Left's "blocked cultural revolution."

50. According to Gramsci, the fight for cultural hegemony was to be directed by what he called, in an echo of Machiavelli, "the modern prince"—the party. Such an idea surely would have met with widespread hostility within the New Left. See Antonio Gramsci, *Selections from the Prison Notebooks*, ed. Quintin Hoare and Geoffrey Nowell Smith (New York: International, 1971), 123–201. Although American rightists since the 1960s have not coordinated their cultural agitation through a single vanguard party, their activities on the cultural front have been far more organized than parallel efforts from the left, owing in part to the long-ago experience of some of the most diligent rightist cultural activists in the CP.

F i v e

The White Panthers'
"Total Assault on the Culture"

Jeff A. Hale

The White Panther Party (WPP) of Detroit and Ann Arbor, Michigan, was a radical counterculture group that became a major target for the FBI's counterintelligence (or "COINTELPRO") program between 1968 and 1971.[1] In October of 1970, the FBI referred to the White Panthers as "potentially the largest and most dangerous of revolutionary organizations in the United States."[2] However, just three years earlier, the group's leaders hosted a "Love-In" on Detroit's Belle Isle, presided over by John Sinclair, whom the *Detroit News* proclaimed "High Priest of the Detroit hippies."[3] In recounting the story of how and why the White Panther collective evolved from primarily cultural, avant-gardist beginnings into one of the Midwest's influential political extremist groups, this essay will address an important (and largely unresolved) historiographical issue: why some segments of the counterculture progressed from strictly nonpolitical ideologies to positions of radical extremism. A case study exemplifying this development, it is hoped, will contribute to a historiographical reassessment of the counterculture, documenting its diversity and complexity.

The White Panther Party grew to become a professedly political organization that was dedicated to the confrontational strategy of "a total assault on the culture by any means necessary." Its formation during the fall of 1968 owed much to both local and national influences. On the local front, Michigan State and Detroit Police surveillance, harassment, and intimidation of left-wing activists reached unprecedented levels in the wake of the Detroit riots of 1967, as well as in reaction to the popular success of the WPP's "house band," the MC5. National influences, especially the allure of the Black Panthers and the Yippies, also played an important role in the politicization of the group. The dynamics of, and interplay between, these (and other) influences are of critical importance because the existing historiography of the 1960s, still dominated by former participants in the various struggles, offers no useful model for explaining the White Panthers' progression toward radical extremism. To cite just one example, the former SDS leader Todd Gitlin explains the New Left's step-by-step evolution from "protest" to "resistance" and ultimately "Revolution" as emanating largely from the Movement's impatience and frustration with the continuing Vietnam War.[4] In dramatic contrast, the Vietnam issue was inconsequential to the evolution of the White Panthers; the forces and motivations underlying the group's "radicalization" are to be found elsewhere, as we shall see.

The White Panther story is, in many respects, synonymous with the life of John Alexander Sinclair, one of the Midwest's most influential Sixties counterculture leaders.[5] He was born on October 2, 1941, in the town of Flint, Michigan, the birthplace of General Motors. His father was a career employee at the local Buick plant, starting on the assembly line in 1928 and eventually advancing to a midlevel management position; Elise, his mother, was a homemaker. John, his brother, David, and sister, Kathy, enjoyed a comfortable middle-class upbringing in Davison, a small town located a few miles from Flint. The closest thing to radicalism that John experienced growing up was drinking beer on Friday nights, listening to rock and roll on a black Detroit radio station, and occasionally "crashing" all-black rhythm and blues shows in Flint with his friends. He graduated from Davison High with good grades and attended Albion College, a small Methodist institution in southern Michigan. It was at Albion that he first came into contact with the beatnik culture that would later define his life. Befriending the college's lone hipster, Sinclair became an instant and obsessed devotee of avant-garde jazz (à la John Coltrane) and Beat poetry (Allen Ginsberg, Lawrence Ferlinghetti, Gregory Corso, etc.). He also discovered marijuana, which had been part of the black urban jazz scene in America since the twenties, before the beatniks introduced it to white culture. Sinclair believed that "weed" heightened his awareness of the world around him, promoted togetherness, and expanded his creativity. It is a credo from which he has never wavered.[6]

After two years at Albion College, Sinclair dropped out and moved back to Flint, where he continued his exploration of black culture in the jazz and blues clubs located in the town's North Side ghetto. Like his beatnik predecessors, Sinclair saw the expressive and communalist culture of urban African Americans as an appealing alternative to the individualistic dominant culture of the postwar United States. Some years later, reflecting upon Norman Mailer's book *The White Negro*, Sinclair asserted "I was a White Negro in a purer sense. By the time that [book] came out, I was on the streets, I was hangin' in the barbershops, in the pool rooms . . . [I was] doing it."[7]

After completing a bachelor's degree at the Flint branch of the University of Michigan in spring 1964, Sinclair moved to Detroit, enrolling in the graduate school of Wayne State University (WSU). His drug connections in Flint, as well as his bohemian sensibilities, led to rapid acceptance in the city's small and exclusive "hipster" community, located near the WSU campus. Here, at beatnik hangouts like the Red Door Gallery, Sinclair first came into contact with the jazz musician Charles Moore, the poets George Tysh and Allen Van Newkirk, and other hipsters. And through these new connections, Sinclair also met his future wife, Magdalene "Leni" Arndt, a gifted artist-photographer from East Germany who had emigrated to Detroit in 1959 and was also attending WSU.

During that fall, John and Leni and their friends and acquaintances began discussing the possibility of starting an organization of area poets, musicians, and other artists, with the immediate goal of providing a meeting place outside of the WSU campus. A "document of self-determination" was drawn up, which among other things preached the virtues of not succumbing to the dominant "square" culture. Soon afterward, the Artists' Workshop was established on the ground floor of a two-story house on the corner of John Lodge and Warren Avenue. Every Sunday, the workshop held an open house, with poetry readings, jazz performances, exhibitions of photographs and original art, and screenings of avant-garde films. Sinclair and Charles Moore performed together in an experimental jazz quartet, known as the DC-4, and Leni began experimenting with photography and filmmaking.[8]

Over the next two years, the Artists' Workshop flourished. The organizational skills of the group's leadership were immediately evident. The Artists' Workshop Press developed into an alternative publishing house, eventually producing first books by John Sinclair, George Tysh, Bill Hutton, J. D. Whitney, Ron Caplan, and John Kay.[9] Members of the collective also published some of the first underground newspapers in the Midwest, including *Guerrilla*, a journal whose masthead read "A Newspaper of Cultural Revolution." Sinclair's activities were the most prolific of all; in addition to attending graduate school, he managed several area houses (subletting rooms to artists and microentrepreneurs), wrote jazz reviews for *Downbeat*, *JAZZ*,

John Sinclair and Magdalene "Leni" Sinclair, 1972, pictured one year after his release from prison where he had been serving a ten-year sentence for having given two marijuana cigarettes to an undercover policewoman. Along with several others, the Sinclairs helped organize the White Panther Party in 1968, inspired by the Black Panther Party for Self-Defense. The White Panthers' 10-Point Platform called for "Total assault on the culture by any means necessary, including rock and roll, dope, and fucking in the streets." Courtesy of Leni Sinclair.

and other national music magazines, and wrote and published three books of poems: *This Is Our Music*; *Fire Music: A Record*; and *Meditations: A Suite for John Coltrane.*[10]

The ideology of the Detroit hip community reflected a voluntary isolation from, and utter contempt for, the outside society. As Sinclair recalls: "Jazz, it's all we did. We used to sit around and smoke dope . . . .You didn't want to go out too much, because, you know, people were a drag. They might see you [laughs]. You weren't a pleasant sight to them. There weren't too many places you wanted to go. . . . Besides, this was what was happening." In its commitment to creating a totally new cultural existence, the Artists' Workshop exhibited elitist tendencies; flyers advertising their events were distributed only to those who "looked hip."[11] The idea of turning on the masses of American youth to a cultural revolt—the White Panther credo—was antithetical to the group's analysis.

While isolating itself from the dominant culture in Detroit, the Artists' Workshop interacted regularly with other bohemian/hip communities on the two coasts. Attending the Berkeley Poetry Conference in 1965, Sinclair met Allen Ginsberg, Ed Sanders, Charles Olson, and others—an experience that led him to conclude that the Artists' Workshop was as hip as many of the other beatnik "scenes" in the country. And, by hosting numerous poets and avant-garde performers who toured the Midwest, the Artists' Workshop acquired hip credentials.[12]

The spectacle of increasing numbers of beatniks congregating near WSU soon caught the attention of Detroit's police, who had a long history of aversion to nonconformity.[13] Frank Donner finds that from the thirties onward, Detroit had one of the nation's most repressive police forces. The Detroit "Red Squad," or "Special Investigative Bureau" (SIB), was created in 1930, ostensibly to "work on the Bolshevik and Communistic activities in the city." This special unit quickly evolved into an abusive surveillance machine, monitoring all shades of political activity under the guise of hunting "radicals." A long-term ally for the SIB appeared in 1950, with the establishment of the "Security Investigation Squad" (SIS), a Michigan State Police countersubversive unit, whose primary objective was discouraging employers from hiring suspected radicals. The two Red Squads established a close collaborative relationship, characterized by unprecedented information sharing and joint intelligence operations.[14] By the mid-1970s, when the full scope of their activities was first made public in a landmark Michigan court case, the Red Squads had amassed dossiers on more than 1.5 million citizens.[15]

In light of the Detroit police force's historical role as praetorian defender of the status quo, it was not surprising that it used many of the same surveillance and intimidation tactics against the Artists' Workshop (and its successor, "Trans-Love Energies") that the force had successfully employed against suspected "subversives" since the turn of the century. A favored tactic employed against artists, beatniks, and leftist utopians was Michigan's draconian marijuana statutes, which listed possession of even trace amounts as a felony offense. John Sinclair's first marijuana arrest occurred on October 7, 1964, when he and two friends were "set up" in a Detroit Police sting operation. Given two years probation and a $250 fine, Sinclair continued his work with the Artists' Workshop, refusing to give the incident much thought. However, the bust was an important harbinger of future events: Detroit's Red Squad immediately opened files on him and his associates and began to take special interest in the beatnik community.[16] The following summer, Detective Vahan Kapagian of the Detroit Police Narcotics Bureau infiltrated the Artists' Workshop, an assignment that was facilitated by the group's open invitations to the public for Sunday poetry readings. Dressing in street clothes and calling himself "Eddie," Kapagian repeatedly pestered Sinclair with requests for assistance in locating marijuana. On August 16, 1965, Sinclair finally relented, driving Kapagian to a friend's house for a "score." Upon their return to the Artists' Workshop, a detail of twenty-five officers from the Narcotics Bureau raided the house at 4825 John Lodge, arresting seven people, including John and Leni Sinclair. John was convicted of second-offense marijuana possession on February 22, 1966, and later sentenced to six months in the Detroit House of Corrections. Detroit's newspapers portrayed Sinclair as the leader of a WSU campus dope ring.[17]

In addition to Sinclair's six-month incarceration, the events of 1966 brought considerable change to the Artists' Workshop. The Detroit scene underwent a radical transformation, as a number of core members moved away from the city for a variety of reasons, including fear of the police and a desire to experience San Francisco's emerging hip community. Writing from prison, Sinclair advised them against abandoning Detroit: "You have it in your power now to create a vital living situation here in Detroit—if you have the will and commitment to such a situation . . . we are all going to have to start working with each other and take advantage of what our local possibilities [are]."[18] Upon his release from jail on August 6, Sinclair immediately began acting on his commitment to local organizing. The fruit of these labors was the eventual creation of Trans-Love Energies (TLE), an attempted union of counterculture, student, and other alternative groups in Detroit, named after a line in a song by folk-rock artist Donovan, urging listeners to "Fly Translove Airways, get you there on time" (the song was later popularized in live performances by the San Francisco rock troupe The Jefferson Airplane).[19]

The creation of Trans-Love Energies during the first half of 1967[20] owed much to two simultaneously occurring phenomena: the arrival of LSD and the flower children. A sea change had occurred in the WSU community during the six months of Sinclair's imprisonment, as large numbers of baby boom progeny, now coming of age, congregated in and around the campus. Many became regulars at the Artists' Workshop. Facilitating the union between older beatniks and younger hippies was LSD-25, which had just arrived in Detroit. For both groups, "acid" ended pessimism concerning the possibility that American society would ever break out of its state of cultural stagnation. As Sinclair explained: "When beatniks started taking acid, it brought us out of the basement . . . the fringes of society—and just blew us apart. From being cynical and wanting to isolate yourself forever from the squares . . . one was suddenly filled with a messianic feeling of love and brotherhood. . . . LSD made you realize that you had ties with the rest of humanity."[21] Beatnik elitism quickly disappeared, and a plethora of alternative organizations and micro-enterprises sprang up—essentially creating a new alternative culture, with its own economy outside of mainstream Detroit society.

TLE tried to unify a diverse student-hip community into an umbrella organization, or "tribal council." Cofounders Sinclair and the artist Gary Grimshaw attempted to get representatives from all of the area's hip organizations to meet on a regular basis, for the purpose of discussing how better to use their talents and services for the benefit of the hundreds of young people converging on the area. Some of the support services provided included free housing, job information, concerts, transportation in and around Detroit, and a cooperative booking agency for performers and organizations. Although TLE never became the unified model of interorganizational cooperation originally envisioned, Trans-Love Energies, Unlimited, the central business unit, became quite successful, organizing local cultural events and hooking up with other hip enclaves across America to bring in well-known artists and performers such as Allen Ginsberg, the Grateful Dead, and the Fugs.

The Trans-Love organization, like most other counterculture collectives, paid much lip service to the egalitarian "no leaders" concept. In theory, the organization was composed of numerous avant-garde and alternative groups, all possessing equal status on the tribal council; each individual was therefore encouraged to be his or her own leader. In reality, the core group within the Artists' Workshop was the driving force behind the TLE collective, due to its energy, organizational abilities, and commitment to making the experiment work. By the same token, Trans-Love Energies' embrace of hierarchical organization and charismatic leadership (namely, Sinclair) contrasted dramatically with other elements of the evolving counterculture, such as San

Francisco's Digger collective. These differences, viewed by many (then and now) as contradictions, would continue to characterize Sinclair's group through the White Panther period. They underscore both the diversity of counterculture forms that emerged during the latter half of the 1960s and the continuing danger of stereotyping historical movements too narrowly.

As TLE underwent expansion, its core membership changed. John's brother, David, signed on, having passed up a full football scholarship at Dartmouth. Two additional 1967 arrivals who would later assume leadership positions in the White Panthers were "Pun" Plamondon and Genie Parker. Lawrence Robert "Pun" Plamondon was born in Traverse City, Michigan, the illegitimate son of a "half-breed Ottawa [Indian] and a long-distance operator." He was adopted as an infant by upper-middle-class foster parents who were well respected in Traverse City. Despite his comfortable upbringing and excellent academic potential, Pun exhibited a rebellious streak from an early age. At sixteen he ran away from home, hitchhiking across the country, and eventually working with migrant farm workers in California. He moved to Detroit in 1967, was introduced to the Artists' Workshop/TLE, befriended Sinclair, and joined the group just in time to take his first LSD trip at the "Love-In" on April 30 (discussed later). With TLE he found an appropriate outlet for his enormous energy and increasing social consciousness. He and Sinclair soon became close friends; eventually Pun assumed a leadership position in the organization.[22] Genie Parker, the daughter of an army colonel with Vietnam combat experience, arrived at the TLE house shortly after the Love-In. An "army brat" who had been raised in Texas, Georgia, and New Jersey, her attraction to the Sinclairs was immediate, and she moved in with the group her first day in Detroit. Within a few months, she and Pun became inseparable, and the two of them gradually became well known in radical circles throughout the country.[23]

Two of Trans-Love Energies' most significant modes of cultural expression were the underground press and the rock band MC5. By early 1967, Sinclair was writing regular columns for the *Fifth Estate*, while also contributing to the sporadically published *Warren-Forest Sun*, the "official" TLE newspaper. He and *Fifth Estate* editor Peter Werbe participated in a dialogue with alternative press editors from across the country, which would eventually spawn the Underground Press Syndicate, a national system of alternative news acquisition and distribution, run primarily by college-age people. As a result of these connections, the *Fifth Estate*'s coverage of the emerging New Left, Black Power, and counterculture movements became extensive.

The union of the MC5 and Trans-Love Energies in mid-1967 contributed to major changes for the collective, including the rapid acquisition of mass youth appeal. Sinclair's association with MC5 members Rob Tyner, Fred Smith, Wayne Kramer, Dennis Thompson, and Michael Davis began in 1966, when the band first used a TLE house as free rehearsal space. At the time, only Tyner and Davis were out of high school. Over the next two years, the quintet would develop and perfect a unique, hard-driving rock and roll sound, widely credited with influencing (some say pioneering) later punk and heavy metal rock genres.[24]

The MC5 began as a collaboration between Kramer and Smith, two junior high school students from the blue-collar Detroit suburb of Lincoln Park. Things began to happen for the guitarists after Kramer hooked up with vocalist Rob Tyner, two years his senior. A devotee of avant-garde jazz and Beat culture, Tyner had only recently discovered the potentialities of rock and roll. After adding drummer Dennis Thompson (who was the newspaper delivery boy in Kramer's neighborhood) and bass player Michael Davis (Tyner's friend) to their lineup, the group settled upon the name MC5, which Tyner, its author, believed sounded like an industrial serial number for a race car engine; only later did he realize the name could also stand for the "Motor City 5." Playing at local clubs and high school dances, the group gradually created a high energy electric sound, which reflected the combination of rock, rhythm and blues, and experimental jazz influences. One special feature of their sound, its deafening loudness, was made possible by the acquisition of a $3,000, state-of-the-art, Vox public address and amplification system. The group's experimentation with the new system resulted in the regular use of "feedback" in their performances, as well as several trademark Tyner stage antics, such as plunging a microphone into a loudspeaker for effect. By mid-1967, the MC5 had built a substantial local following and cut its first 45-rpm single.[25]

The marriage between the MC5 and Trans-Love Energies was rooted in the many social and cultural changes occurring in Detroit, circa 1967. A strict jazz aficionado only a year before, Sinclair rediscovered rock music via the younger hip crowd and rapidly recognized its potential for attracting youth to the TLE banner. The MC5 saw in him an older, experienced artist with indisputable hip credentials. Thus, when Sinclair offered to manage the group, they accepted immediately. An additional contributing factor to the band's rapid acceptance was the opening of the Grande Ballroom, a large Detroit rock club modeled after the Fillmore West in San Francisco. Russ Gibb, the club's "hip capitalist" owner, hired the MC5 as the house band, which guaranteed the group weekly exposure headlining for the top British and American touring acts of the day. Soon, the entire TLE commune became part of the act, providing psychedelic light shows, outstanding psychedelic concert posters and handbills by Gary Grimshaw, and even master of ceremonies duties from "Brother" J. C. Crawford. From this platform, Trans-Love Energies would recruit hundreds—perhaps thousands—of followers.[26]

The peak of this optimistic period for Sinclair and his group came on April 30, 1967, when they staged a "Love-In" at the large metropolitan park on Belle Isle, on the Detroit River. Influenced by San Francisco's Human Be-In the previous January, as well as the trend of similar counterculture celebrations happening in hip enclaves across the country, Trans-Love Energies promoted the event as a gathering of "peace and love," where hippies and straights could come together to celebrate a new vision of society. The *Detroit News* and *Detroit Free Press* gave the Love-In significant coverage, and on the day of the event several thousand "freaks" were in attendance, smoking marijuana, dropping LSD, singing, chanting, and enjoying themselves with minimal disturbances. Although the police were out in significant numbers, they kept a low profile until dusk, when the arrest of a motorcyclist encouraged taunting and rock throwing. The result was a full-scale riot, with numerous arrests, ostensibly for "damaging police vehicles." The resulting press coverage was almost unanimously on the side of the police, portraying Sinclair and TLE as mindless hedonists, more interested in picking a fight with police than in "peace and love."[27]

The Belle Isle experience had a profound impact upon the later development of Trans-Love Energies. The hippie philosophy of getting high, creating alternative institutions, and waiting for the capitalist machine to rust away was proving to be an inadequate analysis. Sinclair later admitted: "[We had] a simplistic picture of what the 'revolution' was all about. . . . [We] said that all you had to do was 'tune in, turn on, and drop out,' as if that would solve all the problems of humankind . . . and what we didn't understand, spaced out as we were behind all that acid, was that the machine was determined to keep things the way they were. . . . [B]y this time there was a full-scale suppression campaign underway."[28] Sinclair struggled with the realization that the local police were responding to cultural revolt with *political* repression. Gradually, over the course of the next year, he came to the conclusion that the counterculture forms espoused and lived by Trans-Love Energies were actually political statements. In response, TLE's activities focused on educating youth regarding both the positive, liberating aspects of the new cultural forms, and also their potential risks. Sinclair began appearing at area colleges, high schools, and other youth gatherings, urging people to join in a "total assault on the culture"—a William S. Burroughs phrase from the early Sixties, popularized by New York poet-artist (and future Yippie) Ed Sanders.[29] The collective also stepped up distribution of its newspapers and other propaganda at

MC5 concerts, warning of police surveillance and hassles. Still another initiative involved assisting high school students with publishing alternative newspapers, activity that again earned Sinclair a hostile mainstream press response.[30]

Although TLE was still a long way from advocating militant action against police and "the state," the group nonetheless delighted in taunting police and other symbols of authority with antiestablishment (often tongue-in-cheek) writing in its newspapers, street theater actions in public, and inflammatory rhetoric at MC5 concerts. And in a city like Detroit, where racial tensions were always high and police rarely appreciated humor perpetrated by hippies at their expense, Trans-Love Energies' actions heightened police interest in the group. The end result was increasingly severe reprisals.

John Sinclair's third marijuana arrest occurred on January 24, 1967, when a force of thirty-four law enforcement officers, representing local, state, and federal agencies, raided the group's commune (still officially known as the Artists' Workshop), arresting fifty-six persons. The raid was the culmination of a four-month-long sting operation, once again facilitated by the wily (and newly bearded) Detective Vahan Kapagian, who infiltrated the organization posing as "Louie" the hip candle maker. Assisting him was a fellow narcotics detective, Jane Mumford, who faithfully wore miniskirts in her portrayal of "Peg" the counterculture "chick." As helpful and friendly as "Louie" and "Peg" were, they remained unable to purchase any marijuana for several months. The police were ultimately forced to move with little hard evidence: two minor pot purchases from WSU students only peripherally associated with the Artists' Workshop and Sinclair's "gift" of two marijuana joints to Detective Mumford shortly before Christmas, 1966.[31] The impact of Sinclair's third arrest would be delayed for two and a half years, as his attorneys, Sheldon Otis and Justin "Chuck" Ravitz, skillfully fought the constitutionality of the state's marijuana statutes. Sinclair remained free to lead Trans-Love Energies through the most turbulent years of the 1960s.[32]

A significant turning point in the history of Detroit was the bloody rioting of July 24–31, 1967, the worst in America's history. Following the riots, the attitudes of Detroit police moved farther to the right, reflecting the growing siege mentality prevalent among many of the city's whites. During the winter and spring of 1968, the situation became unbearable for Trans-Love Energies. Sinclair summarized his feelings during the period: "Nothing was happening but the police. They had everything covered, and if you moved after dark you were snatched up and taken to jail without bail. If you stayed inside they came in after you, kicking down the doors and ransacking everything in sight. . . . Detroit was Police City, baby, and you never forgot it—not for a minute."[33] The last straw came in response to the assassination of Dr. Martin Luther

King Jr. on April 4, when Detroit's police, fearing another major riot, established a "protective curfew" in the city after dark. Since Sinclair's group earned most of its operating funds producing MC5 concerts and related events that usually took place during the evenings, the curfew threatened their very livelihood. Therefore, in May 1968, TLE relocated some forty-five miles to the west, to the college town of Ann Arbor.

The new Trans-Love Energies commune consisted of twenty-eight people, including three children and the MC5 members.[34] Together they occupied two old houses at 1510 and 1520 Hill Street, on the outskirts of the University of Michigan (UM) campus. Two new members of note were nineteen-year-old Ken Kelley, a UM student from Ypsilanti, Michigan, and Milton "Skip" Taube, a Detroit native who first attended UM in 1965 and had since become closely associated with SDS. Kelley edited one of the campus's first underground newspapers, the *Argus*, and immediately recognized in Sinclair a kindred spirit. Taube had recently become disillusioned with the split in the local SDS organization. Two of his closest friends, Bill Ayers and Diana Oughton, led the new SDS splinter group "Jesse James Gang," which would later evolve into the Weather Underground.[35]

Trans-Love Energies' immediate focus was music, which had recently become a local source of conflict. During the winter of 1968, the Ann Arbor City Council had passed an ordinance banning amplified music from city parks. When Sinclair decided to hold an MC5 concert in defiance of the law, the small Ann Arbor police force threatened to arrest all involved. Sinclair did not back down. Thanks to press coverage from the *Michigan Daily*, the campus community got involved. Two weeks later the City Council relented, granting TLE permission to hold a series of free concerts at Gallup Park, on the outskirts of town.[36] This was a big turning point for the group. Trans-Love Energies had stood up to the police and other "authority figures" and won. In Sinclair's view, the incident demonstrated conclusively the potential power of organized youth revolt. Henceforth, TLE's members pursued a recruitment strategy characterized by arrogant, militant posturing toward authority figures and flaunting (in print and on stage) the fact that they were "getting away with it."

Freed from the stifling, repressive atmosphere of urban Detroit and fortified by its success in the Ann Arbor free concert struggle, Trans-Love Energies initiated a "total assault on the culture" throughout the summer. The spearhead of its attack was the MC5, which, thanks to Sinclair's managerial prowess, became a regionally successful touring group. Each MC5 concert was a multimedia event, with psychedelic lights, rear-screen projection, and the spiritual rantings of "Brother" J. C. Crawford. The supercharged electric music of the MC5 was punctuated by Sinclair's radical speeches, urging youth to

The MC5, considered pioneers of punk rock, at the Grande Ballroom, Detroit, Michigan, 31 October 1968, while recording their debut album for Elektra. *Kick Out the Jams* reached the number twenty spot on the charts in 1969. Under the management of John Sinclair, the Motor City band became an instrument for fomenting cultural revolt throughout the country, particularly among high-school-aged youth. Their modus operandi included performing free outdoor concerts that were punctuated by Sinclair's political exhortations. Courtesy of Leni Sinclair.

pursue personal freedom to the utmost extremes. The MC5's shows successfully fused two very new countercultural forms: alternative, electric rock and roll music and a rhetoric of youth culture liberation. Ken Kelley's recollections of his first MC5 concert provide insight into the energy and excitement surrounding the band:

I'll never forget the first time I saw the MC5 perform that hot June night in 1968 at the Grande Ballroom. . . . The ozone scent of anticipation quickened my pulse as Rob Tyner jumped to center stage and shouted "Kick out the jams, motherfuckers!," the opening rant into The 5's anthemic underground hit song. As Tyner squirmed and sang, behind him were two sparkle-sequined guitarists [Fred "Sonic" Smith and Wayne Kramer] who traded-off lead in a fervid fusillade of fiery notes. . . . When Fred played solo on his trademark-tune, "Rocket Reducer No. 62," you knew why he got his name "Sonic"—the only word that packed enough "G-force."... He leaped up and down ... in swirling orgiastic gyrations of musical frenzy.... When Fred played, sex itself exploded on stage.[37]

Stephen Stills's antiestablishment lyrics from the previous year—"There's something happening here. What it is ain't exactly clear"[38]—seem equally appropriate for the unprecedented countercultural amalgamation Trans-Love Energies and the MC5 were forging in America's heartland during the year of the barricades.

TLE's political economy was far removed from that of most other hippie collectives. Earnings from MC5 shows financed the entire Trans-Love operation, including two communes, several dozen core members, and a very active propaganda machine. This uniqueness reflected the history and evolution of the group; from the first days of the Artists' Workshop, Sinclair had juggled such seemingly contradictory tasks as organizing free Love-Ins and being responsible for collecting rent from tenants in several buildings he managed. And in much the same manner, the Trans-Love commune in Ann Arbor booked most MC5 gigs for pay, while also playing many free concerts and benefits. Sinclair defended the group's political economy by asserting that the MC5 was a true "people's band," playing as many benefits and free shows as possible. He added that the funds acquired from paid shows were used primarily "to spread the word that there was another way of doing things . . . to bring the new world order into being."[39]

The MC5's growing popularity did not escape the attention of the local Ann Arbor Police, the Washtenaw County Sheriff's Office, or the Michigan State Police. Throughout the summer, an increasing number of what Sinclair called "creep scenes" occurred, in which police presence at MC5 shows led to arrests, near arrests, and an intimidating cat-and-mouse surveillance and evasion game. Sinclair's biweekly *Fifth Estate* articles, titled "Rock and Roll Dope," chronicled both the MC5's growing popularity and what Sinclair believed to be an escalating counterattack from the forces of the conservative establishment. The police response included marijuana busts in the parking lots, pressure on club owners (in response to the MC5's desecration of American flags and frequent use of profanity onstage), and a steadily increasing presence. On several occasions, the police turned off the electricity at clubs to prevent the band from playing; in one bizarre incident, the MC5 was issued a ticket for being "a noisy band." In June, TLE leaders Gary Grimshaw and "Pun" Plamondon were charged by the Traverse City Police with marijuana possession and sale in their community the previous March, an incident that sent Grimshaw fleeing to another state and resulted in the imprisonment of Plamondon (a $20,000 bond, far in excess of the group's resources, kept him in jail for three months awaiting trial). The unpredictability and insanity of the summer of 1968 peaked on July 23, when Sinclair and MC5 guitarist Fred "Sonic" Smith were arrested by Oakland County sheriffs in Leonard, Michigan and charged with "assault and battery on a police officer." While he was in prison, the Oakland County authorities cut off most of Sinclair's long hair. Three days later, the MC5 were arrested by the Ann Arbor Police and charged with "disturbing the peace" for playing at a free concert in West Park.[40]

The harassment by law enforcement officials was undoubtedly motivated by several factors, including their repulsion at the sight of long-haired hippies using drugs, mutilating the nation's flag in public, and in the process influencing other young people to imitate their counterculture lifestyle. As had been the case in Detroit, police in the hinterlands of Michigan were ill prepared to face resistance and blatant antipolice hatred from rebellious, white, middle-class youth. However, the police overreaction was also influenced by TLE's provocations on stage and in the pages of the *Fifth Estate* and the *Sun*. Seeking to (in the terminology of the times) "expose the repressive nature of the mother-country system," Sinclair and MC5 lead vocalist Rob Tyner regularly informed crowds of hyped-up youth about the various police (and club owner) hassles they were facing. Audience reaction often bordered on riot. In addition, Sinclair baited the police in article after article of the *Fifth Estate*. He realized that the newspaper was now required reading for many local police officers, as part of their intelligence gathering. The following passage is typical of Sinclair's invective that summer:

> We matched our magic against the pigs' brute tactics and it
> worked—any respect any of the people there might have had for "law
> and order" as represented by the Ann Arbor police just disappeared,
> and their futile tricks were exposed to the light. All this bullshit was
> totally unnecessary—we just wanted to do our thing and let the peo-
> ple do their thing with us, but the police just won't let that happen
> without trying to stomp us out one way or the other. . . . People are
> getting hip to all of the old people's lies and perversions, and they
> aren't going to stand for it much longer. *We* sure aren't.[41]

The defiantly political tone of Sinclair's writing was intentional and demonstrated the continuing evolution of his ideology. He theorized that "our culture itself represented a political threat to the established order, and that any action which has a political consequence is finally a political action."[42]

However, Sinclair also recognized that the typical MC5 fan was largely uneducated as to the nuances of political versus cultural revolt and generally despised "politics" of the conventional and/or New Left variety. Therefore, TLE began using its growing popularity to educate young people regarding the politics of their new culture and movement.

National events, such as the expansion and convergence of the New Left, Black Power, antiwar, and counterculture revolts into a single "Movement" for radical social change, also played a role in the increasing politicization of Trans-Love Energies. By virtue of their national underground newspaper connections and their extensive touring with the MC5, Sinclair and his cadre were better informed than more isolated counterculture groups about the Movement's increasing resistance to the establishment. Detroit's *Fifth Estate*, along with the Ann Arbor–based TLE papers *Sun* and *Argus*, gave extensive coverage to Black Panther shoot-outs with police, campus revolts, and the increasing numbers of street battles between police and "freeks" that were happening across the country. The importance of this process cannot be overstated, as members of Detroit's hip community would now begin relating the events in their lives (such as drug usage/acceptance, alternative institution building, and deteriorating police relations) with similar developments in other hip communities across the United States. The national underground media network, a first-of-its-kind phenomenon, would become a catalyst for the future merging of radical movements.

Trans-Love Energies' previous interaction with counterculture enclaves on the East and West Coasts also provided a platform for increasing national awareness. By 1968, Sinclair had befriended fellow avant-garde artist-poets Ed Sanders and Allen Ginsberg, and through them had met Youth International Party ("Yippie") activists Jerry Rubin and Abbie Hoffman. The street theater antics of the New York Yippies had much in common with the MC5's shocking stage antics. Therefore, when Ed Sanders invited Sinclair and the MC5 to perform at the Yippies' Festival of Life in Chicago in late August, they accepted without hesitation. Sinclair recalled the band's Sunday, August 25, performance—and the disturbance it provoked:

> As it turned out, we were the only ones in the country who showed up to play . . . The Fugs [Sanders's band] wouldn't even come. . . . They were terrified! . . . [the Yippies] didn't have a stage. They didn't have a permit. They didn't have power. . . . So we set up on the grass. We plugged into a hot dog stand. . . . We played one set on the grass, just like in Ann Arbor at the free concerts . . . [and then] Abbie Hoffman decides that this is the time to start the shit. He

Genie Parker and Lawrence Robert "Pun" Plamondon, ca. 1968–1969. Founding members of the White Panther Party, the Plamondons were put under surveillance by the Detroit Red Squad and the FBI, who soon charged Pun, the WPP's "Minister of Defense," with the 1968 bombing of a CIA-recruiting office in Ann Arbor, Michigan. Charges were later dropped when the U.S. Supreme Court, in a landmark decision, ruled unanimously that surveillance of domestic political dissidents conducted solely by the executive branch and without judicial warrants was unconstitutional. Courtesy of Leni Sinclair.

had this big flat bed wagon that was going to be used for the stage, but they wouldn't let him bring it in. So he decides, "Fuck it, I'm going to bring it in." He knows that this is going to provoke a confrontation. . . . He started to bring this wagon through and that attracted thousands of people. Then he comes up and takes the mike between sets and starts ranting and raving. . . . The police were already starting to advance on the park. . . . So I just got my equipment men and started to take down the equipment and pack it in the van. . . . The police were getting closer and closer. . . . When we pulled out, the police were swarming all over the area, and that's when the shit really started. We just drove straight back [to Ann Arbor].[43]

Sinclair came away from the Chicago debacle convinced of two things. First, the police responded vastly out of proportion to any real threat posed by the gathering of "freeks," New Leftists, antiwar activists, Black Power supporters, and others. For Sinclair, this meant that the Movement—including the counterculture—would have to get *politically* organized for self-defense purposes or face repression by law enforcement agencies. Second, after experiencing the Yippies' less than prolific organizational skills, Sinclair became convinced that Trans-Love Energies possessed the requisite organization, experience, and popular following to present a viable model for politicizing the youth culture on a national scale. The creation of the White Panther Party (WPP) as the political wing of TLE, formally announced on November 1, 1968, represented the culmination of these lessons.

The selection of the name White Panthers, which demonstrated a close identification with the Black Panthers, might appear as something of a contradiction, considering TLE's mostly white membership and sparse record of attention to black causes in Detroit. However, Sinclair never strayed from his close identification with black culture (especially its music), and the Artists' Workshop had been a multiracial organization. Most TLE members envied and respected the Black Panthers' armed self-defense strategy and disciplined organizational model. Yet the most influential Black Panther advocate within the collective was Pun Plamondon, who spent the summer in a jail cell in Traverse City reading works by or about Black Panther leaders Huey Newton and Eldridge Cleaver. At this time, the Black Panthers were actively seeking alliances with "white mother country radicals" in the New Left, counterculture, and peace movements. For Plamondon, the Black Panthers' call for white allies, essentially white Black Panthers, was a revelation. Upon his return to Ann Arbor in September, he lobbied Sinclair to form a white support group for the Black Panthers.[44] The timing of Plamondon's request, just after Sinclair had returned from the "stomp scene" in Chicago, was crucial: the Black Panthers appeared to have just the sort of national model of political organization TLE was seeking. In addition, the title "White Panthers" gave the group instant radical credentials and, they hoped, credibility as a "vanguard" white revolutionary organization.

At first, the WPP was little more than a paper construct. The organization's "ten point program" displayed a Yippie-esque mixture of counterculture themes and "fantasy politics." The platform included such things as full endorsement of the Black Panther Party's ten–point program and platform; a "total assault on the culture by any means necessary, including rock and roll, dope, and fucking in the streets"; free food, clothes, housing, drugs, music, bodies, and medical care; and freedom from "phony" leaders—"everyone must be a leader—freedom means free every one."[45] The tongue-in-cheek nature of the early White Panther slogans is something that few people outside the

Movement, most important, neither the police nor the FBI—realized. In fact, the WPP was originally conceived as "an arm of the Youth International Party." The naming of a "central committee" demonstrated Sinclair's penchant for Yippie-inspired theatrics, with positions such as "minister of religion" and "minister of demolition."[46]

Another feature of the early WPP that paralleled the Yippie model was its attempt to co-opt the straight (commercial) media. Just as the Yippies had attracted international press coverage for the Chicago Festival of Life, so too did Sinclair hope to recruit America's youth with both conventional and alternative media coverage of the WPP, generated by its own propaganda machine. "We can work within those old forms, infusing them with our new content and using them to carry out our work," he asserted.[47] Sinclair had also learned from the Yippies that there was a direct relationship between the level of sensationalism in the message to the media and the degree of media coverage. Early White Panther press releases and propaganda were intentionally overstated: "If you make it outrageous enough," Plamondon later recalled, "the networks will pick it up."[48]

All propaganda and wishful thinking aside, the White Panthers did possess one potential ticket to national visibility that fall: the MC5. On September 26, 1968, Elektra Records signed the band to record a "live" album at the Grande Ballroom in Detroit. Elektra's young publicity director, Danny Fields, apparently recognized the potential commercial value of youth in revolt. The MC5's debut album, "Kick Out the Jams," as well as a 45–rpm single (same title, with B-side "The Motor City Is Burning") were released in early 1969 and immediately entered the Billboard Hot 100. The album went to number 20 on the Billboard charts; the single to number 82.[49] *Rolling Stone* put lead vocalist Rob Tyner on its January 4, 1969, cover. Few at the time realized the significance of radical counterculture musical expressionism achieving popular acceptance.

For Sinclair, a national recording contract with Elektra, complete with $50,000 advance, represented neither a "sellout" nor a surrender to capitalist commodification of "the people's music." In his 1972 book *Guitar Army*, he provided an ideological justification for the action, focusing upon two key aspects of Trans-Love's "total assault on the culture" thesis. First, Sinclair stressed that successful revolutions require the participation of the masses. He hypothesized that in order to reach the maximum number of prerevolutionary youth the WPP should use as many of the "old establishment forms" as possible, including the media, radio stations, and of course record companies. Second, Sinclair believed that by disguising itself as a simple economic force like a rock band, the MC5 could work parasitically from within the capitalist recording industry to challenge its dominance of national music distribution; he added, " . . . we're determined to change the structure of . . . the pop music scene—and the people whose lives it shapes, as we pass through it on our way to building a whole new structure on our own."[50] Finally, Sinclair predicted that once the MC5's record was released and gained national acceptance, the WPP, working with other radical groups and "people's bands" across the country, could establish an alternative recording and distribution system to rival, and eventually replace, the existing capitalist structure.

The details surrounding the MC5's contract with Elektra would seem to support Sinclair's position that the WPP was in fact "putting something over on the old people," rather than selling out. The most obvious evidence for this was Sinclair's liner notes on the album, which boldly stated: "The MC5 *is* the revolution. . . . The music will make you strong . . . and there is no way it can be stopped now . . . [so] Kick out the jams, motherfucker!" Equally significant, Elektra allowed the album to be originally released with an uncensored version of "Kick Out the Jams," complete with Tyner's use of profanity. Thus, while Elektra's primary motivation was undoubtedly record sales, that is, an attempted commodification of the new counterculture music, by consenting to Sinclair's demands that the White Panthers' core philosophies be included in the record, the company became a willing accomplice in disseminating the WPP gospel to a national audience. And when one considers that the precise parameters of the relationship between record companies and hip rock bands were still being established in 1968, it is therefore not unreasonable to ask: "Who commodified whom?"

The first year of the WPP coincided with Richard Nixon's election to the presidency and an atmosphere of increasing confrontation nationwide. The FBI initiated COINTELPRO (a nationwide secret counterintelligence initiative) specifically designed to disrupt and destroy the New Left and affiliated groups. In 1969 came the fragmentation of SDS and the first incident of National Guardsmen shooting unarmed hippies and students during the People's Park riots at the University of California, Berkeley. Other campus confrontations paralyzed universities across the country. The Beat poet Allen Ginsberg, a favored speaker on the college circuit, claimed that the police and National Guard were gassing and beating so many students "it's like they're manufacturing violent radicals by the milliard."[51] Todd Gitlin accurately summed up the atmosphere of mounting social disorder:

In the year after August 1968, it was as if both official power and movement counterpower, equally and passionately, were committed to stoking up "two, three, many Chicagos," each believing that the

final showdown of good and evil, order and chaos, was looming. . . .
The once-solid core of American life—the cement of loyalty that
people tender to institutions, certifying that the current order is
going to last and deserves to—this loyalty, in select sectors, was
decomposing . . . underneath [it all] grew a sublime faith that the
old sturdy-seeming ways [of the ancien régime] might be papier-
mâché and that the right trumpet blast—the correct analysis, the
current line, the correct tactics—might bring them crashing down.[52]

Nixon did not disguise his intent to use the full force of the nation's police,
military, and intelligence establishments to smash all shades of dissent, including the counterculture. What is more, his administration's willingness to
define the enemy with ever-wider strokes of the brush empowered and
emboldened the praetorian forces of authority. In this environment, the mere
act of advocating "revolution" was looked upon by police and the FBI as tan-
tamount to committing a violent, treasonous act.

The worsening relationship between police and the Movement in southeast Michigan paralleled the national trends. The police might have acted
with greater restraint if radical rhetoric and posturing had been all they were
up against. However, memories of the riots of 1967 lingered and, in fall 1968,
a wave of bombings took place, targeting unmanned police cars and other
symbols of the establishment, including a clandestine CIA recruiting office in
Ann Arbor. The individual responsible for much of the destruction was "hip-
pie-turned-mad bomber" David Valler, whose philosophy had evolved from
LSD to TNT over the course of a few months.[53] Not surprisingly, the Valler
bombings influenced many local police and FBI to begin looking at all hippies as potentially violent.

In this atmosphere of mounting tensions the White Panthers presented
their analysis of a pending revolution in increasingly militant terms.
Plamondon emerged as the most radical of the group, issuing statements like:
" . . . get a gun brother, learn how to use it. You'll need it, pretty soon. Pretty
soon. You're a White Panther, act like one."[54] For his part, Sinclair presented
a "youth colony" thesis, which asserted that the hip youth of America were in
fact a persecuted "colony," with similarities to both urban blacks and Third
World anti-imperialist movements, such as the Vietcong (National Liberation
Front) in South Vietnam. "Our culture is a revolutionary culture," he stated,
adding "we have to realize that the long-haired dope-smoking rock and roll
street-fucking culture is a whole thing, a revolutionary international cultural
movement which is absolutely legitimate and absolutely valid." Opposing the
youth colony, Sinclair saw a "pig power structure," reflecting the "low-energy

death culture" of American capitalist society, which he believed would even resort to "kill[ing] us if they can get away with it."[55]

The culmination of this increasingly militant posturing was the creation of a "White Panther Myth," by which the group portrayed themselves as genuine revolutionaries who would not hesitate to take the struggle to the next level—violence against the state. The White Panther Myth contained both offensive and defensive components. Rhetorically, Sinclair and Plamondon promised to "attack" and "assault" the capitalist power structure; they boasted of their creation of "high-energy rock and roll bands" for the purpose of "infiltrating the popular culture."[56] Yet their propaganda also spoke of being "dragged into the struggle" against their will, due to increasingly severe police harassment.[57] The image of formerly peace-loving hippies who were forced to fight back (which paralleled the Black Panthers' raison d'être) was therefore an important aspect of the White Panther Myth. However, aside from their written and oratorical bombast, and the occasional pose for photographs with guns clutched clumsily in hand, the White Panthers were far removed from the revolutionary violence that characterized groups such as the Weathermen and the New Year's Gang; their "assault" existed primarily in the cultural realm. But over the next two years, as a result of heightened police, FBI, and Justice Department interest in the group, the militant, offensive side of the White Panther Myth acquired a more potent basis in reality.

Events of 1968–69 confirmed Sinclair and the Plamondons' "death culture" suspicions, as police surveillance increased and the WPP faced a staggering number of "creep scenes." Within a few weeks of the release of the MC5's album, Elektra Records, apparently under pressure from industry executives, removed Sinclair's liner notes from all future editions of the album and released a censored version of the single "Kick Out the Jams." Many stores had refused to carry the album due to its profanity. Angry and frustrated, the White Panthers requested that fans kick in the doors of shops that refused to sell the MC5's music. Elektra responded in kind, dropping the group altogether in spring 1969. The MC5's first big eastern city tour also ended ominously after an ugly incident in a club inspired the hip capitalist promoter Bill Graham to blacklist the band nationally. Police hassles worsened, and WPP members continued to be arrested on a variety of charges.[58]

The FBI's interest in the White Panthers, which had started in late 1968,[59] remained minimal until the so-called Ann Arbor riots of June 16–18, 1969, which featured three days of pitched battles between rock-throwing freeks and a massive contingent of riot gear-clad police. For FBI Director J. Edgar Hoover, who had been incensed by what he termed "filthy" and "obscene" lyrics by the MC5, the mere presence of White Panthers at the riots was proof that they had coordinated the revolt. After reading reports on the riot, Hoover ordered that actions be taken to monitor, disrupt, and damage the WPP.[60]

The group's worst setback to date came on July 28, 1969, when Detroit Recorder's Court Judge Robert J. Colombo sentenced John Sinclair to nine and a half to ten years in prison for his third marijuana offense, dating back to January 1967. Rubbing salt in the wound, Judge Colombo refused to set bond, arguing that Sinclair displayed "a propensity and a willingness to further commit the same type of offenses while on bond."[61] The impact on the WPP of Sinclair's incarceration was enormous, and the situation soon went from bad to worse. On October 7, 1969, a federal grand jury in Detroit indicted Sinclair, Pun Plamondon, and Detroit WPP chapter member Jack Forrest on conspiracy charges stemming from the September 29, 1968, CIA office bombing in Ann Arbor.[62] The inclusion of David Valler as an unindicted co-conspirator in the indictment demonstrated that the former antiestablishment bomber would be the government's star witness.[63] However, the U.S. attorney had to wait more than a year to start the trial, because Plamondon went underground to elude capture.

During the first half of 1970, the White Panther Myth reached its fullest expression. Now on the FBI's Ten Most Wanted list, Plamondon moved with ease in the underground, hiding out on the West Coast for a few months, then moving on to Canada, northern and central Europe, and finally to Algeria, where he met with Eldridge Cleaver, the Black Panther leader in exile, whose philosophy of black-white cooperation in the Movement had been instrumental in the creation of the White Panthers.[64] Returning to the United States during the late spring, Pun hid out in the woods of northern Michigan, collecting weapons and writing inflammatory articles, one of which asserted "I don't want to make it sound like all you got to do is kill people, kill pigs, to bring about revolution . . . [but] it is up to us to educate the people to the fact that it is war, and a righteous revolutionary war. . . . It's up to the vanguard to start taking on activity."[65] On the national scene, Weathermen bombings and the spectacle of Ohio National Guardsmen shooting to death four unarmed student protesters at Kent State University caused many to question whether the social fabric of America was unraveling. For the WPP, the timing of Plamondon's underground capers could not have been worse; the group achieved national visibility at precisely the moment when the Nixon administration was seeking to make examples of as many radical groups as possible.

The remaining White Panthers faced the continued imprisonment of Sinclair, the government's bombing conspiracy indictments against Sinclair, Plamondon, and Forrest, and ever-worsening police and FBI surveillance and harassment. Abandoned by the MC5, who departed to make less revolutionary music with the novice producer Jon Landau, the WPP faced a debilitating financial crisis. Somehow, the leadership of Leni and David Sinclair, as well as Genie Plamondon, Skip Taube, and Ken Kelley, managed to hold the collective intact. Even more miraculously, this embattled core group found the time and resources to correspond with and tutor dozens of emerging White Panther chapters nationwide and in England,[66] and it entered into discussions with the Yippies concerning a possible merger.[67] The "Free John" movement merged with a larger CIA conspiracy trial defense, which attracted support from such notables as Jane Fonda, Donald Sutherland, and Allen Ginsberg. And famed Chicago conspiracy trial lawyers William Kunstler and Leonard Weinglass signed on with Detroit National Lawyers Guild attorney Hugh "Buck" Davis to ably defend the White Panthers in their upcoming CIA conspiracy case.[68]

Considerable debate took place within WPP ranks about taking the struggle to the next level—that is, actualizing the White Panther Myth. From his prison cell, Sinclair began to express doubts about the violent "adventurism" now being advocated by Eldridge Cleaver and the Weathermen. Other WPP members, including Skip Taube and Jack Forrest, expressed support for the goals behind the violent actions, while struggling with the utility and consequences of actually committing them. Several WPP members began openly brandishing rifles and other firearms, engaging in target practice at rural locations on the outskirts of Ann Arbor.[69] These activities were influenced by a mysterious new arrival, Dennis Marnell, who assumed the title of deputy minister of defense and went to great lengths to make the group feel more comfortable handling and using weapons. The available evidence strongly suggests that Marnell was a government agent provocateur, who infiltrated the WPP commune for the purpose of gathering intelligence on Plamondon's whereabouts and possibly setting the group up for future arrests. Infiltration along these lines was a common COINTELPRO tactic during the period.[70] In any event, Marnell was scared off by wary White Panthers before he could complete his presumed assignment.[71]

Another turning point for the WPP came with Plamondon's capture by the Michigan State Police on July 23, 1970, near Cheboygan, Michigan. Press reports quoted FBI agents as stating that Plamondon had a .38 caliber Derringer pistol, a rifle, a shotgun, and "two cartons of dynamite" in his possession. Bail was set at $100,000, and Pun was soon transported to Detroit for arraignment in the CIA conspiracy case. Traveling with Plamondon at the time of his capture were Taube and Forrest, each of whom were charged with harboring a fugitive and held in lieu of $25,000 bond.[72] The shock of losing three more WPP leaders might have been bad enough—but materials allegedly found in the Volkswagen van in which the three were traveling would ultimately have much greater long-term consequences for the group.[73] The FBI's new special agent-in-charge in Detroit, Neil J. Welch, meticulously studied the materials, eventually preparing a 107–page report for FBI headquarters, completed on September 3, 1970. Within weeks of the report's issuance, Hoover elevated the WPP to the status of one of the most dangerous militant organizations in America and brought them to the attention of Nixon's attorney general, John N. Mitchell.[74]

Information concerning the "ultraradical" White Panthers was welcome news to the Nixon administration that fall. Congressional elections, the most divisive in years, were heating up. Hoping to overturn Democratic majorities in Congress, Nixon assumed a major role in the campaign, delivering highly partisan speeches associating Democrats with hippies, Black Panthers, and Charles Manson-esque radicals. Obsessed with acquiring more intelligence on radicals, Nixon directed Hoover's FBI to expand its COINTELPRO dragnet against the Movement, and the Bureau's Ten Most Wanted list was expanded to sixteen, with nine slots occupied by Movement radicals.[75]

Events came to a head on September 9, 1970, when a "national security" wiretap—installed without a court order—was initiated on the WPP's Ann Arbor commune; it would remain in operation through January 26, 1971. On September 22, 1970, Nixon, Mitchell, Hoover, and Michigan Congressman Gerald Ford discussed the White Panthers in a White House meeting.[76] Three days later, the Senate Judiciary Committee's Internal Security Subcommittee heard testimony regarding the WPP from Sergeant Clifford Murray of the Michigan State Police.[77] It wasn't long before nearly the entire spectrum of U.S. government and military intelligence agencies (FBI, CIA, Defense Intelligence Agency, National Security Agency, and National Security Council) were actively investigating the group.[78]

The White Panther saga took another unexpected turn late in the year, when the Nixon administration became interested in the group for more than its militancy. Using the WPP's federal CIA conspiracy trial as a test case, the Justice Department attempted to acquire Supreme Court sanction for a sweeping, unconstitutional wiretapping plan, known as the Mitchell Doctrine (so named due to Attorney General Mitchell's delivery of the legal briefs before U.S. District Judge Damon J. Keith in Detroit). The Mitchell Doctrine asserted that the president possesses the "inherent constitutional power" to wiretap "domestic radicals" *without a court order* if he, and he alone, believes them to be threatening to the national security. Ultimately, a Supreme Court with several Nixon appointees voted unanimously (8–0) against the doctrine in June of 1972, in the landmark *U.S. v. U.S. District Court* (also known as

"Keith") decision. The WPP case was subsequently dropped, as were many other federal conspiracy trials involving Movement groups that involved illegal government electronic surveillance.[79]

Freed from prison, Sinclair and Plamondon returned to Ann Arbor and established the Rainbow People's Party, a nonmilitant, grassroots organization whose activities mirrored the Movement's entrance into mainstream politics after 1970. Sinclair's marijuana case received belated, yet critical, attention from the Michigan Supreme Court, which overturned the state's draconian pot statutes. The national trend of marijuana decriminalization during the Seventies owed much to the two and a half years John Sinclair had spent behind bars in Michigan.

The White Panthers represent a clear example of a Sixties counterculture group that evolved into a militant political organization. Their metamorphosis was due to a combination of factors, including: (1) the preternaturally conservative southeast Michigan environment—in particular, the inflexible, often repressive police, who overreacted to cultural radicalism; (2) the group's considerable success in recruiting a popular following, via the MC5's music and youth culture propagandizing, which imbued the WPP's leadership with a dangerous "we can get away with anything" attitude; (3) the organizational abilities of the group's leadership, which allowed them, through such means as the underground press and other organizing, to remain well-informed concerning national trends in the Movement—and also made them susceptible to the allure of militant political organizing after the Chicago riots; and (4) the U.S. government's dedication to prosecuting and jailing the group's leadership, which provided all the proof the WPP needed that its self-created myth of revolutionary vangardism had a basis in reality.

How real were the White Panthers' revolutionary aspirations? The answer depends upon one's definition of "revolutionary." If judged by the standards of the time, the much-envied Che Guevara model of armed revolt, the WPP, with the possible exception of Plamondon, failed to live up to the White Panther Myth of Movement radicalism. In the final analysis, much of the White Panther message was confined to Yippie-like posturing. However, the *cultural* assault formulated by Sinclair and carried out by the WPP—the national propaganda campaign involving alternative newspapers, rock music records, and live shows—had very real revolutionary potential (which, more than any other factor, may explain why Sinclair was repeatedly denied bond). Prior to Sinclair's imprisonment and the departure of the MC5, the White Panthers possessed both the means and the message to radicalize millions of youthful baby boomers.

Did the WPP have a strategy beyond blowing young peoples' minds? Or was its main goal merely radicalizing youth and, like the Yippies, waiting for Armageddon to trigger "action in the streets"? Sinclair admits that at the time he possessed "a vision of instantaneous, violent, and apocalyptic change."[80] However, in the turbulent period between 1968 and 1971, such visions were not uncommon, both within the Movement and among the police, FBI, and Justice Department. The White Panther Party's strategy began with a commitment to turn on as many young people as possible to all facets of the new counterculture lifestyle, including its political implications (such as the likelihood of police reaction/repression and how to fight back). From here, the WPP sought to further politicize the counterculture by injecting political content—the doctrines and messages of radical groups such as the Black Panthers and the Yippies—into their avant-garde, rock and roll–inspired message. And by adopting a political framework that was, in Sinclair's words, "looser and more far out"[81] than that of their more doctrinaire contemporaries in the New Left, the White Panthers believed they could reach the millions of disaffected youth who may not have otherwise responded to a radical *political* message. For Sinclair, the recruitment of this large and growing segment of the population was a prerequisite for achieving a genuine mass revolution in the United States.

The fact that the utopian vision of Sinclair's White Panthers may appear maniacal or largely unfulfilled more than three decades later does not denigrate its significance. As Theodore Roszak states, the counterculture in America during the Sixties had few domestic historical models of successful leftist rebellion and organization to draw upon, as opposed to their European peers. American counterculture radicals, he adds, assumed positions that were "more flexible, more experimental, and . . . more seemingly bizarre" than any of their historical predecessors.[82] By declaring that rock music, marijuana use, and "fucking in the streets" would bring about revolution, the White Panthers introduced a new chapter in American radical utopianism. They took a pre-rock model of beatnik hedonism, added LSD, marijuana, and high-energy electric music, and concluded that the act of liberating young people from traditional societal inhibitions would bring about a new culture.

The White Panther saga contains many ironies. None of these is greater than the fact that a group of counterculture "freaks," who, in search of radical certification, created a largely fictional White Panther Myth—only to end up being portrayed by the Nixon administration as the epitome of a domestic national security threat and embroiled in a landmark constitutional case. It is hard to disagree with Sinclair's reflective assessment: "The Government . . . should have been *paying* us for what we were doing!"[83]

NOTES

1. For a more detailed history of the White Panthers, as well as the Nixon administration's focus on the group as part of a complex legal strategy to obtain expanded "national security" wiretapping authority, see the author's Ph.D. dissertation: *Wiretapping and National Security: Nixon, the Mitchell Doctrine, and the White Panthers* (Ann Arbor, Mich.: University Microfilms, 1995) [hereafter cited as "Hale, *Wiretapping and National Security*"].

2. FBI memorandum, R. L. Shackelford to C. D. Brennan, 8 October 1970, 62-112678-125.

3. *Detroit News*, 2 May 1967, 18-A.

4. Todd Gitlin, *The Sixties: Years of Hope, Days of Rage* (New York: Bantam Books, 1987), 229, 380–82.

5. The information concerning John and Leni Sinclair's early lives through the Artists' Workshop period comes primarily from the following sources: John Sinclair, *Guitar Army: Street Writings/Prison Writings* (New York; Douglas, 1972), 7–9, 56–58, and 188–200; John and Leni Sinclair Papers, Michigan Historical Collections, Bentley Historical Library, University of Michigan [hereafter cited as "JLS"]; Leni Sinclair personal interview, 21 and 23 July 1992, Detroit; Bret Eynon, "John Sinclair: Hipster," unpublished biography, 21 November 1977, Hunter College, American Social History Project, 9–18, located at the Michigan Historical Collections, Bentley Historical Library, University of Michigan, "Contemporary History Project Papers [hereafter cited as "ASHP Interviews"]: John Sinclair," box 1, topical file: John Sinclair [hereafter cited as "ASHP-Sinclair Biography"]; and John Sinclair interview with Bret Eynon, 1977, ASHP Interviews, box 239-J [hereafter cited as "ASHP-Sinclair Interview"]. Bret Eynon's work with the American Social History Project in Ann Arbor during the late Seventies resulted in extremely thorough oral history documentation of the White Panthers (and other Movement participants). I am grateful to him for allowing access to these documents.

6. Sinclair, *Guitar Army*, 185; ASHP-Sinclair Interview, 44; John Sinclair, "Musical Memoir," [unpublished article in author's possession], 1991.

7. ASHP-Sinclair Interview, 18; Norman Mailer, *The White Negro* (San Francisco: City Lights, 1957).

8. The Leni Sinclair Collection (in her possession, New Orleans). Her enormous collection of photographs, which documents the evolution of Detroit's beatnik and counterculture communities during the Sixties, is available for research and commercial use.

9. The internationally known author and National Public Radio commentator Andre Codrescu frequented the Artists' Workshop as a student at WSU in the mid-Sixties.

10. Sinclair, *Guitar Army*, 56–58, 188–91; Leni Sinclair personal interview, 21 July 1992, Detroit.

11. ASHP-Sinclair Interview, 6–7.

12. Leni Sinclair personal interview, 21 July 1992, Detroit, Michigan; Sinclair, *Guitar Army*, 191–92.

13. In a city that was 35 percent black, only 5 percent of police were African-American. Two-thirds of the police were from blue-collar families. Training in the handling of modern urban problems was lacking, and the end result was very poor police-community relations. See the following: Dan Georgakas and Marvin Surkin, *Detroit: I Do Mind Dying: A Study in Urban Revolution* (New York: St. Martin's Press, 1975), 105, 186–87; Peter K. Eisinger, *The Politics of Displacement: Racial and Ethnic Transition in Three American Cities* (New York: Academic Press, 1980), 57; James A. Geschwender, *Class, Race, and Worker Insurgency: The League of Revolutionary Black Workers* (Cambridge: Cambridge University Press, 1977), 18, 25, 58–64; and Sidney Fine, *Violence in the Model City: The Cavanagh Administration, Race Relations, and the Detroit Riot of 1967* (Ann Arbor: University Of Michigan Press, 1989), 95.

14. Frank Donner, *Protectors of Privilege: Red Squads and Police Repression in Urban America* (Berkeley: University of California Press, 1990), 53–58, 290–95.

15. *Benkert et al. v. Michigan State Police et al.*, No. 74-023-934-AZ (Wayne County Circuit Court, Michigan). The John and Leni Sinclair "Red Squad Files" [hereafter cited as "Sinclair Red Squad Files"], obtained via the case's "disbursement program" (and graciously made available to the author), contain hundreds of pages of documents spanning the years 1964 through 1974. See *Detroit Free Press Magazine*, 4 November 1990, 8–10, 16–21; and *Detroit Free Press*, 14 September 1990, 20.

16. Sinclair Red Squad Files. The Detroit Police "setup" involved a friend of Sinclair's from Jackson, Michigan, who had been arrested on drug dealing charges. In return for a reduced prison sentence, the friend-turned-informer arranged to purchase marijuana from Sinclair and a friend in a sting operation orchestrated by the Detroit Police. See also Sinclair, *Guitar Army*, 189–90.

17. ASHP-Sinclair Interview, 19–20; *Detroit Free Press*, 18 August 1965, 3.

18. ASHP-Sinclair Interview, 18–19.

19. Donovan's original studio version of "The Fat Angel" appeared on his 1966 album *Sunshine Superman* (Epic BN-26217). Subsequent live cover versions of the song have appeared on Jefferson Airplane compilations, including the 1987 release *2400 Fulton Street* (RCA C-214830).

20. The Artists' Workshop existed for a time within the larger TLE collective. However, by late 1967 the Artists' Workshop closed and the group's energies focused almost exclusively on the TLE organization.

21. ASHP-Sinclair Interview, 19–20.

22. Kathleen Stocking, "A Personal Remembrance: Ann Arbor's Famous Radicals, Then and Now," *Monthly Detroit* 5 (February 1992): 78 [hereafter cited as "Stocking, A Personal Remembrance"].

23. Genie Parker interview with Bret Eynon, 1977, ASHP Interviews, box 239-J [hereafter cited as "ASHP-Genie Plamondon Interview"].

24. *Goldmine*, 17 April 1992, 16–22; *Rolling Stone*, no. 25, (4 January 1969): 7; see also no. 632, (11 June 1992): 35–36.

25. Wayne Kramer interview, published in the online magazine *Addicted To Noise (ATN)*, issue 1.02, parts I–IV, February 1995, URL address: http://www.addict.com/issues/1.02/Features/MC5/Wayne_Kramer; [hereafter cited as "Kramer ATN Interview"]; *Goldmine*, 17 April 1992, 16–22.

26. Kramer ATN Interview.

27. *Detroit News*, 1 May 1967, A-1; see also 2 May 1967, 18-A.

28. Sinclair, *Guitar Army*, 25–27.

29. Ed Sanders telephone interview with author, 10 May 1998.

30. *Detroit News*, 27 April 1967, 17-C.

31. Sinclair Red Squad Files, Detroit Police Department, Detective Division, Narcotics Bureau, Arrest Report, 27 January 1967; Leni Sinclair interview with author, 23 July 1992, Detroit.

32. It was also during this period that John and Leni, who had lived together since 1965, decided to get married. At the time, Leni was pregnant with Sunny, their first child.

33. ASHP-Sinclair Biography, 48.

34. Eve Silberman, "The Hill Street Radicals," *Ann Arbor Observer*, May 1991, 45–53.

35. Ken Kelley interview with Bret Eynon, 1977, Hunter College, New York, American Social History Project, 3, located at the Michigan Historical Collections, Bentley Historical Library, University of Michigan, ASHP Interviews, box 239-J; Milton "Skip" Taube interview with Bret Eynon, 1977, Hunter College, New York, American Social History Project, 14, located at the Michigan Historical Collections, Bentley Historical Library, University of Michigan, ASHP Interviews, box 239-J.

36. ASHP-Sinclair Biography, 48–49.

37. Ken Kelley interview, published in the online magazine *Addicted To Noise (ATN)*, issue

1.02, page 2, February 1995, URL address: http://www.addict.com/issues/1.02/Features/MC5/Kick_Out_The_Jams/.

38. Buffalo Springfield's "For What It's Worth" (a hit single), appeared on their 1967 debut album, *Buffalo Springfield* (Atco SD-33-200-A).

39. Sinclair, *Guitar Army*, 307–08.

40. ASHP-Sinclair Biography, 50–51; Sinclair, *Guitar Army*, 73–95.

41. Ibid., 86.

42. Ibid., 74.

43. ASHP-Sinclair Interview, 41–42.

44. Sinclair had also been deeply moved by a 1968 Huey Newton interview, in which the Black Panther leader mentioned that whites should support the BPP by organizing their own revolutionary cadres. Genie Plamondon recalls that on John's recommendation, she took this newspaper article to Pun in prison. See ASHP-Genie Plamondon Interview, 9; and ASHP-Sinclair Biography, 57.

45. Sinclair, *Guitar Army*, 105.

46. Ibid., 101.

47. Ibid., 116.

48. Quoted in Silberman, "The Hill Street Radicals," 49.

49. Joel Whitburn, *Top Pop Artists and Singles, 1955–1978* (Menomonee Falls, Wis.: Record Research, 1979), 277; *Goldmine*, 17 April 1992, 16–22.

50. Sinclair, *Guitar Army*, 125.

51. Michael Schumacher, *Dharma Lion: A Critical Biography of Allen Ginsberg* (New York: St. Martin's Press, 1992), 541.

52. Gitlin, *The Sixties*, 342–45.

53. For press coverage of the Valler bombings in 1968, see *Detroit News*, 2 September, 1-A; 10 September, 1-A; 12 September, 17-A; 20 September, 1-A; 30 September, 1-A; 15 October, 3-A; 12 November, 1-A and 18-A; 20 November, 2-A; 22 November, 4-A; 24 November, 2-A; and 27 November, 3-B.

54. *Fifth Estate*, 31 October—13 November, 1968.

55. Sinclair, *Guitar Army*, 147–53.

56. Ibid., 48.

57. Ibid., 42.

58. Ibid., 98–100, 109–11.

59. SAC, New York to Hoover, 31 December, 1968, 62-112678-2. This document, as well as the hundreds of additional pages of WPP materials the author obtained via the Freedom of Information Act (FOIA), have not been released in their entirety, thanks to two of the FBI's widely abused FOIA exemptions under Title 5 of the U.S. Code: section 552, subsections (b)-7-c and (b)-7-d. The author's appeal was successful, but at press time the documents had not yet been released, allegedly due to FOIA "backlogs."

60. Hoover to SAC, Detroit, 25 June, 1969, 62-112678-22; SAC, Detroit to Hoover, 21 May, 1969, 62-112678-14.

61. Quoted in Sinclair, *Guitar Army*, 169.

62. Considerable documentary evidence exists to support the conclusion that Sinclair's inclusion in the CIA conspiracy indictment was bogus—a result of FBI pressure on David Valler to "revise" his sworn affidavits vis-à-vis Sinclair's level of involvement. See Hale, *Wiretapping and National Security*, 407–11.

63. This was confirmed in a series of interviews between the author and the former Detroit U.S. Attorney Robert Grace, 20 July, 1992 and 1 April, 1993, Ann Arbor, Mich.

64. *Detroit Free Press*, 5 May, 1970, 1; Stocking, "A Personal Remembrance," 81.

65. Quoted in *Argus* 2, no. 4 (May 23, 1970).

66. An estimated fifteen to twenty fully operational WPP chapters, and up to fifty "poten-

tial tribes," existed across the United States and in Europe. This estimate is based on three sources: (1) FBI Report, 23 October, 1970, "RE: White Panther Party (WPP) National Convention September 23–25, 1970," 22–23, Sinclair Red Squad Files; (2) various lists of WPP chapters, circa 1970–71, located in JLSP, box 17, folder 31, "Chapters"; and (3) ASHP-Genie Plamondon Interview, 20. For a fascinating account of communal life and struggle inside the Chicago regional and Ann Arbor chapters and the perspective of a veteran female member, see Leslie Brody, *Red Star Sister: Between Madness and Utopia* (St. Paul: Hungry Mind Press, 1998).

67. Throughout the first half of 1970, a number of discussions were held between WPP and YIP leaders concerning a possible merger. However, a formal YIP-WPP merger was never consummated. At one point in the discussions, David Sinclair expressed his frustrations as follows: ". . . 'merger' is not a correct term in the first place, because you can't really have a merger between a political party and an image. . . . The fact is there are fundamental differences between ourselves and our politics and those of Abbie [Hoffman] and Jerry [Rubin] and their 'followers'" ("Report to the Chairman on the Central Committee Meeting of 27 February 1970, Prepared by Chief of Staff," 27 February, 1970, JLSP, box 17, folder 21, "WPP Ideology").

68. Kunstler's involvement in the White Panther case is summarized in William M. Kunstler (with Sheila Isenberg), *My Life as a Radical Lawyer* (New York: Birch Lane Press, 1994), 205–10.

69. *Sun/Dance*, 4 July, 1970.

70. See, for example, Paul Cowan et al., *State Secrets: Police Surveillance in America* (New York: Holt, Rineholt, and Winston, 1974), 59–76; Ward Churchill and Jim Vander Wall, *Agents of Repression: The FBI's Secret Wars against the Black Panther Party and the American Indian Movement* (Boston: South End Press, 1988), 47–48, 65–77; Donner, *The Age of Surveillance*, 132–38; and Ward Churchill and Jim Vander Wall, *The COINTELPRO Papers: Documents from the FBI's Secret Wars against Dissent in the United States* (Boston: South End Press, 1990), 139–40, 222–26.

71. Marnell arrived at the WPP commune during the summer of 1970 and soon exhibited classic agent provocateur behavior. Claiming to have had combat experience in Vietnam, he conducted regular "armed self-defense" classes with WPP members. He shunned cameras and would not allow his name to appear in any WPP publications. After being ousted by the WPP, Marnell attempted to set up the attorney Leonard Weinglass with conspiratorial plans to break Sinclair out of prison. See the author's personal interview with Genie Plamondon, 31 March, 1993, Detroit; and author's telephone interview with Weinglass, 29 November, 1992.

72. *Detroit Free Press*, 24 July, 1970, 1; *Detroit News*, 24 July, 1970, 3-A.

73. According to the FBI report, the materials found in the group's possession included a detailed address list of underground contacts, floor plans of a bank in northern Michigan, and a letter advocating the kidnapping of Gerald Ford and/or Spiro Agnew for political ransom. The latter document was actually an anonymous letter sent *to* the Detroit WPP chapter—another FBI COINTELPRO tactic commonly employed against radical groups. See Hale, *Wiretapping and National Security*, 523–26.

74. FBI Report "Re: Plamondon," 3 September, 1970.

75. *New York Times*, 28 November, 1970, 13; Mark Sabljak and Martin H. Greenberg, *Most Wanted: A History of the FBI's Ten Most Wanted List* (New York: Bonanza Books, 1990), 179–81.

76. Hoover to Ford, 25 September, 1970, 62-112678-102, located in the Gerald R. Ford Congressional Papers, Ford Presidential Library, University of Michigan, Ann Arbor, box D-102, folder "Radicals/White Panthers/Protest."

77. U.S. Senate Committee on the Judiciary, Subcommittee to Investigate the Administration of the Internal Security Act and Other Internal Security Laws, *Extent of Subversion in the "New Left,"* testimony of Clifford A. Murray and Richard M. Schave, part 8, 25 September 1970, 91st Cong., 2d Sess. (Washington, D.C.: U.S. Government Printing Office, 1971), 1221–22.

78. Report, SAC, Detroit to Hoover, 17 September 1969, 62–112678–29; "CIA

Memorandum for the FBI Re: White Panther Party," 2 June, 1970, 62-112678-59; Department of State "Airgram," from American Consul in Montreal, Canada to the U.S. Department of State, June 11, 1970, 62-112678 [unnumbered].

79. For a detailed history of the *Keith* case (407 U.S. 297) and the evolution of the Mitchell Doctrine, see Hale, *Wiretapping and National Security*; see also Arthur Kinoy, *Rights on Trial: The Odyssey of a People's Lawyer* (Cambridge, Mass.: Harvard University Press, 1983), 1–38.

80. ASHP-Sinclair Biography, 62.

81. ASHP-Sinclair Interview, 40.

82. Theodore Roszak, *The Making of a Counter Culture: Reflections on a Technocratic Society and its Youthful Opposition* (Berkeley: University of California Press, 1995 [1969]), 4.

83. Quoted in Sinclair, *Guitar Army*, 349.

Section Three
Identity

Introduction

The plethora of names associated with those who participated in the counter-culture—hippies, freaks, Flower Children, "urban guerrillas," "orphans of Amerikkka"—underscores the degree to which Sixties cultural radicals had a revolving-door approach to identity, appropriating and shedding roles and personas at a dizzying pace. While the Beat Generation often identified with the black underclass, and particularly with dissident black jazz musicians, the countercultural wave of the 1960s cast a much wider net in the search for "otherized," marginalized groups to mimic with the view of crafting an authentic oppositional identity.

As Phil Deloria explains in his essay "Counterculture Indians and the New Age," Native Americans were a major cultural fount for white counterculturists seeking to craft a 'tribal' identity. In this respect, the Sixties counterculture situated itself within a long American tradition of whites "playing Indian." But this experiment in appropriation only underscored the racial tensions, stereotypes, and contradictions within the predominantly white movement. The crucible of countercultural identity is further plumbed in Lauren Onkey's essay "Voodoo Child: Jimi Hendrix and the Politics of Race in the Sixties." Hendrix, who held a decidedly liminal status as a black rock legend with an overwhelmingly white following, faced extraordinary obstacles in attempting to forge a hybrid racial identity within a counterculture that had supposedly transcended conventional stereotypes. Black militants pressed him to be more "authentically" black, while his white hip following seemed to want him to somehow "transcend race." Lastly, Robert McRuer in his essay "Gay Gatherings: Reimagining the Counterculture," makes it apparent that the declaration of independence at Stonewall in 1969 was only the opening gong in a protracted process of gay identity formation. The initial phase of differentiation, in which gay men and women sequestered themselves from the core straight society in an expressly countercultural stance, evolved into a community-building process that fortified the gay community for the crises it would face in the 1980s. All told, their methodology owed much to the countercultural style of establishing flamboyantly liberated spaces in the urban milieu.

Six

Counterculture Indians and the New Age

Philip Deloria

I stood at the entrance to the Beverly Hills Hotel. The warm wind
from the south rippled like clean silk on my skin. The air smelled like
honeysuckle and I took a deep breath.

Every book is rewritten by the reader. If you read a book, it becomes
your personal teacher. You bring to it what you are.

—*Lynn Andrews,* Flight of the Seventh Moon: The Teaching
of the Shields *(1984)*[1]

In 1971, a small but dedicated commune lay in the woods outside a college
town in the Pacific Northwest. On occasion, my parents would leave for a long
weekend, depositing my brother and me with the friends who helped run it.
Located on an old farm, the commune had several residents living in the rus-
tic main house and a shifting array of folk wandering in for meals or com-
panionship. In the trees to the south, for instance, a friendly young man had
strung together twenty extension cords to power a small circular saw, the only
electrical tool he would use to build an octagonal house. Across the nearby
stream and up a small hill lay the Indian camp, a set of three Plains tipis that
housed a reassembled "family" of non-Indians who eked out a living making
Aleut-modeled soapstone carvings.

I liked to visit the Indian camp, where people in headbands, fringed leather jackets, and moccasins padded quietly about, calling each other names I cannot quite recall but that had a kind of faux Indian ring—Rainbow, maybe, or Green Wood—that I would later associate with suburban tract developments. The tipis were pleasant enough, although they tended to leak when it rained. Perhaps the "Indians" had been mistaken in choosing the Plains tents, so inappropriate to the wet climate, over the stately and comfortable cedar-log Indian homes one learned about in the local schools (not to mention the clapboard and shingle homes that housed contemporary people on the nearby reservation). But the tipis were inexpensive and easy to set up and that was important on a small communal housing budget. More significantly, they carried a full cargo of symbolic value. Tipis shouted "Indian," and all that it entailed, in a way that Northwest coast log homes, even those blessed with Indian totem poles, never could.

Heirs of the white middle class of the 1950s, the communalists worked hard to counteract their parents' America, perceived in terms of consumptive excess, alienated individualism, immoral authority, and capitalism red in tooth and claw. As an antidote, they promoted community, and at least some of them thought it might be found in an Indianness imagined around notions of social harmony. The commune, safe to say, was one of hundreds of places in which counterculture rebels turned to Indians to think about a better way of living together. New Mexico's famous New Buffalo Commune, for example, was rife with tipis. Explaining its name, longtime member George Robinson set up a chronology of Indian-white ethnic succession that echoed that of Lewis Henry Morgan and made communalists heirs, not to the 1950s but to nineteenth-century Indians. "The buffalo was the provider for the Plains tribes," observed Robinson. "This [commune] is the new buffalo." Ironically, though the members adopted a Plains Indian "ancestry," they looked for actual subsistence not to the bison but to the corn-beans-squash combination favored by more sedentary native people.

The communalists at New Buffalo and at similar communes across the United States, according to a breathless observer, William Hedgepeth, admired "the Indian's feeling of non-acquisitive contentment, his lack of dog-eat-dog Americanized drive, and his tribal sense of sharing and group ritual." Hedgepeth was one of a legion of journalists who hopped from commune to commune, relaying often prurient tales of drugs, free love, and communal euphoria to a curious public. Many communalists wanted to publicize their example, and they offered such writers compelling performances of "tribal" lifestyles. When Hedgepeth left New Buffalo for the nearby Lorian community, for example, he found fifteen communalists sitting around a campfire near several tipis: "[The] males clap or slap at their chests and yell 'Yi Yi Yi Yi Yi,' Indian-style, real loud with each voice dropping out when a beer can or joint is passed."[2]

Despite such gestures, most communes disintegrated quickly under the pressures of individual wants and wills. Even as an adolescent, I could easily see the fissures in the communal facade. Preparing for the "Princess and the Frog" guitar duo concert, for example, someone swept the floors of the main house but did not feel like picking up the enormous dustpile. No one else did either, so we laid a piece of tar paper over it and did not mention the peculiar mound in the living room. And it was one thing to think in the abstract about the "warmth of sharing"; a very different thing to think about sharing the same unwashed cereal bowl, spoon, and bottom-of-the-bowl milk with ten other people.

Whenever white Americans have confronted crises of identity, some of them have inevitably turned to Indians. What might it mean to be not-British? The revolutionaries found a compelling array of ideas in Indianness. What did it mean to be American? What did it mean to be modern? To be authentic? Using furs and feathers, headbands and hair, generations of white Americans have, at many levels and with varying degrees of intent, made meanings, and with them, identities. In the world of the communalists, however, meaning itself was often up for grabs. Driven by continuing social transformations—the baby boom, civil rights struggles, consumer culture, the engagement in Vietnam—older, cold war quests for personal brands of authentic experience gave way to increasing doubts about the existence of God, authenticity, or reality itself. In the 1960s and early 1970s, many Americans turned to a new question: What was the meaning of meaning? Suppose truth had simply dried up and blown away in the blasting wind of nuclear anxiety, cultural relativism, and psychological self-reflexiveness? What if, as the Beatles had suggested, the world was like Strawberry Fields, a mystical, drug-hazy place where "nothing [was] real"?[3]

Academic theorists have since devised a vocabulary to describe such skepticism toward meaning. Among that vocabulary, one word—"postmodern"—has come to serve as a popular, generic shorthand, describing a complicated social world, an equally complex set of intellectual debates, and the interaction between the varied branches of each. That's asking one word to do a great deal of work, and, not surprisingly, postmodernism has proved extraordinarily slippery, its varied definitions emerging from phenomena as diverse as architecture, linguistic theory, philosophy, aesthetics, popular culture, social relations, and global economics.[4]

Why should there be any distinction between the class-bound modernist high culture of the gallery/museum and the vulgar advertisements of mass consumer culture? If language was an arbitrary system of signs, was there any reason to think that the realities it framed were not, in some measure, *created* by the language itself? Why not chop up those signs and rearrange them into a new reality? Was it legitimate to impose the dichotomous worldview of Western philosophy on the rest of the planet? Why was the United States so insistent about global military hegemony? These were questions for oppositional actors ranging from Andy Warhol to Stokely Carmichael to the communalists at New Buffalo. Likewise, they have also been questions for a host of intellectual critics seeking to understand and describe a culture in which each was also an actor. In 1972, for example, the theorist Fredric Jameson noted the connections, suggesting "a profound consonance between linguistics as a method and that systematized and disembodied nightmare which is our culture today."[5] At the center of this complicated tangle of ideas and social transformations are three sensibilities that necessarily underpin this essay: a crisis of meaning and a concomitant emphasis on the powers of interpretation, a sustained questioning of the idea of foundational truth, and an inclination to fragment symbols and statements and to reassemble them in creative, if sometimes random, pastiche.

What concern me even more, however, are the ways in which a contradictory notion of Indianness, so central to American quests for identities, changed shape yet again in the context of these postmodern crises of meaning. On the one hand, the refigurings of Indianness produced by the counterculture and the New Age reflect a unique historical moment. On the other hand, the diverse practices we often subsume under the word "postmodern" may well reflect the familiar toying with meaning and identity that may be seen in a long tradition of Indian play.

Playing Indian serves as an ultimate tool for grabbing hold of such contradictions, and it has been constantly reimagined and materialized when Americans desire to have their cake and eat it too. "Indians" could be both civilized and indigenous. They could critique modernity and yet reap its benefits. They could revel in the creative pleasure of liberated meanings while still grasping for something fundamentally American. It should come as no surprise that the young men and women of the 1960s and 1970s—bent on destroying an orthodoxy tightly intertwined with the notion of "truth" and yet desperate for truth itself—followed their cultural ancestors in playing Indian to find meaningful identities in a world seemingly out of control. Not only in the communes but in politics, environmentalism, spirituality, and other pursuits, Indianness allowed counterculturists to have their cake and eat it. In these arenas, we can also witness the continued unraveling of the connections between meanings and social realities. And, as usual, these disjunctures became most obvious when white people in Indian costume turned and found themselves face-to-face with native people.

Even in the reformist utopias of the communes something was not quite right, and it had everything to do with the soggy tipi on the hill and the well-used communal milk at the bottom of the cereal bowl. The gap between communal intention and personal experience quickly widened as contradictions between individual freedom and social order turned into conflict. The doubledness of Indian meanings reflected perfectly the contradictory dimensions of communalism. Indians signified social harmony—one thinks of the stereotype of the peaceful native village, people interacting in seamlessly pleasant and ordered ways. These were the well-worn antimodern Indians of Ernest Thompson Seton and John Collier. But Indianness also carried a full complement of countermeanings. Dating back to the Revolution, these meanings were tightly linked to the very different idea of radical individual freedom.

At the same time the communalists sought social stability, they rejected any notion of authority, a precondition to organizing such stability. Authority was "not only immoral, but functionally incompetent" according to the apologist and social critic Paul Goodman. Young people, he said, "are in an historical situation to which anarchism is the only possible response."[6] Communal life, as it turned out, was usually incompatible with anarchy, yet many communes existed to take individual autonomy to its anarchic edge. In place of a social contract that protected individual freedom through agreed-upon social restraints, communes offered a collective commitment to "doing one's own thing." A powerful counterculture mantra, "do your own thing" conflated social order—even social consensus—with authority and rejected both.[7] The communalists used Indianness hoping to establish a particular kind of organic community, political in its exemplary social nature and self-transforming in practice. What many of them found instead was an individualism—represented equally powerfully by Indian names, costumes, and tipis—that became supercharged by the very experience of living collectively.

It should come as no surprise that while many communes toyed with symbolic Indianness, they remained largely disconnected from Indian people. Communalists searched reservations for authenticity and inspiration, but their visits rarely went as well as those made by many hobbyists. Native communities, often unexpectedly socially restrictive, did not accord well with the aggressive individualism of many communes. And native people grew weary of constantly reeducating flighty counterculture seekers. Very few of these encounters satisfied either party. Communalists might have learned something about individualism and social order from Indian people, but most preferred a symbolic life of tipis and buckskins to lessons that might be hard-won and ideologically distasteful. The New Buffalos, for example, called their corn-beans-squash experiment a "Navajo diet," ignoring the nearby Pueblos (who had perfected this agriculture) for more symbolically powerful Indians. Doubly ironic, the real Navajo relied not on buffalo or planting for their food but initially on raiding and trading and, later, on sheep and goats.[8]

Although there were certainly exceptions, communalists tended to value Indian Otherness and its assorted meanings more than they did real native people. Nor were they alone. Communal tipis pointed to a broad cultural ethos emphasizing the power of symbolic work over actual labor. When Andy Warhol presented a Campbell's Soup label as art, he suggested that the manipulation of symbols had replaced the work of painting and sculpture. When composer John Cage placed radios on the stage and randomly turned the dials, he did the same, offering up a chance pastiche of sound in place of a practiced performance. Multinational bankers, advertising designers, politicians, and many others followed similar paths. In this kind of world, the meanings of Indianness drifted away from actual Indians more quickly and thoroughly than ever.[9]

This dissipation of meaning became particularly clear when Indians showed up in political discourse. Communalism and New Left politics occupied very different wings of the counterculture, but they shared similar tendencies to play with the limits of meaning. In politics, Indianness carried special resonance for antiwar protesters, and it appeared frequently in the collages of symbols they cobbled together with often creative abandon.[10] The story of nineteenth-century native resistance provided a home-grown model for opposition to the American military imperialism that protesters saw in Vietnam. A popular series of posters, for example, paid tribute to Sitting Bull, Geronimo, and Red Cloud, imagined forerunners of the contemporary protest movement. For Mitchell Goodman, the spirit of impending revolution was akin to that of "primitive" culture. "Blacks, Vietnamese, Indians," Goodman observed. "From them the young in America have something to learn—and they know it. The young are a *class*, in the neo-Marxian sense—abused, processed, exploited—and they have come to see their common interest. But more important, they are a primitive tribe." And after breaking the LSD guru Timothy Leary out of jail, the would-be warriors of the Weather Underground announced that "LSD and grass, like the herbs and cactus and mushrooms of the American Indians, will help us make a future world where it will be possible to live in peace."[11] When it came to the war, the semantic and semiotic linkages could hardly have been more appropriate. Racially "red" Indians matched up well with the ideologically "red" Vietcong, and both joined "youth" as pure, antimodern primitives. Guerrilla warfare, practiced to

"Pow-Wow—A Gathering of the Tribes for a Human Be-In," 14 January 1967, Golden Gate Park, San Francisco. This poster by Rick Griffin helped launch his career designing psychedelic dance concert posters. The guitar-playing Indian, surrounded by the names of counterculture luminaries, demonstrated the movement's tendency to symbolize their rebellion by means of an imagined traditional American Indian "tribal" society. Courtesy of Stewart Brand.

great effect by the Vietnamese and advocated domestically by some radicals, had its parallels in the ambushes and raids of Red Cloud, Geronimo and others—at least as they were half-imagined and half-remembered from generic western films.

One of the most popular antiwar films of the time was anything but generic, and it used Indianness to model a whimsical postmodern style of resistance and to launch a critique of American military adventurism. In *Little Big Man* (1970), a white-Indian cross-dressing Dustin Hoffman wanders through the imperial conquest of the West, constantly crossing and breaking down boundaries of race, gender, and nation. As a white pioneer boy, he is adopted by the Cheyenne. As a Cheyenne, he is first "adopted" and later saved by the vainglorious General George Custer. Flexible boundary hoppers with multiple modes and meanings, the Indians are funny, smart, and sexy. Their playfully serious postmodern nature stands in direct contrast to Custer and his army, who die from rigidity and imperial arrogance at the Little Big Horn. Audiences had little trouble figuring out with whom they were to identify.[12]

The notion of an oppositional political culture linked to Indianness attracted young Americans, many of whom had been schooled on the iconic nationalism of the Boston Tea Party.[13] Those original rebels had used Indianness to shift the location of their identities from Britain to America. Since the early twentieth century, people had put on Indian clothes to search for authenticity in a modern America more alienating than welcoming. Now, countercultural rebels became Indian to move their identities *away* from Americanness altogether, to leap outside national boundaries, gesture at repudiating the nation, and offer what seemed a clear-eyed political critique. Donning the symbols of the Indian—the long hair so visible in the poster image of Geronimo and maybe a bandanna headband to go with it—signified that one's sympathies lay with both the past and the present objects of American foreign policy. To play Indian was to become vicariously a victim of United States imperialism. For those confronting National Guardsmen and Army Reserves in the streets, such a position inevitably carried a powerful emotional charge.[14]

Yet, if being Indian offered one an identity as a critic of empire, that position was hardly uncomplicated. Indianness may have lain outside the United States' social boundaries when it came to the exercise of imperial power, but it was also at the very heart of the American identities inherited by the predominantly white, middle-class antiwar protesters. Playing Indian replicated the contradictory tensions established by the Revolution. An interior Indianness that signified national identity clashed with an exterior Indianness linked with the armed struggle to control the continent. The only significant

When in Spring 1969 Berkeley's politicized countercultural community seized a vacant lot from the University of California and proceeded to convert it into a "People's Park," civil authorities retaliated by calling in the police and the state highway patrol. Soon afterward, Governor Ronald Reagan activated the National Guard and dispatched them along with three battalions of the 49th Infantry Brigade into "Berzerkely." Frank Bardacke's manifesto of defiance prominently featured the Apache warrior Geronimo as a long-haired sign of imperial victimization and stalwart resistance, while it textually linked white counterculturists to the long since vanquished Coastanoan Indians of the Bay Area. Courtesy of Frank J. Bardacke.

point of difference was the inversion that marked modernity: nineteenth-century savages had become authentic twentieth-century victims and critics.

Real Indian people, many of whom were fighting as American soldiers in Vietnam, complicated the picture still further. The contradictions between real and imagined Indians have always pointed to other contradictions bound up within the contours of Indian Otherness itself. One could read the Geronimo poster, for example, in terms that were not oppositional but patriotic. Indianness represented native, "American" martial skill as well as it reflected the resistance of national enemies. Indeed, such an interpretation was likely among native people, for whom patriotism and military service have been, and continue to be, highly valued.[15]

Still other Indian people challenged the United States politically themselves, not only on the war but on native civil rights issues as well. Again, the connections were easily made. "When I walk down the streets of Saigon," observed the Tuscarora activist Wallace "Mad Bear" Anderson, "those people look like my brothers and sisters." With white radicals appropriating Indian symbols and native people reinterpreting those symbols and launching protests of their own, Indianness became a potent political meeting ground. White antiwar political organizers who sought to harness Indianness often found themselves edging along the periphery of a burgeoning Red Power movement. White radicals helped with logistical details of food and transportation during the "Indians of All Nations" seizure of Alcatraz Island, for example, and Indian resistance movements appealed to all sorts of non-Indian sympathizers. The actor Marlon Brando reflected that appeal when he sent Shasheen Little Feather to refuse his 1973 Academy Award with a Red Power speech attacking the film industry's portrayals of native people. Brando, she said (hoping to counter charges of trendiness and yet pointing in exactly that direction), had been "a friend of the American Indian long before it was fashionable to pile on the turquoise and the feathers." Eager non-Indians showed up at fishing protests, the Trail of Broken Treaties caravan to Washington, D.C., and, of course, Wounded Knee (where Brando himself thought he could be of most use). By the same token, Indian leaders sometimes linked hands with other political movements in gestures of solidarity. In 1968, for example, Indians participated in the Poor People's Campaign, a march on Washington planned by the Southern Christian Leadership Conference that included blacks, Latinos, and poor whites.[16]

But just as often as they engaged real Indian people, white radicals joined the communalists in placing their highest premium upon a detached, symbolic Indianness. Different perspectives on rebellion and rights—Red, Black, and Brown Power, antiwar, and women's liberation movements, for example—produced sets of symbols that, for all their distinctions, shared similarly mobile meanings. Red Power drew ideological weight from the far more visible Black Power movement. Indeed, the habit of placing any number of themes with the word—peace power, love power, people power—points to a certain migratory tendency on the part of the signs of revolt. Sixties rebellion rested, in large part, on a politics of symbol, pastiche, and performance. Influenced by media saturation and the co-optative codes of fashion, the emblems of social protest were plucked from different worlds and reassembled in a gumbo of new political meaning. That headband might mean Geronimo, but it also meant Che Guevara and Stokely Carmichael. Indeed, it meant many things, depending on its context and its interpreters. Sacred pipes, Black Power fists, Aztlan eagles, peace signs, Hell's Angels, beers and joints, Peter Max design—everything fed into a whole that signified a hopeful, naive rebellion that often had as much to do with individual expression and fashion as it did with social change.[17]

While, in the 1950s, Indian lore hobbyists had sought personal freedom by leaping across the boundaries of a behaviorially defined notion of culture, by the mid-1960s, symbolic border crossings of culture and race had become so painless that the meanings defined by those boundaries began to disintegrate. With them went a certain kind of social awareness. In 1957, for example, Norman Mailer's celebration of the "White Negro" transgressions of the Beats still carried a sense of the outrageous. The social world worked differently for blacks and whites; everyone knew it and they recognized that difference. Now, however, one might lay claim to the more heavily laden word "nigger" without blinking an eye. Paul Goodman argued that his homosexuality had "made [him] a nigger." Writing as a Yippie named Free, Abbie Hoffman claimed the word for young white activists harassed by police. The California professor Jerry Farber suggested that students themselves were enslaved niggers. Marginalized by antiwar planners, Hoffman and Jerry Rubin complained that they had been treated like niggers. And John Lennon and Yoko Ono would soon pronounce that "woman is the nigger of the world."[18]

Similar dynamics characterized the more positive meanings being attached and detached to Indianness. White radicals sought political power by appropriating and cobbling together meanings that crossed borders of culture and race. In the process, they devalued words like "Indian" and "nigger" and deemphasized the social realities that came with those words. Such attempts to create political solidarity worked to the benefits of whites, but they could have negative political consequences for Indians and African Americans. After all, it was those social realities that underpinned civil rights protests. And if whites claimed and then diluted the very words that described those social worlds, they could only offer in return a "power" that was more linguistic than actual.

This looseness of symbolic meaning, with ideas, statements, and signs chopped up and reassembled in bold antiestablishment collages, pervaded oppositional rhetoric. Indeed, it characterized not only the counterculture but much of American culture itself. Children might continue to dress Indian in Camp Fire and Order of the Arrow groups, but when Scouts turned to crafts work, they also found themselves cutting up magazines and gluing together picture and word collages, the meanings of which were both personal and evasive. In politics and Scout patrols, such pastiches could be read in multiple ways, depending on angle of view and the identity one half-glimpsed when one passed by a mirror. No one owned—or could even lay claim to—long hair and an Indian headband, much less its myriad meanings. So while some counterculture rebels sought to use Indianness to express antiwar sentiments or revolutionary identities, they found that those identities had power only as the symbols crunched together around an ill-defined, culturally centered notion of rebellion. Otherwise, meaning resided with individuals and their interpretations. "Revolution for the hell of it?" asked Hoffman. "Why not? It's all a bunch of phony words anyway. Reality is a subjective experience. It exists in my head."[19]

Hoffman's key notions—an empowered individualism and a flyaway sense of meaning—were not unrelated. As individuals insisted upon the power of their own interpretations of symbols, those symbols began to lose their collective meanings. At the same time, as symbols and signs became increasingly open, individuals found themselves asserting the validity of their right to interpret and to find meaning. While the hobbyists had embraced an open, relativist understanding of culture, oppositional Indian play went further, assuming that not only behavior but also meaning itself could be relativistic.

The world looks different on the far side of the 1960s, for the diverse ambitions of the counterculture did in fact produce significant changes in American society. Nonetheless, the movement often worked most effectively in the realm of cultural gesture. "Expressly political concerns," suggests the historian Peter Clecak, "existed fitfully, even secondarily." And Charles Chatfield observes that "symbolism was used to challenge social and cultural conformity in general. This left the antiwar movement open to extraneous attack, since the contest over the war was waged more on the level of symbols than on issues."[20] As the signs of rebellion—that bandanna headband, for instance—had filled with an array of common revolutionary meanings, the groups that used those signs followed fragmented social agendas. Indianness had a certain heft for many white, middle-class men and some white women, but like Black Power or antiwar protest or feminism, its meanings, uprooted from social realities, could not bring together people separated by fault lines of gender, race, and ideology. Red Power, for example, which sought to refocus Indianness on larger audiences, came eventually to matter more to Indian people than to non-Indians. In building the political movement, young Indians looked to elders and "traditionals," fundamentally altering the ways subsequent native people would construct their identities.

As meanings became liberated from their social moorings, what began to matter most was the relationship between the interpreter and the text being interpreted, be it book, rally, disobedient act, or piece of clothing. In that relationship, individuals found new ways to define personal identities. Perhaps nowhere were the powerful interpretive links between a text and its readers (as opposed to authors and their intentions) so visible as in the counterculture's environmentalist wing, which made its own a speech purportedly given by the Suquamish/Duwamish leader Seattle in 1855. Widely quoted and reproduced, the speech offered an emotionally powerful manifesto for living on the land and a set of instructions for white Americans:

> Every part of this earth is sacred to my people . . . we are part of
> the earth and it is part of us. . . . Whatever befalls the earth, befalls
> the sons of earth. If men spit upon the ground, they spit upon
> themselves. This we know. The Earth does not belong to man.
> Man belongs to the earth. This we know. All things are connected
> like the blood which unites one family. When the last red man has
> vanished from this earth and his memory is only the shadow of a
> cloud moving across the prairie, these shores and forest will still
> hold the spirits of my people. For they love this earth as a new born
> loves its mother's heartbeat. So if we sell you our land, love it as we
> have loved it. Care for it as we have cared for it. We may be brothers after all.[21]

Offered up as the Indian death speech so familiar to nineteenth-century audiences, Seattle gave his blessing and a gentle admonishment to white successors. Yet while the speech offered a classic tale of succession, it also permanently implanted Indians—spiritually at least—in the American landscape. And at the same time it set up distinct Indian and white American epochs, it also linked people together in one "aboriginal," nature-loving family. Like the "vanishing Indian" plays of Jacksonian America, Seattle's words erased contemporary social realities and the complicated and often violent history of Indian land loss. Instead, all people were one, bound by a universal web of blood connections and their relations to the earth. The speech, which pasted together the classic tropes of Indian Americanism, proved one of the most powerful artifacts of the time.

Yet as the words journeyed through American popular culture, jumping from magazine articles to posters to Sierra Club calendars to collective folk wisdom, the fact that Chief Seattle never uttered them fell easily by the wayside. In truth, "Seattle" spoke only for a white screenwriter from Texas, and his moving words were the single highlight of an obscure 1972 television script on pollution produced by the Southern Baptist Convention.[22] What really mattered, however, was not the author but the words themselves and the people who encountered them, interpreted them, and produced meaning and import from their emotionally charged cadences. The text seemed to float suspended above the social world of Indians and whites, environmentalists and screenwriters, generating its own culturally resonant meanings. Those meanings could then be acted out in familiar ways—the tipis at New Buffalo, the Geronimoesque headband, the "Yi Yi Yi Yi Yi" chant, the reassuring purchase of a beautiful calendar.

But Indianness has always been about contradictions, and its uses were hardly confined to this creative, confusing world of free meanings. Indeed, in such a decentered world, many people found themselves searching for something fixed, real, and authentic. Paul Goodman concluded that what really drove the counterculture was a crisis of meaning that was spiritual at base and that "in the end it is religion that constitutes the strength of this generation and not, as I used to think, their morality, political will, and common sense."[23] Playing Indian gave the counterculture the best of both worlds. On the one hand, Indianness—in the form of a headband, a communal tipi, or a speech by Chief Seattle—seemed as open and unfixed as a sign could be. It could mean whatever one wanted it to mean. Such openness had characterized two centuries of playing Indian. On the other hand, and almost alone among a shifting vocabulary of images, Indianness could also be a sign of something unchanging, a first principle. This other kind of Indianness also had a powerful, if often half-conscious, American history.

After World War II, these twinned desires gained power relative to the other, for each proved critical to the construction of identities. If everything was fair game, including Indianness, then desire for something fixed—also represented by "the Indian"—increased proportionately. Seattle's speech, with its mystical evocation of edenic nature and aboriginal Americanness, pointed the way to a particularly spiritual form of Indianness. Likewise, Goodman's revelation came after meeting a young hippie: "He was dressed like an (American) Indian, in fringed buckskin and a headband, with red paint on his face. All his life, he said, he had tried to escape the encompassing evil of our society that was bent on destroying his soul." Although much of the counterculture search for spiritual insight would revolve around hallucinogenic drugs and Eastern mysticism, playing Indian also offered a familiar and powerful path to the reassuring fixity of ultimate enlightenment.[24]

In the 1960s and 1970s, spiritual seekers turned to Sun Bear, Rolling Thunder, and other "medicine people" for guidance in questing after "the Great Spirit." There was nothing pure about these searches. In an oppositional culture, one easily targeted Christianity as part of authoritarian structure and sought to make one's escape. And as we saw in political and communal discourse, the symbols and practices of many countertraditions blurred and overlapped. Hallucinogenic drug use could be knit quite tightly with Plains Indian vision quest rituals, known for the intense experiences that came with their mental and physical deprivations. The 1972 paperback edition of John Neihardt's *Black Elk Speaks*, for example, promised eager seekers an account of a "personal vision that makes an LSD trip pale by comparison," and books like *Lame Deer, Seeker of Visions* by John Fire Lame Deer and *Seven Arrows* by Hyemeyohsts Storm were steady sellers.[25]

Indians reflected spiritual experience beyond representation. Ironically, books and instruction proved the standard means of gaining access to that experience. The hobbyists of the 1950s had used texts, but many had also turned to real Indians. Counterculture spiritualists sought out Indians, to be sure, but, like the communalists, the number of people who actually "studied with" Indian teachers was small relative to the many more who read and interpreted the books and periodicals. Nor was the path always clear for those who engaged Indians. The ambiguities of textual mediation became even more confused when one turned to teachers like Rolling Thunder or Sun Bear. As cultural boundaries opened up, the role of mediator, already difficult to pin down, proved almost impossibly slippery. Non-Indians began taking up permanent Native identities in order to lay claim to the cultural power of Indianness in the white imagination. Likewise, many Native people found empowerment in a white-focused, spiritual mediator's role and they acted accordingly. It quite rapidly became difficult to sort out who was whom along this continuum, and the question of mediators' Indian identity has been fiercely and frequently contested ever since.[26]

Sun Bear offers an instructive example. In the late 1960s, his *Many Smokes* magazine had a small circulation of Indian readers. Sun Bear editorialized on all manner of native issues, from Office of Equal Opportunity policy to the role of claims settlement money in economic development.[27] Yet he was clearly already a mediating figure—his masthead photo showed him playing an Apache on the television show *Death Valley Days*. In the 1970s, however, the nature of Sun Bear's intercultural brokerage changed, and *Many*

Smokes metamorphosed into a full-blown New Age periodical aimed at a much larger, non-Indian audience. In 1986, it changed its name to *Wildfire* and offered up a by-now-familiar montage of articles dealing with Christian theology, crystal magic, spirit channeling, vision questing, land brokering, smudging one's computer, Afghan relief, and natural childbirth. Catalogue goods were always on sale, as were stock offerings for the "Bear Tribe," which, in a 1980s move, became a visible collective through legal incorporation.[28] The Bear Tribe, primarily a collection of non-Indian followers, offered a path to tribal Indianness that relied, not upon spiritual experience, cultural crossing, or accidents of birth, but upon economic exchange. Not surprisingly, many Indians rejected Sun Bear and his enterprise.

Like its counterparts in communalism, politics, and environmentalism, this brand of countercultural spiritualism rarely engaged real Indians, for it was not only unnecessary but inconvenient to do so. Ambivalent people like Sun Bear proved acceptable, for they served not to reveal the lines between Indian and non-Indian but to blur them even further. The most prominent landmark in this ambiguous tradition of texts and mediators may have come in 1968, when Carlos Castaneda published *The Teachings of Don Juan: A Yaqui Way of Knowledge*, a faux encounter with a Yaqui sorcerer whose spiritual insights and desert adventures were presented as "true" ethnography rather than fiction. *The Teachings of Don Juan* became required reading for spiritual seekers, and Castaneda continued to dish out Don Juan's insights in a series of books published throughout the next two decades.[29] Although one heard occasional reports of seekers waiting futilely at grimy downtown bus stations in the Southwest for Don Juan's arrival, most followers were more than content simply to buy the books and discuss them among themselves. Likewise, while many traveled to Harney Peak and Bear Butte, holy places named in other Indian books, they rarely engaged the Lakota or Cheyenne people who also visited these places. Even in a quest for fixed meaning, Indian people were basically irrelevant. Indianness—even when imagined as something essential—could be captured and marketed as a text, largely divorced from Indian oversight and questions of authorship.

The disconnections of the 1960s and 1970s may have reached peak development in the activities of the New Age, a movement for an aging counterculture. Like "counterculture" itself, "New Age" spans an ambiguous time period and serves as a general rubric for a wide range of practices. Although one might point back to the counterculture or to the self-actualization movements of the 1970s, it was not until the early 1980s, with the popular writings of Shirley MacLaine and the noodlely music of Windom Hill recording artists like George Winston and Will Ackerman, that New Age first became visible under that name. Heavily based in self-help and personal development therapies, its proponents await a large-scale change in human consciousness and a utopian era of peace and harmony. In New Age identity quests, one can see the long shadows of the counterculture and of certain strands of postmodernism: increasing reliance on texts and interpretations, runaway individualism within a rhetoric of community, the distancing of native people, and a gaping disjuncture between a cultural realm of serious play and the power dynamics of social conflict. New Age thinking tends to focus on ultimate individual liberation and engagement with a higher power, with little interest in the social world that lies between self and spirit.[30]

Take, for example, the "Church of Gaia/Council of Four Directions," a gathering of spiritual seekers in my hometown who found themselves easy targets for a *New York Times* writer:

> In an ancient rite of American Indians, wisps of smoke rise from
> burning herbs in prayer to Mother Earth and Father Sky, as the
> woman with the pipe intones solemnly, "Creator, we come to you in
> a sacred manner." There were Indian chants of "ho," a song about
> the return of the bison and some reverent words offered for "the red
> nation." All that was missing in this gathering on the second floor
> of an office building over a Boulder pizzeria was an Indian.[31]

When the article was reprinted in Boulder's local paper, Stephen Buhner, one of the church's board members, responded in kind. Emphasizing the pedagogical qualifications of the authors of New Age texts and his own First Amendment rights, Buhner captured the mix of interpretation and self-focus that has characterized many New Age pursuits. "Sun Bear and Ed McGaa," he argued, "[were] given the right to teach traditional Native religious ways by their teachers. That right has never been rescinded." According to Buhner, McGaa's Vietnam combat record and medicine "training" legitimated his text, *Mother Earth Spirituality*, while Sun Bear's role as Medicine Chief of the Bear Tribe Medicine Society (recall its corporate status) made his a worthy voice.[32]

These are, one should note, particularly Western views of the ways in which spiritual knowledge can be understood and transmitted. Even as the Church of Gaia sought Indian spiritual essentials, then, its members disengaged themselves both physically and intellectually from Native people. Adopting the behavioralist dynamic of the hobbyists, Buhner suggested that spiritual insight resulted from a teacher-learner encounter and that it was manifested through a certification process in which one's qualifications might be revoked for cause. Yet in many Native societies, and especially among the

Plains people so beloved by New Age seekers, real spiritual authority comes not so much from tutelage as from spiritual experience itself. Buhner valued Sun Bear and Ed McGaa not for their spiritual experiences but for their compiling of cultural knowledge—texts that could be purchased, interpreted, mastered, and materialized.[33]

What mattered most was Buhner's claim to be able to acquire and practice sacred traditions. He made the claim not in terms of his *own* training or experience but by calling on essential Americanisms—freedom of religion and equal opportunity—that rang with a legitimating intensity equal to that of McGaa's military service. "Our church" claimed Buhner, "believes that no person because of their skin color, should be prohibited from worshiping God in the manner they choose."[34] Indianness—coded as a spiritual essential—was the common property of all Americans. Yet for Native people Buhner's argument could hardly have been more ironic. Indian First Amendment rights, protected only by a congressional vow of good faith and long the target of white reformers, came under severe attack during the 1980s. In a series of legal decisions, the Supreme Court gutted the already weak American Indian Religious Freedom Act, curtailing the exercise of Indian religious freedom in favor of federal environmental law, tourism, and hydropower production, Forest Service—supported logging operations, and state regulation of controlled substances. Coming from a man who lived in a solar home on thirty-five acres of pricey Boulder real estate and did as he pleased with regard to Native spirituality, the claim of discrimination had to ring hollow.[35]

And yet, was Buhner really wrong? Not in a world in which contingent meanings mixed with the power of individual interpretation, endless information, and good intent. And if New Age followers graze freely on proliferating information about other cultures, they usually do so with a sense of compassion and concern. Like the communalists, they tend to be good people bound up in contradictions. Ed McGaa caught the sincere tenor of New Age participants from a sympathetic Indian perspective: "If we want the white man to change, we must teach him." And, echoing Chief Seattle, "We're all brothers."[36] In this universalist interpretation, cultures inevitably bump up against each other and, when they do, they exchange and share cultural material, each becoming a kind of hybrid. Making sense of this hybrid world is less a social activity than a personal one, and individuals should be able to use every available tool in doing so. In a world of free-flowing information and multicultural mixing, no group of people has exclusive rights to "culture," even if they bound and define it as their own.

Buhner's final argument drew on such multicultural information, at once universally accessible and personally meaningful: "The religious war in the former country of Yugoslavia, fought over just such differences, should be warning enough of the wisdom of the First Amendment."[37] Moving quickly from global crisis to individual rights, Buhner skipped his own social milieu. It was apparent to most Indians that the Church of Gaia/Council of Four Directions—economically powerful and racially unmarked—was probably the last group needing to wage war in order to practice its religious beliefs. Despite its misleading nod to Muslims, Serbs, and Croats, Buhner's argument was both superficial and common: self-creative cultural free play was the prerogative of individuals, and it had little to do with the relations between social groups or the power inequities among them.

But if Buhner's suggestion was superficial, it was hardly simple. Rather, it drew upon an important, cosmopolitan strand of multicultural thought, forcing it into an uncomfortable alliance with a postmodernism that emphasized the openness of meaning. The nation's strength, suggested multiculturalists from the critics Randolph Bourne and Horace Kallen to the historian Gary Nash, lay not in the genteel tradition of white America but in its diverse array of different peoples and traditions. Difference, they argued, was not to be rejected but rather embraced. First framed in the early twentieth century, confronted more directly in the post–World War II years, and quasi-institutionalized during the 1970s and 1980s, multiculturalism had become a key idea around which social meanings could be negotiated. And yet, multiculturalism itself was hardly clear-cut. Bourne, suggests the historian David Hollinger, spoke for a cosmopolitan tradition that emphasized dynamism and openness. Kallen, on the other hand, planted the seeds for a sterner pluralist focus on the autonomy and singularity of ethnic groups. In the wake of the Civil Rights movements of the 1960s, this latter, pluralist form of multiculturalism came to share a persistent linkage with the questioning of unequal power and opportunity for the nation's diverse peoples.[38]

With its focus on difference and rigid categorizations, cultural pluralism proved troublesome to those who lived identities along more complicated racial-ethnic, gender, sexual, occupational, and geographic lines. Indeed, the breaking down of inequities and social restrictions enlarged the numbers of people who fit multiple categories at the same time: one might be Swedish, Dakota, and Latino all at once. A cosmopolitan focus on culture crossings and simultaneities suggested that one's identity was not so much a matter of descent but of consent and choice. This particular kind of multiculturalism gained increasing power and visibility during the 1980s. And yet, placed in the context of a postmodernism that emphasized relativism and openness, it was easy to read cosmopolitan multiculturalism as a license for *anyone* to choose an ethnic identity—Indian, for example—regardless of family, history, or tribal recognition. When non-Indian New Age followers appropriated and altered a cosmopolitan understanding of Indianness, they laid bare a slow rebalancing away from the collective concerns with social justice that had emerged in the 1960s and toward the renewed focus on individual freedom that has characterized America since the 1980s.[39]

New Age adherents have found numerous ways to push the scales toward individual liberty, materialized, in this case, through the consumption of other cultures. Committed, sincere people like Stephen Buhner have surveyed the traditions the world has to offer, mixing together Indian spiritual practices with Zen Buddhism, tantric exercise, wicca, druidism, and other exotic brands of knowledge. The New Age men's movement, for example, offers up a complex brew of interpersonal psychology, group therapy, and sensitivity training in Indian-tinged settings. Gathered out-of-doors, men's movement participants make and wear masks, seek out totem animals (usually big, masculine animals), pass an Indian "talking stick" around as they share repressed experiences, and meditate alone in the wild in a sort of well-tempered vision quest experience. The focus is on healing a wounded Self. Women's groups have similar bonding rituals, often centered around an essentialist vision of women's intrinsic connection to the earth. And, of course, New Age followers of both sexes bond together around someone else's cultural knowledge in situations ranging from conferences at swank hotels to sweat lodge ceremonies in backyards.[40]

Like their countercultural predecessors, New Age devotees rely on books to package the cultures they consume. In the mid-1980s, New Age writing exploded, and followers have had a wide array of mediating texts to teach them the ways of Indianness. A familiar format involves an old Indian person who, for whatever reason, turns, not to other Indians, but to a good-hearted white writer to preserve his or her sacred knowledge. John Neihardt's moving and sympathetic *Black Elk Speaks* set the trajectory in 1932, and, if the quality of the writing has deteriorated, the model remains the same. Lynn Andrews's *Medicine Woman* series, for example, began with this format and has now expanded to include other world cultures. It stands at thirteen books, with no end in sight. Andrews's pastiche accounts leap wildly around native North America as she finds, for example, a Choctaw woman living near a Canadian Cree community in a Pawnee earth lodge, described in such a way as to sound suspiciously like George Catlin's 1832 paintings of Mandan houses. And it is her Cree teacher, "Agnes Whistling Elk," who collapses ancient wisdom with postmodern insight: "Every book is rewritten by the reader. . . . You bring to it what you are."[41] Numerous other books gave readers the opportunity to imagine identities through such rewriting. Clarissa Pinkola Estes suggested ways women could "run with the wolves," Robert Bly and Sam Keen offered up equivalent myths for men, and James Redfield's abominable *Celestine Prophecy* showed heroic whites learning deep secrets from disappearing South American Indians amid an insignificant backdrop of social struggle. Readers of such texts then put the words into concrete forms, performing them through vision quest weekends and pipe ceremonies in National Forest hideaways, many of which carried the heady price tag that signified "conspicuous consumption."[42]

The tendency of New Age devotees to find in Indianness personal solutions to the question of living the good life meant that Indian Others were imagined in almost exclusively positive terms—communitarian, environmentally wise, spiritually insightful. This "happy multiculturalism" blunted the edge of earlier calls for social change by focusing on pleasant cultural exchanges that erased the complex histories of Indians and others. Even lingering nineteenth-century images of bloodthirsty savagery have been rendered ambivalent or positive. Despite almost twenty years of Indian protest against his team's nickname (to cite the most egregious example) Washington Redskins owner Jack Kent Cooke insisted that the name "honors" rather than degrades Native people.[43] For hundreds of years, Indianness had been an open idea, capable of having its meanings refigured by Americans seeking identities. The Orwellian pronouncements of people like Cooke, however, suggested that, for many, postmodern Indianness had become so detached from anything real, it was in danger of lapsing into a bland irrelevance.

What are we to make of this transformation? Since the colonial era, Indian Others had been objects of both desire *and* repulsion, and in that raging contradiction lay their power. Now, they were almost completely flattened out, tragic victims who brought the last powerful remnants of their cultures as ethnic gifts for a pluralistic American whole. Non-Indians have constructed Indian Others along two different scales: first, an axis of *distance* on which Indians could appear anywhere between a remote inhumanity and a mirror reflection of one's Self, and second, an axis of *value* on which Indians appeared in gradations of positive and negative. Now, these lines of difference and value threatened to disappear. The social boundaries that marked Indianness as either inside or outside America almost vanished before an all-encompassing universalism. For Stephen Buhner and Lynn Andrews, *everything* was inside. Likewise, the axis of value occupied by savage and noble Indians also shrank in importance as Indians became genial objects of fashion, style, and cultural play. What was there not to like about Indians?

In the sense that everything in a postmodern world could be seen as a game or a project, "playing" Indian had quite literally reached its contradictory apotheosis. It retained its proven creative power—play *is* a crucial way we shape identity and meaning—but, at the same time, its substance tended to slip away. For while play is a critical experience, it is also a powerful metaphor for that which is frivolous and without significant meaning. Postmodernity— as both concept and cultural moment—embraces play, perhaps, because one of its ultimate modes is almost humorously ironic: a firm belief in the contingency of meaning. Such belief might lead one to argue that the way meanings are made and materialized is vitally important. On the other hand, if no meaning is any better than any other, it might also suggest that the practice of meaning-making matters very little.[44]

New Age meaning-making was reflected in the concrete experience of Native costume, always a crucial element in Indian play. It was perhaps indicative of the nature of the movement that its followers tended to play Indian in ways that were surprisingly low grade. A bandanna headband, an assumed name, a personal fetish—any one would suffice. Many Indian objects were deeply embedded in the conspicuous consumption campaigns that took shape around "Santa Fe Style" and "American Country West."[45] In contrast, the hobbyists (who had made authenticity into their own kind of fetish) had experienced a particularly *social* kind of interaction. They had sought out Indians and made and worn painstaking reproductions of Native clothing. In the New Age, authenticity had few material or social forms. Rather, it resided—like all good, unknowable essentials—in a person's interpretive heart and soul. Yet putting on costumes had always been an essential element in Indian play. "We do not stir a step until our equipment is right," insisted Lewis Henry Morgan. The Camp Fire Girls' self-designed Indian dresses, expressing personal character in a material way, underpinned their entire pursuit. The Improved Order of Red Men cherished the smoky canvas costumes that went into the storage locker after a night's ritual. Costume had been the badge of meaning for Tammany paraders and cold war hobbyists alike.

The concrete nature of clothing had always insured that even in the midst of creative play, a thread of social connection bound real Indians to those who mimed them. And indeed, it was the social *reality* of authentic, aboriginal Indians that gave Indian play meaning and power. When the New Age turned to disjointed signifiers—a headband rife with associations, a stylized pipe influenced (one would almost swear) by Tolkien, a set of tropes from one's personal library—adherents allowed some of the true creative power of Indianness to slip away. Yet most New Agers, confronting the contradictions between a self-focused cultural world of creative free play and a social world of struggle, hatred, winners, and losers (with Indians usually numbered among the latter) understandably tended to the former.[46]

Indianness retained a certain degree of power, however, and that power suggests that some markers of difference remained in place. Ironically, the social realities that New Age devotees tended to avoid helped fuel the sense of Indian-white difference that made Indianness meaningful. Indians lived poverty-stricken lives on faraway reservations—and their poverty and geographical distance made them different and thereby authentic. Incorporative multiculturalism, on the other hand, has tended to focus on distinctive *cultural* contributions, and to attenuate even those cultural differences within a larger "human" whole. The asymmetrical relationships of power that undergird the system linger in the uneasy collective unconscious. Mexican food, for example, is a more palatable ethnic gift than Mexican agricultural stoop labor, although in its concrete expression of social inequality and physical distance, it is the latter that defines the "authentic."

Native people who reject this kind of cultural incorporation find themselves in a curious and contradictory position, shunted outside the boundaries of a universalism that purports to be *without* boundaries. Reluctant to share their cultural heritage as a common property, they are marked as exterior. Like the Mexican agricultural worker, it is the social difference of these Indians that guarantees Indian authenticity. In this relentlessly contradictory interplay, such people are simultaneously granted a platform and rendered voiceless. In the summer of 1992, for example, the Indian-published newspaper *Indian Country Today* ran a series of articles indicting many New Age "medicine people" as frauds and inviting their response. Most refused to grant any legitimacy to the critiques and failed to respond. Some did, and they were rebutted effectively. But the newspaper's detailed investigative reporting had no appreciable effect on New Age audiences. Indian presence was noted. Complaints, however, were ignored and suggestions rejected.[47]

Yet while these oppositional Indians were ignored, it was nonetheless important that they *speak*—and speak critically, for in doing so, they offered one of the only indicators of authentic difference functioning in the world of texts, interpretations, and unchained meanings. Where Sun Bear and "Medicine Woman" Lynn Andrews inhabited a cultural world easily shared by Indians and non-Indians, oppositional Native people focused on social and political worlds, where the difference between the reservation, the urban ghetto, and the Beverly Hills Hotel, with its silky breezes and honeysuckle air, stood in stark relief. When they tried to force non-Indians to translate from the cosmopolitan language of open cultural meanings to the pluralist languages of power, struggle, and inequality, they rethreaded the material connections that made Indianness so *real*. And so one multicultural tradition—that of cultural pluralism—provided the "reality" that empowered a distorted, postmodern version of a more cosmopolitan multiculturalism. Indian reality fed back into the textual world, increasing the power of Indianness, even as it contradicted the particular form that Indianness took. The presence of multicultural images and statements, however, let Indian players claim a sincere, but ultimately fruitless, political sympathy with Native people. Indeed, the New Age's greatest intellectual temptation lies with the wistful fallacy that one can engage in social struggle by working on oneself.

As the hobbyists demonstrated so clearly, a multicultural order requires markers of pure difference in order to make its blurrings of that difference meaningful. Even as it is often ignored, then, the critical voice offered by *Indian Country Today*'s Tim Giago—an interestingly middle-of-the-road voice, one should note—matters more to both New Age postmodernism and materialist social criticism than that of Dirk Johnson, the *New York Times* reporter who went after Stephen Buhner's church. Racism, poverty, poor health care, underfunded educational facilities, pollution and toxic dumping, domination by extractive industries—these are the ways in which social and political power has figured difference in Indian Country. When the Indian staffers of *Indian Country Today* report on these issues, they reflect that difference, so easily ignored by postmodern multiculturalism and yet so vital to the authenticity of its Indianness.

The quicksand dynamics of power link these two worlds in intimate and confusing ways, for the power that dominated Indians could, at the same time, be turned to their advantage. *Indian Country Today*, which features Giago's frequent attacks on the lack of Indian voices in the mainstream media, has been partially funded by the Gannett Foundation, a mainstream institution. There was certainly no mistaking the meaning and the money when the paper left behind its original name, *The Lakota Times*, for a connection with that most postmodern of print news outlets, *USA Today*. And yet, *Indian Country Today* is, at the same time, a significant power base for Native people. If Indian people found themselves disempowered in one social realm—the mainstream press—they also *found* power in that same place. It is, paradoxically, the same power, and it makes a difference that it flows through different channels. One channel maintains a social hierarchy; the other maintains a contradictory ethic of multicultural egalitarianism. The power to define and exclude, the power to appropriate and co-opt, and the power to speak and resist are sometimes one and the same, and that power flows through interlocked social and cultural systems, simultaneously directed and channeled by humans and yet often beyond strict human control.[48]

Indian people have, for over one hundred years, lacked military power. Being militarily defeated, they found that social, political, and economic power were often hard to come by as well. Native people have been keenly aware, however, that, in their relations to white Americans, they do in fact possess some mysterious well of cultural power. When the Red Power activists of the late 1960s and early 1970s took over Alcatraz, marched on Washington and trashed the office of the Bureau of Indian Affairs, and sniped at the besieging army at Wounded Knee, these were not simply military or revolutionary actions. Above all, they were cultural acts in which the participants sought social and political power through a complicated play involving white guilt, nostalgia, and the deeply rooted desire to be Indian and thereby aboriginally true to the spirit of the land. Among American ethnic and racial groups, Indians have occupied a privileged position in national culture, and Native people have often put the power that came with this exceptionalism to political and social ends.

That such a politics of culture resonated so thoroughly—even in a world where symbols had spread their meanings so hopelessly thin—suggests the continuing depth and power of Indianness for white Americans. Community and individualism, spiritual essence and precarious meanings, cultural universalism and social difference—paradoxes like these continue to drive contemporary Indian play just as surely as the problem of Briton and aborigine drove the original revolutionaries. Likewise, if the Indian plays of the counterculture and the New Age reflect the crazy-quilt cultural moment we have called postmodern, they also reveal the ways in which those same practices have a longer, more complex history. There is little about the postmodern—linguistic relativism, epistemological crisis, pastiche and bricolage—that has not appeared in the past.[49] Indeed, many of these interpretive tropes have shown up in the history of Indian play. Indian costume has been the site of a host of language games and remade meanings, and people like Lewis Henry Morgan and Ernest Thompson Seton have used it to rethink the very ways they understood the world. Writers, fraternalists, Boy Scouts, and bohemian reformers have all chipped off fragments of Indianness, put them into new contexts, and turned them to new uses.

My weekends visiting the tipi camp and slurping used milk from the collective cereal bowl were part of something new in the sense that Indian play has always taken on new shape and focus to engage the most pressing issues of a particular historical moment. I too was an actor in a world in which questioning the common sense of everyday life was bidding to *become* the common sense of everyday life. But in other, and perhaps more crucial, ways I was participating in a long and unbroken tradition in American history. My communal Indian friends were attempting to redefine themselves and their local community. In doing so, they hoped, in some small way, to offer an example to the nation as a whole. Like many before them, they had turned to Indianness as the sign of all that was authentic and aboriginal, everything that could be right with America. But they had also turned to Indianness as a way of making an absolutely new start. The communalists were hardly alone in seeking to have their cake and to eat it too. Like those who had come before, they found that Indianness inevitably required real Native people and that those people called everything into question. Playing Indian, as always, had a tendency to lead one into, rather than out of, contradiction and irony.

ACKNOWLEDGMENT

The author and the editors wish to thank Yale University Press for permission to reprint this essay in slightly modified form from its first appearance in Philip J. Deloria, *Playing Indian* (1998).

NOTES

1. Lynn Andrews, *Flight of the Seventh Moon* (New York: Harper and Row, 1984).

2. William Hedgepeth, with photographs by Dennis Stock, *The Alternative: Communal Life in New America* (New York: Macmillan, 1970), 73, 84, 81. For corn, beans, squash, see Robert Houriet, *Getting Back Together* (New York: Coward, McCann, and Geohegan, 1971), 170–71. Although my understanding of countercultural communalism relies on certain personal experiences, I have also drawn upon Keith Melville, *Communes in the Counterculture: Origins, Theories, Styles of Life* (New York: William Morrow, 1972); Richard Atcheson, *The Bearded Lady: Going on the Commune Trip and Beyond* (New York: John Day, 1971); Lewis Yablonsky, *The Hippie Trip* (New York: Pegasus, 1968); Timothy Miller, *The Hippies and American Values* (Knoxville: University of Tennessee Press, 1991); Benjamin Zablocki, *Alienation and Charisma: A Study of Contemporary American Communes* (New York: Free Press, 1980); Laurence Veysey, *The Communal Experience: Anarchist and Mystical Communities in Twentieth-Century America* (Chicago: University of Chicago Press, 1978), 279–406.

3. The Beatles, "Strawberry Fields Forever," *Magical Mystery Tour* (EMI, 1967).

4. In thinking about this cluster of ideas, I have been informed by, among others, Andreas Huyssen, *After the Great Divide: Modernism, Mass Culture, Postmodernism* (Bloomington: Indiana University Press, 1986), especially 141–221; David Harvey, *The Condition of Postmodernity: An Enquiry into the Origins of Cultural Change* (Cambridge, Mass.: Blackwell, 1989); Fredric Jameson, *Postmodernism, or The Cultural Logic of Late Capitalism* (Durham: Duke University Press, 1991); Hal Foster, ed., *The Anti-Aesthetic: Essays on Postmodern Culture* (Port Townsend, Wash.: Bay Press, 1983); Jean Baudrillard, *Simulacra and Simulations*, trans. Sheila Faria Glaser (Ann Arbor: University of Michigan Press, 1994); Jean-Francois Lyotard, *The Postmodern Condition: A Report on Knowledge*, trans. Geoff Bennington and Brian Massumi (Minneapolis: University of Minnesota Press, 1984).

5. Fredric Jameson, *The Prison House of Language: A Critical Account of Structuralism and Russian Formalism* (Princeton: Princeton University Press, 1972), ix.

6. Goodman, as quoted in Melville, *Communes in the Counterculture*, 114. See also Goodman, *The New Reformation: Notes of a Neolithic Conservative* (New York: Vintage, 1969), 143–54; Veysey, *Communal Experience*, 3–73. On Paul Goodman, see Theodore Roszak, *The Making of a Counter Culture: Reflections on the Technocratic Society and Its Youthful Opposition* (Berkeley: University of California Press, 1995 [1969]), 178–204; Morris Dickstein, *Gates of Eden: American Culture in the Sixties* (New York: Basic Books, 1977), 74–83.

7. See, for example, Abbie Hoffman [pseud. Free], *Revolution for the Hell of It* (New York: Dial Press), 10 for "Do your own thing" as a mantra; Goodman, *New Reformation*, 145.

8. Stewart Brand, "Indians and the Counterculture, 1960s–1970s," in *Handbook of North American Indians: Volume Four, History of Indian–White Relations,* ed. Wilcomb Washburn (Washington, D.C.: Smithsonian Institution Press, 1988), 570. For "Navajo," see Houriet, *Getting Back Together,* 170.

9. For Warhol, see Robert Rosenblum, "Warhol as Art History," *Andy Warhol: A Retrospective,* ed. Kynaston McShine (New York: Museum of Modern Art, 1989), 25–36, 183–197. See also John Cage, *Imaginary Landscape No. 4* (for twelve radios, twenty-four players, and conductor), 1951, with performances in 1951 and 1959; Cage, *Radio Music* (for one to eight radios), 1956. On Cage, see *John Cage Catalogue* (New York: Henmar Press, 1962), 36, 38; Eric Salzman, "Imaginary Landscaper," and Richard Kostelanetz, "John Cage as *Horspielmacher,*" in *Writings about John Cage,* ed. Richard Kostelanetz (Ann Arbor: University of Michigan Press, 1993), 1–7, 213–21. See also Douglas Crimp, "On the Museum's Ruins," *Anti-Aesthetic,* ed. Hal Foster, 43–56.

10. For the antiwar movement, see Todd Gitlin, *The Sixties: Years of Hope, Days of Rage* (New York: Bantam, 1987), especially 242–60, 285–304; William Chafe, *The Unfinished Journey: America Since World War II,* 2d ed. (New York: Oxford University Press, 1991), 320–28; Tom Engelhardt, *The End of Victory Culture: Cold War America and the Disillusioning of a Generation* (New York: HarperCollins, 1995), 244–46; Nancy Zaroulis and Gerald Sullivan, *Who Spoke Up? American Protest against the War in Vietnam, 1963–1975* (Garden City, N.Y.: Doubleday, 1984); Charles DeBenedetti with assistance from Charles Chatfield, *An American Ordeal: The Antiwar Movement of the Vietnam Era* (Syracuse: Syracuse University Press, 1990). For the relationship between antiwar and counterculture protest, see David Farber, "The Counterculture and the Antiwar Movement," in *Give Peace a Chance: Exploring the Vietnam Antiwar Movement,* ed. Melvin Small and William D. Hoover (Syracuse: Syracuse University Press, 1992). For a general survey, see Farber, *The Age of Great Dreams: America in the 1960s* (New York: Hill and Wang, 1994).

11. Mitchell Goodman, "What's Happening," *The Movement toward a New America: The Beginnings of a Long Revolution (A Collage) A What?* (Philadelphia: Pilgrim Press/Knopf, 1970), vii. For LSD, see Farber, "Counterculture and Antiwar," 19.

12. *Little Big Man,* directed by Arthur Penn (Fox, 1970).

13. Naomi Feigelson, *The Underground Revolution: Hippies, Yippies, and Others* (New York: Funk and Wagnalls, 1970), 7, 64; Free, *Revolution for the Hell of It,* 37.

14. See Hoffman, *Revolution for the Hell of It,* 71–73, for appropriation of racial victim identity. For crossing to the Vietnamese position, see Gitlin, *The Sixties,* 261–82. See also "You Don't Need a Weatherman to Know Which Way the Wind Blows" (1969) in William H. Chafe and Harvard Sitkoff, *A History of Our Time: Readings on Postwar America* (New York: Oxford University Press, 1983), 235–38.

15. See Tom Holm, *Strong Hearts, Wounded Souls: Native American Veterans of the Vietnam War* (Austin: University of Texas Press, 1996), 118. One should note as well the tendency of American ground troops to reprise nineteenth-century Plains warfare, designating North Vietnamese territory "Indian country." See Holm, 129.

16. For Indian activism, see Indians of All Tribes, Peter Blue Cloud, ed., *Alcatraz Is Not an Island* (Berkeley: Wingbow Press, 1972); Adam Fortunate Eagle, *Alcatraz! Alcatraz! The Indian Occupation of 1969–1971* (Berkeley: Heyday Books, 1992); Vine Deloria Jr., *Behind the Trail of Broken Treaties: An Indian Declaration of Independence* (Austin: University of Texas Press, 1985); Stanley David Lyman, *Wounded Knee 1973: A Personal Account* (Lincoln: University of Nebraska Press, 1991); Paul Chaat Smith and Robert Allen Warrior, *Like a Hurricane: The Indian Movement from Alcatraz to Wounded Knee* (New York: New Press, 1996). For Anderson, see Troy R. Johnson, *The Occupation of Alcatraz Island: Indian Self-Determination and the Rise of Indian Activism* (Champaign: University of Illinois Press, 1996), 32. For Brando, see "Brando Has Long Backed Rights of Racial Minorities," *New York Times,* 28 March, 1973, 40. For Poor

People's Campaign, see Paul Cowan, "Indians Meet the Press: It's Pride vs. Prejudice," in Goodman, *Movement toward a New America*, 249–50.

17. Fiegleman, *Underground Revolution*, 11; Free, *Revolution for the Hell of It*, 164, for pastiche poster. For revolutionary bandanna, see Jerry Avorn, Robert Freedman, et al., "Up Against the Ivy Wall," in Chafe and Sitkoff, *Our Time*, 246. For bandanna in drug and communal culture, see Yablonsky, *Hippie Trip*, 64, 74, 80. See James Clifford, *The Predicament of Culture: Twentieth-Century Ethnography, Literature, and Art* (Cambridge: Harvard University Press, 1988), 346, for Indianness encoded in a bandanna headband. For the compression of high and popular culture, see William L. O'Neill, *Coming Apart: An Informal History of America in the 1960s* (Chicago: Quadrangle Books, 1971), 200–227, 245–49.

18. Paul Goodman, *New Reformation*, 194; Hoffman, *Revolution for the Hell of It*, 71–73; Jerry Farber, "Student as Nigger," in Goodman, *Movement toward a New America*, 303–04; Farber, "Counterculture and Antiwar," 17; John Lennon and Yoko Ono, "Woman is the Nigger of the World, *Shaved Fish* (EMI, 1972).

19. Hoffman, *Revolution for the Hell of It*, 9.

20. Peter Clecak, *America's Quest for the Ideal Self: Dissent and Fulfillment in the 60s and 70s* (New York: Oxford University Press, 1983), 117; Charles Chatfield, "The Antiwar Movement and America," *American Ordeal*, 396.

21. As quoted in Rudolph Kaiser, "Chief Seattle's Speech(es): American Origins and European Reception," in *Recovering the Word: Essays on Native American Literature*, ed. Brian Swann and Arnold Krupat (Berkeley: University of California Press), 517.

22. For a tracing of the speech's diffusion, see Kaiser, "Seattle's Speech(es)," 497–536, especially 515.

23. Goodman, *New Reformation*, 59.

24. Goodman, *New Reformation*, 54; Feigelson, *Underground Revolution*, 50–51, 64–65; Roszak, *Making of a Counter Culture*, 124–77.

25. John Neihardt, *Black Elk Speaks: Being the Life Story of a Holy Man of the Oglala Sioux* (New York: Pocket Books, 1972); John Fire Lame Deer and Richard Erdoes, *Lame Deer: Seeker of Visions* (New York: Simon & Schuster 1972); Hyemeyohsts Storm, *Seven Arrows* (New York: Ballantine, 1972). On drugs, see William Braden, *The Private Sea: LSD and the Search for God* (Chicago: Quadrangle Books, 1967); Melville, *Communes in the Counterculture*, 223–27; Veysey, *Communal Experience*, 437–39, 442–44.

26. Doug Boyd, *Rolling Thunder: A Personal Exploration into the Secret Healing Powers of an American Indian Medicine Man* (New York: Random House, 1974); Sun Bear, *The Medicine Wheel: Earth Astrology* (Englewood Cliffs, N.J.: Prentice Hall, 1980); *Walk in Balance: The Path to Heathy, Happy, Harmonious Living* (New York: Prentice Hall, 1989). See also James Clifton, *Being and Becoming Indian: Biographical Studies of North American Frontiers* (Chicago: Dorsey Press, 1989).

27. Editorial, *Many Smokes* 2, no. 1 (1st quarter 1967): 3; 2, no. 3 (3rd quarter 1967): 3.

28. I make these observations after reading several issues of both *Many Smokes* and *Wildfire*. For specific examples listed, see *Wildfire's* inaugural publications, I, nos. 1, 2 (spring–summer) and I, nos. 3, 4 (fall–winter).

29. Carlos Castaneda, *The Teachings of Don Juan: A Yaqui Way of Knowledge* (Berkeley: University of California Press, 1968); *A Separate Reality: Further Conversations with Don Juan* (New York: Simon & Schuster, 1971); *Journey to Ixtlan: The Lessons of Don Juan* (New York: Simon and Schuster, 1972); *Tales of Power* (New York: Simon & Schuster, 1974); *The Second Ring of Power* (New York: Simon & Schuster, 1977). To date, four other books follow, the most recent being *The Art of Dreaming* (New York: HarperCollins, 1993).

30. MacLaine, *Out on a Limb* (New York: Bantam, 1983); *Dancing in the Light* (New York: Bantam, 1985). Artists on the tastefully packaged Windom Hill label included the pianists George Winston and Bill Quist, the guitarist Ackerman, and the bassist Michael Manring, among many others.

31. Dirk Johnson, "Spiritual Seekers Borrow Indians' Ways," *New York Times*, 27 December, 1993, A1. Also printed as David Johnston, "New Age Rites Seen as Robbery," *Boulder* [Colorado] *Daily Camera*, 27 December, 1993, 5C.

32. Stephen Buhner, "Protecting the Right to Worship," *Boulder Daily Camera*, 3 January, 1994, 2C. See also Ed McGaa, *Mother Earth Spirituality: Native American Paths to Healing Ourselves and Our World* (San Francisco: Harper and Row, 1990); *Rainbow Tribe: Ordinary People Journeying on the Red Road* (San Francisco: Harper-San Francisco, 1992).

33. I do not mean to suggest that there are not teacher-student relationships in Native religious traditions. It is important, however, to distinguish between healing and spirituality, the former relying more heavily on teaching. Sacred bundles and spiritual power were in fact subject to transfer, although as often in an economic or kinship exchange as a master-learner one. See, for example, Peter Nabokov, *Two Leggings: The Making of a Crow Warrior* (New York: Crowell, 1967), 143–54. For Plains spiritual tradition, see James Walker, *Lakota Belief and Ritual*, ed. Raymond J. DeMallie and Elaine A. Jahner (Lincoln: University of Nebraska Press, 1980); Lee Irwin, *The Dream Seekers: Native American Visionary Traditions of the Great Plains* (Norman: University of Oklahoma Press, 1994); Raymond J. DeMallie, "Lakota Belief and Ritual in the Nineteenth Century," in *Sioux Indian Religion* ed. Raymond J. DeMallie and Douglas R. Parks (Norman: University of Oklahoma Press, 1987), 25–44; Joseph Epes Brown, ed., *The Sacred Pipe: Black Elk's Account of the Seven Rites of the Oglala Sioux* (Norman: University of Oklahoma Press, 1953).

34. Buhner, "Protecting the Right to Worship."

35. See, for example, *Badoni v. Higginson* 638 F2d 172 (1980) *United States v. Dion* 476 US 734 (1986); *Lyng v. Northwest Indian Cemetery Protective Association* 485 US 439 (1988); *Employment Division, Department of Human Resources of Oregon, et al. v. Alfred L. Smith et al.* 494 US 872 (1990). See John Wunder, *"Retained by the People": A History of American Indians and the Bill of Rights* (New York: Oxford University Press, 1994), 180–99.

36. Johnston, "New Age Rites."

37. Buhner, "Protecting the Right to Worship."

38. Randolph Bourne, "Trans-National America," in *War and the Intellectuals: Essays, 1915–1919* ed. Carl Resek (New York: Harper Torchbooks, 1964), 107–23; Kallen, "Democracy versus the Melting Pot," *Nation* 100 (18–25 February, 1915): 190–94, 217–20. See also Gary B. Nash, "The Great Multicultural Debate," *Contention* 1 (spring 1992): 1–28; and Nash, "The Hidden History of Mestizo America," *Journal of American History* 82 (December 1995): 941–64. See also Hollinger, *Postethnic America: Beyond Multiculturalism* (New York: Basic Books, 1995), 11; Lawrence W. Levine, *The Opening of the American Mind: Canons, Culture, and History* (Boston: Beacon Press, 1996), 105–20 and passim.

39. See, for example, Werner Sollors, *Beyond Ethnicity: Consent and Descent in American Culture* (New York: Oxford University Press, 1986).

40. I make this summary after years of reading Boulder's New Age periodicals and talking with friends who have been involved in New Age activities. Particularly useful have been *Men's Council Journal, Nexus, The Eagle's Cry: A Journal for Holistic Experiences, Wisdom, and Education*, and the national-circulation magazines *Shaman's Drum* and *New Age Journal*.

41. Andrews, *Flight of the Seventh Moon*, 26. For others in the series, see, for example, *Medicine Woman* (San Francisco: Harper and Row, 1981); *Jaguar Woman and the Wisdom of the Butterfly Tree* (San Francisco: Harper and Row, 1985); *Star Woman* (New York: Warner, 1986); *Shakki: Woman of the Sacred Garden* (New York: HarperCollins, 1992).

42. Estes, *Women Who Run with the Wolves: Myths and Stories of the Wild Woman Archetype* (New York: Ballantine, 1992); Robert Bly, *Iron John: A Book about Men* (Reading, Mass.: Addison-Wesley, 1990); Sam Keen, *Fire in the Belly: On Being a Man* (New York: Bantam, 1991); Diane Stein, *Dreaming the Past, Dreaming the Future: A Herstory of the Earth* (Freedom, Calif.: Crossing Press, 1991); James Redfield, *The Celestine Prophecy: An Adventure* (New York:

Warner, 1993); Michael Rossman, *New Age Blues: On the Politics of Consciousness* (New York: Dutton, 1979). For more analytical treatments, see Michael Schwalbe, *Unlocking the Iron Cage: The Men's Movement, Gender Politics, and American Culture* (New York: Oxford University Press, 1996); Michael York, *The Emerging Network: A Sociology of the New Age and Neo-Pagan Movements* (Lanham, Md.: Rowman and Littlefield, 1995). Numerous other authors, ranging from "Indian" mystery writers Tony Hillerman and Jean Hagar to high-culture writers like M. T. Kelly and W. P. Kinsella, have assumed the literary voice of "the Indian." Others, such as Jamake Highwater and Forrest Carter, have taken Indian identity as their own.

43. For mascots, see Philip Deloria, "Mascots and Other Public Appropriations of Indians and Indian Culture by Whites," in *Encyclopedia of North American Indians*, ed. Frederick Hoxie (Boston: Houghton Mifflin, 1996), 359–61; Dennis Banks, Laurel R. Davis, Synthia Syndnor-Slowikowski, and Lawrence A. Wenner, "Tribal Names and Mascots in Sports," *Journal of Sports and Social Issues* 17 (April 1993): 1–33. For Redskins, see, for example, Ward Churchill, "Crimes against Humanity," *Z Magazine* (March 1993): 43–47.

44. On play, see Johan Huizinga, *Homo Ludens: A Study of the Play Element in Culture* (Boston: Beacon Press, 1955), 8.

45. Christine Mather and Sharon Woods, *Santa Fe Style* (New York: Rizzoli International, 1986); Mary Emmerling and Carol Sama Sheehan, *American Country West: A Style and Source Book* (New York: Clarkson N. Potter, 1985).

46. This is not to say that New Age followers have offered no political help to Native people, nor to suggest that they have completely failed to engage Indians. Rather, it is the nature of the engagement that is at issue. New Age participation in Plains Sun Dances, for example, has been so overwhelming and so lacking in etiquette that many dances have been closed to non-Indians.

47. *Indian Country Today* 13, no. 3 (14 July 1992): 1, 2, and subsequent editions throughout the months of July and August.

48. On cultural difference, see Homi K. Bhabha, *The Location of Culture* (New York: Routledge, 1994). On power, I have been influenced by Michel Foucault, *The History of Sexuality, Volume I: An Introduction,* trans. Robert Hurley (New York: Random House, 1978); *Discipline and Punish: The Birth of the Prison,* trans. Alan Sheridan (New York: Pantheon, 1977); *The Foucault Reader,* ed. Paul Rabinow (New York: Pantheon, 1984).

49. See especially Huyssen, *After the Great Divide*, viii–x, 178–221.

Seven

Voodoo Child

Jimi Hendrix and the Politics of Race in the Sixties

Lauren Onkey

He was unabashedly sexual. He didn't apologize to black people for being wild,
and he . . . certainly didn't ask permission from white people. He laid down a
gauntlet, you know, he said "are you prepared to be free?"
—*Vernon Reid*[1]

As the sun rose over "Woodstock Nation" at Max Yasgur's farm on the morning of August 18, 1969, Jimi Hendrix took the stage. He was supposed to
close the momentous three-day festival the previous night, but the concert ran
so far behind schedule that he ended up saluting the dawn instead. With the
crowd having thinned to about 30,000 from its estimated peak of a "half a million strong," Hendrix looked out on a field in which it was difficult to distinguish between people and debris. Those who had stuck around to catch his set
saw a different Jimi Hendrix from the one who burst on the scene at the
Monterey Pop Festival a mere two years earlier. For starters, his band, the Jimi
Hendrix Experience, was no more. They had performed their final show in
June, and Hendrix had been holed up during the summer jamming with new
musicians and pondering his future direction. He came to Woodstock with a
five-piece band that he introduced as the "Gypsy Sun and Rainbows." It
included bassist Billy Cox and guitarist Larry Lee, whom Hendrix had played
with during his army days in Tennessee, and drummer Mitch Mitchell from

the Experience. Two additional percussionists, Juma Sultan and Jerry Valez, had been enlisted by Hendrix to expand his power trio sound. Although Hendrix flicked his tongue at his guitar now and then, he was physically subdued on stage. This performance showcased Hendrix the guitar virtuoso. The set mixed hits ("Fire"), blues ("Hear My Train A-Comin'"), and new songs ("Message to Love") with some extended improvisations ("Jam Back at the House"). Hendrix's appearance was most memorable, however, for his astonishing interpretation of "The Star-Spangled Banner," which was used to close the 1970 film *Woodstock*. By default it was also to be a fitting close for a tumultuous decade.

The image of Hendrix playing the national anthem has become symbolic of the counterculture. He looked as funkily elegant as always, sporting an Afro banded by a red silken scarf, an Indian-fringed suede jacket, blue velvet bell-bottom pants, beads, and silver earrings in both ears. Hendrix began his instrumental version of the song by flashing a peace sign to the audience. Then accompanied only by Mitch Mitchell's psychedelic jazz drumming, he played the first few verses of the song, adhering closely to its familiar form. When he got to the line "and the rockets red glare," Hendrix let loose with a carefully orchestrated sonic assault on the audience in which his shrieking, howling guitar riffs, modulated and distorted with feverish feedback, attained the aural equivalent of Armageddon. The bombs bursting in air and ear transformed Yasgur's placid cow pasture into the napalmed and shrapnel-battered jungles of Vietnam. As the song drew to a close, Hendrix solemnly intoned a few notes of "Taps," memorializing not just the slain but perhaps his own former pro-war stance that dated back a few years to his hitch in the army.[2]

The crowd was struck dumb by this bravura deconstruction of our national hymn, which managed to simultaneously evoke chauvinistic pride for and unbridled rage against the American way of life.[3] These seemingly incompatible feelings found a tenuous resolution in the early morning air of a day in late summer during the Nixonian denouement. When asked a few weeks later why he played the song at, of all places, the Woodstock Festival, billed as "3 Days of Peace & Music," Hendrix responded, "Because we are all Americans. . . . When it was written it was very nice and beautifully inspiring. Your heart throbs and you say, 'Great, I'm American.' Nowadays we don't play it to take away all the greatness that America is supposed to have. We play it the way the air is in America today. The air," he continued in an understated fashion, "is slightly static."[4] Hendrix's "Star-Spangled Banner" signified a proud and revolutionary voice at the end of this successful, cooperative festival.

Three weeks after Woodstock, Hendrix participated in a benefit for the Harlem United Block Association on 139th Street at the urging of the Allen

Twins (a.k.a. The Ghetto Fighters), longtime friends of Hendrix's from the neighborhood. The UBA ran day care centers and tutorial programs for poor Harlem residents. It was the first time Hendrix had played in a community benefit of any kind. His band shared the bill with the rhythm and blues stars Big Maybelle and J. D. Brown. To promote the show, he conducted a press conference in Harlem at Frank's Restaurant on 125th Street where he talked about the "crusade" of fusing the festive countercultural spirit of Woodstock with the gritty reality of the inner city, because, as he put it, "a lot of black people . . . haven't been included yet."[5]

> [Woodstock] just spread harmony and communication, and there was no violence at all out there which is completely different. . . . This whole thing is done [for] the benefit of the UBA. And we hope to do some more gigs for it you know, some more benefits. . . . 'Cause a lot of kids in the ghetto . . . don't have the money to travel across country to see these different festivals. . . . I mean, seven dollars is a lot of money. So . . . I think more groups that are supposed to be considered heavy groups should contribute more to this cause.[6]

The different responses to Hendrix's show in Harlem and Woodstock revealed the racial polarization of the times. At Woodstock, Hendrix was an undisputed star, the highest paid of all who performed there. He was one of very few musicians of color playing for an adoring but predominantly white audience. In Harlem, by contrast, he faced a small, primarily black, and somewhat hostile audience that was largely unfamiliar with his music.[7] On a truck bed stage in the street, Hendrix, flanked by Mitch Mitchell and Billy Cox, played a similar set to the one in Woodstock, including "Voodoo Child (Slight Return)" (which he introduced as "the Harlem national anthem") and "The Star-Spangled Banner." Arthur Allen described the tension in the air at the beginning of Hendrix's set: "He started making some kind of distortion out of his guitar . . . like throwing something at [the public]. And . . . someone threw an egg out a window and it really freaked him out. He started playing like he never played before and blew everyone's mind, had everyone on their toes. And that was his first communication with black people and they dug him."[8] Gerry Stickells, Hendrix's road manager, remembers that a few Black Panthers in the crowd intimidated the band's road crew: "All of the white guys had to hide in a burned out, defunct laundry until it was time to go on. We had to put the gear up quickly because people were throwing stuff and spitting on us."[9] Hendrix biographer David Henderson reported that "As he was walking back to the equipment truck after the set, a black nationalist type came up to Jimi and said, 'Hey, brother, you better come home.' Jimi quickly replied, 'You gotta do what you gotta do and I gotta do what I gotta do *now.*'"[10]

The vast differences between Hendrix's reception at these two parallel events suggest the complexities of race surrounding his career. Like Elvis Presley, whom the young Hendrix admired, his iconic stature served as a lightning rod for the race debates of his time. The highlight of the Rock and Roll Hall of Fame and Museum's exhibit commemorating the thirtieth anniversary of Hendrix's death was a series of crayon and pencil drawings Hendrix did while still in high school. One stands out like the bent F chord that opens "Foxy Lady": a crayon and pen drawing of Elvis, dated 1958, on simple notebook paper. Elvis is depicted wearing a bright red jacket, his hair high and wild, cradling his guitar while crooning into a microphone. Shooting out of his body in all directions are some twenty song titles. Elvis had clearly left his mark on the fourteen-year-old Hendrix after he saw him in concert in Seattle in September of 1957. Presley wasn't the only thing that led Hendrix to his first guitar in 1958 and his first band, the Rocking Kings, in 1959.[11] Hendrix remembered being captivated by blues and R & B on the radio and his parents' record collection. But the Elvis drawing suggests that he was particularly taken with the rocker, which isn't surprising. In 1957, Elvis possessed what Hendrix desired: flamboyant and energetic stage shows, unapologetic sexual appeal, and a racially hybrid musical sound. It turned out that he inherited his volatile racial status in American culture as well.

Like Elvis, Hendrix raises questions about the meaning of integration in the post–Civil Rights era. In *Elvis after Elvis,* Gil Rodman explains that the popular view of integration doesn't necessarily correspond to the positive meaning associated with Dr. Martin Luther King's crusade. "For many whites, racial integration was (and is) seen as a nightmare to be avoided rather than a dream to be embraced, while for many blacks, integration was (and is) nothing more than a code-word used to disguise the destruction of black culture through its forced assimilation into white culture."[12] Debates over Hendrix's racial status have been in play ever since the rock critic Robert Christgau called him a "psychedelic Uncle Tom" following his performance at the Monterey Pop Festival in 1967 and the rock critic Michael Lydon wondered whether he was the "black Elvis" in the *New York Times* in 1968. Hendrix and the racial politics of his largely white counterculture audience challenge ideas about racial authenticity and the meaning(s) of integration in the late 1960s.

Race permeates many discussions of Hendrix's career, as scores of critics have tried to account for the artist's greater appeal to whites than blacks during the Sixties.[13] Two arguments dominate. The first is that he "sold out" to a white audience with his highly sexual performances and psychedelic music, which are coded as "white," and had begun to embrace a more pure "black" identity in the last year of his life. This argument, rooted in essentialist notions of identity, is used to expose the counterculture's purported bourgeois racism. The counterculture appeared to welcome Hendrix's experimentation, but ultimately disdained it as commercial pandering. [14] The second is a utopian claim that Hendrix "transcended race." George Lipsitz exemplifies this argument in his assertion that Hendrix was one of the "outsider" heroes for the counterculture who were "able to transcend their personal histories and build new identities in an openly multiracial musical environment." [15] "Transcendence" in this usage can signify a desire to avoid race altogether, which was certainly easier for whites than blacks. White desire to "transcend race" can too often mean avoiding the unconscious ways whites perpetuate racial norms. [16] In the end both of these interpretations limit our understanding of the complex relationship between Hendrix and the counterculture. Hendrix consciously attempted to mix sometimes contradictory racial elements. [17] His achievements cannot be accounted for, perhaps cannot even be seen, in tropes of racial authenticity or racial invisibility.

Hendrix's story can be read as a barometer of racial consciousness in the counterculture, from the halcyon celebration at Monterey, where (problematically) race was not a referent, to the impact of black nationalism in 1968 and '69, when Hendrix and his audience were called to account for the role that race played in their relationship. His story reveals the fissures and ultimate break in relations between African Americans and the counterculture; indeed, it suggests that a utopian attempt to ignore race can reproduce racism in unforeseen ways. Even before he made it big, Hendrix sought places where his music, ideas, and performance would not be judged by binary definitions of black and white music or identity. The counterculture's spirit of musical, sexual, and lifestyle experimentation was a productive site out of which Hendrix could emerge, a place where he could find acceptance and sympathetic collaborators. The critic Paul Gilroy characterizes Hendrix as an artist of the "black Atlantic" world, the world of movement and exchange between Europe, Africa, and North America once defined by the slave trade. He describes Hendrix's music as one of the "stereophonic, bilingual, or bifocal cultural forms originated by, but no longer the exclusive property of, blacks." [18] Gilroy offers a way to see Hendrix's story as one of exchange between blacks and whites, and between black blues traditions and new technological forms. Hendrix's negotiation between black art, white counterculture, and, crucially, commercial pop music success suggests the possibility and dangers of hybridity. [19] Stomping on the idea of authenticity and origin, aware of racial limitations but glimpsing alternatives, Hendrix emerged at a moment in

Western history when it was possible for such radical forms to gain mass appeal—to help, in other words, fashion a counterculture.

Hendrix's biography repeats a familiar story of black migration and reveals the various racial and ethnic ancestries subsumed under "blackness." His path was not linear: he did not travel from "authentic" black musical roots to mainstream success; instead he veered between a variety of sites, drawing inspiration from anyone who sparked his interest. He grew up in Seattle following the Second World War, the son of former vaudeville dancers; his ethnic background was a patchwork of Cherokee, Irish, white, and African-American ancestries.[20] Seattle was then predominantly white but included a racial mix of Native Americans and Asian Americans and a vibrant, experimental music scene. [21] In 1961, his tour of duty in the army transformed into an encounter with the musical roots of rock and roll. During his time in Tennessee, he played with Gorgeous George Odell, Curtis Mayfield, Little Richard, and Lonnie Youngblood on the "chitlin' circuit." After being honorably discharged following his injury from a parachute jump, Hendrix headed for the black metropolis of Harlem in 1964, where he hooked up with the Isley Brothers and got a taste of pop success. He headed back on the road, moved to Hollywood in early 1965, where he played with black soul/psychedelic singer Arthur Lee, and then returned to New York, where he joined Curtis Knight and the Squires, a small-time R & B band. Hendrix's genius was that he never saw contradictions between, for example, traditional blues and Little Richard's androgynous flamboyance; indeed, he intuitively grasped how these disparate styles could meet and explode into new musical landscapes.

He took his penchant for showmanship and his guitar virtuosity on a journey to three sites that would soon propel him into pop stardom: New York's Greenwich Village in early 1966, "Swinging London" later that same year, and the Monterey Pop Festival during the next year's "Summer of Love." In these three countercultural centers, Hendrix fused music, fashion, and theatricality into an apex of psychedelic creativity. In these places, he honed his uniquely "bifocal" art: playing Howlin' Wolf's "Killing Floor" at Monterey; laying down smooth Wes Montgomery jazz licks in the psychedelic sci-fi "Third Stone from the Sun"; mixing Little Richard's look with London's Carnaby Street finery; jamming with jazz horn player Roland Kirk (who could play three horns simultaneously) at the height of English psychedelia. Yet his success was regarded by both mainstream and counterculture critics alike as somehow constituting "white" success. There were minefields on this hybrid path that ultimately revealed that race could not be ignored either by Hendrix or his audience.

Race was always a factor on Hendrix's path. His decision to leave the Curtis Knight band and relocate to Greenwich Village in 1966, for example, was an act of rejection against fixed definitions of "blackness." He felt unwelcome in Harlem. Arthur Allen, a friend whom he met soon after his arrival there, remembers that Hendrix was at odds with conservative black culture: "He would wear blues hats like the old masters. . . . Then he would put buttons on them to make them his style. He wore pins. My brother and I began wearing bell-bottom pants because of him. Most blacks associated bell-bottom pants with clowns."[22] His interest in the blues roots of R & B and in white musicians like Bob Dylan and the Beatles also set him apart from the Harlem music scene.[23] In the Village he could express himself more freely, especially on the electric guitar.[24] Hendrix quickly became part of the scene, carrying his guitar with him everywhere and sometimes playing on the street. In an interview early in 1968, Hendrix compared the two neighborhoods: "In the Village people were more friendly than in Harlem where it's all cold and mean. Your own people hurt you more. Anyway, I had always wanted a more open and integrated sound. Top-40 stuff is all out of gospel, so they try to get everybody up and clapping, shouting 'yeah, yeah.' We don't want to get everybody up. They should just sit there and dig it."[25] Hendrix relished the tradition of open jamming in Village clubs; he could play long, open-ended songs to a willing audience any night of the week. The scene also gave him exposure to revolutionary guitarists from England such as Jeff Beck and Eric Clapton, the avantgarde jazz of John Coltrane and Ornette Coleman, and a ready supply of psychedelic drugs.[26] But as the Hendrix biographer David Henderson recalls, Hendrix's relocation to the Village was perceived in Harlem as a step down: "Hanging out down in the Village with all those beatniks and hippies. . . . The slick veneer front of the R & B musician destroyed for him in the Village. Disdain from his friends 'uptown'—'he's looking scruffy and acting crazy.'"[27]

Hendrix assembled a couple of white sidemen and performed regularly as Jimmy James and the Blue Flames at the Café Wha?, a dive on MacDougal Street over the Players Theater, where the Fugs often performed.[28] He was seen there by Bob Dylan, the Rolling Stones, and white bluesmen Mike Bloomfield and John Hammond Jr., among other notables. Interestingly, during this period he also met Mike Quashie, a Trinidadian singer and limbo dancer who specialized in fire walking. Hendrix often borrowed clothes from Quashie, who seems to have been another key influence in the development of Hendrix's flashy clothing style.[29] It wasn't long before Hendrix was spotted at the Café Wha? by Chas Chandler, the bassist in the Animals, a band from the English coal mining town of Newcastle that had produced some of the best British R & B records of the early 1960s. Chandler, in a career move from musician to manager, realized that London, with its blues fanatics and flourishing pop scene, would be the ideal place for Hendrix to hit. Hendrix quickly agreed, and they were off, less than three months after their initial meeting.

Swinging London was then a world capital of fashion and music. Hendrix reveled in a place where guitar experimentation was everything, and an extravagant pop fashion scene stoked his eclectic tastes. He tapped into the fashion scene of Carnaby Street, decking himself out in military jackets and paisleys. He let his hair grow even longer than he had in the United States, creating a proto-Afro that was part Little Richard, part Bob Dylan. His hairstyle figured prominently in posters and advertisements for the rest of his career. His flamboyant look celebrated the pastiche approach to creative self-expression that exemplified hippie counterculture during its "flower power" phase. And while some say he adopted "white" fashion, one contemporary observer offers a reading of Hendrix's look that suggests the revolutionary potential of Hendrix's style for blacks:

> With their mutton-chop sideburns, droopy moustaches and flowing hair, English rock stars were effectively spoofing the Victorian officer class whose finery they donned. But a grinning, crazy-haired Hendrix in hussar's jacket suggested something else entirely—a redskin brave showing off the spoils of a paleface scalp, perhaps, or a negro "buffalo soldier" fighting on the side of the anti-slavery Yankee forces in the US Civil War.[30]

Hendrix quickly put together a band consisting of the white English rockers Noel Redding on bass and Mitch Mitchell on drums. Chandler hooked up with Mike Jeffrey, who managed the Animals, to begin promoting the newly christened Jimi Hendrix Experience. Chandler, Jeffrey, and Hendrix jumped willingly into the pop fray; they set out to make hits rather than to entertain the burgeoning bohemian scene in London. The historian Jonathan Green sees Hendrix as one of the many rock musicians whose involvement in the business was at odds with the anticommercial wing of the nascent counterculture:

> Chas Chandler . . . and Track, Chris Lambert and Kit Stamp's record label, were no hippies. . . . How much the bands felt any genuine fellowship with the freaks is debatable. There was lip-service, undoubtedly, and for a while even the top stars liked to see themselves as part of the underground. But there was a real gulf, and as the bands became increasingly famous and rich, it could only widen."[31]

The Experience didn't play such new underground clubs as the UFO and Middle Earth. According to Mitch Mitchell "they didn't want to know us at that time anyway. Looking back we might seem to have had more in common with that audience, but maybe Chas thought they were rather marginal and wanted to build some kind of base for us."[32]

The aggressive marketing of the Jimi Hendrix Experience in London set the stage for the problems Hendrix would have with his racial image. People involved on the scene during the mid-Sixties argue that London was remarkably free of racial prejudice, which explains why Hendrix was welcomed there so easily. As Kathy Etchingham, Hendrix's first white girlfriend in London, remembered it: "Here, in those days, a lot of people couldn't see colour. It wasn't a point of contention at that time."[33] However, Hendrix's arrival had been preceded by nearly two decades of West Indian immigration and subsequent racial tension, including race riots in the Notting Hill district; by the mid-Sixties, there was increasing white protest against the presence of these black immigrants. Indeed, Hendrix was represented graphically with *British* racial stereotypes in the London press, which referred to him variously as the "Wild Man from Borneo" (a former British colony), a "Mau-Mau" (Kenyans who fought a guerrilla war for independence from the British in the mid-1950s), and "a wild-eyed revolutionary from the Caribbean." Race, as it was figured in the history of British colonialism and played out in the reception of nonwhite immigrants, was in actuality a very prominent part of London society in the 1960s.

Despite this contentious reality, Hendrix was received as more of a curiosity—an exotic bird from another land—than a threat. He was regarded like an Indian or African displayed at court under colonialism, designed to titillate but not disturb people. His promoters intuited that this racial exoticism could *sell* the Experience, as the biographers Shapiro and Glebbeek argue: "Chas wanted to establish Jimi's image as mean, moody and magnificent, so photos of Jimi were chosen to make him look ugly."[34] Noel Redding points out that Hendrix's race helped him garner popular attention: "The fact that Jimi was black guaranteed him notice in England, even more so when he was playing next to two white guys."[35] Hendrix's initial popularity in England derived nothing from the supposed "invisibility of race" but rather owed much to the exoticism of American blackness that found its place in the aesthetics of Swinging London.

It was during his London sojourn that Hendrix developed his signature eroticized and over-the-top performance style. He played guitar with his teeth, behind his back, on his back, flicked his tongue in the air repeatedly and dry-humped both his instrument and his amplifiers. His antics brought him swift notoriety in England and in Europe, but they also engendered charges that he was fulfilling white stereotypes of black male sexuality and violence. In 1968, Eric Clapton, an early admirer of Hendrix, described his performances as exploitative: "You know English people have a very big thing towards a spade. They really love that magic thing. . . . Everybody and his brother in England still sort of think that spades have big dicks. And Jimi came over and exploited that to the limit . . . Everybody fell for it. . . . I fell for it."[36] Such criticisms, however, fail to recognize that Hendrix's shtick had its roots in black popular music; his exoticism obscured his sources. When asked where he got the idea to play guitar with his teeth, Hendrix replied that he learned it while performing on the club circuit in Tennessee: "Down there you have to play with your teeth or else you get shot. There's a trail of broken teeth all over the stage."[37] As the biographer David Henderson argues:

> While the young white rock 'n' rollers had often managed to copy and cajole the correct changes of black music, they nevertheless failed to present in their stage presentation "The Show." "The Show" was the staple of every performance, especially on the southern tours and at places like the Apollo. "The Show" was when the artists or band would do some wild, wild, way-out stuff. "The Show" was the height of the performance, and like the saxophone "honkers," this display often put both the audience and the performer in a transcendental state where improvisation came to the fore and the unexpected took everybody out. Very much akin to the building emotional patterns of black holiness churches, this crescendo, once reached, could be stretched and augmented and built upon all night if necessary. But for the true followers of black music, it was this transcendental moment everyone waited for. [38]

While Hendrix's "Show" wasn't recognized as a staple in black popular musical performance in England, it was nonetheless welcomed and promoted there. It was itself an exoticized practice, taken out of its original context. And consequently when Hendrix returned stateside, his flamboyance on stage was not understood as signifying "black."

The Monterey Pop Festival in June of 1967 launched Hendrix's American career; when he arrived in San Francisco, his first album had not yet been released in the USA.[39] Monterey, the first major outdoor rock festival, featured both L.A. pop groups like the Mamas and the Papas, Buffalo Springfield, and The Byrds and the less well known "San Francisco sound" of the Grateful Dead, Janis Joplin, and Country Joe and the Fish. Despite efforts to include numerous black artists on the bill, only Hendrix, Otis Redding, and Hugh Masekela appeared. Monterey was a great artistic success that in retrospect may be seen as the high-water mark of the possibilities and creativity of the counterculture. Hendrix's image dominated all others in discussions of the festival, just as the image of him setting his guitar on fire before a stunned audience there dominated later images of Hendrix. [40]

He showcased the hybridity of his repertoire, performing the blues (Howlin' Wolf's "Killing Floor" and B. B. King's "Rock Me Baby"); Bob Dylan's counterculture anthem "Like a Rolling Stone"; a range of his own startling psychedelic songs from *Are You Experienced?* ("Foxy Lady," "The Wind Cries Mary," "Can You See Me?," and "Purple Haze"); and ending with the British garage classic "Wild Thing." As famously featured in the 1968 documentary *Monterey Pop*, Hendrix ended the show by lighting his guitar on fire and then smashing it to bits. Hendrix was wildly, openly sexual in a way that disturbed even this supposedly hip audience: he humped his amplifiers, simulated cunnilingus on his guitar, and also brandished it as an extension of his penis. The film zooms in on two women sitting up front who looked completely stunned, and more than a little scared. He carried all the flamboyance and pyrotechnics of the black popular music scene and the London underground to the West Coast and then brought his heady cauldron of influences to a boil.

The creativity and excitement of this performance, however, were buried under a language of racial essences. Hendrix received a number of negative reviews, especially from members of the emerging rock press who saw his performance as pandering to white teenyboppers rather than as an expression of black tradition or a new kind of art form.[41] Robert Christgau reviewed the festival for *Esquire*, and he astutely addressed the festival's racial politics, defining the "love crowd" as white, uncomfortable with black music, and insecure about its own abilities to imitate it. He argued that the audience responded to three "preconceived symbols—the spade, the supergroup, the guru." [42] The "spade" was a figure of hypersexuality that allowed whites to feel sexually free but conformed to stereotypes of blackness that made whites comfortable. Christgau's argument implied that in the United States, Hendrix was exoticized by the festival's elision of race. He then continued, savaging Hendrix's performance:

> He was terrible. Hendrix is a psychedelic Uncle Tom. Don't
> believe me; believe Sal Silver of the *East Village Other*: "Jimi did a
> beautiful Spade routine." Hendrix earned that capital S. Dressed
> in English fop mod, with a ruffled orange shirt and red pants that

outlined his semierection to the thirtieth row, Jimi really, as Silver phrased it, "Socked it to them." Grunting and groaning on the brink of sham orgasm, he made his way through five or six almost indistinguishable songs, occasionally flickering an anteater tongue at that great crotch in the sky. . . . He had tailored a caricature to their mythic standards and didn't overdo it a shade. . . . I suppose Hendrix's act can be understood as a consistently vulgar parody of rock theatrics, but I don't feel I have to like it. Anyway, he can't sing.[43]

Christgau revealed his disdain for rock theatrics in this review, which was a growing trend at the time. As rock moved from matching suits, haircuts, and choreographed stage routines to the festival and the jam session, theatrics came for some to represent inauthenticity, especially to the new rock press, which covered (and created) primarily white artists. But what was it about Hendrix's performance that could be construed as "Uncle Tomming"? Uncle Toms try to please and entertain whites by conforming to white stereotypes of black behavior, but there is nothing dangerous or particularly sexual about an Uncle Tom. In Christgau's analysis, a "psychedelic Uncle Tom" fulfills the counterculture's desires for more open sexuality, but in stereotypical ways. Christgau's review trivialized the real demands that Hendrix made on his audience. Hendrix challenged his audience to see race as a process of cross-pollination, and in so doing he created a new kind of black expressive culture. As Mablen Jones argues: "His arrogant stage performances were the antithesis of the stylized black vaudeville of Motown as well as the gospel self-humiliation of [James] Brown. He looked and sounded egotistical, maniacal, and weird."[44] Hendrix's Monterey performance could have been seen, should have been seen, as an original hybrid, especially to someone like Christgau who recognized the racial problems of the festival. While he cannily perceived the counterculture's evasion of race, he still defined race in essentialist terms.

Although there was much to celebrate, the Monterey Pop Festival and the reception of Hendrix there revealed racial divisions underlying the rhetoric of integration dominant in the first half of the decade. The critic Craig Werner argues that blacks "didn't much care" about the San Francisco scene: "Monterey, and the scene that gave birth to it, was mostly a white thing. You could see it—the *Monterey Pop* crowd shots rarely manage to capture more than a couple of black faces in any frame—but you could also hear it. Janis Joplin, one of the few Southerners to perform, blew the crowd away with 'Down on Me' and 'Ball and Chain' partly because she didn't have to compete with KoKo Taylor or Aretha Franklin."[45] Where did this leave Hendrix and the new black pop stardom he created? The race riots of the mid-to-late-Sixties made it clear that blacks had little use for the hippie dropout lifestyle. That tension played out in the rest of Hendrix's short, successful career. If Hendrix left Harlem for musical freedom in the counterculture, it was quickly apparent that that freedom came at the cost of racial identity.

After Monterey, Hendrix carried with him all of the traces of his countercultural milieu to rock stardom: musical and sartorial experimentation on the one hand and racial polarization on the other. He produced prodigious amounts of groundbreaking music in a very short period. His first album, *Are You Experienced?*, was released in the United States in August 1967 and ultimately reached number 5 on the charts (it remained on the *Billboard* charts for 106 weeks). His second album, *Axis: Bold as Love,* was released in December in the United Kingdom (number 5) and in January of 1968 in the United States (number 3). *Electric Ladyland* followed in autumn. All three albums exemplify his nouveau hybridity: traditional blues of "Red House," the sonic experiments of "1983," jazz beats of "Rainy Day, Dream Away," the Curtis Mayfield–style soul of "Electric Ladyland," straight rock of "Spanish Castle Magic," as well as his tour de force "Voodoo Chile," in which he translated the figure of the bluesman into psychedelic terms:

> Well the night I was born / Lord I swear the moon turned a fire
> red / Well my poor mother cried out 'Lord, the gypsy was right!'/
> and I seen her fell down right dead / Well, mountain lions found
> me there waitin', / and set me on a eagle's back / He took me past
> to the outskirts of infinity, / and when he brought me back, / he
> gave me Venus witch's ring / And he said "Fly on, fly on" / 'Cause
> I'm a Voodoo Chile baby, Voodoo Chile.

Hendrix became obsessed with studio technique, developing an artistic persona atypical of black artists at the time and more associated with the experimentation of white artists like the Beatles and Brian Wilson of the Beach Boys.[46]

The Jimi Hendrix Experience performed more than 150 shows in the U.S. alone between Monterey and the breakup of the original Experience in June 1969. But especially in the United States—in both mainstream and underground reception—Hendrix's fame was articulated in terms of race. He appealed to a wide cross-section of audiences: from those genuinely interested in fashioning an alternative to the Establishment to those who may have just liked to indulge themselves momentarily in the seductive world of sex, drugs, and rock and roll. He played not only in large urban centers but also in provincial towns such as Tuscaloosa, Alabama; Muncie, Indiana; and Davenport, Iowa. This frenetic touring introduced a live radical sound into some very square places. Hendrix's race was emphatically *not* invisible on his American tours. In Dallas, the Experience was threatened with violence if they played "The Star-Spangled Banner"; they were refused hotel rooms in Tuscaloosa because there were too many white women around Hendrix; and Hendrix knew that he could not enter many restaurants down South. Mitch Mitchell argues that the Experience was disturbing not only because Hendrix was black but because they were an integrated band.[47] Hendrix's popularity dramatized both the potential and limits of integration. In this environment the marketing of Hendrix had transformative results by flaunting his blackness and his integrated band. His extensive touring claimed the right of an African American to play with white musicians and consort with white women whenever and wherever he chose.

But the rampant commercialism of the Experience also exploited racial stereotypes, especially Hendrix's aggressive and supposedly dangerous sexuality. His management had control over merchandising (posters, programs, etc.), which became an important source of income for the visually exciting Experience. Jim McDermott argues that Jerry Goldstein, president of The Visual Thing, the company with exclusive rights to Hendrix's posters and program, "understood the potential of marrying merchandising techniques of the teen idol area with psychedelic artists—especially one as exotic as Hendrix. . . . Sales of memorabilia, right from the outset, were strong."[48] Perhaps the most striking example of this marketing was the use of Ron Raffaelli's photo of Hendrix, stripped to the waist, standing astride with two white women, also stripped to the waist, and Redding and Mitchell framed between Hendrix's legs looking on behind them. This provocative image was reproduced in the form of several different posters as well as in a book titled *Electric Church: A Visual Experience*, which was sold at the Experience's 1969 U.S. shows.[49]

Hendrix crafted and exploited this image for some time, and he certainly attracted an array of white lovers and groupies. Yet when he attempted to impose certain limits on what he considered to be acceptable exposure, he could find himself overruled. Against Hendrix's wishes, the British version of *Electric Ladyland* featured twenty-one naked women of diverse races on the cover, holding pictures of Hendrix. Playing up his incendiary potential, the inside cover showed Hendrix against a flaming backdrop.[50]

The image of the highly sexual black man surrounded by naked white women played on the stereotypes and fears of mainstream white America. The above-ground press emphasized his sexuality as if to ridicule him; in a special issue of *Look* from early 1969 devoted to examining black-white relations, there

Jimi Hendrix with two unidentified models, and Noel Redding and Mitch Mitchell of the Experience on the island of Maui, 6 October 1968. Ron Raffaelli was hired by the Experience's management company in fall 1968 to visually document the group's every move. His photographs were then incorporated into a book entitled *Electric Church*, which was sold at the group's American concerts that following year. This shot prefigured the antihero protagonists of blaxploitation film as well as the later "thug life" poses of gangsta rap artists. Hendrix's virile petulance in a subordinated white world was deliberately crafted to capitalize on the presumed ensuing sex panic.
Michael Ochs Archives.

is a picture of Hendrix at a hotel pool with several lovely white women around him; the caption reads "Cooling it poolside with California birds." Hendrix is quoted in the article as saying, "Race isn't a problem in my world."[51] The underground press, too, read Hendrix's sexuality as his limitation. In 1968 a reviewer for the *East Village Other* lambasted his show at the Fillmore East:

> The great Jimi Hendrix Experience blessed the stage of the Fillmore last Friday . . . but what a drag it was that Hendrix was so penis oriented that night. The greatest musician in the world really doesn't have to hump his guitar. Playing with his teeth is cool, but doing his guitar is a little out of the question and kind of silly. The strange thing was that the audience responded to this the most. . . . [It was the] closest thing to mass hysteria I've ever seen.[52]

If Hendrix intended his image to represent sexual and racial freedom, it was more often received as pandering to commercialism and racial stereotypes instead. The historian Brian Ward argues that while Hendrix "played" with white stereotypes of black sexuality and therefore gave himself some element of control over them, he "left pervasive white assumptions unchallenged and tacitly endorsed."[53] Subsequently, Hendrix began to feel uncomfortable with his eroticized image. Not because he felt it signified "Uncle Tom," but because he felt it was distracting his audience from fully appreciating the complexity of his work: "I never wanted it to be so much of a visual thing. When I didn't do it, people thought I was being moody, but I can only freak when I feel like doing so. I can't do it just for the sake of it."[54] With the loss of control over how the meaning of his image was negotiated with his audience, Hendrix had to come to terms with race more consciously. He had come to realize that the hybridity of his act wasn't communicating what he wanted it to either to counterculture or mainstream audiences.

A box set of previously unavailable Hendrix material, *The Jimi Hendrix Experience* (2000), includes an early 1969 jam among Hendrix, Buddy Miles, and Larry Young titled "It's Too Bad." It's a blues tune that slyly comments on his complex racial positioning in the culture: "So I go way across the tracks, and man they treat me the same as you do/ They say, man until you come back completely black, go back from where you came from too." Hendrix follows this poignant expression of his rejection by blacks with a dismissive giggle and a searing guitar solo. The lyrics, the laugh, and the fierce playing are all part of Hendrix's articulate retort to those who wanted to deal with him in only "racially pure" terms, as "completely black" or "Uncle Tom." The previous year in an interview with England's *Melody Maker*, Hendrix appeared confident that his success allowed him to avoid racial politics: "I just want to do what I'm doing without getting involved in racial or political matters. I know I'm lucky that I can do that . . . lots of people can't."[55] Hendrix soon realized the naivete of his stance. In the volatile and violent racial climate of the late 1960s, the career of this highly visible black musician was being defined whether he liked it or not as a "white thing."

After the release of *Electric Ladyland* in late 1968, Hendrix tried to artic-ulate his relationship to blues as a way to sort out his growing sense of dis-comfort with a mostly white audience:

> The background of our music is a spiritual-blues thing. Blues is part of America. We're making our music into electric church music—a new kind of Bible, not like in a hotel, but a Bible you carry in your hearts, one that will give you a physical feeling. We try to make our music so loose and hard-hitting so that it hits your soul hard enough to make it open. It's like shock therapy or a can opener. Rock is technically blues-based. Rock is like a young dragon until the establishment gets hold of it and turns it into a cabaret act with the big voice and the patent-leather shoes and the patent-leather hair. Almost anyone who has the power to keep their minds open listens to our music. Black kids think the music is white now, which it isn't. The argument is not between black and white now. That's just another game the establishment set up to turn us against one another. But the black kids don't have a chance too much to listen—they're too busy trying to get their own selves together. We want them to realize that our music is just as spiritual as going to church.[56]

Hendrix situates his music as a "spiritual-blues thing" here specifically to make connections with black listeners, almost in direct contradiction to his rejection of gospel and church when he talked about what attracted him to the Village. His comments reveal, too, that he saw the rock music industry as the culprit in commercializing music and creating divisions between blacks and whites. His experiences with the rock business had taught him that record companies, radio formats, and the growing concert business had little interest in breaking down racial divisions. Clearly his career was at a turning point.

Little evidence exists that African Americans in the 1960s considered Hendrix a sellout; rather, he's remembered as a distant oddity. His longtime friend and sometimes lover Faye Pridgeon (who's black) described her reac-tion to his 1967 Central Park show: "I guess I liked it, but it just wasn't black music. I was a funky person. I came from Jimmy Reed, Guitar Slim, Muddy

Waters and Lightnin' Hopkins. This is what had blown me away about Jimi—he wasn't your average John Q. African American. He was a real blues fanatic. . . .When he went into rock 'n' roll, it kind of knocked me for a loop."[57] Nelson George attributes black indifference to Hendrix solely to musical style: "problem was, you just couldn't dance to it. Maybe if you were stoned at a light show the Jimi Hendrix Experience could be boogie fodder. Maybe if the grass was flowing at a local love-in you'd dance. However, to the audiences of Stax and Motown and James Brown, "Purple Haze" and "Hey Joe" just didn't do the do."[58] Hendrix received no radio exposure in black markets, so there was little opportunity for black audiences to hear him in the context of other black music.[59]

But for some African Americans Hendrix represented the possibility of a new kind of black/counterculture identity: proud, experimental, and hybrid. Soul singer Bobby Womack felt that a "new breed of blacks" would connect with Hendrix and that when he saw young black men dressing like Hendrix, he realized that Jimi had helped create the "black hippie."[60] Frank Gilliam, a UCLA political science professor and member of the Black Rock Coalition, reflects that "When we were growing up, rock was not cool music for black kids to enjoy. Either you listened to 'soul' music or else you were considered 'whitewashed.'. . . Jimi personified the 'transculturation' of America for middle-class blacks. He validated our position in society, the fact that we were proud to be black, but also not enslaved by black experience."[61] Bob Davis, the creator of the "Jimi Hendrix Black Experience" website argues that Hendrix was a symbol of pride and equality for black fans: "Hendrix in his lifestyle, demeanor and willingness to 'crossover' and actually deal with white people on an equal footing, had become such a powerful symbol for the achievement of the objectives of the American Civil Rights Movement of the 1960's, that the chief beneficiaries of that movement sought to emulate him in the strongest way possible."[62] None of these fans saw Hendrix as pandering to whites or to young people; they instead talk about the revolutionary potential of his music and image.

But the possibilities of Hendrix's prototypical black hippie were hard to see in an era of a burgeoning black nationalism. Black artists and musicians were consciously developing a black art and a black aesthetic, turning to Africa as a source of inspiration for creating a more "authentic" blackness. By the summer of 1968, the Black Power movement had gained mass musical exposure when James Brown scored a hit with "Say It Loud—I'm Black and I'm Proud." The rhetoric of integration and transcendence was on the back burner. Therefore Hendrix's transformative hybridity put him at odds with the Black Panther Party. He was repeatedly lobbied by members of the Panthers for financial support and more direct political involvement. Members of his management organization and his bandmates in the Experience describe Hendrix as feeling overwhelmed and embattled by his encounters with the Panthers, although he did introduce "Voodoo Child (Slight Return)" as the "Black Panther national anthem" at several shows in 1969. He also told *Rolling Stone* in March of 1970, "I naturally feel part of what [the Black Panthers] are doing." But, he added cautiously, "In certain respects. . . . not the aggression or violence or whatever you want to call it. I'm not for guerrilla warfare."[63] He had rejected violence earlier in "House Burning Down" from *Electric Ladyland*, a song that seems to comment on the many riots that had ripped apart American cities: "I said 'Oh baby why did you burn your brother's house down?'/Look at the sky turn a hell-fire red, Lord/Someone's house is burning down down down/Well, someone stepped from the crowd/He was nineteen miles high/He shouts, 'We're tired and disgusted/So we paint red through the sky.' I said, 'The truth is straight ahead/So don't burn yourself instead/Try to learn instead of burn." Hendrix was intrigued by the Black Power movement and excited about the possibilities of new black identities. His discomfort came from a reticence about politics, but also a reluctance to align himself with any kind of racial essentialism.

Hendrix attempted to reach out to a black audience in 1969, although not at the expense of the hybridity that was always the hallmark of his career. His effort to create a more racially conscious identity came at a time when he also felt a growing disenchantment with the demands of pop music success. Woodstock marked the beginning of a new path for Hendrix, a period of racial and sonic reinvention. In addition to his post-Woodstock performance in Harlem, he recorded with the black nationalist group The Last Poets in November 1969 and formed an all-black band, the Band of Gypsys, for shows at the Fillmore East on New Year's Eve of 1969. Hendrix recorded the proto-rap song "Doriella du Fontaine" with Buddy Miles and a member of The Last Poets, Jalal Nurriddin.[64] The Last Poets had formed in May of 1968 and maintained political ties to the Black Panthers. Their aggressive street poetry, chanted over African drums, expressed frustration with both white society and bourgeois blacks. On "Doriella du Fontaine" Hendrix laid down a funky R & B riff over Miles's in-the-pocket drumming; the backing track would be at home on a James Brown record. Nurriddin takes on the persona of a pimp telling the story of one of his women, their adventures, and her subsequent death. The track's producer, Alan Douglas, explained that "This piece was from a suite of things we were doing called *Jail Toasts*, like older black convicts would rap in prison. It started with 'Dear John' letters they would receive and in order for them to turn around and have some fun, they would create poetry out of them."[65] The song, as David Henderson suggests, is a contemporary folk expression, glorifying the pimp and the whore's style.[66] The song is a fascinating mix of a traditional R & B beat with an insurgent voice of black nationalism. Although the track was not released until 1984, it suggests that Hendrix could now collaborate with artists whose overtly political agenda he might have earlier found off-putting.

Hendrix achieved arguably his greatest artistic success in this period of more self-realized racial politics with his new Band of Gypsys, featuring Buddy Miles on drums and Billy Cox on bass. Although each of the musicians happened to be African American, Hendrix's main purpose was not in assembling an all-black band.[67] The Band of Gypsys created a new vehicle for expressing Hendrix's ideas that in turn produced his most overtly political music. The band recorded a number of songs in the studio that marked a new era for Hendrix: he continued his guitar experimentation, but Miles brought the call-and-response of black blues and gospel and the more straight-ahead drumming style from R & B to ground that experimentation in a more danceable, funkier beat. The band all referred to their sound as providing "earth" for Hendrix's sky church sounds. (In fact, they recorded a song called "Earth Blues" in late 1969). Their only live concerts were at the Fillmore East on New Year's Eve, 1969, and New Year's Day, 1970. The show featured new songs and Hendrix's wildest guitar playing, accompanied by a throbbing, protozoic light show. He dedicated "Voodoo Child (Slight Return)" to the Black Panthers and "Machine Gun" to "all the soldiers fighting in Chicago, and Milwaukee, and New York . . . oh yeah, and all the soldiers fighting in Vietnam," making explicit connections between race riots, antiwar protests, and the Vietnam War. It was the first time he had mentioned the war from the stage. The song depicts soldiers as pawns in the game of "evil men": "Evil man make me kill ya/ Evil man make you kill me/Evil man make me kill you/ Even though we're only families apart." In Hendrix's world, powerful, evil forces keep people from seeing their common bonds, whether it be between blacks and whites in the United States, between Americans and the Vietnamese, or between antiwar protesters and American GIs. The music was startlingly violent; Hendrix's guitar conjures a cacophony of gunfire and bomb blasts, while Miles and Cox lay down a relentlessly menacing rhythm underneath, interrupted only by Cox's machine gun shots on his snare drum. "Machine Gun" demands listeners to reckon with the fact that a revolutionary counterculture is facing corrupted, divisive foes. Hendrix had reached a point where he could articulate his politics through his music, in part because he had begun to consciously address the meaning of his conflicted racial status.[68]

Hendrix's legacy has been in the multiple, hybrid spirit the best of his music possessed.[69] In one of his last interviews before his untimely death in 1970, he posited a tantalizing plan for the future:

> with the music we will paint pictures of earth and space, so that the listener can be taken somewhere. It's going to be something that will open up a new sense in people's minds. They are getting their minds ready now. Like me they are going back home, getting fat, and making themselves ready for the next trip. You see music is so important. I don't any longer dig the pop and politics crap. That's old fashioned. . . .When there are vast changes in the way the world goes, it's usually something like art and music that changes it. Music is going to change the world next time.[70]

Hendrix suggests here that if the revolution were to succeed, it would need to take hold in the imagination apart from the commercial and political realms. He reflects back on the two paths that had tripped him up—the "pop" Experience that transformed him into a racial caricature, and the attempts by the Panthers to push him toward claiming a pure "blackness"—and tries to imagine a new third way. Having been through a remarkable four years, Hendrix held out the possibility of a psychedelic, imaginative reordering of the world. He still avoided talking about race very directly because he had found a way for "blackness" to emerge more overtly in his music and performance during the last year of his life. Because he held tenaciously to that vision despite a series of uncomprehending audiences, he remains emblematic of the best hopes of a revolutionary counterculture.

Notes

1. Reid soundbite in "'Purple Haze': The 100 Most Important American Musical Works of the 20th Century," *All Things Considered*, National Public Radio, 18 September, 2000.

2. Hendrix enlisted in the army in the spring of 1961 after dropping out of high school. He had few job prospects and was fighting with his father, so the army seemed a logical way out. He fulfilled his wish of being a parachutist, training in California and ending up stationed in Tennessee. When asked about the war by a Dutch journalist in 1967, Hendrix expressed his belief in the cold war "domino theory": "The Americans are fighting in Vietnam for a completely free world. As soon as they move out, they [the Vietnamese] will be at the mercy of the communists. For that matter the yellow danger [China] should not be underestimated. Of course, war is horrible, but at present it's still the only guarantee of peace." Quoted in Harry Shapiro and Caesar Glebbeek, *Electric Gypsy* (New York: St Martin's Press, 1995), 387.

3. Hendrix recorded a studio version of the song in March 1969, and played it at many shows in late 1968 and early 1969. He introduced the song at a concert at the Los Angeles Forum in April of 1969 by saying, "Here's a song that we was all brainwashed with." The studio version was never released in Hendrix's lifetime; it is included in the box set *The Jimi Hendrix Experience* (MCA Compact Disc 088 112 317 2-5, 2000). For a moving depiction of the force of Hendrix's version of the song, see Sherman Alexie's short story "Because My Father Always Said He Was the Only Indian Who Saw Jimi Hendrix Play 'The Star-Spangled Banner' at

Woodstock," in *The Lone Ranger and Tonto Fistfight in Heaven* (New York: Atlantic Monthly Press, 1993).

4. John McDermott with Eddie Kramer, *Hendrix: Setting the Record Straight* (New York: Warner Books, 1992), 222.

5. Ibid.

6. "Jimi Hendrix Speaks at the United Black Association Press Conference," www.soul-patrol.com/funk/jh_speaks.htm, 20 August, 2000.

7. The shows also function differently in our cultural memory. The Woodstock performance is captured on several official audio and video recordings, but only poor quality bootleg tapes and a few photographs exist of the UBA benefit.

8. Shapiro and Glebbeek, *Electric Gypsy*, 393.

9. McDermott, *Hendrix: Setting the Record Straight*, 222.

10. David Henderson, *'Scuse Me While I Kiss the Sky: The Life of Jimi Hendrix* (New York: Bantam Books, 1981), 287.

11. Dave Marsh describes the Seattle scene as inherently eclectic: "Seattle's resistance to trendiness is a prime characteristic of its rock scene from the late fifties straight through to the grunge of the early nineties. In fact, the best Pacific Northwest bands did not reject anything at all, including what [Larry] Coryell believed to be 'Madison Avenue pop,' but maintained an elastic attitude that incorporated everything it heard in idiosyncratic ways: This is as true of Jimi Hendrix as it is of Quincy Jones. . . . Out of this stew of influences a Pacific Northwest rock aesthetic began to emerge. It boiled down to a willingness to try anything, make any unlikely noise, adapt all available resources in the service of shaking the spirit." *Louie Louie: The History and Mythology of the World's Most Famous Rock'n'Roll Song* (New York: Hyperion, 1993), 53.

12. Gil Rodman, *Elvis after Elvis: The Posthumous Career of a Living Legend* (New York: Routledge, 1996), 54–55.

13. For example, the July 2000 issue of *Uncut* included a series of articles that addressed his racial politics; Charles Shaar Murray wrote a similar piece in the November 1999 special "Black Power" issue of the British music magazine *MOJO*. There is even a "Jimi Hendrix Black Experience" website, which situates Hendrix in the history of black music and black culture (www.soul-patrol.com/funk/jh.htm, 20 August, 2000).

14. The cultural critic George Lipsitz maintains that "white youths could not or would not embrace black culture and politics directly; for the most part they preferred to fashion alternative cultures and communities that spoke more to the alienations of middle-class life than they did to the racial and class inequities of American society. The music of the counterculture employed traditional blues techniques and devices, but its emphasis on electronic distortion (through feedback, reverb, and wa-wa pedals on electric guitars), the focus of its lyrics on alienation and drug use, and the extended length of individual songs and concerts all reflected the concerns and interests of an emerging (mostly) white subculture." "Who'll Stop the Rain," in *The Sixties: From Memory to History*, ed. David Farber, (Chapel Hill: University of North Carolina Press, 1994), 218.

15. Lipsitz, "Who'll Stop the Rain?" 217.

16. Jeremy Wells makes a similar argument in his discussion of the relation between race and heavy metal in studies of Hendrix: "The race-transcending guitarist who helped define heavy metal seems somehow nonidentical with the black man who once played backup for Little Richard" ("Blackness'Scuzed: Jimi Hendrix's (In)visible Legacy in Heavy Metal," in *Race Consciousness: African-American Studies for the New Century*, eds. Judith Jackson Fossett and Jeffrey A. Tucker (New York: New York University Press, 1997), 52.

17. In *The Black Atlantic: Modernity and Double Consciousness*, Paul Gilroy critiques forms of cultural nationalism "which present immutable, ethnic differences as an absolute break in the histories and experiences of 'black' and 'white' people"; he offers instead a "more difficult option:

the theorisation of creolisation, métissage, mestizaje, and hybridity. From the viewpoint of ethnic absolutism, this would be a litany of pollution and impurity. These terms are rather unsatisfactory ways of naming the processes of cultural mutation and restless (dis)continuity that exceed racial discourse and avoid capture by its agents." *The Black Atlantic: Modernity and Double Consciousness* (Cambridge: Harvard University Press, 1993), 2.

18. *The Black Atlantic*, 3.

19. Nelson George sees Hendrix as a "cultural curator" or "historical critic" because he worked in a pop idiom: "By taking established black forms, preserving their essence but filtering these textures through an ambitious creative consciousness, they made astounding music that is in the tradition yet singular from it." *The Death of Rhythm and Blues* (New York: Pantheon Books, 1988), 108.

20. For the most exhaustive discussion of Hendrix's family, including a family tree, see Shapiro and Glebbeek, *Electric Gypsy*, 5–33, 746–47.

21. Buddy Miles, who played drums with Hendrix in 1968–69, felt that an integrated environment helped contribute to Hendrix's comfort with racial mixing: "Jimi was from Seattle, a city that had not only American but Canadian blacks, so he could fit into the mainstream much easier than rural blacks. I was from Omaha, Nebraska, where you also had a good racial mix of people." McDermott, *Hendrix: Setting the Record Straight*, 68.

22. Ibid., 192.

23. Dylan was an important influence on Hendrix's writing and singing. Hendrix was always self-conscious about his vocal abilities, and Dylan's unconventional singing style allowed him to see the possibilities of his own voice. During his career, Hendrix covered four Dylan songs: "Like a Rolling Stone," "Drifter's Escape," "Can You Please Crawl Out Your Window?" and "All Along the Watchtower."

24. Nelson George attributes this change to Hendrix's musical style: "Unfortunately, Hendrix fatally damaged his connection with black audiences because of his innovative brilliance on the electric guitar, an instrument that, with the declining black interest in blues, fell into disfavor. But in rock, lead guitarist extravagance was crucial to the music and the supporting culture. It was the perfect accompaniment to LSD and other chemicals of choice. . . . In essence, Hendrix was the revenge of the r&b sideman, one with the ability to turn the voices inside his head into music." *The Death of Rhythm and Blues*, 108.

25. Michael Lydon, "'The Black Elvis?'" *New York Times*, 25 February, 1968, 19–20.

26. Charles Shaar Murray contends that "whether or not he actually attended the jazz clubs and sat at the feet of Sun Ra, Coltrane, Mingus, and Coleman, their presence was inescapable. In fact, it really doesn't matter whether Hendrix can be *proved* to have checked these men out or not. It is a matter of record that he arrived in London with a battered copy of Roland Kirk's *Rip Rig and Panic* in his luggage, and Billy Cox . . . has attested to Jimi's knowledge of lounge-bar standards such as 'Misty,' 'Moonlight in Vermont' and 'Harlem Nocturne,' which featured chords and scales more sophisticated than those used in standard blues-rock." *Crosstown Traffic: Jimi Hendrix and the Post-War Rock 'n' Roll Revolution* (New York: St. Martin's Press, 1989), 192).

27. Henderson, *'Scuse Me While I Kiss the Sky: The Life of Jimi Hendrix*, 149.

28. He also played often at the Café Au Go Go on Bleecker, The Loft on Hudson Street, and especially the Night Owl Café on West Third, a club that "leaned toward the psychedelic, drug-oriented music" and also featured afternoon jam sessions that provided the musicians lunch. Robbie Wolliver, *Hoot! A 25-Year History of the Greenwich Village Music Scene* (New York: St. Martin's Press, 1986), 139.

29. Shapiro and Glebbeek, *Electric Gypsy*, 104.

30. Neil Spencer, "Lord Kitchener's Valet," in *The Ultimate Experience*, eds. Adrian Boot and Chris Salewicz (New York: MacMillan, 1995), 195. Hendrix's look also suggested androgyny, which Robert Wyatt, drummer for the London psychedelic band The Soft Machine, argues was

a dominant aesthetic on the London scene at the time: "Macho was less of a big thing generally in England. The ideology and culture back then was much more hermaphrodite, pre-Raphaelite, boys being like girls and so on. . . . Hendrix was very interested in that more English way of looking at things, musically and aesthetically." David Stubbs, "Public Image Unlimited," *Uncut,* July 2000, 54.

31. Jonathan Green, *All Dressed Up: The Sixties and the Counterculture* (London: Pimlico, 1998), 429.

32. Mitch Mitchell and John Platt, *The Hendrix Experience* (New York: De Capo Press, 1998), 32.

33. Mark Prendergast, "Racial Rehabilitation," *New Statesman and Society,* 28 April 1995, in *The Jimi Hendrix Companion: Three Decades of Commentary,* ed. Chris Potash (New York: Schirmer Books, 1998), 183. In his autobiography, Mitch Mitchell remembers that "colour never entered into it at all, certainly not in England. English audiences were used to integrated bands and maybe that was a difference for Hendrix, experiencing that possibly for the first time outside Greenwich Village." Mitchell, *The Hendrix Experience,* 36. While fellow band member Noel Redding concurs that race wasn't an important issue at the time, in his memoirs he was unable to recall another racially integrated group performing in England at the time of Hendrix's arrival.

34. Shapiro and Glebbeek, *Electric Gypsy,* 136.

35. Noel Redding and Carol Appleby, *Are You Experienced? The Inside Story of the Jimi Hendrix Experience* (New York: De Capo Press, 1996), 27.

36. Shapiro and Glebbeek, *Electric Gypsy,* 136.

37. Don Menn, "Jimi's Favorite Guitar Techniques," *Guitar Player,* September 1975, in *The Jimi Hendrix Companion,* ed. Potash, 84.

38. Henderson, *'Scuse Me While I Kiss the Sky: The Life of Jimi Hendrix,* 77. For the best discussion of Hendrix's roots in black music, see Murray's *Crosstown Traffic,* especially chaps. 4–8.

39. U.S. fans had heard very little of Hendrix before Monterey. "Hey Joe" was released as a single in May of 1967, and "Purple Haze" on the first day of the festival. The album *Are You Experienced?* was not released in the United States until August 1967.

40. For example, Joel Selvin introduces his study of the festival by arguing that "No single performance has been more deeply embedded into the firmament of rock than Hendrix at Monterey . . . he walked onstage a nobody and walked off a major star." *Monterey Pop* (San Francisco: Chronicle, 1992), 3. Jeremy Wells concludes that "Historically, mythically, and imagistically, the performance does represent Hendrix's emergence as a dominant cultural force" ("Blackness 'Scuzed," 57–58).

41. For example, Albert Goldman described Hendrix as not entirely black in a 1968 story for *New York magazine*: "Like the last generation of jazzmen, who transcended their Negro origins to become figures in the international music avant-garde—playing to almost exclusively white audiences, working with white sidemen, studying with white masters, and consorting with white women—Hendrix's blackness is only skin deep." "SuperSpade Raises Atlantis: Jimi Hendrix," in *Freakshow* (New York: Atheneum, 1971), 86.

42. Robert Christgau, "Secular Music," in *Any Ol' Way You Choose It: Rock and Other Pop Music, 1967–1973* (Baltimore: Penguin Books, 1975), 23. He argues for instance that the crowd's enthusiastic reception for Buddy Miles was an example of this fascination with "the spade" : "Miles got it because he was, as the Los Angeles *Free Press* so delicately put it, 'a raunchy black mound'—the spade." Robert Christgau, "Secular Music, "25. Presumably Ravi Shankar is the guru and the Byrds and Mamas & Papas are the supergroup in Christgau's formulation.

43. Christgau, "Secular Music," 32.

44. Mablen Jones, *Getting it On: The Clothing of Rock 'n' Roll* (New York: Abbeville Press, 1987), 84.

45. Craig Werner, *A Change Is Gonna Come: Music, Race, and the Soul of America* (New York: Plume, 1998), 92.

46. The rock press seemed much more smitten with Hendrix as a studio and guitar genius than with Hendrix's stage show. Studio experimentation was the mark of the "rock *artist*," a concept that emerges in the late Sixties in magazines like *Rolling Stone* and *Crawdaddy.*

47. Mitchell, *The Hendrix Experience*, 37.

48. McDermott, *Hendrix: Setting the Record Straight*, 139.

49. Caroline Coon, "Jimi Hendrix—Experienced?" in *The Ultimate Experience*, ed. Adrian Boot and Chris Salewicz (New York: Macmillan, 1995), 153.

50. See Shapiro and Glebbeek for Hendrix's handwritten letter to the record company suggesting a specific design for the American edition of *Electric Ladyland*, 305–06. They did not create exactly the design he wanted, but they did use a different cover. The American album featured the British cover shot as a separate poster included inside.

51. George Goodman, "Jimi Hendrix Experience: Black & White Fusion in the Now Music," *Look*, 7 January, 1969, 37–38.

52. *East Village Other*, 17 May, 1968, 18.

53. Brian Ward, *Just My Soul Responding: Rhythm and Blues, Black Consciousness, and Race Relations* (Berkeley: University of California Press, 1998), 246.

54. Roy Hollingworth, "Hendrix Today," *Melody Maker*, 5 September, 1970, in *The Jimi Hendrix Companion*, ed. Potash, 37.

55. Alan Walsh, "I Felt We Were in Danger of Becoming the U.S. Dave Dee," *Melody Maker*, 20 July 1968, in *The Jimi Hendrix Companion*, ed. Potash, 17.

56. Henderson, *'Scuse Me While I Kiss the Sky: The Life of Jimi Hendrix*, 214.

57. McDermott, *Hendrix: Setting the Record Straight*, 79.

58. George, *The Death of Rhythm and Blues*, 108.

59. The Harlem deejay Eddie O'Jay attributed Hendrix's lack of a black audience partly to the preprogrammed radio format he and other disc jockeys had to follow: "My not being able to play the kind of records that I'd wanted to hear on the radio meant that few people had heard of Jimi Hendrix. I don't think the black masses were appreciative of Hendrix's music because we were not exposed to it that much" (McDermott, *Hendrix: Setting the Record Straight*, 223). Geoffrey Stokes argues that the emergence of FM widened the racial divide: "Most black pop musicians . . . continued to work within AM's traditional expectations. . . . As AM stations found themselves confronted with a wave of unconventional new sounds, they increasingly relied on Motown's tried-and-true product as the backbone of their playlists. As a result, however, the emerging FM progressives looked elsewhere for their black artists. . . . This policy meant, in essence, that the bulk of the music that was most popular with black listeners (and to some degree with younger teens of all races) wasn't played on the stations that were drawing an ever-increasing white youth audience." "Love for Sale," in Ed Ward, Geoffrey Stokes, and Ken Tucker, *Rock of Ages: The Rolling Stone History of Rock & Roll* (Englewood Cliffs, N.J.: Rolling Stone Press, 1986), 378. For a discussion of the place of black radio in the black pride movement, see Nelson, *The Death of Rhythm and Blues.*

60. Murray, *Crosstown Traffic*, 82.

61. Chuck Philips, "Experiencing Jimi Hendrix," *Los Angeles Times*, 26 November, 1989, in *The Jimi Hendrix Companion*, ed. Potash, 168. The Black Rock Coalition is a group of musicians and activists sponsoring "black rock" concerts and conferences.

62. Bob Davis, "Me & Jimi & Funky DC 1972," 16 June, 1997, www. Soul-patrol.com/funk/jh.htm, 20 August, 2000.

63. John Burks, "The End of a Beginning Maybe," *Rolling Stone*, 19 March, 1970, in *The Jimi Hendrix Companion*, ed. Potash, 28.

64. There is some confusion over which of The Last Poets Hendrix recorded with. John McDermott says it was Nurriddin; this is supported by the fact that when the record was finally

released in 1984, it was done so under the name "Lightnin' Rod" and Nurriddin recorded several other songs as "Lightnin' Rod." However, both David Henderson and Shapiro and Glebbeek credit the track to Alafia Pudim.

65. McDermott, *Hendrix: Setting the Record Straight*, 234.

66. Henderson, *'Scuse Me While I Kiss the Sky: The Life of Jimi Hendrix* , 295.

67. For a thorough account of the Band of Gypsys, including interviews with Cox, Miles, the Allen Twins, and Hendrix's producer Eddie Kramer, as well as live footage from their Fillmore East shows, see *Jimi Hendrix: Band of Gypsys*, Bob Smeaton, director (MCA Music Video, MCAV-11931, 1999).

68. Roger Steffens argues that Hendrix appealed to black and white soldiers alike in Vietnam, because he "gave us the melody of war, raw and off-key, the ragged guys who'd been shot in the field." Roger Steffens, "Nine Meditations on Jimi and Nam," in *The Ultimate Experience*, ed. Adrian Boot and Chris Salewicz (New York: Macmillan, 1995), 113.

69. In addition to his powerful influence on rock guitar players, Hendrix's work has also made its mark on hip-hop. DJs like Q-Bert modeled their early deejay battles on Hendrix's performances as they scratched needles across rather than within the grooves of a record. Hendrix has been sampled extensively by artists such as Ice-T, Chuck D, Digital Underground, A Tribe Called Quest, the Beastie Boys, and Monie Love. In "Jimmi Diggin' Cats," the New York hip-hop/jazz band the Digable Planets imagine that Hendrix would have given them his blessing: "Yo, everybody's goin' retro, right? Word/ And I was thinking that if the 60s and 70s were now, Isaac Hayes would have his own 900 number/ I know, and MC Hammer would have been a pimp, right? /And Jimi? Jimi would have dug us, right? Word."

70. Hollingworth, "Hendrix Today," 36.

Eight

Gay Gatherings
Reimagining the Counterculture

Robert McRuer

Everything seemed to come alive for me then, like it had never been before. I
was gay! Gay! With ribbons streaming and bells ringing. It was not just the sexual awakening; I was still very shy about that. Rather it was the experience of
self-validation that so excited me. As I continued to go to GLF meetings and
meet gay people, I listened to what they said and saw a viable way to live as a
gay person. I accepted my new identity. I had come out in the movement.
—*John Knoebel, "Somewhere in the Right Direction:*
Testimony of My Experience in a Gay Male Living Collective" (1972)

In 1972, John Knoebel wrote of his experiences living as part of the 95th Street
Collective. This group of five gay men in New York City was, apparently, the
first gay male living collective in the United States. The group's decision to
experiment with an alternative, communal living arrangement fit well within
larger understandings of what it meant to "come out" in the early 1970s—
indeed, Knoebel's story (titled, after all, "Somewhere in the Right Direction")
would almost suggest that, for him, the trajectory from coming out to collective living was inevitable. Knoebel first detailed the individual isolation he
experienced growing up in the Midwest and attending religious schools, but
then wrote of a transformation that was much more than individual: "I was gay!
Gay! With ribbons streaming and bells ringing. . . . I had come out in the

movement."[1] For Knoebel and many others at the time, the coming-out experience was fundamentally a collective experience: one came *out* of the closet, certainly, but even more important, one came out *to* a community or movement (in Knoebel's case, the Gay Liberation Front, or GLF) involved in the process of reimagining and reshaping the world.[2] The burgeoning gay movement made possible the formation of new identities, individual and collective, and because of this, communal living could indeed be seen as a natural part of some people's coming-out process in the early 1970s. Although the standard, bourgeois American dream offered an extremely limited repertoire of identities (the dominant culture's image of success was the white and middle-class heterosexual couple, living a private existence with their children in the suburbs), both coming out and functioning as part of a collective marked a refusal to live according to those terms set by straight society.

The men involved in the 95th Street Collective were committed to shaping ways of being sexual together, even though the actual sexual experimentation within this particular group during its existence was quite limited. Virtually every other aspect of the men's lives, however, was collective: they made decisions about finances and meals together, took care of the apartment, worked out conflicts through regular group discussions, organized activism within the larger gay liberation movement (including staffing a telephone and providing space where GLF men could hold meetings), and even walked together holding hands in Riverside Park. Like other gay men of the period, they were strongly influenced by feminism and attended several consciousness-raising (CR) groups in the community in addition to their regular discussions within the collective. The CR groups in the community helped them develop an analysis of their own oppression that they subsequently brought back to the collective: for instance, they were critical of, and struggled against, both individualism (which they understood as supporting competitive, patriarchal ways of relating that limited the possibilities of emotional, sensual, and sexual bonds between men) and the couple form (which they understood as supporting sexist and heterosexist ideas of possessiveness and hierarchy).

Of course, as this description of their experiment should underscore, the "straight" society that Knoebel and his friends were refusing was not simply "heterosexual" society. It was, more broadly, the same "straight" society that various facets of the counterculture had been critiquing and rejecting throughout the 1960s. Indeed, the "ribbons streaming and bells ringing" that Knoebel associated with coming out and being gay are directly reminiscent of the colorful alternatives proffered by the counterculture more generally to what they perceived as a gray and lifeless American society (the gray flannel suit of the "organization man" had come to represent the homogeneity and emptiness of white middle-class corporate life).[3] During the famous "Human Be-In" in San Francisco's Golden Gate Park in January 1967, thousands of hippies with streamers, flamboyant costumes, music, and drugs held a festival celebrating their vision of a peace and love they believed could transform the world. Through this event and other colorful "happenings" in the 1960s, the counterculture imagined and performed alternatives to middle-class conformity and materialism.

Although the counterculture was extremely varied, in general the young people involved, like the men in the 95th Street Collective, valued community over individualism and peace and harmony over competition and dissension. Members of the counterculture encouraged young men and women to "drop out" of, or reject, a society focused on greed and the exploitation of others and to explore the different, heightened kinds of consciousness that music, drugs, and sexual experimentation could bring. And although the counterculture as represented by hippies and by events like the Human Be-In flourished for only a short time (roughly the last half of the 1960s), its impact on youth cultures extended far beyond that period. Countercultural values, for instance, were clearly helping to shape the 95th Street Collective and similar gay and lesbian communities.

The counterculture had a complicated and often problematic relationship to race, gender, and sexuality, however, and because of this, other factors were equally decisive in shaping the new gay and lesbian communities. Timothy Miller contends that "Black radicals (Malcolm X, W. E. B. Du Bois) were countercultural heroes because they refused to compromise with the white and prosperous Establishment."[4] Nonetheless, despite a supposed affinity with African American cultures (or, more properly, white ideas or fantasies about African American cultures), the counterculture was predominantly white and male. It was often, indeed, not only predominantly male but openly sexist; as Miller explains, "women were commonly 'chicks'; when they were in relationships with men, they were 'old ladies.'"[5] The historian Terry H. Anderson recounts that "sales of underground papers soared when they began publishing 'personal' columns in which men would advertise for 'groovy chicks who like to smoke weed and ball.'"[6] Hippies, due to their long hair and more "feminine" appearance, may have been conflated with gay men in the popular imagination, but this conflation did not necessarily mean that the counterculture explicitly endorsed or participated in homosexual activity. On the contrary: despite the abstract rhetoric of love and sexual freedom that dominated the movement, the privileging of masculinity through an emphasis on "groovy" heterosexual performance meant that the counterculture was often homophobic as well as sexist. This homophobia undoubtedly qualified the degree to which the counterculture could have a direct influence on living experiments like the 95th Street Collective. The influence the counterculture had on such experiments was consequently always mediated through other factors: feminism, as I have already suggested, but also other political movements connected to the New Left, such as the antiwar, student, or Civil Rights movements.

The counterculture and the New Left in some ways represented opposing tendencies during the period. As the historian Theodore Roszak famously put it,

> To one side, there is the mind-blown bohemianism of the beats and the hippies; to the other, the hard-headed political activism of the student New Left. Are these not in reality two separate and antithetical developments: the one (tracing back to Ginsberg, Kerouac, & Co.) seeking to "cop out" of American society, the other (tracing back to C. Wright Mills and remnants of the old socialist left) seeking to penetrate and revolutionize our political life?[7]

However, almost all of the new gay and lesbian communities—communities that were both imagined and actualized in the 1970s—descended in some way from both varieties of youth culture. Roszak himself went on to suggest that the counterculture and the New Left were, in fact, deeply connected; as Todd Gitlin puts it, "there was a direct line from the expressive politics of the New Left to the counterculture's let-it-all-hang-out way of life."[8] For gay liberationists, this connection between the counterculture and the New Left was undoubtedly particularly pronounced. In his account of the 95th Street Collective, Knoebel highlights how his participation in it resulted from his prior participation in the New York Gay Liberation Front. Like the collective, the GLF itself emerged from the confluence of countercultural values and the radical political values animating the various other movements of the 1960s.[9]

In this chapter, I want to look more closely at a selection of "gay gatherings" in order to trace this confluence. After briefly surveying the meanings of "gathering" and community more generally, I first consider, as a type of gathering, the very anthology in which Knoebel's description of the 95th Street Collective first appeared. *Out of the Closets: Voices of Gay Liberation*, edited in 1972 by Karla Jay and Allen Young, was one of the first publications of its kind and was itself, like the communal experiment Knoebel wrote about, a gathering of politicized voices influenced by both the counterculture and the New Left.[10] Second, I examine the emerging women's cultures of the 1970s, taking as my particular example the Michigan Womyn's Music Festival. The Michigan Womyn's Music Festival was founded in 1975 and initially drew about 2,000 women; the event was designed to provide a space where women could experience a new kind of freedom, openness, and creativity. Alice Echols, in *Daring to Be Bad: Radical Feminism in America, 1967–1975*, labels such events "cultural feminism"; Echols's contention is that cultural feminism diluted an earlier and more political "radical feminism."[11] Although I will not wholly dispute this argument, I will qualify it by considering the complex (and somewhat contradictory) mix of radical and countercultural impulses that contributed to the establishment of annual gatherings such as the Michigan Womyn's Music Festival.

Third, and perhaps more unexpected, I consider the successful campaign for a seat on San Francisco's Board of City Supervisors waged by Harvey Milk in 1977. A political campaign like Milk's would appear to be a more traditional and liberal "gay gathering," but I argue that the campaign's commitments to communities coming together and ties to events such as the annual gay pride parade (known in San Francisco at the time as "Gay Freedom Day") connect even such a seemingly liberal gathering to both radical and countercultural roots. Finally, I briefly examine the emergence of disco. Commentators often position disco cultures of the 1970s, like the counterculture of the 1960s, at odds with the more radical liberationist politics of the period. I challenge this by suggesting that the fluid, communal identities that emerged from the dance floors (identities that represented, significantly, new ways of being both black and gay) were precisely the kinds of identities that were needed to face the political crises, including the AIDS epidemic, of the 1980s and beyond.

COMING TOGETHER: COMMUNITIES AND GATHERINGS

In *Keywords: A Vocabulary of Culture and Society*, Raymond Williams writes that from the nineteenth century, "*Community* was the word normally chosen for experiments in an alternative kind of group-living." This sense of the term, as Williams understands it, marks a contrast between "the more direct, more total and therefore more significant relationships of *community* and the more formal, more abstract and more instrumental relationships of *state*, or of *society* in its modern sense."[12] The sharp contrast between *community* and *state* or *society*, as well as the more alternative or experimental sense of the former, has been lost somewhat in the last few decades. Jan Zita Grover, for instance, discusses the ways in which the term has been appropriated during the AIDS epidemic: when heterosexuals began describing themselves (or were described by the mainstream media) as "the heterosexual community," the more critical sense of *community* was lost. As Grover puts it, "Particularly since the mid-1960s in the U.S., the term *community* has been most frequently invoked in oppositional terms to identify a local, ethnic, racial, or political variant to the mainstream. To find the mainstream defining itself as a variant is therefore surprising."[13] What is missing from conservative deployments of *community* is the sense of directness and totality that political and countercultural movements in the 1960s and 1970s sought—for those movements, shaping community specifically entailed forging the more focused "significant relationships" Williams describes.

The forging of significant relationships occurred through a process of *gathering*, which the *Oxford English Dictionary* defines as "A bringing together or coming together of people."[14] Members of the counterculture understood straight society as reproducing mindless conformity, a conformity which they believed was responsible for the isolation and alienation that was endemic to American life. If the priorities of mainstream society ultimately did nothing but pull people apart and dull their ability to think and feel deeply, the counterculture would bring people together, offering them rich sensory experiences and alternative ways of living and relating. The Human Be-In, the 95th Street Collective, and other communities shaped in opposition to the dominant culture were gatherings in the sense that they created spaces where people could come together in new relations of nurturance and interdependency.

OUT OF THE CLOSETS
Such new relations were precisely what the contributors to *Out of the Closets: Voices of Gay Liberation* offered readers in 1972. In language that directly evoked countercultural values, Karla Jay wrote in the introduction to the first edition of *Out of the Closets*, "This book is written for gay brothers and sisters by gay brothers and sisters as an act of love and communion."[15] The closet, as the contributors to *Out of the Closets* understood it, was a space that separated people from each other by refusing or denying them community, and thus it was a space that served the needs of an individualistic and competitive culture. *Out of the Closets* was compiled to provide evidence of gay and lesbian alternatives to the culture that had created the closet.

Jay named the struggle that lesbians and gay men faced "a class struggle" and identified the "oppressor" as "white, middle-class, male-dominated heterosexual society."[16] In the rest of the collection, numerous other contributors extended her critique and identified capitalism, patriarchy, and imperialism as the systems gay men and lesbians opposed. Through their denial of community and "communion" more generally, these systems sought to negate the very existence of the cultures gay men, lesbians, women, people of color, and the working class had shaped. The negation of the existence of these thriving cultures made more possible and efficient the exploitation of individuals within them. *Out of the Closets*, however, as an unprecedented gathering of lesbian and gay voices that was both affirmative and creative, resisted this negation. Jay wrote:

> If we do share one idea . . . it is that *gay is good*. We affirm our uniqueness. We are proud to be lesbians and homosexuals, and we offer no apologies or explanations of why we are what we are. We will not give in, consider ourselves sick in any way, or conform to "straight" standards of dress or behavior. If homosexuals are your worst fear, then you have a problem. Our self-love and our love for our gay sisters and brothers are the core of our revolution, and this love ultimately binds us together no matter what our exterior differences or opinions.[17]

The refusal to conform in dress and behavior, the rhetoric of revolution through love, and the idea that love can bring different kinds of people together in unexpected ways were all signs that these "voices of gay liberation" were simultaneously voices of the counterculture.

Out of the Closets was divided into ten sections, focused on such topics as "Gay People vs. the Media," "The Man's Law" (on the police and the prison system), "Gay People vs. the Professionals" (on medicine, psychotherapy, and health care systems generally), and "Lesbians and the Women's Liberation Movement." The idea that a patriarchal society imposed rigid roles on both men and women was threaded throughout the collection; writers were generally united in opposition to imperialism, racism, and class oppression, but they understood sexism to be at the root of homophobia. Despite a burgeoning separatist sensibility in some of the essays by women, many of the essays also shared a commitment to coalition between women and men (and, of course, the collection as a whole, with its mix of male and female contributors, was also evidence of that commitment). Coalition with other revolutionary movements was also stressed: an entire section, for instance, was given over to the Cuban Revolution, and although the writers in the section expressed ambivalence over what they understood (and experienced) as the extreme homophobia and machismo of the Cuban revolutionaries and their allies on the left in the United States, the general commitment in the movement was to solidarity with the anticapitalist and anti-imperialist struggle in Cuba. Writers also affirmed alliances with groups such as the Black Panthers, Students for a Democratic Society, and the Yippies, even as they criticized these groups' ongoing homophobia. Throughout the anthology, the influence of feminism and the New Left was perhaps most evident in the consistency with which writers identified gay oppression as systemic, rooted in patriarchy and capitalism, and expressed in institutions such as the mass media, government, the legal system, organized religion, or the health care system. The homophile movement that preceded gay liberation—a movement that was, from the mid-1950s on, more likely to stress accommodation with such institutions—was seen by the contributors to *Out of the Closets* as increasingly outmoded.[18]

Although there was not absolute uniformity on the meanings of gay or lesbian identity, in general the contributors to *Out of the Closets* understood being gay as expansive and coming out as transformative. Indeed, gay identity was so expansive to gay liberationists that it was not necessarily limited to "homosexuals." Just as the countercultural call to "drop out" theoretically went out to everybody, so did the gay liberationist call to "come out." In his own contribution to the collection, "Out of the Closets, Into the Streets," Young wrote, "Gay is good for all of us. The artificial categories 'heterosexual' and 'homosexual' have been laid on us by a sexist society. . . . Straights who are threatened by us like to accuse us of separatism—but our understanding of sexism is premised on the idea that in a free society everyone will be gay."[19] In her essay "Gay Is Good," Martha Shelley likewise wrote, "And now I will tell you what we want, we radical homosexuals: not for you to tolerate us, or to accept us, but to understand us. And this you can do only by becoming one of us. We want to reach the homosexuals entombed in you, to liberate our brothers and sisters, locked in the prisons of your skulls. . . . We will never go straight until you go gay."[20] Some commentators have since suggested that gay liberationists in the 1970s were tied to a naive notion of an "essential" identity that preexisted the act of coming out; this identity simply needed to be "liberated," brought out into the open. Contributions to *Out of the Closets* like those by Young, Shelley, and others, however, indicate that gay liberationists had a much more complicated understanding of identity. Gay identity was more a creative *act* than an inert, preexistenting *substance*—that is to say, for gay liberationists, gay identity could be best understood as something one collectively *did* rather than something one already *had*. Given this understanding of identity, it was not clear in advance what gay identity would become—only that it would be something creative and communal.[21]

Carl Wittman's "A Gay Manifesto," one of the major essays not only of *Out of the Closets* but of gay liberation more generally, made explicit the ways in which this idea of an expansive and transformative gay identity was tied to, and emerged from, not only feminism and the New Left but also the broader counterculture:

> A major dynamic of rising gay liberation sentiment is the hip revolution within the gay community. Emphasis on love, dropping out,

being honest, expressing yourself through hair and clothes, and smoking dope are all attributes of this. The gays who are the least vulnerable to attack by the establishment have been the freest to express themselves on gay liberation. . . . The hip/street culture has led people into a lot of freeing activities: encounter/sensitivity, the quest for reality, freeing territory for the people, ecological consciousness, communes. These are real points of agreement and probably will make it easier for them to get their heads straight about homosexuality, too.[22]

Through his overview of the "hip revolution," Wittman made it clear that in many ways, the counterculture had laid the groundwork for the expansive understanding of gay identity that other contributors emphasized and extended. His concluding "Outline of Imperatives for Gay Liberation" only underscored this link: "Free the homosexual in everyone: we'll be getting a good bit of shit from threatened latents: be gentle, and keep talking and acting free."[23] The gathering that Wittman and others imagined in *Out of the Closets* both resisted the capitalist and patriarchal "establishment" that isolated people from each other and emphasized new ways of living that would bring people together.

WOMEN'S CULTURE, WOMEN'S MUSIC

The emerging lesbian separatist sensibility that was evident in some of the essays in *Out of the Closets* could itself be understood as a countercultural impulse. As the 1970s continued, more and more women were publishing work—with titles such as "Leaving the Gay Men Behind" or "Goodbye, My Alienated Brothers"—that expressed frustration with the gay male movement.[24] As the counterculture more generally had been urging both men and women for almost a decade, so too were these writers urging readers to "drop out" of the dominant culture—only this time the audience was specifically women and the "dominant culture" was often the gay movement itself. Increasingly arguing that their primary alliance was with feminism and not with gay liberation, lesbians in the 1970s began to break with gay men. Given the ways in which feminism was providing women with critical tools for analyzing and challenging patriarchy, this split should not be surprising. As John D'Emilio writes in his foreword to the 1992 reissue of *Out of the Closets*, "When the anger of lesbians . . . who were beginning to see the many forms of sexism all around them collided with the ingrained habits of gay men socialized into dominance, the simplest interactions became a minefield."[25] At the same time, just as gay liberation more generally resisted the negation of gay community with creativity and affirmation, so did lesbian feminists in the 1970s resist the marginalization or diminishment of their experiences within the gay movement by shaping vibrant alternative cultures for women.

In 1972, Judy Dlugacz and nine other women formed Olivia Records. This record label would feature women's music and focus on women at the level of both production and consumption, first employing women as engineers and producers and then distributing the music to the growing networks of women's communities throughout the country.[26] As Urvashi Vaid explains, "Olivia was a conscious political strategy aimed at building a lesbian movement and at promoting a lesbian political analysis: if we could not find images of ourselves in the mainstream, we would make them ourselves."[27] Many of the performers who recorded with Olivia Records went on to perform at the outdoor women's music festivals that, by the mid-1970s, had sprung up from coast to coast, and many of the performers at the festivals, in turn, went on to record with Olivia Records. The record label and the music festivals were just part of the new lesbian culture that was attracting women everywhere; what the women involved began to refer to as "Lesbian Nation" also included discussion and CR groups, coffeehouses, athletic teams, bookstores, and—of course—communes and other living collectives.

Lillian Faderman explicitly highlights the connection that Lesbian Nation generally and the music festivals in particular had to the counterculture: "The festivals were modelled on the hippie be-ins of the 1960s, in which counter-culture crowds, in various stages of undress, would dance, get high on LSD or pot, and listen to the music."[28] The most famous festival of all was the Michigan Womyn's Music Festival, which was founded in 1975 by Lisa Vogel, her sister Kristie Vogel, and their friend Mary Kindig. Although the Vogels and Kindig had no prior experience in organizing such an event, they were determined to make it possible for those who attended to hear women's music and participate in women's culture and community. The weekend-long event, on eighty acres of rented land near Mount Pleasant, Michigan, was designated "women-only"—the organizers wanted to provide a safe space where women could remove themselves from men and interact with each other as they chose. Professionalism and other values that might have driven the male-dominated music industry more generally were eschewed; as Lisa Vogel remembers, "It was a radical time in feminist politics, and creating and defining women's culture was a primary focus. It happened as a lark, not as a professional undertaking."[29] Indeed, the performers most popular at the festival were not those who perpetuated a slick, professional image, removing themselves from the audience, but those who presented themselves as part of the community, suggesting to the audience that all the women gathered there were engaged in "creating and defining women's culture" together. Just as those involved in the countercultural gatherings that preceded the Michigan Womyn's Music Festival were aiming for harmony and (theoretically) a leveling of the hierarchies that structured the world outside, so too did the women involved in this event hope it would provide a space where alternatives to patriarchy could be imagined and shaped.[30]

As D'Emilio and other commentators have noted, the new lesbian cultures being shaped at festivals and elsewhere became increasingly utopian in the second half of the 1970s. In fact, one of the only book-length overviews of the music festival phenomenon is titled *Eden Built by Eves*. In that study, Bonnie J. Morris quotes one of the performers, Jean Fineberg, to underscore the utopian sentiment that came to prevail in Michigan:

> Imagine a city where women rule. Where all the roads, all the buildings, the plumbing, the hospitals, the restaurants, the stores are run by women. Imagine a city where all the arts and all the crafts, the dance, the movies, the theatre, the poetry are created by women. Imagine a city where women and children feel free to walk anywhere, day or night, in total safety. Imagine a city where it doesn't matter what we wear, where we're not judged by our clothes, where clothing is optional and our bodies are sacred. Imagine a city of thousands of women, where there's no violence and no weapons, no criminals and no jails, no oppression and no fear. This city has existed in only one place in the history of the earth. We are in that city now. Welcome to Michigan![31]

Utopian ideas like this meant that the emphasis for many lesbian feminists had shifted from engagement with, or transformation of, the outside world, to removal from that world and the structures of patriarchy and capitalism that sustained it. The spatial orientation that gay liberationists attempted to forge encouraged people to move *outward*: from the imagined (isolated, confined) space of the closet to the streets or the world. In contrast, despite the fact that it was an outdoor event, the spatial orientation at women's music festivals was *inward*: Fineberg imagined not a transformed *world* where there would be no oppression and fear, but simply a city. Of course, a city could be understood as an extremely public place, but for Fineberg and others, it was clearly a place to which women could escape. Fineberg's comments pointedly welcomed festivalgoers to Michigan as a private place set apart from the rest of the world.

Ironically, this was precisely the split Roszak identified among youth cultures more broadly—between a bohemianism seeking to "cop out" of American life (or, we might say in this case, patriarchal culture) and a leftist politics seeking to revolutionize American (patriarchal) society. And, in fact, such a reading of lesbian separatism, or "cultural feminism" more generally, is standard at this point, in large part due to Alice Echols's argument that a politicized radical feminism gave way in the mid-1970s to a simple celebration of women's culture and essentialized female differences. Echols writes, in language that in some ways parallels Roszak's,

> Radical feminism was a political movement dedicated to eliminating the sex-class system, whereas cultural feminism was a countercultural movement aimed at reversing the cultural valuation of the male and the devaluation of the female. . . . Thus, we find radical feminists mobilizing women on the basis of their similarity to men and cultural feminists organizing women around the principle of female difference. Moreover, in contrast to radical feminists who believed that feminism entailed an expansion of the left analysis, cultural feminists conceived of feminism as an antidote to the left.[32]

Echols goes on to suggest that a more radical feminist politics was stifled because of the way in which cultural feminists "succumbed to counterculture."[33] As Echols would see it, with their utopian emphasis on escape from the world outside, events like the Michigan Womyn's Music Festival were retreats in several senses of the word.

Echols's analysis has been extremely influential, in large part because it is an accurate and convincing portrayal of the political shifts that occurred in feminism in the 1970s. Saralyn Chesnut and Amanda C. Gable point out, however, that attacks on cultural feminism like Echols's "fail to consider the relationship between cultural production and social change [and] overlook what is arguably the most significant legacy of the lesbian-feminist movement: its creation of a new lesbian subject."[34] Just as the hip/street culture Wittman described had provided spaces where a gay liberationist identity could be forged, so did Lesbian Nation, in Chesnut and Gable's analysis, provide a space where new lesbian identities could be constructed. These new lesbian identities, in turn, made further political engagement and cultural transformation possible. Additionally, Chesnut and Gable argue, critics and historians "have tended to focus on what lesbian feminists wrote rather than on what they did—on theory to the exclusion of practice."[35] This focus has made it difficult to see the ways in which individuals and communities were negotiating, in complex ways, the abstract and increasingly utopian ideas emerging from what Echols calls cultural feminism.

To consider the daily realities of at least one women's community in the 1970s, Chesnut and Gable sketch the history of Charis Books and More, a women's bookstore in Atlanta's Little Five Points neighborhood. They argue that women's movement through new countercultural spaces like Charis Books and More allowed for the development of identities and politics that women could then carry to other locations: "Feminist bookstores . . . served as meeting places and resource centers for the community as well as locations to sell books and journals. Rather than short-circuiting the social-change agenda of radical feminists, in many ways the rise of feminist bookstores and presses allowed feminist ideas, including those of radical feminism, to continue to be developed and disseminated."[36] In other words, the ideas of radical feminism were not simply supplanted by cultural feminism; they were put into print and circulated, and in some cases extended, because of the existence of cultural institutions, like bookstores, that women developed in the mid-1970s. Women's music festivals, similarly, performed a complex function for lesbians in the 1970s. They were spaces of escape, but they were not where women lived their day-to-day lives. The identities and politics that developed from "dropping out" at women's music festivals were put into circulation, as it were, in local communities around the country.

The critique of the male left and of gay liberation notwithstanding, lesbian feminism throughout the 1970s was at least partially connected to both. Gatherings such as the Michigan Womyn's Music Festival allowed women to disengage from mainstream (straight and gay) society and retreat to a city set apart from the dominant patriarchal culture, but many participants simultaneously continued to imagine reshaping the institutions of that culture, not least academic institutions where, as the decade concluded, feminism increasingly gained a foothold. To position women's countercultures as diametrically opposed to political engagement obscures the ways in which many lesbians themselves imagined cultural production and struggle as linked to radical politics. The festivals and other cultural feminist sites were without question limited in what they achieved (and indeed they should be understood as more limited than the radical feminism that preceded them), but—as with countercultural happenings more generally—they nonetheless helped to generate new ideas, identities, and communities.

NEIGHBORHOOD BUILDING: HARVEY MILK AND THE CASTRO DISTRICT

The next "gay gathering" I will consider is the one that would seem to be the least tied to the counterculture and the most tied to more traditional liberal politics. Harvey Milk's campaign for a seat on San Francisco's Board of City Supervisors would not seem to be about "dropping out" of mainstream society at all, but instead about working to secure a place on the inside. If the counterculture had effectively come into existence by *rejecting* the status quo,

San Francisco's Harvey Milk, the "Mayor of Castro Street," ca. 1978, greeting an admirer who's sporting what appears to be a real boa, probably during the annual Gay Pride parade (known in San Francisco at the time as "Gay Freedom Day"). The previous year Milk had become the first openly gay candidate to be elected to the city's board of supervisors. He represented District 5, which included the Castro neighborhood, with its sizable gay population, as well as the hippie enclaves of Noe Valley and the Haight. Milk's tenure in office was tragically cut short when he and Mayor George Moscone were shot to death in November 1978 by a political rival, former supervisor Dan White. Courtesy of Gay Lesbian Bisexual Transgender Historical Society of Northern California/Robert Pruzan.

then a campaign like Milk's, with its explicit *support* for the already existent political system, would by definition not qualify as a countercultural event. Yet Milk's brief tenure on the board of supervisors (which ended when he and Mayor George Moscone were assassinated by Dan White in November 1978) was generative of culture and community in ways that link his campaign and the events that followed it to the other countercultural gatherings I am considering in this chapter. Or, perhaps more accurately, gay countercultures and communities in San Francisco in the 1970s were generative of Harvey Milk.[37]

Moscone was elected mayor in 1976. He was a liberal Democrat who appealed to many diverse groups in San Francisco, mainly because he stood for the interests of local communities and neighborhoods and against the interests of the wealthy, especially wealthy developers. These commitments were evident in his support for Proposition T, a measure that changed the elections for the board of supervisors from citywide to district, effectively giving neighborhoods the right to elect one of their own. Proposition T passed, and in 1977 Harvey Milk was elected to the board of supervisors from District 5, which included the Castro neighborhood, with its large gay population, as well as the Noe Valley and the Haight (which had earlier been one of the prime sites for the development of the Sixties counterculture more generally). The new emphasis on community leadership changed the face of city government in San Francisco: Proposition T also made it possible for the first acknowledged feminist, the first Chinese American, and the first African American woman to sit on the board.

In a televised local interview following the election, a reporter asked Milk, "What's it like being a so-called 'in-person,' as opposed to having been an 'out-person' for a number of years?" With tears in his eyes, Milk responded, "Being one of 'them'? . . . Incredible. The establishment . . . the white, power establishment, non-gay, very wealthy establishment, have to deal with me. It's an incredible position." With characteristic affect that set his performance apart from the slick performances of "establishment" politicians, Milk voiced his commitments: he stood not for the system as it was, but for his community, which had traditionally been shut out of the system.

The boundaries of Milk's community, however, were not fixed; increasingly, he came to be a voice not simply for gay men and lesbians but for all the disenfranchised. In fact, the idea that lesbians and gay men should work at building community across differences was evident in many of Milk's talks or speeches. In a speech that resisted (and reversed) attempts by the dominant culture to cast gays and other marginalized groups as "others," for instance, Milk insisted, "without hope, not only gays, but those blacks, and the Asians, and the disabled, and the seniors—the 'us-es,' the 'us-es'—without hope, the us-es give up. I know that you cannot live on hope alone, but without it, life is not worth living, and you and you and you, gotta give 'em hope." Milk's rhetoric in this speech was clearly influenced by the counterculture that had flourished in San Francisco for more than a decade: what Milk called his "people positions" emphasized groups coming together, positioned "us" against "them" (where "they" represented the "establishment," that ubiquitous target of the counterculture), and worked to build a sense of solidarity in communities and neighborhoods.

The successful campaign against the Briggs Initiative—a statewide bill sponsored by Senator John Briggs that would have prohibited openly lesbian or gay people from teaching in California's public schools—gave Milk more visibility on the level of state, and even national, politics. The commitment to coalition politics that developed through this and other struggles solidified Milk's connection not only to the counterculture but also to the more radical, New Left–influenced politics of gay liberation that had preceded him. As John D'Emilio writes,

Milk's record during his one year in office indicates that he . . . was moving beyond liberalism. He worked hard to cement a coalition among gays, racial minorities, and the elderly. He became a strong advocate of rent control and measures to restrict real estate specula-tion, he opposed the redevelopment plans being pushed by down-town corporate interests; and he introduced a resolution to have the South African consulate in San Francisco closed. During 1978 he helped to push Moscone away from mainstream liberalism and toward a populist-style coalition politics.[38]

In the same television interview I quoted earlier, Milk himself brought together the New Left emphasis on coalition and the countercultural desire for harmony: "There's tremendous harmony developing. . . . I think it's vital that the minorities, the traditional ethnic minorities, and the gays, and the feminists, link together. And possibly the rank-and-file unions, not the union leaders, [but] the rank-and-file, link together, to form a very solid, strong coalition." To Milk, coalition meant working together across divides of race, gender, sexuality, and class (and, in numerous other speeches, age and ability) in order to forge a harmonious community that was not beholden to the pow-erful establishment and the discord and division it perpetuated.

Without question, positions such as these generated new coalitions and new kinds of community in San Francisco in the 1970s. As I suggested, how-ever, it is as accurate to suggest that the influence was in the opposite direc-tion—to suggest, that is, that the gay counterculture in San Francisco generated Harvey Milk. Before moving from New York to San Francisco, Milk had already established himself as antiestablishment, participating in antiwar protests and burning his Bank America card. But San Francisco in the 1970s was a place where gay and lesbian people migrated to find the freedom that eluded them elsewhere—the annual Gay Pride Parade, in fact (in which Milk himself participated), was called "Gay Freedom Day." In their 1984 film *The Times of Harvey Milk*, Robert Epstein and Richard Schmiechen highlight this freedom by positioning Milk's arrival in the city and the development of his campaign against a backdrop of countercultural images: hippies marching in jean jackets and colorful beads and buttons; shirtless men with their arms wrapped around each other; streamers, balloons, and people on the rooftops and window ledges; streets packed with women and men dancing to music. To the strains of disco star Sylvester singing "You make me feel mighty real," Epstein and Schmiechen effectively place Milk's campaign in the context of the expansive sense of gay freedom that many men and women were discov-ering in San Francisco.

The gathering of communities and individuals around Harvey Milk was not as radical as *Out of the Closets*, with its more explicit rejection of capitalism, patriarchy, and imperialism, nor as countercultural as the Michigan Womyn's Music Festival, with its removal to a nonpatriarchal space set apart from the rest of society. Still, Milk's campaign resisted the establishment, especially corporate and development interests that would impede the building of communities and neighborhoods, and in this sense, the campaign was connected to the kind of affirmative and communal gay consciousness usually not afforded by traditional liberal politics. Indeed, Milk's assassination itself could be interpreted as a sign that the alternative community and culture he stood for were in fact threatening to the status quo.

DISCO NIGHTS: GAY AND PROUD, BLACK AND BEAUTIFUL

Following his death from complications due to HIV/AIDS, Sylvester's obituary in *Jet* magazine in January 1989 described him as "the flamboyant homosexual singer whose high-pitched voice and dramatic on-stage costumes propelled him to the height of stardom on the disco music scene during the late 1970s."[39] Expanding on *Jet*'s assessment, Phillip Brian Harper suggests that Sylvester actively worked to shape the disco music scene, and was not simply propelled to the heights within it: "Sylvester was able to help create a disco culture—comprising elements from both black and gay contexts—in which he and others could thrive as openly gay men."[40] As Harper and other queer commentators understand it, Sylvester's performance was about more than the homosexual "flamboyance" *Jet* reported; it was about shaping a space where the very meanings of "black" and "gay" could be expanded. Walter Hughes, for example, writes that "'You Make Me Feel (Mighty Real)' performs the representative hypostatization of [Sylvester's] gay identity. His impassioned repetition becomes as orgasmic as Donna Summer's in 'I Feel Love,' insisting that, for the gay black man, the realization of self can have the ecstatic force of a revelation."[41]

For Hughes and most historians of disco, however, the "realization of self" was in many ways a loss of self: the dance floor was a place where one's individual identity could disintegrate and be absorbed into the larger mass of writhing bodies. The music and lights, as well as the sexual experimentation and drugs that were so much a part of disco cultures, facilitated this disintegration of self and absorption into others. A dominant strand of American individualism from Ralph Waldo Emerson on had celebrated autonomy, self-possession, self-control, and transcendence of the body (Emerson's famous image of a transparent eyeball, located nowhere but seeing everything, was of course unencumbered by embodiment). Just as surely as it inverted the primacy of day over night, disco turned these principles of American individualism upside down and inside out; as Hughes points out, many popular disco songs were precisely about a *loss* of autonomy, about giving possession or control of oneself to larger forces: "The destruction and re-creation of the self must be performed not, tautologically, by the self itself but by some power above and beyond it. . . . Gay men, at the irresistible prompting of a disco diva such as Grace Jones, cropped their hair, dressed alike, and became what she calls 'slaves to the rhythm.'"[42] Disco certainly offered transcendence, but it was transcendence of precisely the disembodied (detached and impenetrable) individual identity Emerson celebrated. Through a refusal of detachment and impenetrability, through an openness to others and to a range of bodily pleasures, the self could be remade.

The "others" involved in this process were invariably gay, black, or both. As Peter Braunstein and others have noted, "For the first half of the 1970s, disco was an extended conversation between black musicians and gay dancers."[43] Disco had developed earlier in the century, but it was in the immediate post-Stonewall era that gay people made it their own. Several factors contributed to the gay transformation of disco culture: the "search for continuous, danceable rhythms," the new popularity of drugs such as poppers, innovations such as an expanded dance floor in gay clubs such as the Sanctuary (formerly a German Baptist church), and an emphasis on "rampant promiscuity and public sex."[44]

Although the metaphor of a conversation might suggest that two separate and fully formed identities met on the dance floor, the conversation between black musicians (often black divas such as Donna Summer or Gloria Gaynor) and gay dancers that Braunstein notes was unique. The collective remaking of the self that disco culture encouraged meant that the "mighty real" black and gay identities suddenly visible on the dance floor came into existence *through* the conversation. Moreover, they were available to a range of people who may not have identified as "black" or "gay" in advance. As Hughes points out,

> Implicit in early disco is the assumption that only a black woman
> can openly vocalize her sexuality, and that only a gay man would
> join her in a free-fall from rational self-mastery. But . . . the negoti-
> ation between usually straight black women and usually white gay
> men seemed to open up and make visible all the various subject
> positions between these previously polarized identities. Since the
> actual author and audience of any disco song are both indetermi-
> nate, disco's racial, sexual and gender identity cannot be finally

fixed as "black music," "women's music," or "gay music." The violence . . . [disco] does to fixed identity results in a doubling, slippage and transference of black and white, male and female, gay and
straight subject positions.[45]

To exemplify this doubling and slippage, Hughes notes that "Grace Jones can
sing of 'feeling like a woman' and 'looking like a man'; Donna Summer can
plead with her lover (or her audience) to 'turn my brown body white.'"[46] And,
of course, just as a Baptist church could become the hedonistic gay Sanctuary,
so too could Sylvester use his origins in the black church and gospel music
(sites where homosexuality might be accepted but only on the condition that
it remain silent) to generate a gay and proud, black and beautiful identity that
refused to be silenced and that could be performed and offered to others.[47]

Disco would seem to be less political than the other gay gatherings I have
examined in this chapter, and is perhaps the gathering that most bears out
Roszak's interpretation of a split between a politicized New Left and a counterculture seeking escape. And, in fact, Andrew Holleran's *Dancer from the
Dance*, one of the premier gay literary works to emerge from the era, positions
the gay men involved in the disco scene as completely uninterested in gay politics. Despite an awareness of that split, *Dancer from the Dance* could be read
as a fairly loving tribute to the men involved in the disco scene.[48] Other
assessments of disco in the 1970s, however, were not so kind. As the decade
continued, bumper stickers emerged that declared "DISCO SUCKS," and even
less hostile judgments understood it as having nothing to do with meaningful
political activity. "Disco," as Hughes explains in a summary of the critiques
that were offered of it, "is 'mindless,' 'repetitive,' 'synthetic,' 'technological' and
'commercial,' just as the men who dance to it with each other are 'unnatural,'
'trivial,' 'decadent,' 'artificial' and 'indistinguishable' 'clones.'"[49]

In defense of disco, however (to borrow a phrase from Richard Dyer), I
would argue that here too the confluence of the counterculture and the more
radical politics of the early 1970s can be seen.[50] As I indicated earlier in this
chapter, after all, for many contributors to the gay liberationist anthology *Out
of the Closets*, it was not clear in advance what gay identity could become; it
was only clear that a truly free society would *encourage* the development and
expansion of gay identity. With the foundational understanding that gay identity would be collective and imaginative, anything was possible. Despite the
charge of "mindless conformity," then, the disco music scene shared many
characteristics with other countercultural phenomena that were about *resisting*
the mindless conformity of straight society more generally. For many black
and white gay men, and for some women, especially black female performers,

expansive gay (and black) identities that were about freedom and about creatively coming together with others came into being on the dance floor.

As I suggested earlier, for many other women, the free society where everyone would be *lesbian* and where (initially) it was not always clear what lesbian identity might become was shaped at music festivals. Of course, neither the stage at Mount Pleasant, Michigan, nor the dance floor at the Sanctuary wholly fulfilled gay liberationist calls for a transformed world, and in many ways, both locations compromised such calls (mainly through a dilution of an analysis of the *systemic* nature of oppression). At the same time, these lesbian and gay sites nonetheless allowed women and men to resist the demands of straight society and reimagine their individual and collective identities.

BACK TO THE FUTURE: REIMAGINING THE COUNTERCULTURE

I want to conclude by positing a continuity between the variety of gay liberationist countercultures of the 1970s and the queer cultures of the 1980s and 1990s that effectively responded to political crises such as AIDS and Reaganism. By positing such a continuity, I intend to resist current ideological understandings of what happened in the decade. A cultural myth is now being consolidated about the 1970s. This myth has gained prominence because of stories told not only by conservatives like Marilyn Quayle (who proclaimed at the 1992 Republican National Convention that despite some of the good that came out of the 1960s, not everyone dropped out, toked up, or dodged the draft) but even by some highly visible gay writers like Bruce Bawer or Gabriel Rotello.[51] To these commentators, the decade was a period of collective childhood or adolescence, but in the 1980s and 1990s, we grew up (as a culture or as a movement). AIDS is, of course, offered by such storytellers as the proof of their narrative—we went wild in the seventies, so the story goes, but paid the price (and learned from it) in the 1980s.

As I have demonstrated, however, the gay gatherings of the 1970s, despite limitations, provided spaces where lesbians and gay men learned to reinvent themselves and their communities in opposition to the dominant culture. This capacity for reinventing identity and community, which was perhaps best exemplified in the 1980s and '90s through the reclamation of "queerness," made resistance possible (or even inevitable).[52] Not long after many groups began to call themselves "queer," Jeffrey Escoffier wrote that "queers are constructing a new culture by combining elements that usually don't go together. They may be the first wave of activists to embrace the retrofuture/classic contemporary styles of postmodernism. They are building their own identity from old and new elements—borrowing styles and tactics from popular culture, communities of color, hippies, AIDS activists, the antinuclear movement, MTV, feminists, and early gay liberationists."[53] The cultural generativity Escoffier identified with queerness clearly had strong roots in the 1970s, given the larger history of most of the "old and new elements" on his list. Even a "new" element such as AIDS activism arguably drew on earlier, countercultural movements: the feminist health movement of the 1970s, the disability rights movement that blossomed in Berkeley and elsewhere, gay liberation.

In a consideration of the specific ways in which gay communities forged new sexual practices in the 1980s, Douglas Crimp identifies a pattern that could, I think, be extended to describe the range of cultural practices lesbians and gay men developed in the 1970s. Crimp writes:

> Our promiscuity taught us many things, not only about the pleasures of sex, but about the great multiplicity of those pleasures. It is that psychic preparation, that experimentation, that conscious work on our own sexualities that has allowed many of us to change our sexual behaviors—something that brutal "behavioral therapies" tried unsuccessfully for over a century to force us to do—very quickly and very dramatically.[54]

The gay gatherings I surveyed in this chapter similarly produced dramatic transformation, effectively laying the groundwork for the challenging decades that were to come. If psychic preparation, experimentation, and conscious work on our sexualities (and identities more generally) are all part of what Crimp calls "promiscuity," then promiscuity could easily describe the "love for gay sisters and brothers" that was at the core of the revolution imagined by the contributors to *Out of the Closets*, the creativity that resulted from women collectively producing music, dance, and art at the Michigan Womyn's Music Festival, the harmony that developed from the "us-es" coming together in an alternative political campaign such as Harvey Milk's, or the communal eroticism performed and explored in the disco music scene. Safe sex and AIDS activism more generally are not the only legacies of these gay gatherings. In the 1980s and 1990s, lesbian and gay curricula in colleges and universities, cultural forms such as vogueing or queer poetry slams, art deemed "obscene" by the right wing as well as communal responses to right-wing attacks, progressive political campaigns such as Tammy Baldwin's for the U.S. House of Representatives (from Madison, Wisconsin) or Tom Ammiano's for mayor of San Francisco, and candlelight marches and vigils protesting governmental responses to AIDS or violence against gay men and lesbians could all be understood as descending, in some way, from such countercultural promiscuity.

This expansive promiscuity has recently been under attack. In part because of the prominence of writers like Bawer and Rotello (but also because of the policies pursued by national organizations such as the Human Rights Campaign), the lesbian and gay movement has been striving for "normalcy," putting forward as overnight "leaders" of the movement celebrity spokespersons such as Ellen DeGeneres or Melissa Etheridge, courting corporate sponsorship for events such as the April 30, 2000, Millennium March on Washington for Gay, Lesbian, Bisexual, and Transgender Rights, and emphasizing issues such as marriage rights or the right to serve in the military instead of emphasizing more sweeping calls for social justice and the reshaping of dominant cultural values.[55]

The current "normalizing" of the movement, I would argue, entails forgetting (or even consciously rejecting) the countercultural (and revolutionary) roots of gay liberation. Current trends in the gay movement are also arguably in line with the "normalization" and commodification of the counterculture more generally. The quintessential countercultural "reunion," for instance, is probably Woodstock 1999, which—with its clear connections to corporate sponsorship—diluted the sharp critique of American society and commodified the alternative lifestyles and worldviews celebrated at the original Woodstock in 1969. Woodstock 1999 would seem to represent a nostalgic desire to reimagine the counterculture, but it does so through forgetting the elements of it that made it an attractive alternative to straight society, thereby eliminating what was most promising about the counterculture in the first place.

Each of the gay gatherings I have examined here have, in some ways, convened similar forgetful "reunions" in the 1990s. In their introduction to the 1992 reissue of *Out of the Closets: Voices of Gay Liberation*, Jay and Young literally apologize for what they label "extremism," disavowing in particular the anthology's rhetoric of revolution and its argument that gay identities were theoretically available to everyone.[56] Over the years, the Michigan Womyn's Music Festival has become famous not for being a site of possibility where new understandings of identity and community could be generated across differences but for being a site where identity is policed. The policy of admitting "only women born women" was developed specifically to exclude transsexual women from participation in the event. Harvey Milk's story has now been produced as an opera, but even more problematic than that is the extreme commodification that currently plagues Castro Street and other historically gay neighborhoods. Far from being sites where the development interests that Milk and Moscone challenged are resisted, such neighborhoods are often the center of urban development. Finally, in films such as *54* and *The Last Days of*

Disco, the definitive black and gay music scene of the 1970s has been white-washed and heterosexualized.[57]

At the turn of this century, however, there are hopeful signs of a renewed convergence of revolutionary and countercultural values as extremely diverse groups of activists have come together in colorful festivals/protests reminiscent of the countercultural/political gatherings of the 1960s and 1970s. These activists, some of whom have explicitly identified as queer, gay, or lesbian, have shut down the streets of cities like Seattle and Washington, D.C., to protest globalization and the greed and unchecked power and exploitation of multinational corporations. Specifically targeting the policies of organizations such as the World Bank and the International Monetary Fund (IMF), protesters have articulated a systemic analysis of the ways in which globalization policies that encourage privatization and benefit multinational corporations are detrimental to non-Western nations and regions, women, the poor and working class, people of color, people with disabilities, and people with HIV/AIDS. The tactics activists have deployed include not only barricades in the streets but also demonstrations by groups such as the Lesbian Avengers, who have bared their breasts and swallowed fire, or impromptu puppet shows in the parks, with IMF and World Bank officials represented as pigs feeding off of the people. The coalitions that are imagined and the communities that are actualized through these protests are similar to the communities imagined and actualized by countercultures and the New Left in the 1970s.

I want to conclude by offering my arguments about the gay liberationist past in the interest of a desirable (and queer) future where the lesbian and gay movement would not forget its countercultural history but reimagine and extend it as a vital and ongoing part of these larger movements. In the early 1970s, John Knoebel, the men of the 95th Street Collective, the Gay Liberation Front, and other individuals and groups imagined "coming out in the movement" as presenting the most "viable way to live as a gay person." The locations generating the radical and countercultural movements Knoebel had in mind have shifted, but the transformative sense of coming out and not knowing in advance what gay identity might become need not be forgotten.

NOTES

1. John Knoebel, "Somewhere in the Right Direction: Testimony of My Experience in a Gay Male Living Collective," in *Out of the Closets: Voices of Gay Liberation*, ed. Karla Jay and Allen Young (New York: New York University Press, 1992 [1972]), 301–15 at 302.

2. For a discussion of the various meanings of "coming out," see John D'Emilio's *Making Trouble: Essays on Gay History, Politics, and the University* (New York: Routledge, 1992), 244–45, and his foreword to the twentieth-anniversary edition of *Out of the Closets*, ed. Jay and Young xx-xxiv, xxviii-xxix. See also the first chapter of my own *The Queer Renaissance: Contemporary*

American Literature and the Reinvention of Lesbian and Gay Identities (New York: New York University Press, 1997), 32–68, especially 32–39.

3. The most famous literary examination of the middle-class "organization man" was Sloan Wilson's novel *The Man in the Gray Flannel Suit* (New York: Simon & Schuster, 1955).

4. Timothy Miller, *The Hippies and American Values* (Knoxville: University of Tennessee Press, 1991), 6.

5. Ibid., 16.

6. Terry H. Anderson, *The Movement and the Sixties* (New York: Oxford University Press, 1995), 261.

7. Theodore Roszak, *The Making of a Counter Culture: Reflections on the Technocratic Society and Its Youthful Opposition* (Berkeley: University of California Press, 1995 [1969]), 56.

8. Todd Gitlin, *The Sixties: Years of Hope, Days of Rage* (New York: Bantam, 1987), 213.

9. David Savran cites Roszak's famous passage and overviews the connections and conflicts between the New Left and the counterculture in *Taking It Like a Man: White Masculinity, Masochism, and Contemporary American Culture* (Princeton: Princeton University Press, 1998), 109–22. Throughout his work, D'Emilio consistently argues that gay liberation emerged from the range of radical and countercultural movements impacting young people in the late 1960s and early 1970s. See D'Emilio, *Making Trouble*, 241, and his foreword to *Out of the Closets*, ed. Jay and Young xvii–xix.

10. Cited in note 1.

11. Alice Echols, *Daring to Be Bad: Radical Feminism in America, 1967–1975* (Minneapolis: Univeristy of Minnesota Press, 1989).

12. Raymond Williams, *Keywords: A Vocabulary of Culture and Society*, rev. ed. (New York: Oxford University Press, 1983), 75, 76.

13. Jan Zita Grover, "AIDS: Keywords," in *AIDS: Cultural Analysis, Cultural Activism*, ed. Douglas Crimp (Cambridge, Mass.: MIT Press, 1987), 17–30 at 24.

14. This is the fourth definition given for the term in *The Compact Edition of the Oxford English Dictionary*, vol. 1 (Oxford: Oxford University Press, 1971), 1121.

15. Karla Jay, "Introduction to the First Edition," in *Out of the Closets*, ed. Jay and Young, lxi–lxii at lxii.

16. Ibid., lxi.

17. Ibid., lxii.

18. On the homophile movement that preceded the Stonewall riots, see D'Emilio, *Making Trouble*, 17–56, 237–39.

19. Allen Young, "Out of the Closets, Into the Streets," in *Out of the Closets*, ed. Jay and Young, 6–31 at 29.

20. Martha Shelley, "Gay Is Good," in *Out of the Closets*, ed. Jay and Young, 31–34 at 34.

21. Simon Watney writes, "Gay culture in the 1970s offered the grounds for the emergence of a social identity defined not by notions of sexual 'essence,' but in oppositional relation to the institutions and discourses of medicine, the law, education, housing and welfare policy, and so on." Quoted in David Halperin, *Saint Foucault: Towards a Gay Hagiography* (New York: Oxford University Press, 1995), 209 n. 114. See also David Halperin's discussion of Michel Foucault's notion of gay identity as a "state of becoming" in *Saint Foucault*, 67–81.

22. Carl Wittman, "A Gay Manifesto," in *Out of the Closets*, ed. Jay and Young, 330–342 at 341.

23. Ibid.

24. Radicalesbians [*sic*], "Leaving the Gay Men Behind," in *Out of the Closets*, ed. Jay and Young, 290–93; Del Martin, "Goodbye, My Alienated Brothers," in *Long Road to Freedom: The Advocate History of the Gay and Lesbian Movement*, ed. Mark Thompson (New York: St. Martin's Press, 1994), 41–42.

25. D'Emilio, foreword to *Out of the Closets*, ed. Jay and Young, xxi.

26. Thompson, ed., *Long Road to Freedom*, 106.

27. Urvashi Vaid, *Virtual Equality: The Mainstreaming of Gay and Lesbian Liberation* (New York: Anchor-Doubleday, 1995), 65.

28. Lillian Faderman, *Odd Girls and Twilight Lovers: A History of Lesbian Life in Twentieth-Century America* (New York: Penguin, 1991), 221.

29. Lisa Vogel, quoted in Kara Fox, "An Unexpected Anniversary: Michigan Festival Surprises Its Founder by Lasting 25 Years," *Washington Blade*, (16 August 2000), 26–27 at 26.

30. On Lesbian Nation and the Michigan Womyn's Music Festival see Bonnie J. Morris, *Eden Built by Eves: The Culture of Women's Music Festivals* (Los Angeles: Alyson, 1999).

31. Jean Fineberg, quoted in ibid., 59.

32. Echols, *Daring to Be Bad*, 6.

33. Ibid., 7.

34. Saralyn Chesnut and Amanda C. Gable, "'Women Ran It': Charis Books and More and Atlanta's Lesbian Feminist Community, 1971–1981," in *Carryin' On in the Lesbian and Gay South*, ed. John Howard (New York: New York University Press, 1997), 241–84 at 252.

35. Ibid., 246.

36. Ibid., 251–52.

37. All quotations from Harvey Milk's speeches in this section are drawn from Robert Epstein and Richard Schmiechen's film *The Times of Harvey Milk* (Black Sand Productions, 1984). I have also found D'Emilio's "Gay Politics, Gay Community: San Francisco's Experience," in his book *Making Trouble*, 74–95, helpful in compiling this account.

38. D'Emilio, *Making Trouble*, 90.

39. Phillip Brian Harper, *Are We Not Men? Masculine Anxiety and the Problem of African-American Identification* (New York: Oxford University Press, 1996), 12.

40. Ibid., 13–14.

41. Walter Hughes, "In the Empire of the Beat: Discipline and Disco," in *Microphone Fiends: Youth Music and Youth Culture*, ed. Andrew Ross and Tricia Rose (New York: Routledge, 1994), 147–57 at 154.

42. Ibid., 150.

43. Peter Braunstein, "Disco," *American Heritage* 50, no. 7 (November 1999): 43–57 at 55.

44. Ibid., 52–53.

45. Hughes, "In the Empire of the Beat," 153.

46. Ibid.

47. For a consideration of black gay identity and the black church, see my analysis of the work of Randall Kenan in *The Queer Renaissance*, 69–115.

48. Andrew Holleran, *Dancer from the Dance* (New York: New American Library, 1978).

49. Hughes, "In the Empire of the Beat," 147.

50. Richard Dyer, "In Defense of Disco," in *On Record: Rock, Pop, and the Written Word*, ed. Simon Frith and Andrew Goodwin (New York: Pantheon, 1989), 410–18.

51. Marilyn Quayle's references to smoking marijuana and draft dodging were made to discredit Bill Clinton in his 1992 campaign for the presidency (since he had been accused of both). Both Bruce Bawer's *A Place at the Table: The Gay Individual in American Society* (New York: Touchstone/Simon & Schuster, 1993) and Gabriel Rotello's *Sexual Ecology: AIDS and the Destiny of Gay Men* (New York: Dutton, 1997) imply that the supposed "excesses" of the 1970s somehow "caused" AIDS and that the gay movement needs to "grow up" in the 1990s and focus on issues such as marriage rights.

52. I discuss redeployments of "queerness" in the late 1980s and early 1990s in my introduction to *The Queer Renaissance*, 1–31.

53. Jeffrey Escoffier, quoted in Lisa Duggan and Nan D. Hunter, *Sex Wars: Sexual Dissent and Political Culture* (New York: Routledge, 1995), 171–72.

54. Douglas Crimp in Crimp, ed., *AIDS*, 253.

55. The "normalization" of the gay movement is discussed most thoroughly by Michael Warner in *The Trouble with Normal: Sex, Politics, and the Ethics of Queer Life* (New York: Free Press, 1999), 88–89. Warner explicitly notes that the normalizing trends he analyzes are antithetical to gay liberationist/queer thought from the 1970s.

56. Jay and Young, "Introduction to the Twentieth Anniversary Edition," in Jay and Young, eds., *Out of the Closets*, xxxix.

57. It is important to stress that every aspect of *Out of the Closets* that Jay and Young disavow in their 1992 introduction is affirmed as positive by D'Emilio in his foreword to the same volume. For instance, D'Emilio writes on p. xx: "The failure of a revolution to materialize should not cause us to dismiss the seriousness with which it was pursued or the depth of political conviction that made many subscribe to it. . . . The revolutionary aspirations of these young lesbian and gay radicals are directly responsible for their signal achievement: their willingness to burst out of the closet and to come out in a public, uncompromising way." The best source on the current commodification of gay identity and community is Alexandra Chasin's *Selling Out: The Lesbian and Gay Movement Goes to Market* (New York: St. Martin's Press, 2000). For a critique of the late 1990s disco revival in the films *The Last Days of Disco* and *54*, see Peter Braunstein, "The Last Days of Gay Disco," *Village Voice*, (30 June 1998), 54–55, 58.

Pop Culture and Mass Media

Of all the dividing lines superimposed on the 1960s cultural landscape, perhaps none has been more persistent than the demarcation between a "mainstream" culture and the "counterculture." Yet binarisms of this sort, as much as they are grounded in a certain reality, often obscure more than they clarify. Not only do "counterculture" and "mainstream" tend to acquire a more monolithic quality as categories when they are arrayed against one another, but this either/or thinking also overlooks the fact that the two formations shared much the same culture. Indeed, what characterizes "counterculture" and "mainstream" during the 1960s and '70s is the astounding, persistent, and rapid cross-fertilization of ideas, sensibilities, and styles between the two worlds. Nowhere is this process of exchange and assimilation more evident than in the remarkable pop culture and mass media of the era.

A pervasive mentality shared by both mainstream and counterculture was what Peter Braunstein in his essay "Forever Young" dubs the "culture of rejuvenation." Sampling 1960s pop culture ranging from fashion to film, discotheque dance culture to Yippie! theatrics, Braunstein argues that mainstream and counterculture alike shared a common mentality that prized "being young again" by reclaiming the psychic vitality of childhood. The porous boundaries between radical and mainstream appear again in David James's essay "'The Movies Are a Revolution': Film and the Counterculture." James explores experimental, underground, and radical documentary filmmakers, but finds that, as much as independent filmmakers in the 1960s and '70s devised a new cinema in opposition to the establishment model, they were never completely able to define themselves outside of Hollywood's terms. The power to set the terms of how to figuratively represent countercultural ideals and taboos is examined in Beth Bailey's "Sex as a Weapon: Underground Comix and the Paradox of

Liberation," which reveals the degree to which the counterculture was anything but monolithic. In attempting to sustain a countercultural value system through sexist narratives in underground comix, the male-dominated counterculture eventually ruptured its fragile internal consensus and inadvertently inspired a new, feminist counterculture. Like cave art was to the Neolithic, like graffiti, chat rooms, MUDDs, and talk radio are to the postmodern, underground comix were a ubiquitous and very public expression of the counterculture's groupmind and psyche. There, in the collective imagination where the iconographic met the pornographic, countercultural artists of all genders and sexual persuasions renegotiated what liberation would look like.

Nine

Forever Young

Insurgent Youth and the Sixties Culture of Rejuvenation

Peter Braunstein

At first glance, the generation gap dividing youth and adult society seems a fit antagonism to place on the mantle alongside such other hallowed 1960s binarisms as Free World versus Communism and counterculture versus mainstream. The image of rampaging youth who rejected the values of their parents and surrogate parents (Lyndon Johnson, university administrators), vowed never to trust anyone over thirty, and hoped to die before they got old has become a deeply entrenched cliché. But the vaunted generation gap was only the flip side of a culture of rejuvenation that encompassed youth and adults alike.

As the LSD historian Jay Stevens has observed, in the 1960s "[i]t was as though the country as a whole was undergoing a late adolescence."[1] By mid-decade, an enraptured media had endowed youth with heroic attributes that would have seemed shocking in the late 1950s, and adults' desire to buy into this new valuation of youth led to a more inclusive conceptualization of the term "youth." No longer simply an age category, youth became a metaphor, an attitude toward life, a state of mind that even adults could access. Sustained by the expansive play element in mainstream 1960s culture, this pervasive rejuvenation mentality went on to imbue the ideology of the late-'60s counterculture. Cultural radicals built upon the decade's ongoing infatuation with youth, redirecting it in favor of a full-fledged, radical critique of wayward adulthood. In doing so, they presented the counterculture with its most intractable irresolution: how to plot the future of a movement that strives above all to live in the moment.

It is typically ironic of this culture of rejuvenation that the youthful tenor of the 1960s was established by two adults. Though forty-two and thirty-one years old, respectively, in 1960, John F. Kennedy and First Lady Jacqueline Kennedy spearheaded the youthful style and aesthetic that eventually became the zeitgeist of the decade. JFK's good looks and charm, his dynamic cabinet and entourage (which included younger brother Bobby), and Jackie's immediate ascension to fashion and style maven provided a vivid contrast with the staid and geriatric Eisenhower administration. In contrast to the slow-moving Eisenhower years (epitomized by Ike's frequent golf course outings), JFK's administration consciously hammered out an image of constant motion always verging on volatility and crisis—which belied its lackluster legislative perform-ance.[2] This energetic style has proved the fodder for long-term memory of Kennedy and, as William Chafe has pointed out, JFK's rhetorical emphasis on "the excitement of danger, the exhilaration of confrontation, and the heroism of sacrifice" provided a behavioral template for his youthful admirers.[3] After his death, JFK was posthumously accorded the role of youth's leader. In a 1965 *Esquire* article on the twenty-eight people who count most with college rebels, JFK came in at number 4, "because he made everybody respect youth."[4]

JFK and Jackie had a running start on actual youth of the 1960s, who until nearly mid-decade were immersed in a 1950s cultural hangover that affected fashion, style, music, and social behavior. Up to 1964, journalists were still remarking on how Sixties youth were a "quiet generation," the University of California at Berkeley president, Clark Kerr, made the retrospectively embarrassing assertion that "employers are going to love this generation" because they're "easy to handle,"[5] and the *Billboard* pop charts featured back-ward-looking teen-angst odes involving premature death, like "Last Kiss" and "Leader of the Pack," or premature marriage, like "Chapel of Love." But the shape of things to come had already emerged across the Atlantic, where England's Mod insurgency in music and fashion pitted youngsters against the older generation and even against youthful peers ("Rockers") still wedded to 1950s tastes in doo-wop music and leather jackets. While American teens seemed like undefined gray nobodies to a media waiting for 1960s youth to announce itself, British Mods had been spreading rejuvenation culture throughout Britain from the teen ground level up since the late 1950s. By 1964 maverick fashion designers like Mary Quant, inventor of the miniskirt, and new bands like the Kinks and the Who had cultivated what would soon become an international style in musical taste, clothing, and sensibility.

The British Invasion, officially launched by the Beatles' takeover of the pop charts (and their subsequent U.S. tour) in January 1964, brought Mod culture to America. "Everything went young in '64," recalled Andy Warhol in *Popism: The Warhol Sixties* "The kids were throwing out all the preppy outfits and the dress-up clothes that made them look like their mothers and fathers, and suddenly everything was reversed—the mothers and fathers were trying to look like their kids."[6] The spectacle of rabid Beatlemania naturally focused the media's attention on teenagers, and the writer Tom Wolfe made a name for himself chronicling how teens had become the driving force behind American culture, the demographic where future fads, fashion, and sensibilities incubated before being spread to the rest of America. Anticipating the hippies before the term was coined, Wolfe argued in 1965 that "now high styles come from low places, from marginal types who carve out worlds for themselves . . . in tainted undergrounds," and "come out of the netherworld of modern teenage life."[7]

Esquire, a magazine geared to college-age males, went even further. The July 1965 cover page asked "Does today's teen-ager influence the adult world? 'Ridiculous,' says Ed Sullivan," who is shown wearing a Beatles wig. An array of articles followed arguing rather persuasively that American teenagers, as consumers, had hegemonic control of the U.S. economy. Marshaling an impressive array of statistics—that youngsters age thirteen to twenty-two possess $25 billion a year in disposable cash, that by the end of 1965 more than half the population will be under twenty-five—essayists concluded that the teen consumer market "is only the stepping-stone for total take-over by youth of the entire United States market." This trend, according to the authors, would last at least a generation, since "that vague no-man's-land of adolescence" has "suddenly turned into a way of life," becoming "a subculture rather than a transition." Youth was not only prolonging itself indefinitely as an age category; it had also become a pervasive consumer identity that inflected adult buying patterns. By emulating the consumption patterns of teenagers, adults could literally "buy young." As the president of Macy's New York department store put it, "In our generation you had to keep up with the Joneses. Today it's more important to keep up with the Joneses kids. In short, in the child-oriented society where we find ourselves, the teen-ager is the new influential."[8]

The culture of rejuvenation that swept America during the Mod era (1964–66) is best illustrated in two venues: fashion and the new dance crazes. Rejuvenation in women's fashion applied to all age groups, as Mod clothing encouraged age regression even among those who were still teenagers. One example was the "Big Baby Look" of 1965, in which teenage girls wore short schoolgirl dresses with puffy sleeves and flat shoes with straps across them. To complete the prepubescent look, as Warhol noted, "lipstick was finished and the big thing was eye makeup—iridescent, pearlized, goldenized—stuff that gleamed at night."[9] Such a look of exaggerated youthfulness expressed the associated sensibility that maturity, in dress or behavior, was a dirty word, a sign of premature death, and therefore something to be warded off as long as possible. As one *New York Times* reporter summed it up, the Mod fashion dictum was that "the young should look like the young. . . . The old could, if they wished, look like the young, but the young must not on any account look like the old."[10] Many adult women acceded to the new power dynamic in the fashion world—Jackie Kennedy's embrace of the miniskirt in 1966 cleared the way for its adoption by American women over thirty—though there was the occasional holdout. Mrs. Loel Guiness, *Women's Wear Daily's* fashion "First Lady of 1963," complained five years later that "[t]oday if you dress like a decent person, you are made to feel a million years old. If you dress young, you look like an idiot. What choice is there?"[11]

Another canonical feature of Mod-era fashion that became a guiding principle for 1960s youth culture generally was the emphasis on mutable identity and role playing. In the manner of children who pretend to be astronauts or hairdressers, Sixties fashion projected individual identity as a slide show of alternating roles, postures, and personalities—a sensibility that could be summed up as "the many moods of me." The 1960s, after all, was the heyday of wig culture, and fashion icons like the supermodel-sprite Twiggy or *femme-enfant* Brigitte Bardot mastered the art of the ever-changing "look" that rendered them perennially unfathomable and elusive. Fashion historian Joel Lobenthal wrote that in the world of 1960s fashion "the individual remade himself daily, trying out new stances of dress and behavior, internalizing some, keeping others at arm's length as theatrical alter egos."[12] Consistent with this fashion orientation was the throwaway paper dress (which occasionally could be purchased with do-it-yourself paint set) meant to be worn to one night's "happening" and then discarded—along with whatever identity came with it.[13] As the paper dress maker Elisa Stone recalled, "I loved the idea that my clothes were not going to last. I thought of them as toys."[14] The corollary of this approach was that keeping the same look for too long—which in some circles meant two nights in a row—was a faux pas and perhaps even a sign of creeping maturity.

The play-acting aspect of Mod culture was also apparent in the numerous dance crazes of the era. The Twist fad of 1959–63 had established the pattern: teenagers invented a new dance step, soon grew tired of it, at which point it was taken up by trendsetting adults and socialites. The dance-craze pace stepped up considerably beginning in 1964, when the European entertain-

Hip fashion photographer (David Hemmings) during a shoot in Michelangelo Antonioni's epochal 'statement' film, *Blow Up* (1966). Sixties fashion projected individual identity as a slide-show of alternating roles, postures, and personalities—a sensibility that could be summed up as "the many moods of me." This mentality pervaded all aspects of the culture, from TV shows like *Batman* and *Get Smart,* to discotheque dance culture and countercultural incarnations like the hippie "Flower Child." In dance or dissent, the charade remained the most pervasive and versatile mode of self-expression of '60s youth. Few films of the era engaged the subject of kaleidoscope identity more fruitfully than *Blow Up*. Museum of Modern Art Film Stills Archive.

ment form known as the *discotheque* took root in America along with British rock music. The discotheque featured programmed music spun by a disc jockey rather than the live bands Americans were used to, and immediately became the testing ground for such new dances as the Frug, the Watusi, the Monkey, and the Go-Go. As with fashion, the organizing principle behind the dances was the charade. A visit to any discotheque in 1965 might involve the spectacle of teenagers, as well as adults in their thirties and forties, doing the Woodpecker (by flapping their hands like wings and bobbing their faces as if pecking wood), the Hitchhiker (by making a thumbing gesture), or the Chickenback (by jumping back to back and shaking in order to remove the invisible chicken from their backs).[15] Tom Wolfe observed that the infantilism of the dances was counterbalanced by the utter seriousness of the dancers, most of whom were "absolutely maniacal about form . . . practically religious about it," to the point that "none of them ever smiled."[16] This form of serious play, or a rejuvenation mentality that obliterated the distinction between play and work, would take on ideological importance as 1960s youth culture evolved.[17]

The role of teens as cultural locomotives led to a new estimation of youth among many adults, readily apparent in media coverage beginning in 1965. Indeed, *Vogue* magazine that year was an ongoing celebration of "Youth," a paean trumpeted in the New Year's Day issue: "Youth, warm and gay as a kitten yet self-sufficient as James Bond, is surprising countries east and west with a sense of assurance serene beyond all years. . . . Under 24 and over 90,000,000 strong in the U.S. alone. More dreamers. More doers. Here. Now. Youthquake 1965." [18] Earlier 1950s-era media characterizations of youth as deviant or nihilistic gave way to a new valuation of young people as valorous, crusading, and brimming with moral vitality.[19] The likening of youth to an army of sorts due to its size and unifying mission was a particularly daunting image in militarist American society, implying that the imposing demographic was a force to be reckoned with ("Youthquake"), a willful body that couldn't and shouldn't be ignored. All of these glowing attributes together crystallized in a new valorization of youth as heroic and redemptive, an image that built on JFK's rehabilitation efforts. Taking up the torch, one young female novelist intoned in *Vogue* that her youthful peers "are being faced with awesome responsibilities and are often forced to make decisions that a generation or two ago would have automatically been left up to their parents. The three who went to Philadelphia, Mississippi last year and never came back attest to this fact. . . . We live in a tense world and we are the ones who will lead it tomorrow. And there are stumbling blocks all along the way." [20] Only youth, the article implied, had the moral zeal, the intelligence, and the force of sheer numbers to save America from peril.

At the same time, young people and adults alike cast youth alternately as an inclusive, age-immune state of mind and as an age-bound, exclusive category closed to adults. One female writer in *Vogue* conceived of youth as "a perfect, separate island in time," while another contended that "real youth, to my way of thinking, is not an age. Rather it is a feeling . . . a way of living, and I fervently hope it shall always prevail." [21] Such contestations over youth's boundaries, as pious, anodyne, or overdramatized as they may have seemed in 1965, pointed the way to two divergent end points of the youth-adult relationship. While the more exclusionary bracketing of youth as age-defined tended inexorably toward the dichotomized generation gap, counterculture-versus-mainstream cosmology of the latter Sixties, the more inclusive, ecumenical notion of youth as state of mind undergirded the blossoming culture of rejuvenation that facilitated rapid adult assimilation of youthful ideas and lifestyles during the same period. These two contradictory conceptualizations of youth coexisted uneasily for the entirety of the decade, the contest between them never fully resolving itself in either one's favor.

Youth in the mid-1960s, a resplendent entity bathed in media attention and suffused with such attributes as energy, ingenuity, and idealism, was the driving force behind American pop culture. Not surprisingly, this type of cultural authority only served to inflate youth's sense of importance, producing an attitude that was at once self-confident and whimsical, holier-than-thou and smart-alecky, and occasionally smug and omnipotent. This youthful zeitgeist is best captured in the caper films that proliferated during this era, among them *Kaleidoscope* (1966), starring Warren Beatty and Susannah York, and *The Jokers* (1966), with Oliver Reed.[22] Superficially, the films involved an elaborate bank, casino, or jewelry heist, but their subtext was a contest between the generations. The premise was the same: someone, usually a young, suave, hip, independently wealthy playboy, plans a daring robbery not because he needs the money, but just for kicks, just to prove that by sheer ingenuity he can outwit the (adult) authorities. Implicit in caper films was the antagonism between the individual and society, a theme that grew more explicit and violent as the genre evolved with such films as *Danger: Diabolik* (1967), with John Phillip Law, and *The Thomas Crown Affair* (1968), starring Steve McQueen and Faye Dunaway. As rejuvenated adult and capricious bank-robbing millionaire McQueen confesses in the latter film, "It's not about the money. It's about me and the system."[23]

But as far as the Mod era is concerned, the caper genre not only illustrates youth's cocky optimism, sense of superiority, and thirst for challenge and adventure, but testifies to the still mildly adversarial relationship between young people and the system that predated the more aggressive counterculture beginning in 1967. The young protagonists in these films, like Warren Beatty in *Kaleidoscope*, are too charming, clean-shaven and poised to be genuine outlaws. Instead, the relationship between the hero-criminal and his authority-figure adversaries, as in the numerous cat-and-mouse crime and espionage films and TV shows of the era (*Batman, The Man from U.N.C.L.E., Get Smart, The Avengers*), conveys a Sixties trope that could be characterized as "hard play": that type of Bond-Blofeld antagonism that is at once playful and serious, lighthearted and deadly, fun-loving and ruthless.

Hard play, like the "serious play" of dance culture, was a cardinal expression of that salient aspect of the culture of rejuvenation: the breakdown of the work-play dichotomy. The extraordinary expansion of the play element in Sixties culture was predicated on the economic bounty of the era; indeed, the

American economic boom of the 1960s was unique in that it reconstituted the material basis for neo-childhood among white, middle-class Americans of all ages. Just as affluent children are sheltered from material considerations and thereby exist in a world in which work and leisure are irrelevant categories, the full-employment economy of the 1960s fueled widespread assumptions that the need for work would eventually disappear in favor of, as one underground journalist put it, "a society based on the needs of the soul (creative time) and not of the flesh (work time) where machines (and not men) regulated by technicians turn out enough food, shelter and clothing for an entire nation, perhaps in all probability the world . . ." [24] As the director of the Western Behavioral Institute mused in January 1966, "The superior man of the future will be the person who can cope with a world without work . . ." [25] Caper film protagonists were this cultural avant garde: purveyors of a truly post-scarcity sensibility, they robbed banks not for material gain but as a creative outlet. The 1960s conflation of work and play, and its affinity for spy and caper film scenarios that confounded the two categories and melted them into one single approach to life, illustrated the rejuvenation mentality which held that adults could be children again: they could play with utter seriousness and "work" with blithe and creative abandon.

In early 1967, the zeitgeist epicenter of youth culture shifted from Swinging London to psychedelic San Francisco, as American and world media trained their cameras on a new, more colorful, and radical incarnation of insurgent youth: the "hippies." The bohemian denizens of San Francisco's Haight-Ashbury announced themselves to the world, quite intentionally, at a festival held on January 14 called "The First Human Be-In." Announcements for the event indicated that youth's self-image as redemptive and heroic had, at least in San Francisco, taken on messianic proportions. One proclamation in the hippie newspaper the *San Francisco Oracle* read: "Now in the evolving generation of America's young the humanization of the American man and woman can begin in joy and embrace without fear, dogma, suspicion, and dialectical righteousness." [26] Another announcement, in the *Berkeley Barb*, made it clear that youth's enormous self-confidence and sense of mission had finally crystallized: "The spiritual revolution will be manifest and proven. In unity we will shower the country with waves of ecstasy and purification. Fear will be washed away; ignorance will be exposed to sunlight; profits and empire will lie drying on deserted beaches. . . ." [27]

Since the purpose of the Be-In was so nebulous and existential (as opposed to, say, a Sit-In), the fact that it struck many observers as having no meaning meant that it probably had cosmic significance. Roughly 20,000 hippies, Berkeley politicos, and interested observers showed up at the Polo

Grounds in Golden Gate Park to drop acid, listen to the Grateful Dead and the Jefferson Airplane, and celebrate the collective act of being. As Buddha, the psychedelic ex-Marine drill instructor serving as master of ceremonies, took the stage, a voice announced, "Welcome. Welcome to the first manifestation of the Brave New World." The audience was a full-color advertisement for the so-called "love generation." Hippies had brought fruit, flowers, incense, cymbals, and tambourines; one could spot various people dressed as shaman, cowboys, and prophets. There were figures wearing Colonial petticoats, buckskins and war paint, madras saris and priests' cloaks, togas, ancestral velvets, and Arabian desert robes. One observer described it as "a medieval scene, with banners flying, bright and uncommitted." The Be-In's unqualified success spurred a media feeding frenzy that broadcast the hippie lifestyle and some version of its value system to the rest of the nation. [28]

While the hippies' affinity for playing dress up appeared innovative, it had its roots in a Mod sensibility that embraced the charade, in dance and fashion, as a way of presenting multiple personas and thereby warding off the stultified uni-identity associated with adulthood and its related bête noire, maturity. The hippies, however, elevated the charade to the status of an organizing principle in their collective ambition of redeeming America via rejuvenation. Their device for accomplishing this task was the short-lived "flower child" phase of youth revolt, which can be understood as a sort of political charade. To understand how a charade involving young people posing as peaceful, loving flower children could function as a radical political stance, one must embed it within the context of 1967 America. By that year, the exuberant optimism of mid-1960s liberalism—as represented by the "triumph" of the civil rights movement with the passage of the Voting Rights Act of 1965, for instance—had devolved into a more turbulent and confrontational political miasma. In the course of 1967, U.S. forces in Vietnam grew from 385,000 to almost half a million; meanwhile, the antiwar movement's ranks swelled with opposing numbers, while the white-black solidarity of the earlier civil rights movement gave way to the Black Power stance and its corollary, the race riot, beginning in Watts in 1965 and increasing in frequency thereafter. Amidst growing violence—in the streets, on university campuses, and in Vietnam—the flower child charade was at once a mockery and a repudiation of this overall climate of aggression.

During the height of the Flower Power phase of hippiedom, the Beat-era activist, poet, and Fugs member Tuli Kupferberg wrote an influential essay titled "The Politics of Love" that distilled the analysis and program of the hippies. Significantly, Kupferberg was forty-four when he wrote this paean to redemptive youth (which included himself), thereby positing "youth" as a mentality-defined, and not strictly age-defined, category. He begins the essay by surveying the "patent failures of the anti-Vietnam war movement, the isolation and trend toward terrorism of the civil rights movement (I mean the Blacks, the whites have always used terror), the failure of SDS or anarchists to develop fast a new viable ideology of revolution, ... the national terror against narcotics, the failure to appear of any liberal of the stature even of JFK [*sic*]." Kupferberg concludes that "the youth (and those older still ALIVE) are presented ... with two seemingly different directions." The first one, political engagement in the style of the New Left or the antiwar movement, Kupferberg discounts because "the society corrupts even those who would overthrow it!," the result being that "they will not become like us—we will become like them." Instead, he advocates a "politics of love" in which youth drop out of the core society and form "primitive communisms," live off the crumbs of affluence, and gradually "corrupt" the hate-filled society through love. Doubting the efficacy, and even the tangibility, of this approach while still espousing it, Kupferberg ends his essay in the form of a Socratic debate. He admits that "we will lose many battles," but counters that "[t]he beauty of our youth will conquer the world ... We will make the ugly beautiful—the sick healthy—the poor rich—the soldiers peaceful." His imaginary interlocutor then chides him by saying, "You are stupid, insane, naive children," to which Kupferberg replies, "Who else can save us?" [29]

A patchwork construction, the flower child "love ethic" as articulated by Kupferberg and his hippie peers drew from Civil Rights nonviolence, the radical pessimism and alienation of the Beats, apostolic early Christianity, peace movement/Ban the Bomb pacifism, and the redemptive millenarianism of the LSD subculture and combined these stances to radicalize rejuvenation culture with a more critical social perspective. To be childlike, in this new construction, meant to be at one with nature, with the earth, with other human beings; to be nonviolent, loving, and (re)sensitized to the violence around you; to consciously regain the simplicity and wonder of childhood as a perceptual prism for reclaiming a society wracked by civil uprisings and war abroad.

Not surprisingly, this hippie love ethic was criticized by the New Left as a watering down of youthful energies, an irresponsible and apathetic stance that mystically promoted societal renewal not via concrete structural changes in the political system but through a nebulous social stance based on love. [30] The New Left, however, provides only one perspective on the issue. When the hippies are assessed from the standpoint of Mod-era popular culture, it is clear that they took a latent, implicit Mod critique of adult society, maturity, and the life cycle and politicized it. While Mod-era youth disdained maturity on a stylistic and aesthetic level, because it reminded them of their parents, the hippie analysis cast maturity and the denial of childhood as a motive force behind militarism, injustice, racism, intolerance, and human aggression. The transition from Mod to hippie in the context of the '60s youth insurgency, then, is a shift from attitude to ideology, from posture to provocation.

Another way in which the hippies radically inflected the culture of rejuvenation was through the philosophy of deconditioning that emerged from their experiences with LSD. Beginning with the writer Aldous Huxley's mescaline experimentation in the 1950s, discerning users began to notice that psychedelics neutralized the brain's filtering mechanisms that ordinarily screened out phenomena deemed commonplace or irrelevant. Indeed, LSD and other mind-expanding drugs incapacitated the discriminating faculties of the brain that placed objects and images in hierarchies of value. Under the influence of LSD, the palm of one's hand, the leaf in the tree, the fabric of one's jacket acquired as much significance as one's parking space, the Dow Jones index, one's spouse. Given that this nonjudgmental openness to phenomena replicated the perceptual vista of the infant or small child, many LSD users tended to describe their trips as rebirths, Huxley referring to his mescaline experiences as a "second childhood." When LSD was still legal in the 1950s, and widely used in therapy by psychiatrists, one patient described her LSD session as follows:

> As I plummeted down, I felt myself growing smaller and smaller . . .
> I was becoming a child . . . a very small child . . . a baby . . . I was a
> baby. I was not remembering being a baby. I was literally a baby.
> (The conscious part of me realized I was experiencing the phenom-
> ena of age regression, familiar in hypnosis. But in this case,
> although I had become a baby, I remained at the same time a
> grown woman lying on a couch. This was a double state of being.)[31]

Whereas the end point of Mod-era rejuvenation was the teenager, LSD culture set its sights on earlier childhood, and even infancy, as optimal regression site.

Gradually, a body of thought began to emerge from such luminaries as Huxley, William Burroughs, Allen Ginsberg, and Timothy Leary, who utilized the insights gained from their LSD-enabled neo-childhoods in the service of erasing adult, middle-class programming. If LSD revealed a world of psychic plenitude, the corollary insight was that adults viewed their surroundings with blinders on. LSD philosophers concluded that adults' perception of their environment was so shuttered, rigid, and one-dimensional that, not surprisingly, their response to stimuli always followed the same dismal pattern, producing war, injustice, poverty, racism, and sexual repression. The antidote to this psychic tunnel vision called maturity was "deconditioning," a term coined by Burroughs.[32]

According to deconditioning philosophy, LSD could help rupture the psychic straitjacket of adulthood and open the door to a new set of behavioral options. As Jay Stevens explained, "deconditioning assumed that LSD allowed you an objective look at your own conditioning, all the categories you had been taught to filter experience into, first as an infant and later as a functioning member of a complex, highly organized society." The implications were earthshaking: "Take LSD and wipe the slate clean of all that Madison Avenue–Big Business–Behaviorist crap." [33] Timothy Leary called this process "breaking set": jettisoning, via LSD use, all the old behavioral patterns and conditioning—mindless consumption, hatred, competitiveness, intolerance— in favor of new, more evolved, more childlike perceptual and behavioral "imprints." "Reimprinting" one's psyche and becoming a child-adult, deconditioning proponents insisted, represented true psychological maturity and was ultimately the route to personal and societal salvation. [34]

In a cultural setting in which being childlike was taken as a sign of mental health, one can appreciate the hippies' affinity for dressing in costumes, adopting colorful nicknames, being playful whenever possible, and fashioning an economic relationship with society that resembled that of a middle-class child with its parents—panhandling as an updated version of asking for one's allowance. Acting childlike in hippie circles was also taken as a heartening sign that one was throwing off the shackles of adult psychic blockage, that the deconditioning was working. In a characteristic statement, Jimi Hendrix once observed that "[a] musician, if he's a messenger, is like a child who hasn't been handled too many times by man, hasn't had too many fingerprints across his brain. That's why music is so much heavier than anything you ever felt." [35] In some notable cases, certain psychedelic explorers felt that simply being around small children would help them break their adult "set" and become more open to their world, because children, as Leary disciple Charles Slack put it, are "already turned on"—they haven't been conditioned yet. [36] In this vein, Leary and his sidekick Richard Alpert took up a brief experiment in collective child-rearing at their estate in Millbrook, New York (based on a scenario taken from Aldous Huxley's book *Island*), hoping to learn from the children and imbibe some of their spontaneity and awe. Unfortunately, the work of overseeing small children became too arduous for the male personnel of the estate, and the experiment faltered. [37] Nonetheless, Leary continued to exalt small children as models for countercultural rejuvenation. In a 1967 hippie summit meeting, he revealed his ultimate drop-out scenario: "I'm going to go away to a beach and live on the beach. I'm going to take LSD once a week and I'm going to take hashish once a day at sunset and I'm going to have babies and I'm going to learn from our babies." [38]

Children, of course, live in the present, while making occasional incursions into the immediate future. So it comes as no surprise that given the hippies' desire to reappropriate the mentality of the very young, presentism—living in the moment—became a central tenet of countercultural rejuvenation. As with other aspects of rejuvenation culture, however, presentism was not a philosophical or lifestyle innovation of the hippies, but a characteristic of Sixties youth culture in general. The pace of momentous events throughout the decade (assassinations, demonstrations, riots, festivities), together with the exhilaration felt by the many historical actors involved in 1960s social movements, made for an era of unprecedented experiential density. Zeitgeist barometer Andy Warhol referred to the "acceleration" factor in the '60s, by which he meant the sheer volume of individual and social activity that made one year seem to last five. He attributed this altered perception of time to drugs, particularly the manic amphetamine culture that engulfed the Factory coterie. "I could never finally figure out if more things happened in the sixties because there was more awake time for them to happen (since so many people were on amphetamine) or if people started taking amphetamine because there were so many things to do that they needed to have more awake time to do them in. It was probably both." [39]

Convinced that the frenzied pace of Sixties life was rendering sleep obsolete, Warhol decided to record it before it disappeared. The result was *Sleep*, his first underground film, a six–hour chronicle of a man sleeping—in slow-motion. [40] Elsewhere, in a 1966 *Esquire* article, David Newman and Robert Benton (who would later write the screenplay for *Bonnie and Clyde*) penned a humorous piece declaring that the 1960s were over, arguing that "[t]he Sixties have been so packed with hysteria, so intense and frenetic, so rocking and rolling, so pop and so op that they have well nigh obliterated all that came before. Of course, one of the reasons for this is that nothing came before." They concluded that people needed a rest: "Let six years be a decade," they announced. "Let the next four be a vacation." [41]

Youth in the 1960s tended a culture of immediacy that prized such elements as spontaneity, frivolity, and amorphousness, a zeitgeist epitomized by phenomena like "Happenings" that eluded categorization. The first Happenings, staged by artists in the late 1950s, were described by critics as "a kind of makeshift, hit-and-run theater," apparently spontaneous, "involving people and objects in unexpected, often non-rational conditions and behavior which challenge our accepted ideas about ourselves, our lives, our environment." [42] One Happening conceived by the artist Claes Oldenberg, for instance, featured a man in flippers soundlessly reciting Shakespeare alongside someone shoveling sand from a cot and then lying down in it. [43] By the mid-1960s, Happenings became a catch-all term to describe any type of free-form, deliberately improvised event—be it festive, commercial, or in the case of the Supremes song "The Happening," romantic. [44] Often, a Happening was equivalent to a wild party—hence the iconic '60s exclamation "It's my happening, baby, and it's freaking me out"—except that the idea was to avoid such pigeonholing. Happenings, along with such -in suffixed events as Be-Ins and Love-Ins, testified to the lure of the unscripted in 1960s pop culture, an aspect of its presentist, immediatist orientation.

At the same time, the bohemian critique of mainstream, adult, middle-class society—articulated in America by the Beats and then the hippies—held as a central tenet the rejection of long-term considerations in favor of a radical embrace of the present. Perhaps the most influential ideological espousal of presentism as countercultural mentality came in Norman Mailer's famous 1957 essay "The White Negro." For all its dated jargon and equation of blacks with righteous primitivism and atavism, the article remains, as the historian Thomas Frank points out, "the most compelling statement by which the over-organized postwar world would be resisted," as well as a "blueprint for the cultural eruption by which the civilization of conformity would be overturned." [45]

Throughout the essay, Mailer describes the psychoexistential orientation of the "hipster," or American bohemian dissident, in terms of both infantile regression and radical presentism. Accepting the atmosphere of immediacy and contingency bequeathed to him by the postwar environment of atomic standoff and soul-killing corporate and state dominion, Mailer's hipster desperately embraces life in the shadow of death, consciously choosing "to explore that domain of experience where security is boredom and therefore sickness, and one exists in the present, the enormous present which is without past or future, memory or planned intention. . . ." [46] Stranded in the solitary present, the hipster engages in a potentially destructive, torturous process of rejuvenation that simultaneously affirms his strongest innermost drives, since "the fundamental decision of his nature is to try to live the infantile fantasy." [47] This infantile regression—which may involve any combination of drug use, sexual promiscuity, and criminal fantasy—is actually a dangerous but evolutionary quest for self-knowledge guided by the principle that, in Mailer's formulation, "if one is to change one's habits, one must go back to the source of their creation." Only by unearthing "the violent and often hopeless contradictions he knew as an infant and a child" and "giving expression to the buried infant in himself" can Mailer's hipster hope to "lessen the tension of those infantile desires and so free himself to remake a bit of his nervous system." [48] Once again, what emerges is one of the most tenacious equations of the counterculture: radical rejuvenation, which requires a presentist orientation, inevitably leads to self-discovery, self-knowledge, self-regeneration.

In one respect, Mailer's assertion that the "Hip ethic is immoderation, child-like in its adoration of the present"[49] simply recapitulates Blake's adage that "the road of excess leads to the palace of wisdom," although it furnishes updated travel instructions as to orientation (presentism) and modus operandi (rejuvenation). At the same time, Mailer's essay is strikingly prescient in anticipating a philosophy that would guide both drug explorers of the 1960s and sexual explorers of the 1970s. It was the hipster's innate understanding that "truth is not what one has felt yesterday or what one expects to feel tomorrow but rather truth is no more nor less than what one feels at each instant in the perpetual climax of the present."[50] Indeed, for Mailer's bohemian, the perfect measure of time is certainly not the week or month, nor even the second or minute, but the (male) orgasm—which contains all the ingredients of immediacy, spontaneity, danger, potency, vulnerability, exaltation, and proximity to death that the bohemian rebel craves, and requires, to stay alive.[51]

Mailer's exposition of the rebel mind, while stipulating a guiding quest (self-knowledge via radical rejuvenation), obviously lent itself to manifold readings and open-ended applications. For anti-bohemians it seemed a perilous philosophy for this very reason, since it seemed to sanction any type of deviant, bizarre, excessive, or self-destructive behavior in the name of self-discovery. Indeed, this philosophy of "therapeutic excess," the idea that all forms of personal and social experimentation were a type of wisdom-foraging and were therefore "good for you," became both the creed and the Achilles' heel of the counterculture (or, for counterculturists, the planks on which the counterculture was crucified).

Hippies spent a great deal of time leveling a contrary indictment: that mortgaging one's present in favor of the future simply out of fear, that remaining blissfully or deadeningly unaware of the sources of one's aggression, was true self-destruction; that the image of the three-martini alcoholic on the commuter train back to his loveless marriage was a more compelling signifier of death-in-life than drug use, which was at least an attempt to transcend the stultifying limitations imposed on the human condition. "Many people cannot understand the hippies' rejection of everything that is commonly expected of the individual in regard to employment and life goals: steady lucrative employment, and the accumulation through the years of possession and money, building (always building) security for the future," one underground journalist intoned. "It is precisely this security hypochondria, this *checking of bank books rather than pulses* . . . that drives the youth of today away." Valuing the future over the present, this indictment concluded, sustained the "rat race" value system that prized lifelong competitiveness, materialism, and avarice. "They [the children] have seen their parents slave for years, wasting away a lifetime to make sure that the house was paid off, that the kids got through school in order to get 'good' jobs so that they could join the frantic scramble, later on. The parents' reward for this struggle is that they wind up old and tired, alienated from their children and just as often each parent from the other."[52]

Ultimately, this line of countercultural thought betrayed a deep ambivalence about teleology per se—the notion that ideas, phenomena, people should be tending *toward* something, heading in some direction. If, as Mailer contended, the hipster's only truth is found in the present, then the future may be just a rumor—at the very least, it's something to be broached with trepidation, suspicion, and skepticism. Which naturally raises the question: How to plot the future of a presentist social movement? What's the proper direction for the counterculture—or, more to the point—should the counterculture have a direction?

This was the counterculture's greatest irresolution, a dilemma inherited from the LSD experience that provided so much of its epistemology. Huxley had called it the problem of "reentry": after having experienced the childlike beatitude of an LSD trip, how does the user take this knowledge, this intimation of a better world, and integrate it into the normative reality that returned on the heels of every acid trip?[53] The psychedelic pioneer Richard Alpert echoed the frustrations of many regarding the non-cumulative, anti-teleological circularity of the LSD experience:

> I had plenty of LSD, but why take it. I knew what it was going to
> do, what it was going to tell me. It was going to show me that gar-
> den again and then I was going to be cast out and that was it. And
> I could never quite stay. I was addicted to the experience at first,
> and then I even got tired of that. And the despair was extremely
> intense at that point.[54]

Writer and LSD proselytizer Ken Kesey, having initially advocated freewheeling, recreational use of "acid," had eventually come to a new understanding of the use of drugs in the psychedelic revolution. Drugs had opened doors and fostered new critical and visionary insights, but repeated use of LSD was like going through the same door over and over again. At a furtive press conference while hiding from the FBI in 1966 he confessed: "I know we've reached a certain point but we're not moving any more, we're not creating any more, that's why we've got to move to the next step."[55]

Plotting the next step proved no easy feat for a counterculture in which eschewing the future and reveling in the moment represented a state of grace. This became obvious at the landmark hippie Houseboat Summit of early 1967, convened specifically to plot the future direction of the counterculture. In typical fashion, those luminaries assembled to ponder the fate of the hippie youth movement were Allen Ginsberg, age forty, Timothy Leary, age forty-six, Alan

Watts, age fifty-one, and Gary Snyder, age thirty-six—all adults, albeit rejuvenated ones. The debate centered around the question of whether countercultural youth should drop out or take over, but it immediately foundered over the meaning of those two catchphrases: Ginsberg repeatedly called attention to the diverse, opaque, and perhaps contradictory or nonsensical applications of Leary's mantra "Turn On, Tune In, Drop Out." More illuminating was the consensus that the hippies should not attempt to take over American society, presumably by wresting control of the political system. Watts insisted that "[w]henever the insights one derives from mystical vision become politically active, they always create their own opposite. They create a parody . . . [W]hen we try to force a vision upon the world, and say that everybody ought to have this, and it's *good* for you, then a parody of it is set up." [56] Resistance to institutionalizing the counterculture clearly centered on the ever-present hippie fear of "psychedelic fascism"—or, as Leary phrased the problem, "How do you have a community . . . organized, or disorganized, just as long as it's effective—without a fascist leadership?" [57] It was the same fear voiced by Kupferberg, that by becoming established the hippies would mutate into their current enemies, that a structured, hierarchy-bound counterculture would become the next coercive power structure. One set of instructions, currently provided by bourgeois capitalist adults, would simply be replaced by another set of "countercultural" instructions—clearly a self-defeating proposition. As a gesture of hippie good faith, Leary immediately suggested dropping the term "leaders" in favor of "*foci* of energy*," which met with general agreement. [58]

The panelists having decided, rather early in the summit, that the idea of the counterculture "becoming" something was inherently dangerous, their discussion could have ended there. The four gurus, however, couldn't resist making certain prognostications and forecasts about the future of the counterculture, just as long as they didn't appear to be *directions*. Since 'taking over' wasn't an option, dropping out seemed more practical—a process that, according to Snyder, involved "cutting down on your needs to an absolute minimum, perhaps establishing small farms that will make some new kinds of machines that will turn people on instead of bomb them," a development that may involve "a lot of potentially beautiful teachers who are unemployed at the moment." [59] From then on, visions of a countercultural future America became more colorful, extravagant, and, at times, surreal:

Snyder: . . . So what I visualize is a very complex and sophisticated-cybernetic technology surrounded by thick hedges of trees . . . Somewhere, say around Chicago. And the rest of the nation a buffalo pasture . . .

Leary: That's very close to what I think.

Snyder: . . . with a large number of people going around making their own arrowheads because it's fun, but they know better . . . (laughter) They know they don't have to make them (more laughter).

Leary: Now, this seems like our Utopian visions are coming closer together. I say the industry should be underground, and you say it should be in Chicago. This interests me. [60]

The summit finally concluded with the enumeration of certain "practical steps" the counterculture could take as a means of sustaining itself, among them "the setting up of meditation centers of tribal landing pads in all cities," the encouragement of "extended family type structures" with "much more permissiveness" than the Judeo-Christian model, capped off by "Be-Ins across Europe, perhaps retracing the steps of the Crusades." [61]

The Houseboat Summit not only confirmed Mailer's thesis that the bohemian rebel's preferred dwelling place is the realm of child fantasy, but also brought to the surface the counterculture's anti-teleological orientation. As Alan Watts observed at one point, "If a culture cannot afford an area in itself where pure nonsense happens, and where it is not practical, it has no objectives, it was for no reason whatsoever . . . then this culture is dead." [62] The hippies' presentist orientation fostered a belief that inserting all phenomena within teleologies of causation and resolution, grading all human experience as "success" or "failure," even asking questions like "what's the next step for the counterculture?" was an epistemological trap, a connivance of Western capitalism. Moreover, expecting the counterculture to specify "aims" and a "program" was in itself a profanation of countercultural ideals, a caving in to straight society's pressure to look forward and think in terms of outcome, to measure and quantify one's present experience for insertion into some future-oriented template. Any question involving the counterculture's legacy, whether it "succeeded" or "failed," has to take into account the anti-teleological orientation of much countercultural thought—given that, from a countercultural perspective, any assertion that begins with "the counterculture *failed* because it never (fill in the blank)" is structurally flawed, a contradiction, sort of like asking a hippie what he wants to be when he grows up. The countercultural dream, in fact, was to inhabit a place called Today, a place where all teleologies ceased, where the seeming antipodes of present and future, being and becoming, success and failure, imploded and became irrelevant. After all, adults are the ones saddled with mere goals; children have dreams.

By late summer 1967, the Flower Child charade of the hippies had begun to wilt, overheated by the media hype it had generated. The advertised lifestyle of communalism, free love, and abundant drugs had enticed young people from across America to the two largest urban hippie enclaves, San Francisco's Haight-Ashbury and New York's East Village, and the crescendo of immigrants soon overwhelmed the hippies' meager resources and ad hoc organizations assembled to aid the newcomers. As a result, the "Summer of Love '67" featured scores of young would-be hippies, many of them confused runaways, victimized by unscrupulous drug dealers, crammed in overpopulated hippie "communes," harassed by police and municipal authorities, and objectified by commercialization and tourism meant to capitalize on the hippie phenomenon. By summer's end, two well-publicized murders in both coastal meccas redirected media scrutiny, which now focused on the "dark underside" of the hippie dream. "The mindblower is not that love is dead in the East Village," intoned Richard Goldstein of New York's *Village Voice*, "but that it has taken this long to kick the bucket. Flower Power began and ended as a cruel joke. The last laugh belongs to the media-men who chose to report a charade as a movement. In doing so, they created one." [63] Many hippies agreed, and staged a Death of Hippie mock funeral in San Francisco where they officially disowned the moniker "hippie" as the device used by a rapacious media to categorize, control, and ultimately entomb a cultural movement it didn't understand. Yet at the very moment that the Flower Power charade ended, a new one began, a charade fertile and mythic enough to last till decade's end. It was suggested by the film phenomenon of the year, perhaps of the decade, Arthur Penn's *Bonnie and Clyde*, which premiered in August 1967. *Bonnie and Clyde* is a veritable parable of radical youth in the late 1960s, a Rosetta stone for deciphering their utopian aspirations, destructive impulses, and revolutionary pretensions.

The film is a perfect example of what Pagan Kennedy has called "guerrilla nostalgia": it uses the past as a way of indicting and invalidating the present. [64] As *Life* magazine noted at the time, in *Bonnie and Clyde* "[t]he parallel between the middle 1930s and the middle 1960s is never too far from the minds of the movie's creators." [65] Indeed, the very choice of the Depression-era 1930s was an act of provocation on the part of the filmmakers, for if there was one decade that traumatized the parents of Sixties youth, that explained their anxieties about financial security and their consequent privileging of the future over the present, it was the 1930s. In parallel fashion, Bonnie and Clyde, as children of the '30s, are thinly veiled mirrors of radical youth in the 1960s. Like 1960s youth, they conduct their activities, deemed criminal by a morally invalid society, with a wide-eyed, childlike innocence. As one filmgoer put it, Bonnie and Clyde "react to a life of crime as a child would react to a toy that releases him from a bout of crying."[66] Their criminality enables a life-affirming creative and imaginative escape from the uninterrupted bleakness of their lives in Depression-era America. Also like their Sixties peers, Bonnie and Clyde have seemingly resolved the dichotomy between work and play. They play at being bank robbers, and it is this "playwork" that provides them with money, self-esteem, and, in their minds, enhanced social profiles. Of course, since play is the organizing principle behind their life of crime, the effects of their violent actions on others are shrouded in unreality. As *Esquire* magazine observed, "In [*Bonnie and Clyde*] pain is shown in two aspects: the unreal pain that a child deals out when he says, 'Bang bang, you're dead', and the reality when he is hurt himself. When Bonnie and Clyde shoot people, it is all in fun, just like an old gangster movie; when they are hit themselves, reality floods in on them."[67]

True to the spirit of the 1960s, Bonnie and Clyde are presentists, "rebels with no cause beyond the moment's rebellion," as *Vogue* magazine put it.[68] They live from one bank job to the next, without any overarching aims or goals, just dreams about settling down when hard times are over. Of the two, Bonnie is the more reluctant presentist. She sounds something like Ken Kesey pondering over the LSD experience when complaining in one scene that "When we started out I thought we was going somewhere. This is it. We're just going." Clyde, on the other hand, is completely wedded to their non-teleological lifestyle. When Bonnie asks him how their lives would be different if they could start from scratch, Clyde suggests that "I wouldn't live in the same state where we pull our jobs."

The two outlaws are obsessed with publicity and, in the words of one critic, "at least as interested in their press clippings as they were in money."[69] Like the hippies and Yippies, they believe that they can "steal the media" and use it for their own ends. In one scene, they capture a Texas Ranger and mull over whether to shoot or hang him, but decide to take a comic photo of him with the Barrow gang instead because it will make an effective publicity gimmick. Similarly, it is the publication of Bonnie's poem "The Story of Bonnie and Clyde" in a newspaper that cures Clyde of his impotence: seeing his life story in print has confirmed the validity of his existence and made him immortal.

The last parallel between Bonnie and Clyde and '60s radical youth lies in their relationship with parents, adults, and with the more abstract, nefarious Establishment. Bonnie and Clyde are what can be called "elective orphans": they abandon their parents and establish a surrogate crime family that, despite its tensions, provides them with a unity and sense of purpose absent from their "real" family. After suffering her mother's repudiation of her new, criminal lifestyle, Bonnie cries, "I don't have no momma, no family either," to which Clyde responds, "I'm your family." Significantly, when Bonnie and Clyde are finally gunned down by concealed lawmen, it is because the father of one of the gang members snitched on their whereabouts: in the end, they are betrayed by their nominal parents.

At the same time, the depiction of police authority in the film prefigures the "Off the Pig" fetish of late-'60s radical culture, while the shoot-outs in particular convey a transplanted Vietnam. In their reliance on overkill—superior firepower and manpower—the film's "lawmen" are stand-ins for U.S. forces in Vietnam; in their affinity for ambushes, for shooting at Bonnie and Clyde from just behind the tree line, for concealment and invisibility, they fit American perceptions of the Vietcong. Adult authority figures throughout the film are depicted as faceless, cold, anonymous, deceitful, and hypocritical, enemies of the very people they purportedly serve. As Clyde brags to the captured sheriff, "Last year poor farmers kept you laws away from us with shotguns. You're supposed to be protecting them from us and they're protecting us from you. That don't make sense, do it?"

Bonnie and Clyde was a cultural hand grenade, a mini–Dreyfus Affair that divided movie audiences and critics alike.[70] Given the film's glamorization of hip, young criminals pitted against morally bankrupt authorities, its reception served as a dress rehearsal for the 1968 Democratic National Convention in Chicago, with the law-and-order crowd siding with the besieged authority figures and counterculturists identifying with the outlaws-cum-revolutionaries. As *Bonnie and* Clyde co-screenwriter David Newman recalled, "[T]he thing we loved about Bonnie and Clyde wasn't that they were bank robbers, because they were lousy bank robbers. The thing about them that made them so appealing and relevant, and so threatening to society, was that they were aesthetic revolutionaries."[71] Indeed, the film immediately launched a nostalgia craze for 1930s fashion, as the Bonnie and Clyde look—for the man, casquette and striped 1930s suit; for the woman, beret, long skirt and scarf—became a favored radical chic look beginning in late 1967. [72]

Whether as an artistic statement, political stance, romantic fantasy, or radical ethos, *Bonnie and Clyde* was a road map for radical youth in the late '60s. Its appearance in fall 1967, at the tail end of the abortive Flower Child incarnation of the hippies, signaled the turn toward an angrier, more aggressive, and violent counterculture. As the film historian Peter Biskind argues in *Easy Riders, Raging Bulls*, *Bonnie and Clyde*'s cultural power resided in:

> the flair and energy with which [it] pits the hip and cool against
> the old, straight, and stuffy. It says "fuck you" . . . to a generation of

Bonnie Parker (Faye Dunaway), armed and stylish in Arthur Penn's *Bonnie and Clyde*
(1967). As co-screenwriter David Newman recalled, "[T]he thing we loved about
Bonnie and Clyde wasn't that they were bank robbers, because they were lousy bank
robbers. The thing about them that made them so appealing and relevant, and so
threatening to society, was that they were aesthetic revolutionaries." The controversial
film hit theaters in Fall 1967, just as the Flower Child incarnation of the hippies was
beginning to lose steam. *Bonnie and Clyde* not only launched a '30s revival in fashion
but gave counterculture revolutionaries new, more violent heroes to emulate. Museum
of Modern Art Films Stills Archive.

Americans who were on the wrong side of the generation gap, the wrong side of the war in Vietnam . . . If the Bond films legitimized government violence, and the [Sergio] Leone films legitimized vigilante violence, *Bonnie and Clyde* legitimized violence against the establishment, the same violence that seethed in the hearts and minds of hundreds of thousands of frustrated opponents of the Vietnam War. . . . *Bonnie and Clyde* was a movement movie; like *The Graduate*, young audiences recognized that it was theirs. [73]

One notable convert to the aesthetic revolutionary faith of *Bonnie and Clyde* was the Yippie cofounder and cultural revolutionary prankster Jerry Rubin, who proclaimed that "Bonnie Parker and Clyde Barrow are the leaders of the New Youth." [74] The Zelig of '60s protest movements, Rubin was an alumnus of Berkeley Free Speech '64, Vietnam Day Committee '65, the Be-In and March on the Pentagon '67, and, most notoriously, Chicago '68, his appearance mutating en route from serious leftie to polymorphous hippie to kitschy Guevara-style revolutionary. Apart from his being all radicals to all people, Rubin's main contribution was the theory and practice of "revolutionary play"—a formulation that, for better or worse, provides a handle on the last, vertiginous years of 1960s radical youth culture. [75] Like his heroes Bonnie and Clyde, Rubin experienced the joys and perils of inhabiting a realm in which revolution, outlawry, fun, violence, and celebrity were seen as interwoven strands of some unitary whole, part utopia and part apocalypse.

In his autobiographical manifesto *Do It!: Scenarios of the Revolution*, published in 1970, Rubin provides one of the most effervescent, dynamic articulations of late-Sixties generational warfare, while simultaneously distilling all the most salient aspects of the culture of rejuvenation that undergirded his generation-gap rhetoric of polarization. In one respect, Rubin's philosophy represents the culmination of the decade-long tension between youth and adulthood: if Mod-era youth disdained adults, and hippies indicted them, Rubin wanted to obliterate them. Radicalized, like many others, by the repressive, violent police and state apparatus unleashed on demonstrators at the 1968 Democratic National Convention in Chicago, Rubin concluded that "our parents are waging a genocidal war against their own kids." [76] To fight back against the inevitable adult counterrevolution, Rubin and Abbie Hoffman continued to improvise their non-organization Yippie! According to Rubin, Yippie! (which stands for "Youth International Party") is, like youth itself, really a state of mind: you "belong" to the Yippies if you think like a child, not an adult. (According to Rubin, the "Party" in Youth International Party—besides being an obvious leftist pun—meant "people trying to have meaning, fun, ecstasy in their lives: a party.")[77] Mind games notwithstanding, Yippie! was the vehicle used by Rubin to propound his ideas about revolution as a form of play. Since "[e]verything the yippies do is aimed at three-to-seven year olds," Rubin's first axiom is that revolution must be "fun"—"Yippies say if it's not fun, don't do it"—to which he adds, "The yippie idea of fun is overthrowing the government."[78]

Yippie!, in one respect, represents the utopian endpoint of rejuvenation culture, an exclamatory posturing meant to conjure up a revolution in which children and rejuvenated adults seize all the power and transform the world into a giant playground. As Rubin put it, "Liberation comes when we . . . do what we always wanted to do as children."[79] Consistent with a child's approach to revolution, the Yippie program is decidedly oriented around dreams, not goals. Since goals are part of the teleological straitjacket of adulthood, Rubin categorically rejects them. "Goals are irrelevant," he proclaims, "People are always asking us, 'What's your program?' I hand them a Mets scorecard. . . . *Fuck programs!* The goal of the revolution is to abolish programs and turn spectators into actors. It's a do-it-yourself revolution, and we'll work out the future as we go."[80] Of course, given a "revolution" like Rubin's where the only goal is goallessness, where the modus operandi is fantasy, and where dreams are the organizing principle, it's not unreasonable to expect outlandish objectives ("we will turn Amerika's colleges into nudist camps"), extravagant rules of thumb ("*When in doubt, burn.* . . . Fire is instant theater"), infuriating negotiation postures ("Satisfy our demands, and we got twelve more. The more demands you satisfy, the more we got"), and stringent membership requirements ("Don't grow up. Growing up means *giving up your dreams.*")[81]

Co-mingled with these absurdist, utopian visions is the destructive, apocalyptic, pyrotechnic strain of Yippie theatrics, one that sees anarchy as the necessary starting point of the new, rejuvenated society. "The Youth International Revolution will begin with mass breakdown of authority, mass rebellion, total anarchy in every institution in the Western world," asserts Rubin, "Tribes of longhairs, blacks, armed women, workers, peasants and students will take over."[82] Behind these chimerical assertions, though, lies a defensive posture, a belief that young radicals were forced into this apocalypse fantasy by a repressive adult power structure that wouldn't leave them alone, that plans to annihilate them and eradicate their lifestyle and beliefs. Utilizing both Holocaust and Vietnam strategic hamlet metaphors, Rubin fashions a hippie extermination thesis:

> Liberated neighborhoods are a great threat to capitalist city life. So
> the forces of Death—the business community, cops, and politi-

cians—conspire to wipe us out. An entire battery of laws—genocidal laws against the young—makes social life in the streets a crime. . . . Once upon a time we thought we could end poverty, racism, and war by nonviolent sit-ins and moral pleas. The days of innocence are over. . . . We live in a land which has declared war on its own children, on its future. . . . *To be young is a crime.* Any crowd of kids automatically constitutes a riot. . . . We are faced with two choices: **OBEY OR PERISH**. We are fighting for our very survival as a generation.[83]

Rubin believed that American youth needed new myths to propel and sustain the revolutionary, rejuvenated culture they hoped to build. Two radical myths that circulated at the time, but were seldom dissected, may provide some insight into the paranoid, frenzied rhetoric that closed out the decade. The first can be called the "orphan myth" of late-'60s radicals: as Rubin proclaims in *Do It!*, "I am an orphan of Amerika"[84] (the radical vogue, circa 1968–70, involved spelling America with a "k" to indicate "fascist America" or "America-gone-evil"). Designating oneself an orphan in 1969 America was, on the one hand, an elective act, a metaphor for one's repudiation of authority structures—parental, governmental—deemed illegitimate, immoral, and hostile.

At the same time, however, the orphan myth lends itself to another reading. Given the deaths of John F. Kennedy, the symbolic father of 1960s youth, followed by Malcolm X, Martin Luther King, and Robert Kennedy, one could make the case that late-'60s youth *had* been orphaned by America: their legitimate leaders (i.e., natural parents) had been brutally assassinated, succeeded by their current, illegitimate leaders (i.e., adoptive/foster parents)-Nixon, Agnew. Their orphan status, then, was part elective, part inherited: radical late-'60s youth were traumatized by a very real crisis of legitimate authority that fueled and justified their defection from the core society, making them "orphans of Amerika." One iconic late-1960s radical poster is telling: it features a gun-toting, countercultural man and woman, standing outdoors, a cross between hippie survivalist communards and Weather Underground, carrying a child. They have renounced the old, decaying society and are attempting to form a new one, an action that makes them certain targets of repression. The accompanying inscription reads: "'If we make peaceful revolution impossible, we make violent revolution inevitable'—John F. Kennedy." The implications are manifold, while the JFK quotation invokes a sense of allegiance to once legitimate, but now vacant, authority.

More prevalent was the "myth of the mock revolutionary," which illustrates a major perceptual pitfall of late-'60s radical culture. While radicals like

This late-'60s photograph of a radical hippie revolutionary family, taken by photographer Alan Copeland, perfectly captures the "Bring the War Home," armed survivalist mentality of many counterculturists after Nixon's victory in the 1968 elections. The photo did, in fact, appear on the cover of the *Berkeley Tribe* and in other publications courtesy of Liberation News Service. In its poster version, the image was accompanied by a caption that read "'If we make peaceful revolution impossible, we make violent revolution inevitable'—John F. Kennedy." It perfectly captured the idea that America's radical youth had been 'orphaned' through the assassinations of their 'natural leaders' JFK, Robert Kennedy, Martin Luther King, and Malcolm X. Copyright © Alan Copeland.

Rubin built their careers on inflammatory threats to "subvert the schools with dope, sex, and dynamite" or overthrow the government, they simultaneously viewed their plight as one of victimization: "Cops patrol the hippie areas the way they patrol black communities," insisted Rubin, "the way Amerikan soldiers patrol Vietnamese villages. . . . How far off is the day when the FBI sets up checkpoints at state borders, examines passports, and prohibits entrance to potential 'rioters'?"[85] Radicals alternated between threatening to destroy "Amerika" and feeling persecuted by the very authorities they marked for destruction, as if threatening to destroy the government *shouldn't* beget a response.

This perceptual discordance can be grasped in part by factoring in the side-effects of subsuming revolution under the banner of play. Just as the pre-radical youth who frequented discotheques some five years earlier had alternated between charade dances like the Bug, the Hitchhiker, and the Chickenback, radical youth of the late 1960s engaged in guerrilla mimickry—alternating between Che/Fidel and Vietcong, Bonnie and Clyde, and Black Panthers. In dance or dissent, the charade remained the most enduring and versatile mode of self-expression for youth in the 1960s. But, as Huizinga put it in *Homo Ludens*, "[i]n play as we conceive it the distinction between belief and make-believe breaks down."[86] Rubin was a make-believe revolutionary: all charades aside, he never made any real attempt to overthrow the U.S. government. But, just as children play with deadly seriousness and adopt the persona of their play role, Rubin also *really believed* he was a revolutionary. Yet when the government responded to his play threats with very real repression, surveillance, indictments, and imprisonment, Rubin felt victimized, hunted, persecuted.

One incident in particular, Rubin's 1969 appearance before the House Un-American Activities Committee (HUAC), summed up his predicament as revolutionary action figure. Having once appeared before HUAC dressed as an American Revolutionary War soldier, Rubin decided this time on an international guerrilla mosaic: he entered the halls of Congress wearing a Black Panther beret, Mexican bandoleer, Egyptian earrings, Vietcong pajamas, hippie beads, and pirate-style headband. To complete the look, he brought along a toy M-16 ("the kind the Viet Kong use after stealing them from Americans," he bragged) loaded with *real* bullets. The police guarding the chamber, just for good measure, forced him to discharge the bullets but let him keep the toy rifle.[87] Real bullets, toy gun: therein lies the essence of Rubin-as-revolutionary. Just like Bonnie and Clyde, Rubin embraced outlawry as a dangerous form of play; to the authorities, however, he was a real menace to society. Once in a while, Rubin acknowledged the paradoxes at the core of his play-revolutionary act: "[W]as yippie trying to make Amerika laugh?," he asked himself while selecting a pig to run as 1968 Presidential candidate, "Or was yippie ready to blow Amerika up?"[88] Of course, for Rubin blowing Amerika up and making it laugh could be one and the same thing; the Nixon administration, however, never got the joke.

"Don't trust anyone over 30": first coined by Jack Weinberg of the Berkeley Free Speech Movement, this became the signature slogan of '60s generation-gap rhetoric. Taken at face value, though, it called for some hard decisions. If adults are inherently counterrevolutionary, if they really can't be rejuvenated under any circumstances, what should kids do with them? One possible scenario appears in the film *Wild in the Streets* (1968). In this high-voltage exploitation movie, a rock star is elected President, at which point he lowers the voting age to fourteen and ships all those over thirty-five to concentration camps where they're forced to take LSD. In the context of actual late-1960s radical culture, this wasn't really that far-fetched. Jerry Rubin in *Do It!* suggested lowering the voting age to five and cutting it off at forty, while debating with Eldridge Cleaver where to set the "Age of Trust": Rubin wanted it raised to age forty, while Cleaver insisted it be lowered to twenty. In fact, Rubin displayed the same ambivalence about youth as a category that appeared in *Vogue* magazine circa 1965. The rabble-rousing propagandist in him knew that defining youth sheerly in terms of age and yelling "kill your parents" made for easily digestible copy, sold books like *Do It!*, and turned heads, mostly because it relied on the same type of inane oversimplifications that fueled, say, the cold war. In more candid moments, though, Rubin admitted that "You're only as old as you wanna be" and that "age is in your head," citing as evidence Nikita Khrushchev, at age sixty, banging his shoe on the table at the United Nations: "You can be a yippie no matter how old you are!", Rubin gushed.[89]

A similar phenomenon was enacted on the larger historical stage. The war between the generations garnered the lion's share of media and public attention, especially after 1967 when it became a quasi-political issue; in doing so, it overshadowed the subtler but steadier processes of rejuvenation that influenced both "mainstream" and "countercultural" lifestyles and ideas. In 1970, the same year that *Do It!* called for generational warfare, Charles Reich published his highly influential *The Greening of America*. In it, he credited youth with nothing less than the founding of a new consciousness with the power and scope to redeem America, featuring such countercultural elements as presentism, post-competitiveness, and communitarianism, and called on his fellow adults to follow suit. Films like *Bob, Carol, Ted, and Alice* chronicled, albeit cynically, the spread of rejuvenation culture to adults infatuated with the hippie, or post-hippie, lifestyle. By the early 1970s, as the generation gap gradually become a non-issue, still hip adults assimilated the rejuvenation ethos so heartily that they gradually lost touch with its provenance, forgetting that it came out of the zeitgeist of the 1960s—when many people discovered, however briefly, the secrets to eternal youth.

Notes

1. Jay Stevens, *Storming Heaven: LSD and the American Dream* (New York: Harper & Row, 1987), 291.

2. William Chafe, *The Unfinished Journey: America since World War II* (Oxford University Press, 1995), 189–92.

3. Ibid., p. 188.

4. "28 People Who Count," *Esquire*, September 1965, cover page, 97.

5. Charles Mohr, "World of Affluent Youth Favors In Dancing at City Hideaways," *New York Times*, 30 March 1964, 31; Clark Kerr quoted in Stevens, *Storming Heaven*, ix.

6. Andy Warhol and Pat Hackett, *POPism: The Warhol Sixties* (New York: Harcourt Brace Jovanovich, 1980), 69.

7. Tom Wolfe, *The Kandy-Kolored Tangerine-Flake Streamline Baby* (New York: Farrar, Straus & Giroux, 1965), 212.

8. Grace and Fred Hechinger, "In the Time It Takes You to Read These Lines the American Teen-ager Will Have Spent $2,378.22," *Esquire*, July 1965, 65, 68, 113.

9. Warhol and Hackett, *POPism*, 69, 115.

10. Joel Lobenthal, *Radical Rags: Fashions of the Sixties* (New York: Abbeville Press, 1990), 13.

11. Ibid., 129.

12. Ibid., 217.

13. Warhol and Hackett, *POPism*, 191.

14. Lobenthal, *Radical Rags*, 92.

15. "Discotheque Dancing," *Life* (22 May 1964), 97–106; for an overview of 1960s discotheque culture see also Peter Braunstein, "Disco," *American Heritage* (Nov. 1999) 45, 49–50.

16. Wolfe, *Kandy-Kolored*, 78.

17. Johan Huizinga, *Homo Ludens: A Study of the Play-Element in Culture* (Boston: Beacon Press, 1955), 8.

18. "Youthquake," *Vogue* (1 January 1965), 112.

19. For negative characterizations of 1950s youth, see James Gilbert, *A Cycle of Outrage: America's Reaction to the Juvenile Delinquent in the 1950s* (New York: Oxford University Press, 1986).

20. Heather Ross Miller, "Youth Is Not an Age," *Vogue* (1 March 1965), 84.

21. Anne Tyler, "Will This Seem Ridiculous?" *Vogue* (1 February 1965), 85; Miller, "Youth," 84.

22. Other caper films during the same period include *Gambit* (1966), starring Michael Caine and Shirley MacLaine, and *Rebus* (1968), with Laurence Harvey and Ann-Margret.

23. Films are used throughout this essay as evidence because of their unique ability to capture and convey the sensibilities of an era, mentalities that are notoriously difficult for historians to recapture without recasting them. Films of the 1960s save these subtle but pervasive tropes for posterity. Of course, that's never to say that film accurately represents social reality. Therefore, I've attempted to validate the various 1960s rejuvenation tropes appearing in movies—hard play, charades, neo-childhood—through similar and supporting "real life" manifestations, like the frenetic charade-dances of discotheque culture or the "Flower Child" incarnation of the hippies.

24. " . . . We Hope That You Enjoy the Show," *East Village Other,* (1–15 July 1967), 4.

25. Quoted in Charles Perry, *The Haight-Ashbury: A History* (New York: Random House, 1984), 248.

26. *San Francisco Oracle,* no. 5 (January 1967), 2.

27. *Barb* announcement quoted in Stevens, *Storming Heaven,* viii.

28. Descriptions of the Be-In can be found in Helen Swick Perry, *The Human Be-In* (New York: Basic Books, 1970); Jane Kramer, *Allen Ginsberg in America* (New York: Random House, 1968), 24–25; *San Francisco Oracle,* no. 6, February 1967.

29. Tuli Kupferberg, "The Politics of Love," *East Village Other* (1–15 May 1967), 4–5.

30. For a oft-cited New Left critique of hippiedom, see Warren Hinckle, "The Social History of the Hippies," *Ramparts,* March 1967, 26.

31. Quoted in Stevens, *Storming Heaven,* 174.

32. See William Burroughs, "Academy 23: A Deconditioning," reprinted in *Notes from the New Underground,* ed. Jesse Kornbluth (New York: Viking Press, 1968), 110–14; Stevens, *Storming Heaven,* 102.

33. Ibid., 246.

34. Ibid., 210–11.

35. Liner notes from *The Jimi Hendrix Experience,* Live at Winterland CD, (RYKO Records).

36. Charles W. Slack, *Timothy Leary, The Madness of the Sixties, and Me* (New York: Peter H. Wyden, 1974), 46.

37. Stevens, *Storming Heaven,* 211.

38. Quoted in "Changes," from *Notes from the New Underground,* ed. Kornbluth, 164.

39. Warhol and Hackett, *POPism,* 33, 194.

40. Ibid., 33

41. David Newman and Robert Benton, "Remember The Sixties?" *Esquire,* August 1966, 109.

42. Grace Glueck, "A Kind of Hit-and-Run Theater," *New York Times,* 9 May 1965, sec. 7, p. 4; Alan Solomon, "Is There a New Theater?" *New York Times,* 27 June 1965, sec. 2, 12.

43. Glueck, "Hit-and-Run Theater," 4.

44. For instance, a commercial hair and fashion show dubbed a "Happening." See Enid Nemy, "A Happening Happens to Replace a Hairdo Show," *New York Times,* 12 July 1965, 31.

45. Thomas Frank, *The Conquest of Cool: Business Culture, Counterculture, and the Rise of Hip Capitalism* (University of Chicago Press, 1997), 12.

46. Norman Mailer, "The White Negro: Superficial Reflections on the Hipster," *Dissent,* 4, no. 3 (summer 1957): 277–78.

47. Ibid., 283.

48. Ibid.

49. Ibid., 289–290.

50. Ibid., 290.

51. Ibid., 279, 284.

52. Guy Strait, "What Is a Hippie?" in *Notes from the New Underground,* ed. Kornbluth, 202.

53. Stevens, *Storming Heaven,* 205.

54. Richard Alpert (Ram Dass), *Be Here Now* (San Cristobal, N. Mex.: Lama Foundation, 1971), unpaginated.

55. Tom Wolfe, *The Electric Kool-Aid Acid Test* (New York: Bantam, 1968), 339

56. Quoted in "Changes," from *Notes from the New Underground,* ed. Kornbluth, 124–25.

57. Ibid., 126.

58. Ibid.

59. Ibid., 131–32.

60. Ibid., 180.

61. Ibid., 140, 151, 159.

62. Ibid., 166.

63. Richard Goldstein, "Love: A Groovy Idea While He Lasted," in *Notes from the New Underground*, ed. Kornbluth, 257.

64. Pagan Kennedy, *Platforms: A Microwaved Cultural Chronicle of the 1970s* (New York: St. Martin's Press, 1994), 9. Richard Schickel, "Flaws in a Savage Satire," *Life* (13 October 1967), 16.

65. Schickel, "Flaws in a Savage Satire," 16.

66. Joseph O'Mealy, in *"Bonnie and Clyde—Facts? Meaning? Art?" New York Times*, 17 September 1967, sec. 2, 7, 9.

67. Wilfrid Sheed, "Films," *Esquire*, December 1967, 46.

68. Judith Crist, *"Bonnie and Clyde*: Triumph," *Vogue*, 15 September 1967, 68.

69. Schickel, "Flaws in a Savage Satire," 16.

70. The controversies surrounding *Bonnie and Clyde*, which involved film critics and audiences alike, are well documented in "Hollywood: The Shock of Freedom in Film," *Time*, 8 December 1967, 67–76, and Vincent Canby, "Arthur Penn: Does His 'Bonnie and Clyde' Glorify Crime?" *New York Times*, (17 September 1967), sec. 2, p. 21. The *New York Times* was particularly affected by scandal surrounding the film. In an unprecedented move, the *Times* film critic Bosley Crowther wrote three separate negative reviews of the film. The *Times* subsequently attempted to counteract this animus by printing an entire section of readers' letters weighing in on Crowther's apparent vendetta. See *"Bonnie and Clyde*—Facts? Meaning? Art?" *New York Times*, 17 September 1967, sec. 2, pp. 7, 9.

71. Newman cited in Peter Biskind, *Easy Riders, Raging Bulls: How the Sex-Drugs-And-Rock 'n' Roll Generation Saved Hollywood* (New York: Simon & Schuster, 1998), 27.

72. For the fashion craze set off by Bonnie and Clyde, see "Bonnie Comes On with a Stylish Bang: Faye Dunaway in a '30s Revival," *Life*, 12 January 1968, 69–74. The style and fashion craze launched by the film soon reached Europe, where it was adopted readily by the French. The renowned French provocateur and singer Serge Gainsbourg and the icon Brigitte Bardot outfitted themselves in 1930s gangster outfits and recorded a hit single and album titled *Bonnie and Clyde*.

73. Biskind, *Easy Riders, Raging Bulls*, 49.

74. Jerry Rubin, *Do It!: Scenarios of the Revolution* (New York: Ballantine Books, 1970), 122.

75. For a contemporary assessment of the play component in 1960s "revolution" talk, see Margot Hentoff, "The Games We Play: The Revolution Game," *Village Voice*, 28 September 1967, 1, 3.

76. Rubin, *Do It!*, 87.

77. Ibid., 81.

78. Ibid., 85–87.

79. Ibid., 122.

80. Ibid., 125–26.

81. Ibid., 87, 112, 125, 127.

82. Ibid., 256.

83. Ibid., 232, 242.

84. Ibid., 13.

85. Ibid., 194, 198–99, 232–33.

86. Huizinga, *Homo Ludens*, 25.

87. Rubin, *Do It!* 203–05. A photo of Rubin as Kandy-Kolored, Tangerine-Flake Guerrilla Baby appears on 205.

88. Ibid., 177.

89. Ibid., 7, 89–90.

Ten

"The Movies Are a Revolution"
Film and the Counterculture[1]

David E. James

In the flowering of participatory social life we have come to call "the Sixties," a number of previously unaccommodated and disenfranchised groups of people began creatively to engage history for themselves, to make it their history. In doing so, they transformed the inherited relationship between politics and the arts, creating an epochal shift in the structure of American national culture. Rather than merely depicting social movements, film began to assume an enlarged role in creating them. As people challenged the boundaries separating art from both public politics and everyday life, at times they were able to turn the culture of everyday life into the culture of politics, showing (as the women's movement best articulated) that the two were—or could be—the same.

Because these new forms were fundamentally opposed to mainstream cultural institutions, especially to the corporate media systems that were increasingly dominating American society, new institutions had to be created: small presses to publish poetry, for example, underground newspapers to report antiwar activism, and eventually guerrilla video collectives where the biases of network television could be exposed and countered. These apparatuses communicated the new participatory political cultures to both insiders and the public at large; but just as important as the news they carried was the news they embodied, the fact that they were themselves popularly mobilized and controlled, and so performing in microcosm the overall social reorganization they hoped to promote. Though they perforce existed in a society in which knowledge and pleasure alike had become commodities, and though many aspects of their own production and distribution interfaced with corporate media industries, nevertheless they were not immediately or completely governed by the priorities of capital. In the popular, participatory practices they sustained, culture was re-created as doing rather than as buying, as sensuous human activity, sometimes private and deliberate, but more often collective and spontaneous. In this, if only for a moment, the concept of popular culture was redefined from one of consumption to one of praxis.

In this revitalized popular culture, film was a privileged medium. As Paul Arthur has written,

> The movies were the perfect setup, a process whereby material was converted into light, a hub around which metaphors of temporality, consciousness (collective and individual), motion, and representation accumulated and were then redeployed in a calculus of politicized rhetoric and direct action. Although it was never supposed that this medium would be the principal agent of transformation, it was given a supporting role by many and a vanguard role by some. In the charged reciprocity between art and life, movies suffused reality, which in turn acquired a cinematic gloss.[2]

For a decade, such attitudes to filmmaking maintained a powerful credibility in white youth cultures; cinema was a cynosure of aesthetic and social aspirations, and the marker of the place where these came together.[3] As radically new forms of visual pleasure and cognition were inaugurated, they appeared to explode the previous languages of the medium, and also the roles that it had played in social life; the new forms of *film* heralded new *cinemas*.[4]

For most of its history, the cinema had been a capitalist industry, all but entirely integrated into the other apparatuses of capitalism, with Hollywood the most successful case of a culture-producing industry ever known. In it, films were manufactured as commodities, and their aesthetic and ideological properties reflected this function, even if they were never entirely reducible to it. But as the various countercultures invented cinema as a popular practice, not only did they discover new sights and new ways of seeing, they also discovered new, non-commodity functions that seemed to herald a renewal of society as a whole. Singer Gil Scott-Heron might have been correct when he declared that the revolution would not be televised, but the filmmakers would be there to photograph it for what the underground film actor Taylor Mead termed their "mongrel, wild, uncouth, naïve, heartless, heartful, pornographic, licentious, insane" movies. They would also be there to live it, for, as he also claimed, for a time it seemed that "The movies are a revolution."[5]

This and similar ideas of film as a leading component within a general cultural and social reconstruction inform the stylistic innovations of the period. But of course, like the attempts at revolution in other spheres, countercultural cinema was also enveloped by the institutions it sought to displace. Hollywood's profits had declined from their all-time high in the years immediately after World War II, when almost three-quarters of those able to do so went to the movies at least once a week and when almost 100 million tickets a week were sold. Television was already challenging film's domination of popular culture, but the movies were still the main arena in which public myths were framed. Though young people of the time had been weaned on television, by the mid-Sixties many were defecting from it.[6] The age was felt to be a film age and, recognizing themselves as "a film generation," youth were a main component of the commercial cinema audience. Hollywood's desire to tap the youth market as the counterculture emerged was reciprocated by youth's desire to see themselves represented on the big screen.

Given the degree to which Hollywood monopolized American culture, it was inevitable that the new film practices would only in rare instances achieve the degree of independence to which the most radical of them aspired. Instead, they were commonly involved with many kinds of dialogues and negotiations with the industry. On the level of film, Hollywood was so powerful a presence, its languages and myths so constitutive of consciousness, that alternative styles could rarely be formulated entirely outside its terms. On the level of cinema, the industry was so comprehensive and its rewards so great that attempts to create alternatives to it were framed by the industrial system and not infrequently made with an eye to finding a way into it.

Given these interconnections between dominant and marginal practices, and given the industry's incomparable position in the popular imagination, Hollywood itself played an important role in the counterculture. Two interconnected but opposite patterns of appropriation resulted: Hollywood's attempt to exploit the youth movement, and the movement's own use of Hollywood. We shall return to these developments, but first must come the story of the counterculture's own cinemas. Two main periods will be distinguished, even though fundamental continuities run through them. The first comprises underground film in the first two-thirds of the 1960s, when the Beat and then the hippie countercultures nourished independent cinemas in which a more intense aesthetic experience was linked to a social program premised on the aestheticization of everyday life. The second period is the late 1960s and early 1970s, when the Civil Rights movement and opposition to the U.S. invasion of Vietnam forced this cultural revolution into the making of political documentaries and other forms of militant confrontation with the imperialist corporate state.

UNDERGROUND FILM

The new cinemas had their roots in the prewar European avant-gardes, especially French surrealism and Soviet constructivism, and in parallel traditions of experimental filmmaking in the United States; but their most important progenitor was Maya Deren. Born in 1917 in Kiev, Deren had been active in the Youth Party of Socialist League in New York in the 1930s before becoming secretary to the dancer Katherine Dunham. On tour with Dunham in Los Angeles, she met Alexander Hamid, a Prague-born experimental and documentary filmmaker, then working in Hollywood as a camera man and editor. The two married in 1942 and the next year, working in their own home with primitive 16-mm equipment, they collaborated on a short film that turned out to be one of the most influential non-studio films in the history of cinema, *Meshes of the Afternoon*. In it a young woman, played by Deren herself, returns to her home in the Hollywood Hills and takes an afternoon nap. In her dream, she suggestively transforms the images she saw just before falling asleep into a delirious narrative in which she confronts minatory images of herself. The historian P. Adams Sitney later designated it a "trance film," one that was structured around a heroine who "undertakes an interior quest. . . . [and who] encounters objects and sights as if they were capable of revealing the erotic mystery of the self."[7] *Meshes* established what became the primary motif of underground film, as well as inaugurating the medium's use as a vehicle of self-discovery. As a generation of young artists began to investigate the possibilities of film, they commonly re-engaged Deren's model and often adapted its images,[8] not just as a means of self-expression but also as a means of self-exploration and self-realization. Such an undertaking achieved additional cultural authority as hallucinogenic drugs began to open hitherto unexplored states of consciousness.

In addition to making this and several other seminal films, Deren established the Creative Film Foundation, a nonprofit organization that made grants to independent filmmakers. She traveled across the country making personal presentations of her work at colleges and nurturing the environment in which young people began to imagine the possibilities of a film culture outside the studio system. In her writings she disseminated the idea of a personal experimental film practice that laid the foundation for subsequent theory. One essay in particular, "Amateur versus Professional," proposed that since the word "amateur" is derived from the Latin for "lover," this should be "the meaning from which the amateur film-maker should take his clue. Instead of envying the script and dialogue writers, the trained actors, the elaborate staffs and sets, the enormous production budgets of the professional film, the amateur should make use of the one great advantage which all professionals envy him, namely, freedom—both artistic and physical."[9] Legitimating a mode of independent filmmaking whose full autonomy from the corporate-controlled film industry was understood as the source not of limitations but of unique capabilities, Deren's formulation of an amateur practice of film was an inaugural moment in the conceptualization of a popular participatory film culture.

Inspired by her and other visionaries, by the late 1950s American cineasts were ardently planning alternatives to Hollywood, laying the foundation for what soon became known as the New American Cinema. The most significant of them was The Group, formed in 1960 in New York as an affiliation of twenty-three independent producers, directors, actors, and theater managers, called together by Lewis Allen, a stage and film producer, and by Jonas Mekas, a Lithuanian refugee who in 1955 had begun a little magazine, *Film Culture*. In their manifesto, "The First Statement of the New American Cinema Group," they proclaimed that "The official cinema all over the world is running out of breath. It is morally corrupt, aesthetically obsolete, thematically superficial, temperamentally boring. Even the seemingly worthwhile films, those that lay claim to high moral and aesthetic standards and have been accepted as such by critics and the public alike, reveal the decay of the Product Film."[10] Presenting itself as the gathering of previous sporadic and uncoordinated manifestations of the new filmmaking, The Group invoked the European New Waves in attacking the Hollywood production and distribution systems and their attendant aesthetic criteria. The statement argued against producers, distributors, and investors; against censorship; against existing methods of financing; and it cited two recent independently produced films about Beat poets and jazz musicians, respectively, *Pull My Daisy* (Robert Frank and Alfred Leslie, 1959) and *Shadows* (John Cassavetes, 1959) as evidence against the "Budget Myth" that good films could not be produced for $20,000–$25,000. To implement an alternative to the industry, The Group planned their own cooperative distribution center, support fund, and a film festival as a forum for the New Cinema from all over the world. The manifesto ended by specifying the one basic difference between The Group and industry organizations such as United Artists: "We are not joining together to make money. We are joining together to make films."

Despite this anti-commodity stance, their claim that "paradoxically, low budget films give a higher profit margin than big-budget films" suggested that, qualitative considerations aside, The Group envisioned using the medium outside the studios while still remaining cognizant of box office considerations. Independent feature production in this mode did continue through the 1960s, and indeed it produced many significant films that reflected and mobilized countercultural energies.[11] But the American cinema ultimately came back to life not by inaugurating a reformed industrial practice based on the feature-length, theatrical narrative, but by pioneering an extra-industrial and in fact anti-industrial use of the medium of the kind whose superiority Deren had proclaimed. Known as underground film, this new practice of cinema fully realized the aesthetics and social vision of the Beat generation and of the countercultures into which it modulated.

Initially, the Beat critiques of the moribund conformity and repressiveness of cold war American culture led them to disaffiliate themselves from it. Suffering "not from political apathy but from political antipathy,"[12] they were anti-political rather than merely apolitical, believing that any systematic attempt to reconstruct mainstream society by rationally derived and progressively implemented programs would only reproduce the instrumentalism and regimentation that they saw as its chief failings. Though the Beat movement was linked to protests against cold war militarism and the threat of nuclear war, it prized spontaneous spiritual transformation over organized social action. Nourished by the traditions of populist transcendentalism and illuminated by drugs and Eastern religions, eventually by the crystal euphoria of LSD, this current of radical Romantic idealism proposed a transformation of individual consciousness as the means to social renovation. Further inspired by modern jazz, Beat filmmaking privileged improvisational energy and quasi-physical intensity in the process of composition, over and against the completed artifact, so that filmmaking became an act of psychic wholeness and ecstasy, a model and mainspring of social renewal, and the vehicle of social dissent.[13]

Since this movement was, as Parker Tyler argued, "a new, radically inspired revision of the home movie,"[14] the essentially amateur nature of its production and the irregular methods of its distribution and preservation make a reliable estimate of its extensiveness impossible. Nor is an exact generic definition in formal terms easy. In 1962, just as the term "underground film" was beginning to acquire currency, Jonas Mekas listed some of the examples of the new movements in independent film generally. Alongside the new forms of documentary instanced by Ricky Leacock's *Primary* (1960), more radical innovations such as Shirley Clarke's *The Connection* (1961), and Stan Vanderbeek's satirical protest films, he emphasized the "Pure Poets of Cinema," including Stanley Brakhage, Marie Menken, and Robert Breer and the "Poetry of the Absurd," instanced by the works of Ron Rice and Vernon

Zimmerman.[15] But he ended his essay by returning to the social aspirations that underlay the formal properties of the new films, affirming that "the new independent cinema movement—like the other arts in America today—is primarily an existential movement, or, if you want, an ethical movement, a human act; it is only secondarily an aesthetic one."[16]

Despite their limitations, formal taxonomies of the kind Mekas proposed do give some idea of the variety and dynamism of the experiments under way.[17] In what is still one of the best essays on underground film, Ken Kelman (1964) argued that its release of energies was a response to the joint repressiveness of American society and Hollywood.[18] Comparing it to the Schoenbergian revolution in music, more radical than and superior to the European New Waves, he saw the new film practice as comprising various strategies of psychic restoration. In this "spiritual medium," Kelman distinguished three main categories: films of "outright social criticism and protest"; "films of liberation, films which suggest, mainly through anarchic fantasy, the possibilities of the human spirit in its socially uncorrupted state"; and "mythically oriented" films created "out of a need to fill our rationalistic void." In a similar vein, in spring 1966, when the energies of underground film were at their zenith, Sheldon Renan claimed that "There are fantastic numbers of people now producing personal 'art films,' and at least a hundred of these are of known significance."[19] Renan argued a basic difference between underground and mainstream film—the former as "a medium of and for the individual, as explorer and as artist, while the latter was "a medium of and for bankers, craftsmen, film crews, and audiences":

> Definitions are risky, for the underground film is nothing less than an *explosion* of cinematic styles, forms, and directions. . . . The underground film *is* a certain kind of film. It is a film conceived and made essentially by one person and is a personal statement by that person. It is a film that dissents radically in form, or in technique, or in content, or perhaps in all three. It is usually made for very little money, frequently under a thousand dollars, and its exhibition is outside commercial film channels.[20]

Along with their controlling reference to personal expressiveness and the oppositional nature of their definitions, Renan's remarks suggest not simply a formal development inside a tradition whose social location is stable, so much as an attempt to involve the medium in new social relationships and serve new social needs. While the influence of Hollywood movies was enormous— remakes of commercial film in more or less amateur formats were always a main current in the underground—the movement took its frames of reference from other art forms that had not been as fully industrialized. Especially common was the notion of the film poem, derived especially from Cocteau and works like his *Blood of a Poet* (1930) to suggest a non-narrative, personal expressiveness, capable of a metaphoric richness and texture not available to the "prose" of the feature film.

Paralleling the Beat attempt to recreate in poetry the aesthetic and social functions of jazz, underground film attempted to open out the entire practice of cinema as a sphere of improvisational countercultural activity. All three phases of the cinematic process—the orchestration of activity for the camera to photograph, the transformation of this activity in photography, editing, and other forms of manipulation of the filmic process, and the social rituals surrounding projection of the completed film—were retrieved from the instrumentality they had in the industrial process and remade as occasions for individual and group expressive performance. To sustain and disseminate these experiments, alternative institutions of production and distribution were established, and alternative critical and journalistic undertakings begun. But inscribed within this search for an autonomous cinema of social authenticity, freed from the compromises of the industry, runs the contrary project: the inevitability of engagement with the dominant cinema. Overall, then, as well as reflecting the immediate values of the subcultures that produced it, underground film was shaped by its function as a vehicle of social dissent and by its ongoing dialogues with the commercial feature film.

The limits of this cultural field and the scope of possible innovations within it are framed by the equally radical but entirely contrary innovations of Stan Brakhage and Andy Warhol. Brakhage was the paradigmatic instance of an artist who reinvented filmmaking as a domestic, artisanal practice, using the medium for psychic self-exploration and as the basis for a community life constructed as far away as possible from Hollywood and state power generally. Warhol exemplified the reverse project: beginning as an extremely radical innovator, he took countercultural film back into the industry, reinstating the division of labor in the manufacture of cultural commodities and returning the medium to its functions within capitalism.

By the time Brakhage made his first film in 1952 when he was still a teenager, film poetry was an established stylistic category, with *Meshes of the Afternoon* and Deren's other films the most powerful model for personal filmmaking. Within three years, his work in Deren's mode had become so distinguished that Jonas Mekas proposed it as "the best expression of all the virtues and sins of the American film poem today."[21] Brakhage's early "trance" films featured a sexually tormented protagonist, usually himself, whose traumatized subjectivity was figured in distortions of the visual field and in interpolated clusters of metaphors that interrupted the unfolding of the narrative. His crucial breakthrough occurred as he came to realize that these heightened visual experiences were not simply evidences of his own sexual anxiety or pathology; rather, they were the contours of a perceptual fullness that had largely been lost to human consciousness generally, but might still exist in those visionaries who had somehow escaped the repressive tutelage of modern society.

The many analogies to his position in the emerging drug culture later resulted in Brakhage's film style becoming the *lingua franca* for the representation of psychedelic experience, even though he himself always spoke against drug use, espousing rather the retrieval of expanded vision by natural means. His initial point of reference was infants, and he began to explore the possibility of their possessing such a prelapsarian vision in *Anticipation of the Night* (1958) (Figure 1). The film offered a lush collage of images centering on extended passages of dreams of magical birds, and especially of a baby crawling across a lawn in a garden with dense foliage. Transformed by the rapid pans of his handheld camera, many of them overexposed, the environment is largely abstracted into rushing arpeggios of light, with the textures of the trees and plants infinitely refracted in the rainbow fountains of a garden hose, all creating a visual intensity that, it is implied, approximates the baby's vision.

Around the same time, Brakhage completed his major theoretical manifesto, *Metaphors on Vision*. In it he argued that the denigration of this kind of vision in rationalized modern culture reflected the imposition of verbally ordered priorities on human sight in general, so that the language of mainstream film reproduced and socially enforced a drastically curtailed visual sensuality. Against this repression of the visual, and to make a place for the kind of seeing he was developing, Brakhage made his case:

> Imagine an eye unruled by man-made laws of perspective, an eye
> unprejudiced by compositional logic, an eye which does not
> respond to the name of everything but which must know each
> object encountered in life through an adventure of perception. How
> many colors are there in a field of grass to the crawling baby
> unaware of "Green"? How many rainbows can create light for the
> untutored eye? How aware of variations in heat waves can that eye
> be? Imagine a world alive with incomprehensible objects and shimmering
> with an endless variety of movement and innumerable gradations
> of color. Imagine a world before "the beginning was the
> word."[22]

While recognizing the impossibility of a return to this pre-oedipal sensuality, Brakhage nevertheless dedicated his life's work to make seeing a fully visual

Celluloid strip from Stan Brakhage's 1958 film *Anticipation of the Night*. This intensely personal film is structured around at least two protagonists, one of them an infant from whose perspective the viewer's heightened perception assays the domesticated wilderness of a suburban garden and the chthonian dreamscape of magical birds. In the 1950s and '60s, Brakhage helped reinvent filmmaking as a domestic, artisanal practice, using the medium for psychic self-exploration and as the basis for a community life constructed as far away as possible from Hollywood and state power generally. © Anthology Film Archives, reproduced by permission.

and visionary act, and in doing so evolved an extraordinarily rich vocabulary of unprecedented social promise.

Most of its elements Had previously been regarded as perversions of proper filmmaking, but, like John Cage using noise and other nonmusical sounds to reinvent music, Brakhage took advantage of everything the camera could let him see. He embraced all degrees of exposure and focus, not just "correct" ones, as well as anamorphic and other lens materials that distorted the photographed image. He pioneered all kinds of handiwork on the material of the film strip itself, including baking it, scratching it, painting it, even burying it in the ground and allowing mold to grow on it. Extremely fast cutting, multiple superimpositions, and other eccentric editing techniques gave extended passages in his work the virtuosic kineticism of modern jazz. Though Brakhage justified these innovations by pointing to their antecedents in silent cinema, they were as radically original and profound as those of any other single artist in the medium. Like Griffith and Eisenstein, he created a new film language that eventually became a general resource, and with it he made a series of masterpieces in the early 1960s. These included *Mothlight* (1963), made without a camera by sticking fragments of insects and grasses on a strip of transparent mylar, then passing the assemblage through the printer; *Dog Star Man* (1961–64), an epic attempt to envision his domestic life via cosmological and biological images; and *Scenes from Under Childhood* (1967–70), a two-and-a-half-hour series of films in which he photographed his own children in an attempt to reproduce the prelapsarian visionary plenitude that, he believed, modern society had destroyed.

Brakhage's reinvention of film language was predicated on a reinvention of the uses to which film could be put, a reinvention of cinema itself. As a young man he had sought teachers and friends in the bohemian artist enclaves of New York and San Francisco, meeting other filmmakers (staying for a time with Maya Deren herself) and especially poets. Then in the mid-1950s, he made fitful attempts at a professional career and even interviewed for an apprentice position on the *Alfred Hitchcock Presents* television show in Hollywood. But the discovery of the premises of his mature mode coincided with his emergence from a period of illness and suicidal depression and his marriage to Jane Collum, after which he moved with his wife and eventually their children to a nineteenth-century log cabin in the Colorado Rockies. Though he maintained personal connections with other filmmakers and his audiences by periodically descending from the mountains to show new work, his rejection of the city and his disengagement from urban society at the very beginning of the 1960s foreshadowed the path often followed later in the decade in the various forms of countercultural rustication. Cinema had always been a city culture, and in general it remained so. Brakhage, however, took it into the wilderness, and there he completed his rejection of its commercial role, and indeed of most previous avant-garde practices as well. He made home movies his essential practice of film.

The ideal of an antitechnological, organically human domestic cinema, entirely separate from rather than oppositional to Hollywood, subsequently circumscribed Brakhage's life, his art, and the peculiarly integral relation between them. Preoccupied with his family in their mountain remoteness, Brakhage used them as the material for an art that he understood as fundamentally a spiritual quest, encompassing "birth, sex, death, and the search for God."[23] Specific films addressed his immediate experience of each of these concerns as they manifested in his family life in the Colorado wilderness, and all their thematic and stylistic innovations were synthesized in *Dog Star Man*. But the fundamental significance of these films and of Brakhage's later oeuvre is that he used the medium, not merely to fabricate personal narratives but to negotiate the crises in the biological cycles of his daily life. By becoming fully an amateur in Deren's sense, he made filmmaking the medium of his being. Bridging the aesthetic and the existential, his practice of film became virtually coextensive with his life, simultaneously his vocation and avocation, his work and play, his terror and his ecstasy.

The intense, complex visual experience that is Brakhage's work and the idea of an artistically sophisticated, domestic cinema he epitomized inspired a tectonic shift in the expressive capacity and the social function of film. His film style provided an infinitely flexible vernacular that several generations of young artists reconstructed with local or idiosyncratic nuances. While he himself remained opposed to drugs, his style proved a fertile resource for the expression of altered states of consciousness; it was often appropriated for the representation of psychedelic vision, not least in Hollywood films that later in the decade commercialized the counterculture, including *The Trip* (Roger Corman, 1967) and *Easy Rider* (Dennis Hopper, 1969). Such films reproduce the trance film structure of a subjective visionary interlude set in an objective narrative frame that Maya Deren had transmitted to the American avant-garde. Finally, Brakhage's reconstruction of the home movie as the most principled practice of cinema and his use of 8 mm, the amateur gauge, for works of serious aesthetic aspiration subsequently supplied the radical possibilities of underground film. As experiments in communal living led young people to find themselves in families very different from the Brakhages, their home movies in turn mobilized visions of the transformation of social life.

Brakhage's elaboration of a domestic, artisanal, and anti-industrial use of the medium was mirrored in reverse by Andy Warhol's similarly remarkable but exactly contrary project. Having made himself a wealthy celebrity in highly successful careers in the commercial and fine arts, he turned to the more glamorous medium of film. He began his work there with radically reductionist investigations of the material fundamentals of the medium that, more or less incidentally at first, also documented the bohemian demimonde who formed his entourage at the time. These two concerns, apparently as dissimilar from each other as they were from Hollywood's use of the medium, soon began to coincide when Warhol's underlying interests became clear: an overall fascination with the nature of subjectivity in a media-saturated environment. His film career subsequently extrapolated quite logically from an interest in film as the medium of his own artistic work to an interest in the modern entertainment industry. As he made the capitalist media system as a whole the terrain of his investigations, he maneuvered the initially amateur practice of underground film back closer and closer to Hollywood—a move whose trajectory he limned when he distinguished "the period when we made movies just to make them" from the subsequent turn to making "feature length movies that regular theaters would want to show."[24]

Warhol's earliest films—works like *Sleep* (1963), the six-hour documentary of a man sleeping; *Blow-Job* (1963), a stationary-camera shot of a man's face while he is being fellated; or, even more notorious, *Empire* (1964), the eight-hour, also stationary shot of the Empire State Building at night—provoked as much scandal and alarm in the world of underground film as accounts of them did in the popular press. In comparison to Brakhage's heavily worked, idiosyncratically assertive montages, Warhol's minimization of content, his prolongation of empty duration, and his refusal to add variety by way of iconographic or textural incident seemed a deliberate affront to the expansive, kinetic visual pyrotechnics associated with the youth cultures. Though people were drawn to screenings by the controversy surrounding them and by Warhol's other publicity stunts, usually they left in outrage. Only when he turned to feature-length narratives and to an overt concern with spectacular sexuality did his films actually become popular on the underground film circuits, which in the later 1960s were in any case beginning to intersect more and more with mainstream movies.

As Warhol clarified his underlying thematics, he began to restage the strategies of his early films (which had isolated a single individual before the camera) in increasingly complex situations. Eventually his scenarios involved the interaction of several people competitively negotiating quasi-fictional roles in ersatz versions of corporate film and television. As he did so, he abandoned the underground, artisanal mode of production in which he had himself performed all the key roles in favor of the industrial mode of production with its division of labor (writer, cameraperson, actors, and so on), retaining for himself a role equivalent to that of the producer in the industry. Exhibition correspondingly evolved from private screenings for friends at the Factory and the underground venues organized by Jonas Mekas, to theatrical distribution, eventually on an international scale. *The Chelsea Girls* (1966) was a pivotal turning point between the different modes. It featured a motley selection of self-absorbed monologues and broken, often hostile conversations among colorful members of Warhol's entourage, projected two reels at a time, side by side. Prominent among them were the transvestites, hustlers, and speed freaks who would be the major figures in his later productions conceived entirely in commercial terms, films like *Lonesome Cowboys* (1967) and *Trash* (1970) that played in suburban theaters. *The Chelsea Girls* summarily restated the formal and social innovations of his first, radically experimental phase, while its run in a midtown Manhattan cinema and its financial returns—it realized around $150,000 in profits—raised the possibility of production on an industrial scale, and hence the return of counterculture cinema to the commodity functions of the industry.

Between contrary projects of the kinds exemplified by Brakhage and Warhol, there flourished in the United States a popular practice of cinema, unique in the history of the medium. The mid-Sixties were, as Paul Arthur has noted, "a time when anyone could, and it was thought that everyone *should* become a filmmaker."[25] To sustain and consolidate this spontaneous cinematic *prise de la parole*, people involved in underground film did create something of an institutional infrastructure alternative to that of the film industry, with its own screening venues and its own distribution agencies such as the Creative Film Society in Los Angeles, the Film-Makers' Cooperative in New York, and Canyon Cinema in San Francisco. Jonas Mekas's *Film Culture* became its journal of record where new critical criteria appropriate to the cinematic innovations were developed. Meanwhile, his vociferously partisan column "Movie Journal" in the *Village Voice*, where developments in the New York scene were celebrated, became the guiding light for a phylum of similar columns in the *Berkeley Barb*, the *Los Angeles Free Press* and similar underground publications across the country.

From all this activity a canon of distinguished artists emerged, whose contributions to the medium have become, albeit in a marginalized fashion, part of film history. Besides Brakhage and Warhol, these included Kenneth Anger, Jordan Belson, Bruce Baillie, Robert Breer, Shirley Clarke, Tony Conrad, Bruce Connor, Ed Emshwiller, Barry Gerson, Will Hindle, Ken Jacobs, Larry Jordan, George and Mike Kuchar, George Landow, Saul Levine, Lenny Lipton, Gregory Markopoulos, Taylor Mead, Jonas Mekas, Marie Menken, Robert Nelson, Pat O'Neill, Ron Rice, Carolee Schneemann, Paul

Sharits, Harry Smith, Jack Smith, and Stan Vanderbeek. The incorporation of some of these filmmakers and of a limited number of their works into the canons of film history is extremely important, both as recognition of their aesthetic achievements and as a means of sustaining awareness of filmic experiences richer and more fully human than those allowed by corporate culture. Yet it fails to register what was centrally important about underground cinema: the great numbers of now anonymous people who made the medium the vehicle of self- and communal expression, outside and opposed to alienated capitalist commodity culture. Within this general social achievement, the mutually sustaining aesthetic and political innovations of three of those mentioned above merit special attention.

After the zenith of the counterculture was past, it gradually became clear that in addition to leading the critical and institutional developments already noted, Jonas Mekas was also one of its most profound filmmakers. Eventually settling on the diary film, a key underground genre, he systematically documented his daily life. When this material was edited some years later, it was found to constitute an unparalleled record of the New York counterculture, of the trajectory of underground film, and of many of the other artistic and political developments of the period. Jack Smith's work was a similarly profound and explicit attack on capitalist cinema. Recognizing the importance of classic Hollywood films in furnishing the popular imagination with its icons and aesthetic values, he attempted to re-create what he took to be their essence. To other people, however, his films appeared to be monstrous parodies, anti-films that simultaneously invoked and denied the industrial cinema. Beginning with *Flaming Creatures* (1963), he created desultory tableaux of transvestites that, though full of a bizarre elegance, were also dada enactments of endless deferment and negativity. Smith's influence on underground film and also theater was profound (Warhol especially was deeply indebted to him), but his opposition to the institutionalizing of the underground led him to withdraw his works from circulation. Only since his death have they become generally available. Finally, Carolee Schneemann's most consummate film is an outstanding testament to the counterculture's vision of utopian sexuality. A painter who made one of the first U.S. films to denounce the invasion of Vietnam (*Viet-Flakes*, 1965), Schneemann quickly thereafter emerged as a pioneer in the feminist art movement. Her film *Fuses* (1964–67), depicting her lovemaking with James Tenney, opened up the notion of the amateur to an entirely eroticized language and practice of film, so intense that it was for many years anathema to both the male-dominated world of avant-garde film and to establishment feminism. Though the works of these three epitomize the counterculture's most radical visions, only recently have we been able to fully comprehend them.

The social momentum of underground film ran from the mid-1950s to the mid-1970s, but it flowered best between the release of *Pull My Daisy* in 1959 and the run of Warhol's *The Chelsea Girls* in New York in the summer of 1966, the most scandalous of the underground's dramatic eruptions. Within the next two years, black uprisings in Chicago, New York, and Watts and the emergence of organized resistance to the invasion of Vietnam offered unprecedented, categorical political challenges to the corporate state. Under the stress of increasing militancy, the balance between the aesthetic and the existential that had allowed the making of art to be both self-validating and the central ritual in a countercultural revolt became increasingly fragile. Underground film came to a crisis in which the combined aesthetic and social projects that had sustained it split apart into two separate currents: Structural film, a largely autonomous aestheticism; and a politically radical pragmatism organized into a number of Newsreels.

That tradition which had been most entranced by the material properties of the medium and its new visual experiences secured itself in the field of the aesthetic itself, affiliating with parallel concerns in the worlds of sculpture and painting. This tradition of aesthetic reflexivity became known as Structural film, again following the terminology of P. Adams Sitney.[26] Michael Snow's *Wavelength*, which began to be shown in late 1967, marked the emergence of this current. It consisted of a single slow forty-five minute zoom across a New York artist's loft, with the film stock changed periodically, so that the film is "about" the way space is differently organized by lenses of different focal length and "about" the way different film stocks register the nature of light. Though Structural film was sometimes understood in relation to the antiwar movement, overall it marked a retreat from the social. Its political content was highly mediated, and often recoverable only via theories of the reconstruction of the medium as a preliminary to a perceptual renovation that might have political implications. At exactly the time of Structural film's emergence, the political component of underground film also seceded and reformulated itself. Affiliating with more militant social groups, it subordinated concerns with the phenomenology of filmic experience to more agitational social programs.

FILM AND THE MOVEMENT

On December 22, 1967 some thirty young filmmakers who had previously been independently documenting political activity met at an underground screening venue in New York, the Film-Makers' Cinematheque. They included Robert Machover, whose *Troublemakers* (1966) had documented Civil Rights workers' attempts to organize a Newark ghetto, and Peter Gessner, whose *Time of the Locust* (1966) had similarly documented the

Vietnamese liberation struggle; the concerns of these two films would initially be the Newsreel's main preoccupations. Since it was believed that opposition to the invasion of Vietnam and other movements for radical change in the United States were consistently undermined and suppressed in the biased coverage of television and the media,[27] the filmmakers decided to join in a cooperative effort to create an alternative newsreel system, one that would serve the needs of "all people working for change, students, organizations in ghettos and other depressed areas, and anyone who is not and cannot be satisfied by the news film available through establishment channels."[28]

As they built upon the underground's tradition of protest film, New York Newsreel and related branches that quickly sprang up in Boston, Detroit, San Francisco, Los Angeles, Chicago, and other places throughout the country also continued the underground's artisanal productive methods and its attempts to innovate non-commodity forms of cinema. Financial motives were, as far as possible, pushed to the side, with films supplied free to community organizing groups that could not afford to pay; and new functions for the medium were proposed:

> Films made by the Newsreel are not to be seen once and forgotten. Once a print goes out, it becomes a tool to be used by others in their own work, to serve as a basis for their own definition and analysis of society. Part of our function, therefore, is to provide information on how to project films in non-theatrical settings—on the sides of buildings, etc. We hope that whoever receives our films will show them to other local groups as well, thus creating an expanding distribution network. We shall also encourage the formation of similar newsreel groups in other parts of the country, so that there can be a continual interchange of news films, whereby people in Oakland can see what happens in New York and vice versa.[29]

Jonas Mekas noted at the time that there was "no difference between the avant-garde film and the avant-garde newsreel."[30] Indeed, this continuity with previous minority cinemas links the documentaries of Beat life and the early amateur documentation of peace marches and civil protest such as Jerry Abrams's *Be-In* (1967) and Anthony Reveaux's *Peace March* (1967) with more concerted attempts to use film in the antiwar effort. The work of Saul Levine, especially his film *New Left Note* (1969–75), a metacinematic meditation on the relationship between counterculture aesthetics and activist politics with strobe-fast montages of two-frame shots, is the most important single oeuvre spanning the two phases (figure 2).

Celluloid strip from Saul Levine's film *New Left Note*, 1969–75. The continuity between the Beat/hippie and the militant cinemas of the 1960s and '70s is exemplified by *New Left Note*. Constructed from extended sequences of extremely rapid parallel montage of documentary film footage of antiwar, Black liberation, and women's movement activity on the one hand and television broadcasts of the war and of Nixon's speeches about it on the other, the film also incorporates such devices as solid color frames, end-holes, and splice bars to interrupt the representational mode. The energy and violence of the filmic activity complement the political energy and violence the film engages. Courtesy of Saul Levine.

Like that of the underground press, independent film's role in the Movement was initially reportorial. Where underground film had picked up from the surrealist and cubist avant-gardes of the twenties, the roots of political filmmaking lay rather in the Soviet agitprop cinema, either directly or as mediated by the Workers Film and Photo Leagues of the 1930s. Indeed, the films were often quite primitive in form, consisting of hortatory voice-overs accompanying simple visual documents of political events. But the provision of an alternative to the biased political reporting of television news also involved the production and self-legitimization of group identity. Protest film was a form of political praxis, itself an act of contestation rather than merely the documentation of contestation taking place in other practices. Two of New York Newsreel's films, *Columbia Revolt* (1968) and *Summer of 68* (1969), exemplify this evolution.

Both films were fundamentally attempts to mobilize alternatives to the mass media's misrepresentation of radical social movements, a misrepresentation that, it was believed, was inevitable given the media's integration in the corporate state generally. The first is a vivid and vigorous documentation of the student strike at Columbia University, when Students for a Democratic Society (SDS) mobilized the occupation of five university buildings by over a thousand students.[31] The film includes extended footage taken inside the occupied buildings and shows the brutality of police attempts to evict the students (which was largely responsible for SDS's success in mobilizing the support of the initially more moderate left-liberal students and faculty). Unequivocally voicing the most militant students' understanding of the rebellion, the film subordinates documentary objectivity to a partisan celebration of their program. The Columbia students overcome their alienation by becoming involved in the collective praxis of resistance, and what a narrative voice-over calls their "electric awakening" is figured in the wedding of two of the students surrounded by their new "family" inside the occupied and besieged buildings. *Columbia Revolt* was designed not as an objective documentation of the strike but to justify the theories of students as a revolutionary "class" in order to encourage students elsewhere to engage in insurrections of their own.

Summer of 68, Newsreel's film about the demonstrations at the Chicago Democratic Convention, is a similarly self-conscious attempt to record a crucial political confrontation and to contest mass-media exploitative misrepresentation of the Movement. It contains extensive analysis of the antiwar movement's plans to use the convention to make a highly visible protest against the atrocities in Vietnam, and it contains plentiful documentation of street demonstrations and of the police rioting that met them. Yet it is guarded about the political use to which these representations are to be put.

On the one hand, the film recognizes their importance in allowing the activists who came to Chicago to overcome their own alienation and feel identity with oppressed people in Vietnam. On the other, it recognizes that the spectacle of the police riots, observed in the film itself but also via corporate media in broadcasts all over the world, obscured the more important issues: the racism at home and the war abroad that were the real object of the demonstrations. It concludes on the need for street-level organizing against the war, but also for additional strategies to overcome the corporate media's exploitation of all Movement politics.

Columbia Revolt and *Summer of 68* are simultaneously documentations of radical political activities and themselves political interventions that aimed to generate changes in the structure of American society. This combination of functions, remarkable as it was, was only part of the innovations in alternative political culture that the Newsreels produced. The social inequities of class, race, and sex that the filmmakers confronted in American culture at large were also soon discovered within the filmmaking collectives themselves. As this was realized and confronted, the social activity of filmmaking became the site of political transformations, a microsociety where the utopian aspirations of the Movement's address to society were internally enacted. The critique and reform of the power relations within the filmmaking collective was projected as a model for new relations between the group and society at large. Paralleling and very often deeply intertwined with the struggles in SDS and the splinter groups into which it disintegrated after the cataclysmic events of 1968, the Newsreels at the turn of the decade tried to create within themselves a quasi-Maoist redistribution of power prefiguring, it was hoped, a more thorough integration of the filmmaking groups within the constituencies they served. The restructuring of social relations within film production and the relations of the film practice to society was not accomplished without intense self-consciousness and self-criticism, for the path from simply making political films to making political films *politically* had hardly been trodden before.

The local political conditions faced by the various Newsreel branches across the country produced specific regional emphases, but there were strong personal interconnections among their members, sustained not only by their frequent meetings with each other but also by the national distribution of all the Newsreel films. Inevitably, then, there were substantial similarities in the way each branch refracted the national and indeed international scope of the emergency, leading them to experience fundamentally similar developments. New York Newsreel's main stages were typical: first the formation of an alternative production and distribution organization dominated by white males; then its reorganization so as to incorporate and empower women and minorities, along with attempts to integrate with working-class communities; and finally their almost catastrophic crisis.

When New York Newsreel began in 1968 as an affiliation of politically minded filmmakers, film production was undertaken on the initiative of individual members, all of whom were free to make their films without approval of the group as a whole. The earliest films naturally reflected the concerns of the original white, male, middle-class nucleus who by virtue of their prior experience or their access to equipment and funds were capable of actually completing works. Eleven of the first thirteen films released were concerned with Vietnam and especially with resistance to the draft. They documented, for example, speeches by notable resistance spokespeople (*Draft Resistance* consisted of an interview with Noam Chomsky); interviews with deserters (*Four Americans* interviewed four sailors who had deserted from a U.S. warship); demonstrations (*No Game* documented the fall 1967 demonstration at the Pentagon); and plans for the actions at the Democratic Convention (*Boston Draft Resistance Group* and *Chicago* were both oriented toward the Chicago convention).

Like the activities they depicted, these first films were by and large agitational, and theorized as analogous to acts of war. Their raw production values, with minimal, unsophisticated voice-over analysis subordinated to confrontational emotional impact, were supposed to reflect the filmmakers' own physical participation in the resistance they were created to mobilize. Since they were not designed for general audiences, they depended less on persuasion or explanation than on visceral strategies or moralistic appeals that would excite already committed viewers to action. As Robert Kramer, one of the founding and most prominent members, argued, "You want to make films that unnerve, that shake assumptions, that threaten, that do not soft-sell, but hopefully (an impossible ideal) explode like grenades in people's faces, or open minds up like a good can opener."[32] In line with this rhetoric, each film ended with the Newsreel logo and the staccato chatter of a machine gun, epitomizing the ideal of film as a weapon in the hands of a filmmaker engaged in physical combat. The documentary, analytic function was conditioned by a participatory, performative one, fully consonant with the confrontational, "Bring-the-War-Home" tone of New Left insurgency in the period immediately after the 1968 Democratic Convention in Chicago.

During 1969, this anarchic production of agitational film was increasingly questioned. Though at first no single, correct, analytic ideology was insisted upon, Newsreel revived the Film and Photo League's practice of sending speakers with the films to lead post-screening discussions. "How the films are presented is as important to us as the films themselves," the 1969 catalog claimed, "We hope you will invite NEWSREEL members to your screenings to help present the films and to participate in audience discussions. Without these kind of discussions, our films would be incomplete."[33] The emphasis in this period on using film as a tool for consciousness raising and organizing, as a "pretext for dialogue, for the seeking and finding of wills" (in the terms of the revolutionary Latin American cinemas the Newsreels influenced)[34], subordinated the film as artifact to the debate that could be generated around it.

At the same time, with the demonstrations failing to bring about a withdrawal from Vietnam and the campaigns of peace candidates in the 1968 elections being equally ineffectual, the need for long-range organizing became clear. After 1968, and especially after the SDS and the Movement as a whole split into increasingly violent fractions, the most militant radical groups began to apply their overall social critique to their own organizations, hoping that self-criticism would transform liberal college students into socially integrated, disciplined vanguard cadres. Similar developments occurred in New York Newsreel; a concern with discussion and theoretical inquiry supplanted the earlier anti-analytic interventionist urgency, creating a context in which the diagnosis of the macropolitical situation could be applied to the microsociety of the filmmaking group. The initial very loose structure was replaced by a more formal one in which democratic procedures were brought into play to secure a means of communal control.

In late 1969–early 1970, what Bill Nichols called a "barometric" reflection "of the thoughts and acts of a large portion of the Movement"[35] produced sessions of intense self-criticism that reverberated with the burgeoning debates outside the group, especially about women's liberation and ethnic nationalism. Recognition that there were almost no non-white members, no working-class members, and few skilled women members discredited the confrontational moralism of the earlier stance and stimulated an internal restructuring that dislodged the white male nucleus. This, in turn, led to even more radical reconsiderations that subsequently split the organization. A central "operations committee" and three "work groups," responsible for Third World, high school, and working-class films were formed. Each had a more strongly democratic internal organization, and it was decided that production skills were to be taught to all members. Resistant to this intense self-analysis or undermined by it, the majority of the original nucleus left, and those who remained formed a collective in which the greater power of women and Third World members allowed a much closer relation with the working class. The films produced in this period, such as *The Wreck of the New York Subway* (about a fare increase) and *Lincoln Hospital* (about the attempt of staff members to run the hospital themselves), were concerned with local and domestic questions, not with war resistance or with issues of national interest. In them analysis and explanation replaced the earlier confrontational mode and newsreel format. Though these films were frequently neither as politically or artistically sophisticated as they aspired to be, they did nevertheless achieve the closer integration of the production group within the constituencies it hoped to serve.

Like SDS, which split over disagreement as to which faction of the proletariat was most proper for students to ally themselves with, New York Newsreel was traumatized by the attempt to integrate itself within the working class. After an unsuccessful attempt to bring more people of color into the group, the central operations committee was disbanded. Amid bitter recriminations about race, gender, and class background, especially as these came to a head over the decision to make a film about the Attica prison rebellion in February 1972, New York Newsreel entered a third stage by splitting into virtually autonomous white and Third World factions. In April 1972 New York Newsreel became Third World Newsreel, with a membership of three women of color. Their next films were all about prison conditions for women and minorities, including *In the Event Anyone Disappears* and *We Demand Freedom*. The other major Newsreels, San Francisco and Los Angeles, followed roughly similar trajectories. As they shifted their focus from immediate issues to exploring the possibilities of radical social change, their attempts to affiliate with the working class—especially the black working class—led to increasing marginalization and crisis. San Francisco eventually regrouped, but the contradictions forced Los Angeles to dissolve, and its chief members went to work in factories and engaged in grassroots organizing where filmmaking had no role. But by this time, the other countercultural cinemas had been drawn into a different kind of politics.

In the early 1970s, women's liberation emerged as the strongest social movement of the period, and feminism and cinema began an extraordinarily fertile relationship. Together with the example of Jean-Luc Godard's films of the late 1960s and other European attempts to create cinemas in opposition to the capitalist film industries, Structural film had been the source for increasingly theoretical reconsideration of all the institutions of cinema. This undertaking was galvanized when feminist exploration of the representation of women in the commercial cinema led them to argue that mainstream film was a major component in patriarchal society, responsible for determining relations between women and men and indeed in constructing sexual identity.[36] These developments created both the need and the possibility of new alternative cinemas that would represent women and gender roles differently.

With strong links to the theoretical feminist work that was being carried on in film and literature departments of the universities, this new avant-garde was to be the most important countercultural force in the next two decades, but one that increasingly abandoned its connections with working-class, minority women that the Newsreels had tried to forge. Though the radical impulses of the Sixties survived there, feminism soon centered on the admission of selected members of minority groups to privileged positions within capitalist society, rather than working for radical changes in its structure.

By the mid-1970s, with the disarray of the radical left and the rise of the New Right and revisionist interpretations of the invasion of Vietnam, the ideal of a popular participatory cinema began to fade from American culture. Elements of popular practice persisted, but what experimental filmmaking remained was mostly sustained by the academy or on its edges, not by grassroots social movements outside it. Overall, the hope that a nonindustrial practice of the medium might be linked to movements of genuine social contestation was swamped in new analyses of the mass consumption of corporate culture as itself involving moments of resistance. Corresponding to a radically depleted sense of social possibilities, these new cultural studies affirmed the status quo, and placed center stage in social resistance what before had been its major obstacle: Hollywood.

THE TRIUMPH OF CORPORATE CULTURE

The move of the counterculture toward the industry, instanced here in the career of Andy Warhol, was mirrored by Hollywood's own appropriations of the youth cultures in the late 1960s. By the 1970s, the film industry became all but entirely integrated with corporate capital by its return to blockbuster spectacles that expressed the values of the resurgent New Right.[37] Of the initial "youthpix," *The Graduate* (Mike Nichols, 1967) had appeared best to catch the spirit of the period. Still, the fact that a protest as timid and trivial as that of Dustin Hoffman's character should have been received as the sign of a generational revolt testifies to the paucity of Hollywood's responsiveness to the crises of the times, but also to the counterculture's ability to rewrite the most innocuous commercial blandishments according to its own desires. The same mechanism allowed other, more apocalyptic, studio films set in the past to be read allegorically. *Bonnie and Clyde* (Arthur Penn, 1967), for example, led Jerry Rubin to proclaim that "Bonnie Parker and Clyde Barrow are the leaders of the New Youth,"[38] and in *Do It!* he reprinted photographs of the original gang (not of Warren Beatty and Faye Dunaway, who played them), recognizing that the film had made them countercultural heroes. The New Left leader Todd Gitlin saw them as "freestanding angels, children of the sixties set three decades back," and thought that the "spirit of Bonnie and Clyde was everywhere in the move-ment—and in the larger youth culture surrounding it."[39] But the film that opened the door to the real exploitation of the counterculture was *Easy Rider* (1969). Though this saga of motorcycle youth, rock and roll, and drugs appro-priated all its distinctive stylistic innovations and narrative motifs from under-ground film, it cynically inverted the underground's utopianism. Exploiting the counterculture's vision of new forms of community, the film made sure that they would be destroyed by reactionary social elements, thereby ensuring that their energies would be neither validated nor sustained.

Noticing *Easy Rider*'s enormous profits—in the first year of its release alone it returned $19 million on a $365,000 investment—the studios began to raid other aspects of the counterculture, always taking care to sanitize them and neu-tralize their oppositional social implications. *Midnight Cowboy* (John Schlesinger, 1969) explored the world of the Forty-Second Street male hustlers that Andy Warhol had first filmed four or five years before, and Warhol himself recognized that in it "people with money were taking the subject matter of the underground, counterculture life and giving it a good, slick, commercial treat-ment."[40] But the relationship was more complicated than a simple one-way appropriation. Warhol was recuperating after having been shot in Valerie Solanas's attempt to assassinate him, so he could not play the role of an under-ground filmmaker in its big party scenes although other members of his entourage appeared in the film. Paul Morrissey made an underground movie to be screened at it, and later followed Schlesinger's lead by making *Trash*, his own slick, color version of the world Warhol had previously documented in grainy black and white. Not even the Newsreels were safe. *The Strawberry Statement* (Stuart Hagmann, 1970), a fictionalized version of the Columbia strike stole lib-erally from *Columbia Revolt*, and *Zabriskie Point* (Michaelangelo Antonioni, 1969) did the same to San Francisco Newsreel's similar film, *San Francisco State: On Strike* (1969)—both without communicating any but the most superficial and alienated sense of what had been at stake in the student movements themselves.

Though Hollywood engaged in parallel, deeply contradictory negotiations with women's liberation that resulted in increased representation of women directors in the industry by the early 1980s, the developments in feminist thought in the 1970s continued to find their most important refraction in the feminist avant-garde. Otherwise, something of the spirit of counterculture cin-ema survived in small pockets of filmmakers, working increasingly in super-8 and especially in the various forms of independent guerilla video production. When allied with ethnic minorities and gay and lesbian identity groups, these sustained some of the momentum for social change and some of the struggles against the reduction of cinema to commodity functions that the counterculture had initiated. But they were increasingly separated from each other by the premises of identity politics, forced to occupy Balkanized reservations on the margins of a culture dominated by corporate capital. After its brief dalliance with the counterculture, Hollywood joined in the revisionist caricatures of 1960s politics mounted by the New Right. This culture found its entirely appropriate apotheosis in the films of the "movie brat" generation, exemplified most fully in *Star Wars* (George Lucas, 1977), a film that exploited a regressive, escapist romance-fantasy, allowing it to endorse "both the traditional structures of racism, sexism and social hierarchy that have helped to create and maintain [the audience's] frustrations, and the monocular attitudes towards technology that form an important part of the whole ideological package."[41]

Underground film would have been lost had not at least some of its stylistic innovations reappeared in the least likely of places: television. As children, the counterculture had been the first generation to be nurtured on television, and in the mid-Sixties, the first to be bored by it. But in certain exceptional cases, television did capture the anarchic spirit of the times. CBS canceled *The Smothers Brothers Comedy Hour* in its third season when, after the 1968 Democratic Convention, the duo became unequivocal in their support for the counterculture. Up to that time the show was an anomaly in what was otherwise a corporate wasteland.[42] Other comedy series, notably *Laugh-In*, maintained a perspective sufficiently aslant of mainstream values to run afoul of conservative censors and critics. But the youth cultures mobilized around popular music continued to be a target audience for television. Two decades later, MTV became the means for this appropriation, and the stylistics and iconography of the underground—even motifs from *Meshes of the Afternoon*—were reengaged: the denaturing of images by non-standard camera angles and shooting speeds, strobe and other exaggerated lighting, multiple superimpositions, textural modification of the film material itself, the representation of marginal or "deviant" subcultures, and the parodying of the tropes of commercial film and television.[43] All these devices—which in their own times had been denigrated as degenerate by mainstream culture, and since then denigrated as elitist by the apologists for corporate culture who dominated university film and cultural studies programs—were newly conscripted for the pleasure palaces, not of liberation, but of corporate America.

Notes

1. Some of the material in this essay has been adapted from my book, *Allegories of Cinema: American Film in the Sixties* (Princeton: Princeton University Press, 1989).

2. Paul Arthur, "Routines of Emancipation: Alternative Cinema in the Ideology and Politics of the Sixties," in *To Free the Cinema: Jonas Mekas and the New York Underground*, ed. David E. James (Princeton: Princeton University Press, 1992), 18.

3. While I have generally followed Theodore Roszak in using the term "counterculture" to refer primarily to white youth and especially to quietist attempts to disengage from dominant society, I have also extended it to the politically activist youth organizations that developed around the struggles for racial justice and in protest against the United States's invasion of Vietnam. More precise sociologies of countercultures have been developed by, for example, J. Milton Yinger in *Countercultures: The Promise and Peril of a World Turned Upside Down* (New York: Free Press, 1983). In respect to his distinction between a subculture and a counterculture proper, it is probably most accurate to think of the filmmaking initiatives discussed here as initially subcultural scenes that prefigured and eventually evolved into countercultural insurgencies.

4. Students of the medium are fortunate in having immediately available a precise vocabulary for these two distinct but mutually dependent projects. "Film" designates the strip of celluloid that passes through the camera and later the projector, including all the information that is imprinted on it and subsequently communicated to the spectator. On the other hand, following especially the semiotician Christian Metz (*Language and Cinema* [The Hague: Mouton, 1974]), "cinema" is used to designate the ensemble of social processes and materials that produce this filmic text: all the workers in the movie industry itself and in the industries that supply it, the studios, the theaters, and the spectators. Film is the medium, cinema is the social relations it generates and sustains.

5. "The Movies Are a Revolution." *Film Culture* 29 (summer 1963): 9.

6. Aniko Bodroghkozy documents the three television networks' anxiety in the mid-to-late-1960s about the fact that the younger generation was "staying away from the medium in droves" in her "Groove Tube and Reel Revolution: The Youth Rebellions of the 1960s and Popular Culture" (Ph.D. diss., University of Wisconsin, Madison, 1994), 223. For "film generation," see Stanley Kauffmann, *A World on Film* (New York: Harper and Row, 1966), 415. Kauffmann acknowledged that his was "a culture in which the film has been of accepted serious relevance, however that seriousness is defined." Yet he reserved his own approval for the European art film, not finding in either Hollywood or "certain experimental films" (which he was careful to disparage) the seriousness that legitimized the medium.

7. P. Adams Sitney, *Visionary Film: The American Avant-Garde, 1943–1978*, 2d ed. (New York: Oxford University Press, 1979), 11.

8. Films in this genre include *Fireworks* (Kenneth Anger, 1947), *Fragments of Seeking* (Curtis Harrington, 1946), and several early films by Stan Brakhage. As will be described below, Brakhage radically extended the representation of the dream state and in doing so provided the single most important film language for the expanded visual experience of counterculture subjectivity.

9. *Film Culture* 39 (winter 1965), 45–46.

10. "The First Statement of the New American Cinema Group," *Film Culture* 22–23 (summer 1961). Reprinted in *Film Culture Reader*, ed. P. Adams Sitney (New York: Praeger, 1970), 73–75.

11. Some of the most important of these are Shirley Clarke's film of Jack Gelber's play about junkies, *The Connection* (1961); her study of African American teenagers in New York, *The Cool World* (1963); and her *Portrait of Jason* (1967), about a black homosexual hustler; Jonas Mekas's exploration of Beat generation angst, *Guns of the Trees* (1961); and his brother Adolfas's zany take on some of the same themes, *Hallelujah the Hills* (1963); Norman Mailer's remarkable meditation on paranoia, presidential politics, and the cinema, *Maidstone* (1968); Robert Kramer's fictionalized account of revolutionary youth, *Ice* (1969); and Haskell Wexler's investigation of social responsibility in an age of mass media, all focused on the 1968 Chicago Democratic Convention, *Medium Cool* (1969).

12. Ned Polsky, "The Village Beat Scene: Summer 1960," *Dissent* 8, no. 3 (summer 1961). Reprinted in *Hustlers, Beats and Others* (New York: Anchor Books, 1969), 156.

13. As well as less explicitly undergirding cultural developments later in the decade, black

Americans generally occupied a privileged position in the Beat imagination, with their supposed sensual vitality and social marginality epitomized in the idealized figures of the post-bebop jazz musician. Though Kerouac's formulation of a Beat practice in writing also owes a good deal to Buddhism's emphasis on attentiveness to the present as a meditational discipline, it was modeled on the jazz musician's strategies for tapping the unconscious roots of creativity: "Time being of the essence in the purity of speech, sketching language is undisturbed flow from the mind of personal secret idea-words, *blowing* (as per jazz musician) on subject of image" ("Essentials of Spontaneous Prose," *Evergreen Review* 2, no. 5 [summer 1958], 72–73).

14. Parker Tyler, *Underground Film: A Critical History* (New York: Grove Press, 1969), 40.

15. Jonas Mekas, "Notes on the New American Cinema," *Film Culture* 24 (spring 1962), 12–13.

16. Ibid., 14.

17. The term "underground film" was first used by Manny Farber in an essay on films that played "an anti-art role in Hollywood," the "huge amount of unprized second-gear celluloid" produced by the "true masters of the male action film—such soldier-cowboy-gangster directors as Raoul Walsh, Howard Hawks, William Wellman, William Keighley, the early pre-*Stagecoach* John Ford, Anthony Mann" ("Underground Films: A Bit of Male Truth," *Commentary*, 24, no. 5 [November 1957], 432). In the fullest elaboration of the relation between the Beats and underground film, Parker Tyler recognized the latter "encourages beatnik expression through its practical rule of universal tolerance" (*Underground Film*, 32). There were many derogatory mass market magazine and newspaper accounts of underground film, but also some insightful ones, such as Harris Dienstfrey's "The New American Cinema," in *Commentary* 6, no. 33 (June 1962): 495–504.

18. "Anticipations of the Light," *The Nation* 11 (May 1964): 490–94.

19. *An Introduction to the American Underground Film* (New York: Dutton, 1967), 18.

20. Ibid., 17.

21. "The Experimental Film in America," *Film Culture* 3 (May–June 1955): 17.

22. Stan Brakhage, *Metaphors on Vision* (New York: Film Culture, 1963), 23.

23. Ibid., 25.

24. Andy Warhol and Pat Hackett, *Popism: The Warhol Sixties* (New York: Harcourt Brace Jovanovich, 1980), 251–52.

25. "Movies the Color of Blood," *Film-Makers' Cooperative Catalogue No. 7* (New York: Film-Makers' Cooperative, 1989), vi.

26. For Sitney's final formulation of this genre, see *Visionary Film*, 369–397.

27. Press underestimation of the numbers attending the October 1967 March on the Pentagon and general denigration of the event's implications were regarded as especially mendacious, and not just in the extreme counterculture; see, for example, Norman Mailer's account of the march in *Armies of the Night: History as a Novel/ The Novel as History* (New York: New American Library, 1968), which is also centrally a critique of the mass media. The book is a brilliant phenomenology of the politicization of the countercultures.

28. These "half-official announcements" were published by Jonas Mekas in his *Village Voice* column "Movie Journal" on 25 January 1968, and reprinted in Jonas Mekas, *Movie Journal: The Rise of a New American Cinema, 1959–71* (New York: Collier Books, 1972), 306.

29. Ibid.

30. Mekas, "Movie Journal," *Village Voice*, 29 February 1968, 40.

31. On the Columbia strike (and indeed for the history of the New Left generally), see especially Nigel Young, *An Infantile Disorder? The Crisis and Decline of the New Left* (Boulder, Colo.: Westview Press, 1977), 212–15.

32. "Newsreel," *Film Quarterly* 22, no. 2 (winter 1968): 47–48.

33. *Newsreel Catalog*, no.4 (March 1969): n.p.

34. For recognition of this influence, see Fernando Solanas and Octavio Gettino, "Towards

a Third Cinema," reprinted in *Movies and Methods*, vol 1, ed. Bill Nichols, (Berkeley: University of California Press, 1976), 62.

35. Bill Nichols, "Newsreel: Film and Revolution" (master's thesis, University of California at Los Angeles, 1972), 51.

36. The seminal work in this area was Laura Mulvey's celebrated essay, "Visual Pleasure and Narrative Cinema," *Screen* 16, no. 3 (autumn 1975): 6–18.

37. For a succinct account of developments in Hollywood in this period, and one that is unusual in being fully informed by contemporary developments in the counterculture and its cinemas, see Kristin Thompson and David Bordwell's *Film History: An Introduction* (New York: McGraw-Hill, 1994), 696–722. Thompon and Bordwell also summarize the absorption of the classic-era studios by corporate capital, eventually by transnational conglomerates: MCA acquired Universal Pictures in 1962 and was itself bought by Matsushita in 1990; Gulf + Western's purchased Paramount in 1966; Coca-Cola bought Columbia in 1982, then sold it to Sony in 1989, and so on.

38. Jerry Rubin, *Do It!* (New York: Ballantine Books, 1970), 122.

39. Todd Gitlin, *The Whole World Is Watching : Mass Media in the Making and Unmaking of the New Left* (Berkeley: University of California Press, 1980), 197 and 199.

40. Warhol and Hackett, *Popism*, 280.

41. This summary is Dan Rubey's in his classic essay "Star Wars: 'Not So Long Ago, Not So Far Away,'" reprinted in *Jump Cut: Hollywood, Politics and Counter Cinema*, ed. Peter Steven (New York: Praeger, 1985), 88.

42. Cf. "No television programme, with the notable exception of the *Smothers Brothers Comedy Hour*, was ever able to garner any degree of youth movement support and regular viewership" (Bodroghkozy, "Groove Tube and Reel Revolution," 139).

43. For an account of some of these appropriations, see my *Power Misses: Essays across (Un)Popular Culture* (New York: Verso, 1996) 234–36.

Eleven

Sex as a Weapon
Underground Comix and the Paradox of Liberation

Beth Bailey

Sex & drugs & rock and roll: the phrase has served as both mantra and epitaph for the incoherent phenomenon of "the counterculture" in America. During the late 1960s and early 1970s, it offered a symbolic center for the centripetal force of the movement/conspiracy/revolution/lifestyle that sought to counter what its members saw as America's war culture, the plastic materialism of American suburban success, and the persistence of a culture of scarcity (seen in the Protestant work ethic and the repression of sexuality) in the midst of abundance. Despite its symbolic importance, however, the meaning of "sex & drugs & rock and roll" was never transparent or fixed, and America's hip communities struggled over the significance of the claims embodied in that phrase throughout the life of the counterculture. Now, decades later, the old slogan of countercultural rebellion (having survived the intervening years with fewer changes than most of its adherents) has been invested with a much less complicated historical legitimacy by the often linked forces of marketing and nostalgia.[1]

Though the slogan sounds facile in retrospect, removed from the complexities of lived experience and stripped of the historical context in which culture seemed perhaps the most significant battlefield of all, "sex & drugs & rock and roll" summed up a set of claims that many members of the counterculture took very seriously. This trinity of experiences, many of America's youth maintained in language that ranged from the purposely obscene to the carefully philosophical, offered transcendence of the spiritual poverty of American culture to those prepared to seek it. Some in the counterculture went further, claiming that even the least self-aware encounters with these experiences might offer a path, however circuitous, to greater freedom and political righteousness. As the White Panther John Sinclair told an interviewer from the *East Village Other (EVO)*, insisting upon the political significance of the MC5: "So you listen to the band . . . you just go crazy and have a good time. Throw away your underwear, smoke dope, fuck . . . Rather than go up there and make some speech about our moral commitment in Vietnam, you just make 'em so freaky they'd never want to go into the army in the first place. . . ."[2] Politics could be accomplished through cultural tools, he claimed, because culture was political. Mind-blowing experiences with sex or drugs or music were far more likely to alter the worldview of America's young than were all the earnest speeches and political exhortations in which the avowedly political strand of the Movement placed so much trust.

Such notions of instrumentality were controversial at the time. Critics all too easily made their point, citing incidences of exploitation, addiction, and the pointless hedonism of lost souls. Many argued that these means did not necessarily lead to the desired ends; seducing youth into mindless pleasure was not likely to help them attain a coherent politics or foster principled opposition to society's wrongs. The debate over means, which often marked the boundaries between political and cultural revolutionaries, was never fully resolved and still echoes in histories and retrospectives today. However, it is important to remember that many men and women saw in their embrace of "sex & drugs & rock and roll" something more than the pursuit of individual pleasure.

While these contested ideas about the instrumentality of culture (and pleasure) were central to the politics created and lived by members of the counterculture, the significance of sex & drugs & rock and roll transcended such self-conscious debates among the most committed of them. For "sex & drugs & rock and roll" became a shorthand for the larger freedom the hip community sought. Throughout America, people understood these experiences as markers of identity. To embrace them was to declare allegiance; smoking pot or believing in "free love" or even just listening to psychedelic rock, many believed, made them a part of some vaguely defined countercultural community.

This essay is not an overview of the sexual behaviors or of the sexual politics of counterculture youth. Instead, it investigates the ways that members of America's counterculture used sex to create a countercultural identity.

Focusing on how members of this diverse community represented the counterculture in the underground newspapers that proliferated during the 1960s and early '70s, it traces the use of sex—usually notated as women's bodies—to graphically represent "freedom." This version of freedom, however, both collided with and helped create a feminist consciousness of women's oppression within the counterculture (as well as within the larger Movement). Some women raised angry voices, insisting that much of what was done in the name of liberation was merely exploitation recast in a hip style.

Sex, however, held a very important place as a symbolic determinant of counterculture identity. Transgressive sexuality offered a visual and verbal language with which to challenge the Establishment. Represented with purposeful, shocking vulgarity, sex served as a weapon against "straight," or non-hip, culture. And within the counterculture, the sex = freedom equation had become such an overdetermined convention that it was sometimes hard to find another language in which to explain the superiority of the hip to the straight. Thus many of the women who struggled with the calculus of oppression and liberation had a difficult time negotiating their positions on "sex." It was not easy to shift either the terms or the iconography of sex, and it also was not easy to jettison a potent weapon and key marker of countercultural identity. The texts that some of these women produced, especially the women's issues of underground papers that began to appear in 1970, are full of bizarre juxtapositions and incoherencies that demonstrate how hard it was to re-create the meaning of sex in the counterculture.

By the end of the tumultuous decade of the Sixties, a new media had grown up in America's counterculture. More than 500 underground newspapers were published on varying schedules; their combined circulations fell somewhere between two million and four and one-half million readers.[3] Distributed free or sold at record stores, head shops, and other gathering places for hippies and (as they came to call themselves) freaks, underground newspapers fostered the growth of the counterculture. By disseminating knowledge and validating shared understandings, these locally produced papers worked to create community by establishing the central elements of that specific community's countercultural identity.

Most cities and towns with any significant countercultural presence had some district in which hippies and freaks concentrated, but the communities these newspapers embraced were not geographically bounded. They included the high school students still living at home but nonetheless identifying themselves as hippies or freaks, those isolated in small towns and rural areas with few like-minded souls, and the huge number of people who never quite "dropped out" but who embraced a countercultural sensibility and so thought of themselves as part of the burgeoning counterculture. These newspapers, linked together by the Liberation News Service and the Underground Press Syndicate, as well as by an extremely casual approach to copyright and intellectual property, also helped tie local communities into an emergent national countercultural community.

The papers themselves varied greatly. A few were avowedly political and generally sober in tone, while others were riotous explosions of psychedelic art and thought. Some were little more than mimeographed broadsides full of xxxed-out typos; many were professionally printed, carefully edited, and well funded by businesses, such as record companies, who saw profit potential in the developing countercultural aesthetic. All of these papers, however, in declaring themselves alternatives to mainstream newspapers and to straight culture in general, faced the problem of how to demonstrate that stance. Those who did the hard work of putting the papers out on a more-or-less-regular schedule were usually quite conscious of the role they had assumed in concretizing and disseminating counterculture, though not always so aware of the implications of what they published. Because these papers were such critical institutions in their varied communities, and because people understood that they played such an important role in creating countercultural identity, underground newspapers became the sites of some of the most crucial negotiations—and confrontations—over the definition of the counterculture. In many cases, sex and gender would be the most explosive issues.

In terms of sex, the aesthetic of the underground press was generally outrageous—especially in those papers that endorsed a revolution at least as much cultural as political. Portrayals of sex in these underground papers had two major purposes. Frequently, contributors and editors attempted to use graphic or otherwise "offensive" representations of sex to confront—and offend—mainstream society. The underground press also used sex as a symbol of freedom and liberation, seeking graphics and language and attitudes that clearly transcended the strictures of a repressive society. In attempting these two tasks, which sometimes blurred in the execution, the underground papers used images that ranged from matter-of-fact nudity to the stylized profundity of backlit couples running naked through meadows to the sexually explicit and often violently perverse comix of artists like Robert Crumb and S. Clay Wilson.

In paper after alternative paper throughout the United States, the graphic representation of freedom was a naked woman. (Most of these papers assumed a heterosexual context, though some would eventually incorporate gay iconography.) In East Lansing, Michigan (home of Michigan State University) *The*

Paper announced "Free University" courses for the winter of 1968 under the heading "FREE-dom in spite of the U." "Freedom" appeared as a line drawing of a woman wearing only a mortarboard and carrying a diploma.[4]

Sometimes "freedom" was literally embodied: that same year the *East Village Other* ran a drawing—no more than a sketch, really, rendered in a few simple lines—of a nude woman reclining, one hand fondling her own breast. Inscribed on her body were the words Laughter, Love, Peace, and Freedom. "Peace" was where her head would have been had the author included it; "Freedom" was written across her belly.[5]

In 1969, *Vortex,* one of several underground papers published in Lawrence, Kansas, accompanied a poetic musing on freedom and the redemptive power of the body with photos of a nude couple in an autumn meadow. "Can't hate naked," the poet wrote. "Squat/take shit together/understand. . . ." In keeping with the off-center sensibility of Lawrence's unsentimental hippies, in one photo the couple sat on a toilet (lid closed) there in the meadow.[6] Also in a warped pastoral mode, the Austin *Rag* illustrated its advertising section, the "Rag Bag," with a sketch of two nude women in balletic poses, frolicking among flowers. Here pastoral innocence was compromised by the bearded and besandled (and fully clothed) male figure who danced between them, his hand barely brushing the nipple of one woman's breast.[7] Naked breasts were common icons, and in the underground press even commercial advertisements used this sex = freedom equation to align themselves with the counterculture. An advertisement in Atlanta's *Great Speckled Bird,* seemingly for "The Secretaries of Atlanta," somewhat inexplicably offered a drawing of a woman in bellbottoms, long hair flowing. She's naked from the waist up, her nipples carefully shaded in.[8]

Even the explicitly political was sometimes merged with sexual symbols. The *Great Speckled Bird* announced the Vietnam Moratorium immediately beneath a photo of a nude woman reclining in a tree.[9] Minneapolis's *Hundred Flowers,* a politically serious paper, produced a "sex supplement" that was actually an (inaccurate) set of instructions for childbirth without the intervention of a physician. The section centered around a photograph of a woman—naked, here, for good cause—who had just given birth to her child.[10] Articles calling for abortion rights, which appeared with increasing frequency in the underground press by the end of the 1960s, commonly included photos of women, naked, and often fairly advanced in pregnancy.[11] These images range from celebration to cheap titillation, and the creators of the childbirth supplement had fundamentally different intentions than the creators of the "Secretaries of Atlanta" ad. Nonetheless, the universe of women's bodies presented in these papers created a larger context for viewing any specific illustrations: they all

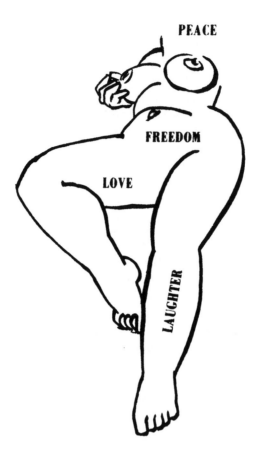

PEACE

FREEDOM

LOVE

LAUGHTER

"Sex as Freedom." Drawing by an unidentified artist that appeared in the *East Village Other* [New York] (1–7 March 1968). Kansas Collection, Spencer Research Library, University of Kansas.

used graphic representations of women's bodies as fundamental symbols of freedom and countercultural identity.

At the same time, some of the images in the underground press moved beyond the sex = freedom equation to treat sex as a weapon. Their creators embraced purposeful obscenity in order to reject the repressive tenets of politeness, respectability, and "sexual morality." Quite a few cultural revolutionaries saw vulgar representations of transgressive sex as a way to challenge what they saw as the hypocritical foundations of the larger culture. As with images that equate sex and freedom, quite different sorts of images worked to a similar end. Images of violent, explicit, or transgressive sex appeared frequently in the underground press, as weapons, because of their shock value in the struggle against "Amerika." So did sexual images that were meant to make viewers think about the hypocrisy of a nation that members of America's hip communities believed had the wrong answer to the question "Is it obscene to fuck, or is it obscene to kill?"[12]

In an episode of "Subvert Comix" from 1968, sex—again represented as a woman's naked body—became, literally, a weapon against repression. An Amazonian figure, drawn from behind, confronted the "DISCIPL'NAR-IAN," a man holding people captive in his authoritarian and repressive frame. In her presence he collapsed immediately: "YECH! DISGUSTING THE NUDE BODY OF A WOMAN I THINK I'M GOING TO RETCH!"[13] In a somewhat similar vein, counterculture celebrity John Sinclair, editor of the *Sun* (Ann Arbor), manager of the MC5, motivating presence behind a "band of artists and lovers," and foremost proselytizer for "rock and roll, dope, and fucking in the streets," was praised in the *Free Press of Louisville* as "the sort of man who caused respectable women to tighten their sphincter muscles and leave the room."[14] Both representations suggest that the power of sex, whether embodied in a naked woman or channeled through a man who enacted the liberating force of "fucking," could easily vanquish the forces of repression.

In many cases these sexual images, while presented as attacks on the establishment, were also a form of macho posturing, a vision of postrevolutionary possibility in which rape played a central role and the word "fuck" was a powerful incantation. In a long tirade of an article in *Vortex* (Lawrence, Kansas), a writer railed about his recent trip to Omaha: "People in Omaha don't fuck," he wrote. "People in Omaha are too damn old or hung-up to fuck." Of course, he continued, "people in Omaha don't know who Paul Krassner [editor of *The Realist*] is" either. "Do you know who Paul Krassner is?" No? "Ask the librarian; if she doesn't know, pinch her tit."[15] The librarian stands for repression and dried-up sexuality, to which the appropriate response is sexual violence.

Such macho posturing appeared in counterculture communities' representations of themselves throughout the nation, but it was raised to an art form by John Sinclair. Though he was not necessarily a representative figure, Sinclair appeared as a culture hero in many underground newspapers in the era, especially after he was faced with a ten–year jail sentence for possession of two marijuana joints.[16] One of their own, Sinclair (who, as noted, edited Ann Arbor's *Sun*) was portrayed in the underground press as an outrageous, larger-than-life figure. He's "one mean motherfucker," wrote D. A. Latimer in *EVO*. "He's big and he's dirty and he was up to recently one of the most busted figures in Hip Culture." Having established Sinclair's bona fides, Latimer offers a transcription of a recent conversation with Sinclair.[17]

Mainly they talked about "tits" and "fucking." The MC5, Sinclair explained, had an "anti-bra campaign" under way. "We hate brassieres, man," he said. "In Ann Arbor, where we live, it's bra city. All these college students who all live in their heads. They all live in Brassieres. . . . You get obsessed: a chick says something to you and all you can say is, 'That's a nice brassiere you got on'. You just wanta yank 'em. 'Cause tits are so wonderful, man." Thus the band's mission was to educate chicks about brassieres, " 'cause they don't know, man, they just put 'em on." When "chicks" came backstage, Sinclair explained, the Five (we're "all notorious ass-grabbers, tit-grabbers. Say hello to a chick by grabbin' her ass") confronted them and explained that bras are just a "ruse": if they don't wear them they'll "really feel good, and besides, when a boy walks up to them he can reach under and feel a real tit."

Sinclair and Latimer mused a while longer about the glories of unfettered tits, until Sinclair, responding to Latimer's mention of fifteen-year-olds, exploded: "With these huge, beautiful fuckin' tits! So fuckin' beautiful! Fifteen-sixteen year old chicks, man! WOW!" The article had no title, but instead an epigraph: "The young, with their ragged hair, their freaky clothes and savage music, come down upon us like the Goths upon Rome." This was no apology for barbarism, but a proud claiming of it. "Say hello to a chick by grabbin' her ass." The macho posturing was interwoven with the claims of liberation, and this was a weapon that did not offer precision targeting.

Another counterculture celebrity, Ed Sanders, also found in sex a potent weapon. He had come from Missouri to New York to attend NYU, and in 1962 had founded *Fuck You: A Magazine of the Arts*. "I'll print anything," he claimed, and so helped lead the way into cultural revolution. Though he saw the dangers of countercultural excess—he once described the counterculture as a noble experiment that nonetheless resembled "a valley of thousands of plump white rabbits surrounded by wounded coyotes"—he continued to embrace excess, especially sexual excess, as a weapon of revolution.[18] In a 1969 "conversation," published in *EVO*, he described a novel he was writing about the riots at the Democratic National Convention in Chicago the previous summer. He called it *"Shards of God"*; it was about "the growth of commie-sequenced suck rape-dope fiend chromosome damaged magico-atheist smut brigade within the fabric of American civilization."[19]

Sanders criticized the rise of low-quality "pornzines" in and around the underground press, but when asked how he positioned his work as "socially redeeming," he gave an answer that might have confused some readers about the difference between his work and the porn to which he was objecting. For example, he said, I might "caption a photo of a walrus fornicating with a girl, with something like, 'This valiant fighter for women's liberation is warding off the rapacious lust of western capitalism.'"

Sanders's critique of the pornzines was rooted in real changes within the underground press. By 1968, the most sordid and sexually explicit material appeared primarily in a new set of alternative papers and publications, of which New York's *Screw* was the most prominent. These publications, fueled by sex ads and personals and full of sexually titillating illustrations and articles, drew readership and revenue away from some of the more "mainstream" underground newspapers. Editors within the alternative press faced some hard choices. Some saw it as a matter of expediency: sex ads paid the bills and kept their papers alive. Some took a firm stance against censorship and slid deeper into the profits and perils of a culture of sexual extremes that, at the time, often was used to symbolize larger counterculture goals of freedom and liberation.[20] A few decided to draw the line somewhere in the continuum of sex and violence, weirdness and nastiness, that threatened to overwhelm their visions of counterculture and community.

Even with alternative venues like *Screw*, however, the boundaries between the sex rags and the mainstream of underground publishing were never hard and fast. Sanders and Sinclair's brand of liberation was published throughout the nation, in a wide range of underground papers. The sexually explicit comix of artists like S. Clay Wilson and Robert Crumb might appear in their joint publication, *Snatch* (no ambiguity there), but they were also published and praised in the many papers that served as arbiters of counterculture lifestyle for their local communities.

Comics offered a venue for various sorts of sexual fantasies. For example, "God Nose," one of the widely circulated and more mainstream comics, offered a storyline in which "man's prurient deeds"—specifically, fondling the enormous "tits" of a series of statues of ancient goddesses representing the world's cultures—released female powers from the past. Represented as naked women, with little in common except the size of their mammary glands, the female spirits met on "the Island of Lesbos" and plotted to turn the world's men into drones, "scrambling for the privilege of servicing [sexually] their queen." "Hereafter," the well-endowed goddess with the snakes coiled around her torso proclaimed, "men shall be kept as cows—to be milked—and most importantly, at *our* pleasure, not theirs!"[21]

A giant step along the sexual continuum from "God Nose" was the work of Zap Comix's Robert Crumb, the foremost artist in what San Francisco's *Love Street* approvingly described as an artistic "movement . . . reeking of violent paranoia, drooling with uncivilized sex lust, smacking of outright insanity, and blustering with diabolical and heavenly larfs."[22] In Crumb's "The Phonus Balonus Blues," subtitled "Another story of life and love in the big city," a drooling, slithering, slathering, slobbering creep confronts a woman on the street: "Hey Cutie! C'mere! I wanna talk to you!" She turns and runs; chasing her, he shouts: "Come back! Why does everybody hate me?" " 'Cause you're sick!" she shouts back, and he runs faster, threatening: "You'll find out how . . . heh heh . . . 'sick' I am!" Her body tilts out of the frame as she runs, and her bottom, caught just at the edge, is simply a larger version of her round breasts. The pervert continues the chase, she dashes down a dark alley (labeled "Dark Alley"), and we all know what is coming. But: "SURPRISE!" she says, bent over so far her head touches the ground, peering at him between her spread legs, no panties. The moral of the story: "Aren't girls unpredictable?"[23]

S. Clay Wilson's cover illustration for a 1966 issue of *The Screw* (Lawrence, Kansas) includes a woman, rising from a welter of bikes and bikers. She prattles on and on:

> I'VE BALLED LEROY
> I'VE BALLED HANK
> I'VE BALLED GEORGE
> I'VE BALLED WILS
> I'VE BALLED MIKE
> I'VE BALLED VAL
> I'VE BALLED GARY
> I'VE BALLED HOWARD
> I'VE BALLED WAYNE
> AND . . .

"All on their bikes too man," says one of the bikers. "Chicks suck," says another.[24]

The Fabulous Furry Freak Brothers, a comic strip about two pot-befuddled hippies plagued by Norbert the Narc, was much more widely circulated than any of the nastier sex comix. But underground papers also publicized the work of Crumb, Wilson, and others; as arbiters of counterculture, these newspapers helped to define hip transgression in such terms. Sex, here, is a weapon against repressive American culture. These representations are patently and avowedly offensive to "mainstream" standards. At the same time, such tools of revolution were part of the community-forging process in which the underground press engaged, and the aesthetics and ideologies of such comics frequently appeared as a central part of hip identity.

Not everyone agreed about such representations, and they were often juxtaposed with other images or arguments that flatly contradicted them. While these juxtapositions often appear simply incoherent today, they were also born of countercultural desires to embrace a certain latitude of lifestyle choice: "Do your own thing." Sometimes, however, the alternative visions cross the line of peaceful

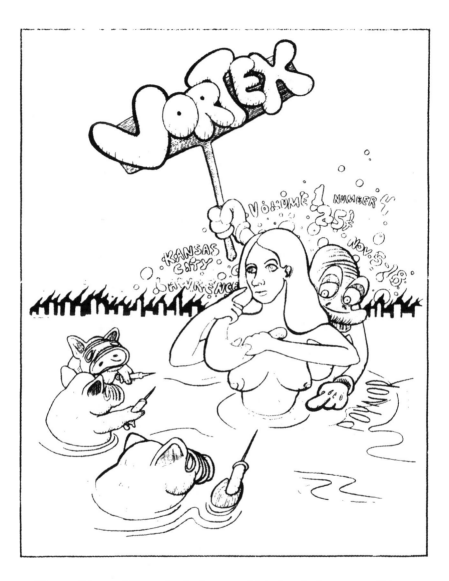

"Sex as a Weapon." Illustration by Poynor, published as the front cover of *Vortex* [Lawrence, Kansas] (5–18 November 1969). Kansas Collection, Spencer Research Library, University of Kansas.

coexistence. Throughout 1969, an advertisement in *EVO* for a new comic publication pictured a hard-looking woman sitting slumped, naked except for the suggestion of fabric draped across her lap. The drawing is in black and white, but her nipples and aureoles are tinted an odd shade of pink. "I'll bet you ten minutes on da nipple that this comic paper really gonna' set precedents in da world of culture," her pimp is saying. When *EVO* ran a major article by feminist Robin Morgan on Women's Liberation as a worldwide phenomenon in July 1969, it was flanked by this ad: "I'll bet you ten minutes on da nipple. . . ."[25]

Thus perhaps it makes sense that one of the first and most significant confrontations between men and women in the underground press, the women's takeover of the *Rat* in January 1970, was precipitated at least partly by representations of sex.[26] Issues ran much deeper than that, of course, for women in the Movement in general too often found themselves relegated to typing manifestos, not writing them, to making coffee and doing "shitwork." Stokely Carmichael had joked in 1966 that the proper position for women in the Movement was "prone," and while comments like that pushed many women to question the status quo within the Movement as well as outside it, sometimes that comment seemed a fairly accurate description of reality.[27] Women commonly found their status determined by what man each was connected to; pressure to demonstrate liberation by sleeping with Movement men was sometimes intense. "The last time I wasn't interested I was called a fridgid [*sic*] bitch," ran the caption to a feminist cartoon in Minneapolis's *Hundred Flowers*. "This time I was a bourgeois individualist."[28]

The takeover of the *Rat* by a group of women including regular staffers and other women from New York's growing radical feminist community, Redstockings, WITCHES, and Weatherwomen, was precipitated by a special issue of the *Rat* on sex and porn. S. Clay Wilson's work was there, of course, and illustrations and articles that looked to some of these women more like the "pornzines" than like a voice of revolution. The politics, sexual and otherwise, of the women's issue were not fully coherent, but it was here that Robin Morgan published her angry manifesto, "Goodbye to All That."

Morgan's essay was a powerful cry of pain and rage. She broke ranks with her brothers in revolutionary struggle, rejecting the macho posturing, the use of sex as a weapon, the exploitative sexuality that reinforced male power. "Goodbye to Hip Culture and the so-called Sexual Revolution, which has functioned toward women's freedom as did the Reconstruction toward former slaves—reinstituted oppression by another name," Morgan wrote. Goodbye to the revolutionary "brother" who "said that groupies were liberated chicks 'cause they dug a tit-shake instead of a handshake." Goodbye to the Berkeley Tribesmen for their part in publishing the comic "Trashman," and to "the reasoning that finds whoremaster Trashman a fitting model, however comic-strip far out, for a revolutionary man." Morgan attacked not only the "male-dominated Left," but also women she believed sacrificed their feminism in a "desperate grab at male approval." The women's editorial collective argued and almost didn't print it, but however controversial and divisive, "Goodbye to All That" did appear in the women's issue of *Rat*. It was reprinted in alternative papers all over the nation, circulated as a broadsheet to other communities, and discussed and debated by women and their men throughout the political and cultural revolutionary movement.[29]

Morgan's farewell may have distilled the anger many women felt, and it definitely served as foundational text for a strand of feminism critics—including feminists—would later identify as "anti-sex." But despite its historical significance, Morgan's polemic was not the first feminist objection to the role of sex in the counterculture or the political left. In the summer of 1969, women who came together from more than a dozen underground papers at the Radical Media Conference in Ann Arbor had resolved that the underground press "must undergo revolutionary changes in its relationship to and *projection of* women" [italics mine].[30]

This resolution called upon the underground press to publish more articles about women's oppression and struggles for liberation. It also insisted that women must have a "full role" in staffing the papers. (Underground papers did, in fact, pay significantly more attention to the issue of women's liberation from late 1969 forward, due in large part to the demands of women staffers.) However, the bulk of the resolution concerned representations of sex. "Male supremacy and chauvinism" must be eliminated from the papers' contents, the resolution's authors asserted, and this could only be achieved by rejecting both "commercial advertising that uses women's bodies to sell records and other products and advertisements for sex, since the use of sex as a commodity specially oppresses women in this country."

Such condemnations of commercial advertising were not especially complicated to make; countercultural sorts had been decrying the appropriation of their culture by the capitalist system ever since for-profit rock concerts. Adding sexism to the critique was simply adding a layer to the existing criticism. But then the women went a significant step further. It was just one sentence, positioned as if an afterthought: "Also, women's bodies should not be exploited in the paper for the purposes of increasing circulation." In effect, they were beginning to question the use of sexual representations as the central iconography of countercultural identity.

So many claims were made in the counterculture through representations of sex and of women's bodies that even women who hated what they saw as exploitation were not sure how to reject this version of "freedom" and revolution without returning to repression, without undermining countercultural identity. Atlanta's *Great Speckled Bird* ran the Ann Arbor resolution in full, accompanied by a response from Maude, one of the women on the *Bird*'s staff. "I am a woman," she wrote. "I demand liberation from the oppression of economic inequalities, male domination, male chauvinism. I also believe that the ultimate health of our society demands sexual liberation—liberation from puritanical attitudes toward sex." To Maude, and to many other women, the issue was not sex but exploitation. It was "puritanical," she insisted, to oppose the "non-exploitative" use of sex in the underground press.[31] Her editorial comment ran beside a series of drawings of women, a kind of anti-sex role argument in pictures. The message of the cartoon was summed up as "I jus' wanna be me," but of the seven women shown, three boasted naked breasts, complete with nipples. One of these is captioned: "Some flunk out of school (some drop out . . .)." Obviously, not everyone agreed on what was exploitative and what was not. But none of these texts—the resolution, the response, or the illustration—can be read in isolation from the others.

The *Bird*'s editorial staff eventually put the resolution to a vote, and the proposal to eliminate "male chauvinist advertising" in their paper was defeated, 10–9. Though the policy was defeated, the editors nonetheless sought to raise public consciousness about this complex issue by publishing arguments in favor of the resolution. One article, signed by the Atlanta Women's Liberation Group, pointed out that "male dominated and product dominated sexual relationships" were not equivalent to sexual liberation. Another, written by the female half of one of the *Bird*'s founding heterosexual couples, defined the problem as "exploitative capitalists"; the author had not a word of criticism for the images of women and sex generated by counterculture celebrities, or by the underground press itself.[32]

This was a common omission, whether based on a distinction between commercial and countercultural origins or simply due to obliviousness. When the Austin *Rag* published a "Woman Talk" feminist glossary, the definition of "sex object" appeared as: "a member of the female sex with prominent mammaries, usually unclothed, used to peddle plastic consumer shit."[33] Just four months earlier, the *Rag* had published the "God Nose" comic (in which men awoke the spirits of ancient goddesses by fondling the "tits" of stone statues) in the special issue on Women's Liberation. Were these images exploitative only if in service of capitalism, only if used to "peddle plastic consumer shit"? Where did "God Nose" fit?

The Ann Arbor *Argus*'s Women's Liberation supplement made a similar, though unarticulated, claim about the relations of sex, exploitation, and capitalism through its cover illustration, which was a collage of images and text from commercial advertisements. "What is the ugliest part of your body?" "How does Mrs. Burke stay as slim as her teenage daughter?" Naked breasts with prominent nipples were pasted onto the image of a model in a white swimsuit. Disembodied breasts were scattered throughout the collage. A Mark Eden breast development ad was reprinted inside. An article on women and self-defense called attention to the ways that "media and advertising" in America's "repressive culture" portray women as "playthings," with "disembodied heads, breasts, legs."[34] In words and images, the *Argus* women attacked capitalism's appropriation of female sexuality in service of commercial culture. The *Argus*, however, was part of the territory of John Sinclair, he who defined liberation as "say[ing] hello to a chick by grabbin' her ass" and raved to counterculture interviewers about the "huge beautiful fuckin' tits" of fifteen-year-old girls. This feminist critique of the sexual exploitation in mainstream culture left such counterculture definitions of sexual freedom unchallenged and uninterrogated.

To some extent, these awkward omissions, the missing criticism, make sense. Throughout the United States, young women and men were rebelling against repressive and often hypocritical rules governing sexual behavior. They were engaged in sexual revolution. In this context, a wide range of sexual images and claims carried the potential for sexual liberation; they both embodied and represented the freedom that many women and men were seeking.

However, the criticisms of the use of sex within the counterculture are not missing *simply* because women in the counterculture saw sexual representations as liberating, for many vehemently criticized what they identified as sexual exploitation outside the Movement. In these cases, women may well have believed that the exploitative images produced by the capitalist, materialist system were fundamentally different from those generated by the counterculture. Or they may have seen those "capitalist" images as a sufficient target, and been concerned that criticizing the counterculture on such grounds would play into the hands of their enemies. After all, many of the radical women who took over the *Rat* in New York were reluctant to publish Robin Morgan's "Goodbye to All That," at least partially because of its scathing attack on sexual exploitation within the counterculture and the political left. Not everyone agreed on the best means to the goal of liberation.

All these explanations are valid to some extent, yet there is another significant piece to this puzzle. Counterculture representations of sex, both as weapons against straight culture and as a quintessential definition of freedom and liberation, were at the heart of the culture and politics of a large portion of the hip community. Sex had become such a critical part of the language of liberation that it was difficult to jettison it, more difficult yet to replace or recast it. While many women tried and some succeeded, others feared that such attempts were merely a return to repression. Thus it was not only in the silences that confusion and ambivalence were manifest, but in the texts and images women themselves produced.

At *Vortex* in Lawrence, Kansas, inspired by news of the women's takeover of the *Rat*, women staffers demanded the right to put out their own women's issue. They didn't write very much of what appeared in it; the issue's centerpiece was a reprint of Morgan's "Goodbye to All That." But they did select the material and control the layout and the artwork, which turned out to be the most complex aspect of the women's issue.[35] The front cover is lovely, a kind of vague vaginal imagery done in a pastel wash, à la Georgia O'Keeffe. There are no written comments to substantiate this interpretation, but perhaps this shift from the usual fetishized breasts (as common in *Vortex* as elsewhere) to an abstractly rendered vagina served as a gendered claim to power, a rejection of male objectification of female bodies by claiming a new mode and site of sexual representation.

Once again, however, one set of images and claims is accompanied by others that contradict it. The back cover of the women's issue of *Vortex* is an unsigned comic, "The Crank Case," which falls squarely into the "sex as weapon" category of countercultural revolution. Two women sit, smoking dope. One is heavy, with hairy legs. She has a phallus and the words "PRICKS FOREVER" tattooed on her left bicep. The other, clearly blonde even in a black-and-white line drawing, is tall and busty and pretty. Suddenly, the pretty one rises and shouts: "I'm sick of it, Edowda Miekunt!! Every magazine shows a bare female ass or tit, but . . . NO CRANKS!"

They take it to court, "Judge Crulius Halfman" (after Judge Julius Hoffman of the Chicago Seven trial) presiding, and charge the "artists of Amerika" with ignoring the desires of women "by showing NO CRANKS." Weeks drag by, "tension MOUNTS," and finally "the case reaches CLIMAX." Judge Halfman erupts: "I WANT FUCK!" Edowda Miekunt shouts, "Climb on! I Can Dig It!" and, kneeling doggie-style, is sodomized by a disembodied "prick." The judge gets the busty blonde, but when she tells him he's a "real bad lay," he reasserts his judicial power. "For that, bitch, I charge you with contempt of court and sentence you to ten years in bed with the Amerikan pig force." The last frame has our blonde heroine spread-eagled on the ground, performing fellatio on one "pig" while another uses his finger for what the *Rat*'s special issue on sex and porn had called "Clit Flit." The moral of the story? "PIG NATION TRIHUMPS again."

The women relinquished control for the next issue, but they got a full page of letters in response to their efforts. All of the writers assumed that the

"Women's Liberation." Illustration by Grant Canfield, published in a special issue of *Vortex* [Lawrence, Kansas] (1–14 April 1970), n.p., on the topic of the Women's Liberation movement and edited by female members of this underground newspaper's staff. Kansas Collection, Spencer Research Library, Unversity of Kansas.

women had not been responsible for that comic but had been somehow sabotaged by hostile men. "Did the guys give you only certain sections of the paper?" asked the Kansas City Women's Liberation Group.[36] The most pointed and articulate criticism came from a man in Manhattan, Kansas, who also assumed that the women were not responsible for that cartoon. Referring to "that excrescence on the back page," he insisted: "Pig nation triumphed throughout that cartoon, not just at the end. Pig nation triumphed when Vortex ran that cartoon, and it will continue to triumph so long as 'underground' papers indiscriminately take anything that offends the old culture as being therefore revolutionary."[37] But the cartoon had not been drawn by men; it was created by two of the *Vortex* women using an accustomed vocabulary of countercultural revolution.

The soft pastels of the watercolor on the cover, Robin Morgan's "Goodbye to All That," and "The Crank Case" strained against one another in the *Vortex* women's issue. One offered an alternate sexuality, one rejected the iconography and practice of sex as a weapon, the third embraced it. These three statements were not presented as the range of options the counterculture offered, but appeared instead as a sign of incoherence, of the fundamental fragility of this cultural community. Sex & drugs & rock and roll? Sex seemed as likely to tear this community apart as to bind it together.

And, increasingly, that was what happened. As more and more women—sometimes joined by gay men—began to insist that the adolescent male fantasies of unfettered "tits" and violent rape did not symbolize their cultural revolutions, the uneasy alliance of communities that had come together to form a counterculture began to dissolve and resolve into new strands. By the end of the 1960s, much of the counterculture aesthetic summed up by "sex & drugs & rock and roll" had become largely synonymous with youth culture. What were formerly markers of opposition now signaled revolutionary intent less than they demonstrated belonging in a vast and powerful peer culture.

Inherent in the exclamation "sex & drugs & rock and roll" was a fundamental belief in freedom, above all else freedom through bodily liberation. Sexual liberation was at the very center of those claims to freedom. But the specific representations of that sexual freedom in the late 1960s and early 1970s counterculture—and in fact much of its practice—eventually were seen by many women and some men as nothing more than a new form of an old sort of exploitation. One of the core beliefs in which hip communities sought to ground their culture had imploded by the early 1970s through this redefinition of "sexual liberation" as sexual exploitation. The counterculture does not disappear because of this confrontation, but it does fragment and emerge in new configurations, including a strand of feminism that was extremely suspicious of (hetero)sex, as well as a strand that embraced a woman-centered version of graphic sexual images.

Those who continued to take cultural revolution seriously had to contend with the legacy of sex in the counterculture. Men and women struggled over the power relations embodied in the sexual images that had suffused the underground press. While these issues were resolved in individual lives, the larger question of the place of sex in the counterculture was put to rest by the demise of this particular countercultural aesthetic, not by any direct resolution.

The lure of sexual transgression as a key to human liberation is a powerful strand of twentieth-century American thought, from Henry Miller to Robert Crumb to Gangsta Rap. Too often, as the experience of America's 1960s counterculture shows, the transgressive does not serve cleanly as a path to liberation; it is also a form of exploitation of those with less power, often within the sub/counterculture itself. That is a lesson worth remembering, as too many academic champions of cultural rebellion today embrace the transgressive, without adequate concern for the proximate targets of that transgression.

NOTES

1. The secondary works most useful to me in writing this article were Abe Peck, *Uncovering the Sixties: The Life and Times of the Underground Press* (New York: Pantheon, 1985); Terry H. Anderson, *The Movement and the Sixties: Protest in America from Greensboro to Wounded Knee* (New York: Oxford University Press, 1995); David Farber, *The Age of Great Dreams: America in the 1960s* (New York: Hill & Wang, 1994); and Ken Cmiel, "The Politics of Civility," in *The Sixties: From Memory to History,* ed. David Farber (Chapel Hill: University of North Carolina Press, 1994).

2. John Sinclair and D. A. Latimer, untitled, *East Village Other* (*EVO*), 4 June 1969, 3.

3. Peck, *Uncovering*, 86, 183.

4. "Free-dom in Spite of the U.," *The Paper* (East Lansing, Mich.), 23 January 1968, 6.

5. Illustration, *EVO*, 1–7 March 1968, 19.

6. Herb Williams, "Naked," and photos by Sylvester Rising, *Vortex* (Lawrence, Kans.), 18 November–2 December 1969, 17.

7. Illustration, *Rag* (Austin), 24 July 1969, 4.

8. Advertisement, *Great Speckled Bird* (*GSB*), (Atlanta), 15 September 1969, 14.

9. Illustration, *GSB*, 13 October 1969, 6.

10. "Sex Supplement," *Hundred Flowers* (Minneapolis), 4 September 1970.

11. For example, see *Argus* (Ann Arbor), 9—23 February 1970, 13.

12. Excerpt from poem by John Siedler, in *Asterisk*, 8 January 1969, quoted in Anderson, *The Movement*, 256.

13. Algernon Backwash and M. Rodriquez, "Subvert Comix," *EVO*, 1–7 March 1968, 17.

14. Paul M. Mayer, "Free John Sinclair," *Free Press of Louisville,* 3 September 1970, 17. Mayer is quoting D. A. Latimer from Countdown 1.

15. "Our Omaha Report," *The Screw* (Lawrence, Kans.), 15 March 1968, 11.

16. John Sinclair, *Guitar Army: Street Writings/Prison Writings* (New York: Douglas, 1972).

17. Sinclair and Latimer, untitled, *EVO*.

18. Peck, *Uncovering*, 15; Anderson, *The Movement*, 286.

19. Jaakov Kohn, "Conversation with Ed Sanders," *EVO*, 30 July 1969, 5.

20. Peck, *Uncovering*, 211.

21. Jaxon, "God Nose," Austin *Rag*, March 1969; reprinted from the *San Francisco Express Times*.

22. Robert Gold, "Alternate Comics," Haight-Ashbury *Love Street*, 2, no. 2, n.d. (1968?), n.p.

23. Robert Crumb, "Phonus Balonus Blues," Haight-Ashbury *Love Street*, 2, no. 2, n.d. (1968?), n.p.

24. S. Clay Wilson, cover, *The Screw*, 18 November 1966.

25. Advertisement, *EVO*, 23 April 1969, 20; with Robin Morgan article: *EVO*, 23 July 1969, 18.

26. See account in Peck, *Uncovering*, chap. 13, and Alice Echols, *Daring to Be Bad* (Minneapolis: University of Minnesota Press, 1989), 248.

27. See the account in Echols, *Daring to Be Bad*, 31.

28. Eileen, Cartoon, *Hundred Flowers*, 18 September 1970.

29. Peck, *Uncovering*, 212; for context, see Ann Barr Snitow et al., eds., *Powers of Desire: The Politics of Sexuality* (New York: Monthly Press, 1983). Morgan's screed is reprinted in *Dear Sisters: Dispatches from the Women's Liberation Movement* eds. Rosalyn Baxandall and Linda Gordon (New York: Basic Books, 2000), 53–57.

30. Resolution reprinted in Atlanta's *GSB*, 4 August 1969, 10.

31. Maude, "Sex Ad Sell-Out?" *GSB*, 4 August 1969, 10.

32. Pam Gwin, "Buy, Sell, Don't Smell—Advertising and the Underground," *GSB*, 15 December 1969, 11.

33. "Woman Talk," Austin *Rag*, 3 July 1969, 11.

34. "Women's Liberation Supplement," Ann Arbor *Argus*, 9–23 February 1970, cover and 11–15. Untitled article on self-defense is by Beth Schneider, 15. The phrase "What's the ugliest part of your body?" is the title of a cut from the Mothers of Invention album *We're Only in It for the Money* (MGM/Verve Records, 1967).

35. Women's Issue of *Vortex*, 1–14 April 1970.

36. Kansas City Women's Liberation, "Dear Sisters," *Vortex*, 1–14 April 1970.

37. Delbert Petrick, "Dear Editors," *Vortex*, 1–14 April 1970.

Section Five
Alternative Visions

Introduction

"Turn On, Tune In, Drop Out": when Timothy Leary coined that signature slogan of the counterculture, he meant it as a precise protocol for altering one's consciousness (see David Farber's essay). But the phrase can equally well apply to incremental degrees of involvement with a countercultural lifestyle. Many people in the "straight"(non-counterculture) world "turned on" to the ideas, lifestyle, and modalities of the counterculture without really adopting them, maybe buying a fringed mohair vest or learning jargon like "groovy" or "I'm hip to where you're at, man," all the while beefing up their stock portfolios and hoping for that "big promotion" at work. Other people "tuned in" to the cultural revolution with more open arms, perhaps migrating to one of the short-lived hippie enclaves scattered throughout the country, consuming vast amounts of pot and LSD, or reading up on Theravada Buddhism. This is what could be called a "Beatles in 1967" level of involvement. But there was a third tier of counterculture diehards, those who didn't wait for the implosion of the "capitalist mother country" to fashion a totalistic alternative way of life. Instead, sizable numbers of Americans did in fact "drop out" of the core society, migrating to communes nationwide and engaging in various forms of pastoral, communitarian experiments. Indeed, for a while in the 1960s and '70s, the commune—whether urban or rural—had replaced the circus as the popular destination of choice for teenage runaways escaping their parents.

As Timothy Miller makes clear in his essay on "The Sixties-Era Communes," the hallmark of back-to-the-land counterculture communes was diversity. While the typical commune emblazoned in most people's minds resembles the desperate utopia depicted in *Easy Rider*, collective living arrangements varied greatly in terms of drug use, religious orientation, and economic structure. Andy Kirk in "'Machines of Loving Grace': Alternative Technology, Environment, and the Counterculture" focuses on a related line of development. The counterculture environmental movement, fed by post-scarcity notions of impending automation, ruptured the neo-Luddite, or technophobic, course of environmental thought in an embrace of radical technological innovation that would undergird the "drop out" scenarios of counterculturists nationwide.

Twelve

The Sixties-Era Communes

Timothy Miller

Communal living is a venerable part of the American past, a patchwork fabric of remote collective villages, progressive social experiments, and millennial religious encampments, among many other threads, that has been continuously present in one venue or another since the seventeenth century. In the mid-1960s communitarian idealism erupted in what was to be by far its largest manifestation ever, when hundreds of thousands, perhaps even a million, of mostly young Americans sought to rebuild from the ground up what they perceived as a rotten, decadent society. Oddly, most of the recent literature on Sixties culture ignores the communes, although they were a critical manifestation of the spirit of the time. That lack of attention helps explain why the communes seem to be rather imperfectly remembered as a phenomenon in American cultural history, and this essay will seek to help straighten some twisted historical assumptions as it describes and depicts the piece of the Sixties that was communal living.

The most common mistake is the presumption that a stereotype called the "hippie commune" accurately represents the historical reality of the day. The error is understandable, because rural hippie communes captured a great deal of media attention in the Sixties era (here defined as approximately 1960 to 1975), what with their funky architecture, outlandish clothing styles, and lifestyles widely believed to be dominated by endemic drug use and free love.

However, like most stereotypes, that one is riddled with problems. It was created largely by sensational media coverage; journalists then as now were always looking for the unusual story, and who could resist such a visually compelling subject, with its great photo opportunities and provocative quirkiness? It's not surprising that the more exotic communes got the attention, and an enduring image of the Sixties commune thus took shape.

But reality was something else. The hip communes were not routinely ravaged by drugs, although pyschedelics were certainly often present. Although most did not condemn unconventional sexual relationships (i.e., anything other than marital heterosex), communards' levels of sexual activity and numbers of partners were if anything lower than those of their noncommunal peers. Some communes were spontaneously created and maintained an open-door policy on residency, but many more were deliberately planned entities that screened potential members. And, importantly, the hip communes were a minority in the overall communal scene. The thousands of religiously committed communes often sharply limited sexual activity and prohibited all drugs, including tobacco, alcohol, and psychedelics. A key to understanding the communes of the Sixties era is that they were enormously, endlessly diverse. Indeed, a more disparable lot of social groups could hardly be imagined. The diversity of the communal world and the difficulty even of defining "commune" precisely was addressed by one reflective Oregon communard:

> Each commune is different. There are communes that live on brown rice, and communes that have big gardens, and communes that buy white bread and frozen vegetables at the grocery store. There are communes with no schedule whatsoever (and no clocks); there is at least one commune where the entire day is divided into sections by bells, and each person states, at a planning meeting at 7 A.M. each morning, what work he intends to do that day. There are communes centered around a particular piece of land, like us, or travelling communes like the Hog Farm, or communes centered around a music trip or a political trip, like many of the city communes.
>
> This diversity raises certain questions. A piece of land that's simply thrown open to anyone who wants to live there, or a place where each family lives entirely in its own house but the land is owned jointly: shall we call these places "communes" or not? Communes differ greatly. . . .[1]

The thousands of intentional communities that embodied the subject at hand included Asian religious ashrams, group marriage experiments, communal rock bands, "Jesus freak" houses, centers of radical politics, and back-to-the-land experiments in agricultural self-sufficiency. The variation was endless, mind-boggling. No one will ever know precisely how many communes there were in the American Sixties era, but they probably ran to tens of thousands. Together they constituted a social phenomenon of remarkable proportions.[2]

FOUNDATIONS

Much that was widely regarded as novel in the Sixties-era communes had actually surfaced in communal experiments as much as a century and a half earlier. Nudity and free love were promoted by more than a few nineteenth-century social radicals and were practiced or at least discussed at dozens of intentional communities; the Home Colony in Washington state, a notable experiment in anarchist communitarianism founded in 1897, had one of its greatest internal conflicts over some members' practice of nude swimming in Puget Sound. Vegetarianism and healthy eating had many communitarian exponents beginning as far back as Bronson Alcott's Fruitlands community, founded in 1843. Political radicals banded together into intentional communities such as the Llano Colony (1916) and the Kaweah Cooperative Commonwealth (1885) to challenge the capitalist domination of society. Hundreds of earlier American communities espoused rural idealism, built their own rude buildings, and thumbed their noses at majoritarian society.

1960s-era counterculturists were romantics and have often been characterized as ahistorical in the sense that they had little awareness of the larger dissenting cultural traditions in which their own social flowering was situated. It is undoubtedly true that many hip young Americans, commune dwellers and otherwise, knew little about the historical lineage into which they were stepping, but again one should not rely overmuch on stereotypes here. As new and unusual as they seemed, the Sixties-era communes actually had clear roots in the American radical and communal past. Many commune dwellers were living links with that past, among them a fair contingent of red-diaper babies; in surprisingly many cases they grew up in families of socialists, communists, or communards, and already knew the vocabulary and spirit of cooperation intimately. Ramón Sender, for example, the first resident at Morning Star Ranch in northern California, was born in Spain the son of a famous writer who had been influenced by the anarchist communes of Catalonia during the Spanish Civil War. In the United States the younger Sender married a great-granddaughter of John Humphrey Noyes, the founder of the Oneida Community in New York state in the mid-nineteenth century. He and his wife embarked on their own communal odyssey by moving for a time into the Bruderhof, a German-founded commune operating in New York state. Community was in his blood when the 1960s rolled around.[3]

Others became ardent students of the history of intentional community in their desire to root the present in the past. John Curl, one of the early residents of the pioneer Drop City commune, became an accomplished historian of cooperation and community.[4] The pages of *The Modern Utopian*, the trade journal of the 1960s communes, were regularly infused with articles on earlier communitarianism. Some communes studied or imitated earlier communes—Israeli kibbutzim, for example, or nineteenth-century radical social reform communities. The members of a San Francisco commune popularly known as Kaliflower studied the nineteenth-century communal classic *The History of American Socialisms* by Oneida's Noyes, and emulated Oneida in some of their own communal practices.[5]

For that matter, the communitarianism of earlier generations had not died out when the 1960s arrived, and living examples of community helped energize the new experiments. Koinonia Farm, for example, the interracial community founded by Clarence Jordan in southern Georgia in 1942, was the destination for many a 1960s pilgrimage. The birthplace of the Habitat for Humanity housing programs, Koinonia was a beacon of the kinds of values the Sixties generation stood for—equality, simple living, moral passion. Quarry Hill, in Vermont, had been founded as a community of artists in the 1940s and served as an inspiration to many of the communes eventually founded in that state. The Catholic Worker movement, which combined communal living, dedicated service to the poor, and devout Roman Catholicism, had been attracting communitarian idealists since the 1930s, and its alumni and alumnae were later found in many of the new communes. Heathcote Center in Maryland, founded at that location by Mildred Loomis in 1965 but rooted solidly in Ralph Borsodi's communitarian School of Living that dated to 1936, attracted many new-generation communards with its pursuit of self-sufficient living and its critique of modern industrial society—so much so that in effect it became a hippie commune.

Moreover, the whole 1960s cultural upheaval had important roots in a long-developing alternative culture that went back at least to mid-nineteenth-century America. Those roots are discussed elsewhere in this volume and do not need to be rehearsed here. The point is simply that the communes were no less historically grounded than any other part of the culture of the day.

New Communal Beginnings

The first stirrings of 1960s communalism came early in the decade. One early outburst of the new communal spirit came with the appearance of the Merry Pranksters, a group of artists and rebels who began to coalesce in Palo Alto, California. At their center was the charismatic author Ken Kesey who had volunteered to be a subject in LSD experiments beginning in 1959; four years later the Pranksters took up residence at Kesey's new home at nearby La Honda. No one ever exactly declared the La Honda property a *commune*, but the ever-changing crowd there (sometime participants ranged from poet Allen Ginsberg to Hell's Angels motorcycle gang members to Jerry Garcia and other members of the band that would become the Grateful Dead) presaged what would soon take place in hundreds of places around the world.[6] Meanwhile, in 1962 a bohemian encampment called Gorda Mountain began to take shape after Amelia Newell opened her land near Big Sur, California to anyone who wanted to stay there, thus inaugurating the first open-land experiment of the new communal generation. In its early years Gorda Mountain was a small and quiet encampment, but with the rise of the Haight-Ashbury scene a couple of hours to the north the settlement burgeoned in mid-decade, reaching a population of around two hundred and inspiring great animosity among its neighbors, who deemed it a social cesspool.

A major foundation stone in the new communal style was laid in 1963 when Huw "Piper" Williams established Tolstoy Farm near Davenport, Washington. Williams, a veteran peace activist who had been influenced by Gandhi, Quaker pacifists, and Catholic Workers, among others, had been inspired by living in an intentional community of radical pacifists in Connecticut and upon returning home organized a self-sufficient collective whose only rule would be that no one could be asked to leave. Still in existence in the late 1990s, Tolstoy could plausibly be regarded as the oldest surviving 1960s commune. It attracted around fifty members its first summer and dedicated itself to simple living. The members worked hard to be agriculturally self-sufficient and to avoid the money economy altogether. Their devotion to not having rules meant that those who wanted to grow marijuana couldn't be stopped, so Tolstoy suffered two major pot busts. But somehow it all worked. People put what little money they came upon into the common treasury, an envelope tacked up on the wall, and after the main house burned down mysteriously in 1968, they just built new little structures here and there and persevered. Thus does a decentralized Tolstoy, its land still in common ownership, survive today.[7]

These scattered and disparate jolts of communal energy turned a collective corner with the founding of Drop City near Trinidad, Colorado, in May 1965. Drop City brought together most of the themes that had been developing in other recent communities—anarchy, pacifism, voluntary poverty, sexual freedom, rural isolation, psychedelics, art—in a flamboyant commune unlike any that had gone before. The founders, Gene Bernofsky, Jo Ann Bernofsky, and Clark Richert, who as students at the University of Kansas had developed an improvisational kind of expression they called "drop art," pooled their meager savings to buy six acres of scrub goat pasture and found an artists' community that would amount to a veritable new civilization. As Jo Ann Bernofsky later articulated their vision,

> We knew that we wanted to do something outrageous and we knew we wanted to do it with other people, because it was more exciting to be with a group than to be just one or two or three people. There was this kind of heady arrogance—talk about arrogance!—that we could just do something so outrageous and so far out, that we could pull it off even though none of us had many resources. . . . It was full of vitality, and it was extremely exciting and wonderful. You had the sense that anything was possible, that the potential was unlimited.[8]

Materially Drop City was desperately poor, but to the Droppers poverty was a state of mind. They anticipated an attitude that would fuel much commune building later in the decade, a conviction that modern society had become so materially productive that real scarcity and want were things of the past, that dropouts could live on the leftovers of an affluent society. As Richert put it, "we were not in a state of poverty mentally, and no one ever went hungry. We owned our land, our buildings, owed no rent, were free of employment, free to create. I felt freer at Drop City than at any other time in my life, and I just can't see that as poverty."

The Droppers lived in near anarchy, sharing their meager food and money, creating art that included visionary paintings and one of the first underground comic books. They built a solar collector to heat a building before many Americans had even heard of the concept of alternative energy. Inspired by the visionary designs of Buckminster Fuller, the Droppers were soon building quasi-geodesic domes from scrap materials, covering them with tops of cars they chopped with axes from junkyard hulks. The fantastic visual presence of the multicolored, funky domes and other artworks, the Droppers' rejection of mainstream American values and attitudes, and an open-door approach to membership attracted media attention and swarms of visitors. As the decade progressed and young Americans began seeking alternatives to mainline culture, Drop City stood as an accessible model of what a new America might look like. To paraphrase Bob Dylan's lyric, something was happening, Mr. Jones.[9]

A major milestone in the new wave of communes came in the spring of 1966 when Ramón Sender and others began to move onto Lou Gottlieb's Morning Star Ranch an hour and a half north of San Francisco. Gottlieb, well known as the bassist for the Limeliters, a popular folk music trio, soon decided that his thirty-one acres would be open to all who would come—indeed, that the universe itself demanded that land not be "owned" by any mortal human but exist as the common possession of all. A freewheeling scene that easily tolerated nudity, free love, and psychedelics quickly developed, and by 1967 and the Summer of Love hundreds were grooving at Morning Star. Irate neighbors tried repeatedly to coerce Gottlieb to shut the place down; he responded by deeding the land to God and preaching all the more passionately his doctrine of open land. Only after lengthy court battles and, finally, a series of bulldozings of the many impromptu dwellings on the property in the early 1970s did the Sonoma County authorities manage to shut Morning Star down. Many of the refugees landed at nearby Wheeler's Ranch, where Bill Wheeler, a convert to the vision of open land, followed Gottlieb's example of opening his property—much more extensive and remote than Morning Star—to all comers. But once again Sonoma County officialdom intervened, and by 1973 the two grand experiments in northern California open-land communalism were history.[10]

The East Coast also saw its share of early Sixties-era communes. Inspired by B. F. Skinner's utopian novel *Walden Two*,[11] which depicted an orderly communal society whose members lived very comfortably while performing agreeable labor, a group of social pioneers founded Walden House in Washington, D.C. in 1965. By 1967 these urban communitarians and others were ready to leave the city and move to a rundown tobacco farm in Virginia. They crammed themselves into the small existing farmhouse, began learning how to grow crops, and, for income, started weaving rope hammocks—a cottage industry that soon became the community's economic backbone. Twin Oaks was the incarnated dream of social engineers rather than a loose confederation of freewheeling hippies (although it soon took on a countercultural aura), and unlike a fair number of other communitarian experiments, Twin Oaks never avoided regulations and structures. It worked out a government involving community planners and managers and required fixed amounts of labor from all its members. On the other hand, members were also provided a great deal of freedom, with flexibility in work schedules and, within broad limits, the liberty to engage in such personal behavior as they chose, including nudity and any sexual relationships that did not disturb community life. The community learned to accommodate a wide range of dietary preferences in its common dining hall. The Twin Oaks economy has always been thoroughly communal; members' basic life needs—food, housing, medical care, recreation—are met by the community, and each member gets a small, equal allowance for such nonessentials as candy, tobacco, and alcohol. A prime example of a community that has survived with its 1960s values pretty much intact, Twin Oaks has grown to a stable population of around one hundred on several hundred acres and has even spawned an offshoot community, Acorn, a few miles away.[12]

THE GREAT COUNTERCULTURAL COMMUNAL EXPLOSION, 1967–75

Between the autumn of 1967 and the early 1970s this modest wave of new communes reached tsunami proportions. The motivations for commune building were many: some hippies abandoned their urban enclaves for more peaceful rural surroundings, especially with the decline of hip neighborhoods in New York, San Francisco, and other cities following the Summer of Love (1967); activists working for social change found community a useful base for the struggle; religious seekers sought to pursue the life of the spirit with others of like mind; Woodstock and other rock festivals offered a slice of heaven that maybe, just maybe, could be made permanent. The sense that Western culture had defeated scarcity was important; an abundantly productive economy produced so many goods and services that those willing to live on the leftovers could actually do very well. (The anti-scarcity theme had by now been well articulated by the Diggers, who preached an anti-money gospel and practiced "garbage yoga" in San Francisco, dishing up free food from society's excess, opening free stores, housing crashers in their communal dwellings, and founding a free medical clinic.) Whatever the exact causes of it all, thousands upon thousands of communes were founded between 1967 and 1975. Only a very few representative examples can be described even briefly here.

California and the Pacific Northwest continued to be major centers of communal life in the late 1960s and early '70s. One notable outpost, and perhaps America's most remote 1960s commune, was Black Bear Ranch, founded in a mountainous part of northern California far from any city by radicals who intended it as an outpost of revolutionary politics—a place surrounded by national forest where rifle practice, for example, could be carried out ten miles from the nearest neighbor. Black Bear had once been a rich gold mine, but its boomtown had been left to ghosts when the seams played out, and by 1968 the site, with several buildings still standing, was for sale for a song. The envisioned radical enclave never really materialized, because many of those who came streaming in were not interested in paramilitary activities. Instead, Black Bear's great isolation caused it to become one of the most self-sufficient communes of them all. Residents gathered vast piles of firewood, butchered animals for food, built a small hydroelectric power system, ran a sawmill, schooled their children, and took care of medical problems with impressive sophistication. Eventually integrating themselves into the surrounding culture to some small extent, several Black Bear members became forest firefighters, and the small bit of occasional income that resulted from that on-demand labor provided enough money to get by. Over time the founders drifted away, but Black Bear lives on, populated by a small but committed second generation of communards.[13]

A communal adobe house-raising bee at New Buffalo, Arroyo Honda (near Taos), New Mexico, August 1967. The act of constructing a communal dwelling served to foster a sense of group cohesiveness, which was essential to an intentional community's survival. Copyright © Lisa Law.

One of the principal magnets for the new communalism was northern New Mexico, and especially the Taos area. An early harbinger of the social revolution was New Buffalo, founded in 1967 a few miles north of Taos by a group of newly arrived New Mexicans deeply interested in American Indian culture who hoped to join a peyote-using church. One of them agreed to spend a good deal of his inheritance on land for the group, and thus they purchased an initial hundred acres. They immediately began to build adobe buildings in the local pueblo style; the main structure had a large oval gathering room with, appropriately, a mounted buffalo head on the wall. Many of the residents lived in tepees around the property. For these communal pioneers New Buffalo was to be what the buffalo had been to the Native Americans, a source of all the needs of life for its people. But it was never an easy life; agriculture was difficult in the arid climate of northern New Mexico, and the cold winters challenged all but the hardiest. As visitors and new members streamed in, the need for making adobe bricks for new buildings seemed endless. Overcrowded in the summer and struggling through the winters, New Buffalo had a remarkably long and stable history, given its circumstances. In the late 1990s its days as an intentional community were apparently coming to an end;

the family of one of the cofounders had recently run it as a hip bed and breakfast but by the latter part of the decade had decided to sell and move elsewhere.[14]

A neighboring community from the 1960s, however, has been more stable. The Lama Foundation was founded in 1967 as a center for spiritual seekers and has remained a nonsectarian religious community since. It has long had a close association with Ram Dass (Richard Alpert), the popular New Age spiritual teacher, and has built an "industry" out of hosting spiritual conferences and workshops for paying attendees. Lama achieved solid countercultural visibility with its publication in 1971 of *Be Here Now*, a spiritual pastiche by Ram Dass and others that sold a reported half million copies and became a countercultural bible.[15] Community members built a central complex with a domed assembly building and a kitchen, and then added scattered private homes and retreat huts around the property. The community's greatest challenge came in 1996 when it suffered a disastrous fire, but it has struggled back and, despite losing some residents (many houses were burned to the ground), has reestablished a solid conference schedule.

Although New Mexico and California seemed to stand out on the national communal map, plenty was also happening in and near the population centers of the East. Packer Corner Farm, in southern Vermont, was home to a group of communal literati who produced some of the counterculture's most eloquent literature, including Raymond Mungo's *Total Loss Farm*[16] and a group volume, *Home Comfort*.[17] The Packer group coalesced in Washington, D. C. and New York City within the staff of Liberation News Service, the chief supplier of copy to the nation's then burgeoning underground press. Tiring of the endless conflict involved in the political movements of the Vietnam era, and hearing, as did so many others, the siren song of country communal living, they pooled their resources to make a down payment on a new communal home in Guilford, Vermont. There they wrote their books, for a time published a periodical called the *Green Mountain Post*, and pursued self-sufficient living. Although most of the original members drifted off the farm over time, some still live nearby, and close friendships remain. The farm itself continues with a newer cast of characters, including some second-generation residents who grew up there in the 1970s and 80s.

The South probably had fewer communes than any other part of the country, but it was the home of the Farm, the largest 1960s-era commune and perhaps the most influential of them all. Stephen Gaskin rose to prominence as a hippie spiritual teacher in San Francisco, where by 1969 thousands were attending the Monday Night Class each week to hear his recasting of ancient truths in contemporary language. At one point Gaskin undertook a speaking tour, and so many of his disciples wanted to go with him that they formed a caravan of dozens of old schoolbuses and other wheezing vehicles in which to accompany him. Back in San Francisco they wanted to make their mobile community permanent, and thus these fervent idealists, after another lengthy caravan, settled in 1971 outside Summertown, Tennessee. There they built a community from the ground up that reached a peak population a decade later of around fifteen hundred. Strict vegans, they were pioneers in the natural foods movement (soybean-based ice cream was but one of their inventions). They were forthcoming about the psychedelic dimension of their spirituality; as Gaskin taught, "We believe that if a vegetable and an animal want to get together and can be heavier together than either one of them alone, it shouldn't be anybody else's business."[18] That philosophy did not carry much weight with the local authorities, and just a few months after their arrival Stephen and three others were arrested for growing marijuana. They spent a year in prison, but things managed to hang together and the Farm had a decade of growth and fame yet ahead. The Farmers learned secrets of low-tech living from their Amish neighbors (indeed, the tie-dyed Farm hippies sometimes called themselves "technicolor Amish") and lived for years in tents and the many school buses that had been parked on the property permanently.

Saving the world headed the Farm's agenda, and the commune soon found itself running a wide range of charitable projects. Always family-oriented and opposed to abortion, the Farm developed a circle of midwives who ran a birthing clinic—one that made this simple but comprehensive free offer: "Hey Ladies! Don't have an abortion, come to the Farm and we'll deliver your baby and take care of it, and if you ever decide you want it back, you can have it."[19] A foundation called Plenty undertook projects that ranged from Third World agricultural education to an ambulance service in the Bronx. For more than a decade the community was a bright beacon to a generation of idealistic, community-minded youth. In the early 1980s a lingering economic crisis led to a radical restructuring of the Farm, and the completely common treasury was abandoned in favor of a system in which members had to pay dues. The community went through a radical depopulation, but after a time it regained some stability and in the late 1990s continued to be the home of some two hundred persons.[20]

INTENTIONAL COMMUNITIES FOR SPIRITUAL GROWTH AND SOCIAL CHANGE

Although the rural hip communes were the most colorful of the genre and got the lion's share of media attention, they were greatly outnumbered by thousands of communal religious and spiritual centers and communes for social change, the latter usually urban. Such communities represented the spectrum of world religions and the gamut of political and social thought. Probably the most numerous of the many new Christian communes were those of the Jesus Movement, populated by Jesus Freaks, as they were commonly called, who took on the clothing and other outward trappings of the hippies while espousing a fundamentalist type of Christianity. The Jesus Movement took shape in the late 1960s; its churches and communes were sometimes independent, sometimes affiliated with an existing denomination or local church. Unlike some other categories of communities, the Jesus communes tended to be structured and often authoritarian, with control residing in a single spiritual teacher or council of elders. In more than a few cases they were strongly patriarchal, interpreting the Bible in a way that relegated women to limited, traditional roles.

The largest of the independent Jesus Movement communal networks was called the Shiloh Youth Revival Centers. Shiloh emerged in 1968 in Costa Mesa, California, when John Higgins, a new Christian convert, began converting others and inviting them to live in his home, which he called the "house of miracles." The following year the group, then numbering about thirty, migrated to Eugene, Oregon, where they bought a ninety–acre tract of rural land for a national headquarters. Shiloh soon had an impressive string of businesses and assets—it owned farms, fishing boats, a logging company, and a twin-engined airplane, among other things—and more than 175 communal residences. For about a decade the optimistic evangelical faith of the members sustained them well. In the late 1970s, however, the membership that had peaked at over a thousand dropped precipitously and businesses and property had to be sold or abandoned. Even the headquarters property was seized by the Internal Revenue Service for unpaid taxes and interest. Soon the largest of the Jesus communes had dissolved.[21]

Other Jesus Movement communes, however, proved more durable. Jesus People USA, for example, has become one of the largest single-site intentional communities in the United States since its somewhat spontaneous ignition within a fundamentalist youth ministry in Milwaukee about 1972. Settling in Chicago by 1974, members began to buy property and businesses and eventually moved en masse into a run-down hotel they had purchased, a building large enough to house their many members and still have space for a low-income retirement home on the upper floors. JPUSA started several successful businesses, some of them involving construction and maintenance work, to support itself, and expanded its evangelism and service programs to include a neighborhood soup kitchen, a homeless shelter, and a magazine called *Cornerstone*, among other undertakings. Its 450 members continue to live simply, on a per capita income that would qualify as poverty-level, as they vigorously live out their demanding faith.[22]

Not all of the Christian communes of the 1960s era came out of the Jesus Movement, and a great many religious communes were rooted in faith traditions other than Christianity. In northern California, for example, an intentional community founded in 1969 grew out of the teachings of Paramahansa Yogananda, an Indian yogi who arrived in the United States in 1920 and built a Hindu-oriented religious organization called the Self-Realization Fellowship. His book *Autobiography of a Yogi* may well be the best-selling Asian religious work of all time in the West.[23] Years after Yogananda's death one of his disciples, Kriyananda (Donald Walters), founded Ananda World Brotherhood Village, which slowly grew to sustain hundreds of resident members. Life was difficult at first, especially because the community attracted quite a few dropouts who did not exhibit the discipline required for the kind of hard spiritual and physical work Ananda required. A devastating fire that destroyed most of Ananda's buildings in 1976 was a further setback, leaving over fifty residents homeless. But slowly the community developed, and with it grew an extensive program of retreats and classes on yoga and a variety of Indian and New Age topics. By the 1990s the members numbered several hundred, and satellite Ananda villages, including one in Europe, were operating as well. With a disciplined program of meditation and study, Ananda Village has become a notable American spiritual center.

If some spiritual communities may be readily categorized as Christian, Hindu, Buddhist, or the like, others are harder to pigeonhole. Many of them simply arose from the teachings of a charismatic leader and have developed identities all their own. The Israel Family of the Seattle area has been such a group; it coalesced around a visionary who called himself Love Israel and reached a peak membership of around four hundred in the early 1980s. Spiritual seekers began moving into Love's house, and eventually more than a dozen nearby houses, in the late 1960s. They all took the last name Israel and new first names as well: Serious, Logic, Meekness, Clean, Understanding. Dressed in biblical robes and sandals and rejecting many of the values of the prevailing society, they troubled the more staid citizens of Seattle and were the focus of a good deal of ongoing conflict. Losing a court judgment to a disgruntled ex-member, the Israel Family declared bankruptcy, sold its urban properties, and retreated to its ranch near Arlington, where it has regrouped, built a dozen homes (several of them yurts) and opened new businesses based on specialized farming operations. A second generation is now having children of its own, and despite local conflicts over zoning and land use on the ranch, the Israels seem destined to live their communal lives for some time to come.

Secular radicals, visionaries, and, occasionally, outright cranks were also major players on the 1960s-era communal fields. While the Vietnam War was at its height many communes dedicated to resisting the war effort appeared, some of them near the Canadian border where they could help draft resisters and deserters slip into Canada. Others worked for racial justice or engaged in extensive social service work, operating soup kitchens, homeless shelters, and other such facilities—sometimes combining those kinds of services with vigorous radical political activism that often included civil disobedience.

Some of the secular reformers sought to change what they saw as outdated social customs. One of the most frontal challenges the 1960s era made to the American status quo was in the area of sexual conduct, and while many communes tolerated unconventional sexual relations and activities, some were based on outright advocacy of new sexual arrangements previously never discussed in polite society. Kerista, established by Jud Presmont and Eve Furchgott in 1971 in San Francisco, was one of the most flamboyant of them. Its centerpiece was a group marriage featuring what its practitioners called "polyfidelity"—faithfulness not to a single partner but to a group in which sleeping partners were rotated daily on a fixed schedule. Claiming to have overcome jealousy, the Keristans engaged in marathon group encounter sessions (the "Gestalt-O-Rama") in which they worked through their hang-ups and conflicts. The Keristans kept from reproducing by the expedient of having all male members undergo vasectomies, and they managed to keep AIDS at bay by keeping sexual activity strictly within the group and stringently screening new members. Economically Kerista was fueled through much of the 1970s and 1980s by its Macintosh computer business. It all came crashing down in 1991, however, Gestalt-O-Rama notwithstanding, when internal conflicts finally tore the community apart. A few members have regrouped in smaller polyfidelitous configurations, and in the late 1990s one band in Hawaii had gone a long way toward recreating the Kerista of a quarter of a century earlier.[24]

Other communities emanated from the 1960s-era sexual frontier as well. As the early 1970s unfolded, homosexuals began to come out of the closet in some numbers, and eventually gay and lesbian enclaves occupied the landscape in communal America, although they were fairly few and often publicity-shy at least until the late 1970s. Gay communal energy was strong enough that by 1974 a quarterly magazine, *RFD*, was circulating among community-minded homosexuals. Lesbians tended to be ahead of gay males in establishing communities; one of the pioneering ventures came in 1974, when WomanShare was founded on twenty-three acres in rural southern Oregon. Although membership has never been large (typically not over half a dozen), WomanShare has become a notable feminist retreat center, a piece of territory off limits to males. Seeking to be as self-sufficient as possible, members learned such traditionally male skills as auto repair and have become an accepted, if distinctive, part of their rural neighborhood.[25]

Environmentalism first became a mass movement in the 1960s era, and several communities dedicated themselves to stopping the world's headlong slide toward environmental oblivion. Some were what later came to be called ecovillages, hamlets planned to minimize automobile use, energy consumption, and pollution on the part of their residents. The most spectacular of them, architecturally, has been Arcosanti, founded in 1970 in the Arizona desert by Paolo Soleri, whose program of "arcology" sees architecture and ecology as inseparably related. Arcosanti's goal was and is ultimately to house five thousand residents largely in one huge structure with solar power, no cars, and no urban sprawl. Progress on this city of the future has been slow, however, since Soleri has chosen to avoid outside support that might force him to compromise his vision. If it ever achieves completion, it will be an impressive community indeed.[26]

IDEOLOGY AND ORGANIZATION

Inherent in the establishment of the new communes was a deep critique of what Western civilization had become by the second half of the twentieth century. The United States, most communards agreed, had become sidetracked from the lofty goals it had embraced at its founding and was no longer the world's hope but its oppressor—a precept confirmed by what they saw as the country's outrageously immoral behavior in its pursuit of the intractable war in Vietnam. Those who chose the communal life were saying no to a system they perceived to be increasingly dominated by greed and materialism. The ultimate culprit, perhaps, was that sacred American icon, individualism. The time had come, communitarians believed, to give up the endless pursuit of self-interest and begin thinking about the common good. They wanted the country to start moving from I to we.

Other ideals were also widespread, if not universal, among the new communitarians. Those who moved to the country embodied the venerable American idealization of rural life. Many who saw the traditional American family breaking down sought to create new family structures, perhaps along tribal lines. Most of these persons, whose generation had grown up with the Civil Rights movement, were committed to racial equality, and that commitment often came to encompass class and gender equality as well. While persons from the higher classes were welcome, and indeed in several cases were the financial angels who underwrote specific communes, in daily life the ideal of classlessness prevailed in virtually all communal environments. Once the ideal of equality for women began to root itself in American society in the early 1970s, it too was widely subscribed to in communal settings, although communal males were, like their noncommunal peers, sometimes slow in putting the egalitarian vision into practice.

It all added up to a vision of nothing less than a new society. The new communitarians were out to save the world and made no bones about it.

Communal governmental structures varied widely. In the Grateful Dead commune, Carolyn Garcia later remembered, leadership rested with the one "who shouted the most and had the best joke."[27] At the other pole, the authority of charismatic leaders could be nearly absolute. At the Farm during its early years one of the conditions for membership was acceptance of Stephen Gaskin as one's spiritual teacher, and his authority was accordingly immense.[28] Some communities were committed to leaderless consensus decision making, which often led to interminable meetings and unworkable compromise decisions. As Rico Reed later recalled of Tolstoy Farm, "Usually, the people who knew the least about the subject would be the pushiest about getting their way. We'd have to do it their way to get their consensus; therefore, the project was half doomed to start with if it required any expertise."[29]

Disdain for money was a popular hippie value—"Use your money as toilet paper," advised counterculturist Jerry Rubin[30]—but like it or not, community had an economic side to it. In surprisingly many cases buying land or paying rent was not a problem; many communes had generous patrons, often hippie benefactors who, with their inheritances, made land freely available to a communal congregation in need of living space. In dozens of cases these benefactors simply donated the money needed for purchasing property to a group; in others they retained title but allowed a commune free use of the land. In the many cases in which commune members had to pay rent or make land payments, the financial burden was still often not heavy, at least on a per capita basis, since run-down old farmhouses were widely available at bargain prices in the wake of the rural depopulation that had taken place in much of the country over the preceding half century.

A good many communities were economically unstructured. People just contributed whatever little bits of money they had, scrounged creatively for supplies of all kinds, perhaps worked a bit when funds ran low, and somehow they all managed to keep body and soul together. Communal living is inherently inexpensive, after all. Sometimes, but not usually, the food stamps or welfare provided by an affluent larger society underwrote a portion of the communal budget. The more organized communes often developed various businesses and industries; the rural ones frequently turned to organic farming for income. But beyond such rational measures, countercultural mysticism posited what was often called "the flow," the remarkable ability of money or needed supplies to appear as needed. Judson Jerome quoted one young woman's experience of the flow thus:

> I mentioned to one woman that I desperately needed birth control pills; I'd run out and had discovered the day before that my prescription couldn't be filled in Canada. She said, "Carol just threw away a six months' supply." . . . I fished the pills out of the trash pile and found they were the very type I'd used for years. I thought of offering to pay her for them, but decided that hippy ethics dictated against offering money for something the Flow had obviously brought to me.[31]

COMMUNAL PEOPLE

Most communes regarded themselves as tolerant and inclusive, but they were usually not very diverse. Racially they were overwhelmingly white; one study on the subject found that communes were less than 1 percent nonwhite, while the American population as a whole was 12 percent nonwhite at that time.[32] The likely explanation is that 1960s-era communes tended to be populated by persons trying to divest themselves of goods they deemed meaningless and bourgeois—voluntary poverty was a strong countercultural theme—whereas nonwhites were disproportionately social have-nots and were searching for a share of the material good life they had never enjoyed. Communes were almost as thoroughly middle-class (or higher) as they were white; their residents were better educated than their average American peers, and they typically came from intact nuclear families.[33]

Despite the homogeneity of communards' backgrounds, the openness and easygoing acceptance many communes exhibited did attract more than a few eccentrics and misfits. Among those who showed up were a fair number of down-and-outers, sometimes mentally ill, who did not pull their own weight, thus discouraging and often driving away the more capable and industrious members any commune sorely needed. Although the negative impact of drugs on communal life has often been overstated, in a few cases users of hard drugs did disrupt specific communes, and sometimes joyous afficionados of psychedelics were prone to spend more time tripping than working. Quite a few communes had residents who were downright quirky: at Morning Star East, Crazy Bill lived in a hole in the ground and ate nothing but dry pancake mix with syrup. At Wheeler's Ranch, Crazy David refused ever to lie down, and even managed to sleep standing up. At Hidden Springs in New Hampshire, one member considered cooking a waste of time and would only eat food directly from cans.[34] Some were just plain dangerous; Hugh Gardner, a social scientist who visited many communes, left Reality Construction Company in fear of his life "after a night spent in a sweat-filled sleeping bag while one of several psychopathic personalities in residence at the time walked around in the dark randomly shooting a rifle at targets unknown, some not very far from my head."[35]

Albert Bates recalled that the Farm in Tennessee once had a "'Tomatarian,' meaning that he ate only tomatoes. We sent him to work on a farming crew, but it was difficult to get much work out of him because he'd take a tomato break every few minutes. He even talked with tomatoes in his mouth. I guess if you are living on tomatoes, you have to eat a heck of a lot of them." But the Farm, like many communes, could also be therapeutic, and sometimes real healing took place. Another Bates vignette:

> One visitor indicated that he was deaf and dumb, so we sent for someone who knew sign language. After they tried signing with him, he wrote that he didn't know how to sign and wasn't really deaf. After several hours of our being really friendly with him, he started talking! He had acted deaf and dumb for years because he was severely inhibited. We sent him to join the farming crew, and he was a better worker than the Tomatarian. He eventually became outgoing, having many stories to tell from the years he was deaf and dumb.[36]

One important social phenomenon of the middle and latter part of the 1960s era was the rise of the contemporary wave of feminism, and reevaluations of gender roles and relationships certainly made an impact on the communes, especially after 1970. More often than not communes were male-founded and male-dominated, and dominant men did not typically fall immediately into gender enlightenment in communal settings any more readily than they did elsewhere. Often gender roles tended to govern daily life and work: men ran the tractors, while women cooked the brown rice and beans and nursed the babies. On the other hand, some communes took deliberate steps to overcome such inbred habits. At Twin Oaks the auto-mechanic crew was deliberately made mainly female, and men often took care of children. The fact that people shared social space intimately actually made even nonegalitarian communes breeding grounds for feminism, since women in close proximity could do mutual consciousness raising fairly readily. Although some of the religious communes remained firmly patriarchal, by the early to middle 1970s most communes were more progressive on gender issues than was American society as a whole.

LIVING THE LIFE

Facilities, activities, and attitudes varied widely among the communes. Most typically a communal group would crowd into an existing house, but in the rural communes enterprising members often built their own shelters, exhibiting great originality in their use of cheap or free materials. In either case people tended to live in close quarters, an enforced proximity that sometimes made for wonderful interpersonal bonding and sometimes drove people crazy. Ken Kesey was eventually among the latter, lamenting, after he dissolved the informal commune that had gathered on his Oregon farm after the breakup of the La Honda scene, "You can't have any of your friends over, you know? There's no way to be a host. You can't go visiting, for fear somebody'll get your bed. It gets so bad it's terrible. And the worst thing about it is that it's with your best friends."[37]

The closeness was aggravated, typically, by visitors, some of them just Sunday drivers who wanted to check out the local alternative scene rather as they would take a trip to the zoo. There were also hordes of would-be communards who wanted to check things out and, if possible, move in. Marty Jezer characterized the visitors at Total Loss Farm over one four-month span as

> Sunday "hippy watchers," high school runaways, newspaper and magazine reporters from both the underground and establishment press, a local farmer who was frightened because his eldest son had expressed a desire to live like us, peace activists passing through, local freaks, a state policeman, hitchhikers wanting a place to spend the night, dropouts wanting a place to live, groups of people planning to start their own communes and schools, and a well-scrubbed young couple who wanted to interest us in manufacturing Ho Chi Minh sandals, which they would market for us, as a cottage industry.[38]

One important countercultural theme from the late 1960s onward, that of eschewing the plastic and artificial in favor of the organic and natural, was heavily present in the communes. Processed foods were frequently disdained in favor of natural foods, and communards often tried to treat illnesses with herbal or other natural remedies. Collective gardening for the production of wholesome food for the group was immensely popular, although few communes approached anything like self-sufficiency in food. In many rural communes and a few urban ones the commitment to the natural along with the liberalized sexual mores of the era meant that nudity was popular. Much of the tending of the garden might take place in the nude, and many communes had group baths, saunas, toilet facilities, and swimming holes. As Gordon Yaswen wrote of nudity at Sunrise Hill in Massachusetts, "The practice of group nudity in the community proved itself a genuinely valuable instrument for the promotion of a sense of warm and frank familiarity among the members. It was—moreover—a symbolic act of communion with—and trust in—each other which helped to cement us."[39] When local voyeurs forced the members of Cold Mountain Farm to start wearing clothes, member Joyce Gardner lamented the situation as "a great loss. It had been such a pleasure to be among ten stark naked people unselfconsciously planting corn in the field. . . . We had all kinds of bodies, of all colors and sizes, and we had grown used to these basic differences without embarrassment. That was important for people who had been raised to regard their bodies with shame."[40]

Nothing epitomizes the Sixties so clearly in the public mind as sex and drugs, and certainly both were present in the communes often enough. "If it feels good, then do it as long as you don't hurt anybody else" was the watchword of the new culture. Outright group sex and frequent, open rotating of sexual partners were rare, the stereotype notwithstanding, but certainly relationships other than conventional marital monogamy were widely tolerated. Similarly, "good" drugs—marijuana, LSD, and the other psychedelics, as opposed to "bad" heroin, alcohol, and amphetamines—were often embraced eagerly or at least tolerated. More than a little marijuana was grown on the more remote portions of communal farmsteads, and a lot of rural communes eventually experienced drug raids.

The Sixties era, communes included, witnessed a good deal of spiritual exploration. Hundreds of the communes were devoted to various specific religious paths, as we have seen, but many of the rest had their spiritual sides as well. Experimentation with Zen sitting, Sufi dancing, meditative chanting, or at least a group "om" mantra before meals went on in a great many communes. Especially in New Mexico, communards befriended local American Indians who led them through peyote rituals. Others produced art with mystical, Asian, and American Indian themes.

Many middle Americans were decidedly uneasy about having a commune pop up in the neighborhood. Local rumor mills were often loaded with wild tales of debauchery and worse. In the Taos area, the scene of the most severe conflicts, communards were shot at and at least one was killed.[41] One original settler at Black Bear Ranch in California many years later asked a neighbor what the locals had thought of the new arrivees back when the commune began, and got a two-word answer: "Charles Manson."[42] Manson, whose communal "family" had outwardly looked like a band of typical hippies while its members were committing serial homicide, was for many Americans a symbol of just what the counterculture could ultimately boil down to, and his grim image chilled a good deal of Sixties-era optimism, communal and otherwise.

Yogi Bhajan leading commune members in Kundalini yoga postures, Aspen Meadows, Tesuque Indian Reservation, New Mexico, Summer Solstice 1969. Those intentional communities that observed a common spiritual practice or belief system often outlasted ones formed around secular ideologies. Copyright © Lisa Law.

But for the communes that survived, toleration came with familiarity. Some communitarians, it turned out, could work and socialize with their new neighbors and become friends. Alpha Farm in Oregon opened a restaurant in a nearby town that became a popular local gathering place. Now, a generation later, ongoing communes are often pillars of their local communities.

INTO THE PRESENT

Most Sixties-era communes are no longer with us. Many fell victim to internal tensions; others lost their more stable members and became populated with down-and-outers who could not keep things going. External pressure often spelled the end, as at Morning Star in California, which could not withstand repeated bulldozings and legal prosecutions. The Clinton Farm in Kansas was forced to give way to a federal reservoir project. MOVE, in Philadelphia, got the ultimate termination notice when city law enforcement agents bombed its house, killing most of the members present. Accidental fires destroyed several communities.

But more broadly, the tenor of the times changed. The assumption that the age of scarcity was past turned out to be misguided. The war in Vietnam wound down, and group-centered idealism gave way to materialism and self-ishness among the young. And anyway, who ever said all the communes would last forever?

That said, terms such as "failure" and "decline" do not provide good ana-lytical tools for understanding the outcome of this incredible episode of com-mune building, because many of the Sixties-era communes do survive and, beyond that, the impact of the communes continues to be felt in American life, especially in the productive ongoing lives of many who lived in them.

Several hundred communes from the Sixties era survive at century's end, a quarter century after the whole episode is generally presumed to have come to an end. Dozens are listed in the 2000 edition of the *Communities Directory*,[43] along with hundreds founded before and since. The Hog Farm, now in Berkeley, Twin Oaks in Virginia, Libre in Colorado, the Sojourners Community in Washington, D.C., and the Farm in Tennessee, among many others, are alive and well and in most cases still adhere fairly closely to their founding Sixties values.

In other cases the land of a closed commune has become a public resource. Earth People's Park in Vermont, once an open-land community, is now, after many twists and turns in its story, a state park. And for that matter a communal resurgence may eventually take place; Stephen Gaskin of the Farm is now building Rocinante, a hippie retirement commune, adjacent to the original Farm property, and other ex-Farm members have purchased a shared vacation/retreat home in Florida. The Mulberry Family of Richmond, Virginia, invested the money it received for its real estate when it broke up and may use it to buy a collective retirement home. Several communities have established permanent land trusts that will keep their property undeveloped or restricted to communal use.

In many places in which communes themselves did not survive, members nevertheless have continued to espouse some of the old communal idealism and live out their lives in ways that the foray into community inspired. Probably the largest concentration of commune alumni and alumnae is in the Pacific Northwest, from California to Washington, where thousands upon thousands of counterculturists, many of them former communards, continue to live in rural isolation, in some cases on the very property that once housed a commune, with little cash income and a lifestyle that still embodies the Sixties-era values of simplicity and separation from the dominant culture. A few marijuana plants still grace an occasional remote field. On a smaller scale that pattern is replicated nationwide.

Virtually none of the hundreds of Sixties-era communards interviewed for the '60s Communes Project, an extensive oral history project conducted in the mid-1990s, regretted having had the experience they did, and many called it pivotal to their lives. The popular notion may be that a lot of former Sixties hippies and radicals now wear power suits and want to get rich, but many more are still trying to work out the better part of the Sixties vision by being good parents and responsible progressive citizens doing work that has social value. Of the communal veterans located for interviews hardly any were corporate lawyers or big-business executives; nearly all were teachers, health care workers, artists, organic farmers, social workers, and the like. More than a few still live simply and work for social change. In those lives the communes may be said to have made their most important and lasting contribution to making the world better.

The communes also deserve some credit for the wider legacy that the Sixties era has deposited in America and the Western world. The cult of the body now so prevalent in society—exemplified by dedication to physical fitness and the consumption of healthy foods—has direct roots in the countercultural Sixties outlook. The large and amorphous constellation of spiritual searches and practices generally called the New Age movement, with its fascinations that range from massage to crystal healing to astrology to channeling, is similarly connected to the mystical spirituality that was so much a part of Sixties life. The rise of socially conscious investing, emphasizing good and ethical business practices, has directly paralleled the maturation of the Sixties generation. Contemporary feminism was nurtured in part by countercultural egalitarianism. And perhaps the most important cultural legacy of all is environmentalism, which neither communards nor Sixties counterculturists invented but which they wholeheartedly promoted. Stewardship of nature was a persistent theme in the communes of the Sixties era.

Many communards saw themselves as world-changers and believed that once everyone saw how sweet life could be without selfishness, militarism, and materialism, a new and enlightened day would surely dawn. The dream of course was never realized, could not have been. Human nature, ever imperfect, manages to interfere with the most beautiful of visions; the communes themselves could not achieve perfection, and in any event the world was not going to be changed by a few noble examples of a different path, any more than it has been changed by the communal religious idealism that has been embodied in monasteries for thousands of years. Nevertheless, the hope that the world can be made better, if not perfect, will remain an ongoing legacy of the Sixties communes.

Notes

1. Elaine Sundancer, *Celery Wine: The Story of a Country Commune* (Yellow Springs, Ohio: Community Publications Cooperative, 1973), 29.

2. For a discussion of communal statistics see my *The 60s Communes: Hippies and Beyond* (Syracuse, N.Y.: Syracuse University Press, 1999), xviii–xx.

3. Sender described the communal influences in his past for the 60s Communes Project, for which Deborah Altus, several volunteers, and I conducted interviews with hundreds of veterans of 1960s-era communes in the mid-1990s under the auspices of the National Endowment for the Humanities. Project materials are currently being processed and eventually are expected to be deposited in a research library for public access.

4. See, among other writings, John Curl, *History of Work Cooperation in America: Cooperatives, Cooperative Movements, Collectivity and Communalism from Early America to the Present* (Berkeley, Calif.: Homeward Press, 1980).

5. John Humphrey Noyes, *The History of American Socialisms* (New York: Hillary House, 1961 [1870]).

6. Extensive accounts of the Kesey/Merry Pranksters scene are contained in Tom Wolfe, *The Electric Kool-Aid Acid Test* (New York: Farrar, Straus & Giroux, 1968), and Paul Perry, *On the Bus: The Complete Guide to the Legendary Trip of Ken Kesey and the Merry Pranksters and the Birth of the Counterculture* (New York: Thunder's Mouth Press, 1990).

7. For more detail on these and other early groups see my *The 60s Communes*.

8. All quotations from the Droppers are taken from interviews I conducted with them between 1984 and 1989.

9. For a more detailed account of Drop City see my "Drop City: Historical Notes on the Pioneer Hippie Commune," *Syzygy: Journal of Alternative Religion and Culture* 1, no. 1 (winter 1992): 23–38.

10. Probably the most extensive account of Morning Star and Wheeler's is "Home Free Home: The Story of Two Open-Door Sixties Communes, Morning Star and Wheeler's Ranch, as Told by Various Residents," ed. Ramón Sender Barayón, manuscript; a copy is at the library of the University of California, Riverside. A copy also appears at www.diggers.org/home_free.htm

11. B. F. Skinner, *Walden Two* (New York: Macmillan, 1948).

12. On Twin Oaks see Kathleen Kinkade, *A Walden Two Experiment: The First Five Years of Twin Oaks Community* (New York: Morrow, 1973); Ingrid Komar, *Living the Dream: A Documentary Study of Twin Oaks Community* (Norwood, Penn.: Norwood Editions, 1983; reprinted by Twin Oaks, 1989); and Kat Kinkade, *Is It Utopia Yet? An Insider's View of Twin Oaks Community in Its 26th Year* (Louisa, Va.: Twin Oaks, 1994).

13. Black Bear's collective autobiography is in two books: *January Thaw: People at Blue Mt. Ranch Write about Living Together in the Mountains* (New York: Times Change Press, 1974), and Don Monkerud et al., eds. *Free Land: Free Love: Tales of a Wilderness Commune* (Aptos, Cal: Black Bear Mining and Pub. Co., 2000)

14. For an early account of New Buffalo see Richard Fairfield, *Communes USA: A Personal Tour* (Baltimore: Penguin, 1972), 187–97.

15. *Be Here Now* (San Cristobal, N. Mex.: Lama Foundation, 1971).

16. Raymond Mungo, *Total Loss Farm: A Year in the Life* (New York: Bantam, 1971 [1970]).

17. *Home Comfort: Life on Total Loss Farm*, ed. Richard Wizansky (New York: Saturday Review Press, 1973).

18. Stephen Gaskin and the Farm, *Hey Beatnik! This Is the Farm Book* (Summertown, Tenn.: Book Publishing Co., 1974), unpaginated.

19. Ibid.

20. For an overview of the Farm's life and Gaskin's teachings see Michael Traugot, *A Short History of the Farm* (Summertown, Tenn.: Author, 1994). Available from the author at 84 The Farm, Summertown, Tenn. 38483.

21. For a brief retrospective overview see Joe V. Peterson, "The Rise and Fall of Shiloh," *Communities: Journal of Cooperative Living*, no. 92 (fall 1996): 61. For an earlier, more detailed study see James T. Richardson, Mary White Stewart, and Robert B. Simmonds, *Organized*

Miracles: A Study of a Contemporary, Youth, Communal, Fundamentalist Organization (New Brunswick, N.J.: Transaction Books, 1979).

22. An account of Jesus People USA is provided in David Janzen, Fire, Salt, and Peace: Intentional Christian Communities Alive in North America (Evanston, Ill.: Shalom Mission Communities, 1996), 104–05.

23. Paramahansa Yogananda, Autobiography of a Yogi (Los Angeles: Self-Realization Fellowship, 1946).

24. On Kerista's life and ideas see Polyfidelity: Sex in the Kerista Commune and Other Related Theories on How to Solve the World's Problems (San Francisco: Performing Arts Social Society, 1984).

25. On WomanShare see Sue, Nelly, Dian, Carol, Billie, Country Lesbians: The Story of WomanShare Collective (Grants Pass, Ore.: WomanShare Books, 1976).

26. For an article that provides an overview of Arcosanti but expresses frustration with the project's slow progress, see Sheri F. Crawford, "Arcosanti: An American Community Looking toward the Millennium," Communal Societies 14 (1994): 49–66.

27. Carolyn Adams Garcia, 60s Communes Project interview, 15 July 1996.

28. In the 1980s, it should be noted, the Farm was restructured and Gaskin gracefully stepped down from leadership and became essentially a regular member.

29. Rico Reed, 60s Communes Project interview, 10 September 1996.

30. Jerry Rubin, "Rubin Raps: Money's to Burn," Berkeley Barb, 19–26 January 1968.

31. Judson Jerome, Families of Eden: Communes and the New Anarchism (New York: Seabury Press, 1974), 94.

32. Angela A. Aidala and Benjamin D. Zablocki, "The Communes of the 1970s: Who Joined and Why?" Marriage and Family Review 17 (1991): 92.

33. Aidala and Zablocki, "The Communes of the 1970s," 92; Benjamin Zablocki, Alienation and Charisma: A Study of Contemporary American Communes (New York: Free Press/Macmillan, 1980), 97.

34. Anecdotes from 60s Communes Project interviews.

35. Hugh Gardner, The Children of Prosperity (New York: St. Martin's Press, 1978), 119.

36. Albert Bates, "The Farm: Tie Dyes in Cyberspace," Shared Visions, Shared Lives, ed. Bill Metcalf (Forres, Scotland: Findhorn Press, 1996), 78–79.

37. "The Ken Kesey Movie," Rolling Stone, 7 March 1970, 29–30.

38. Marty Jezer, "The DRV," WIN 4, no. 1 (1 January 1969): 13.

39. Gorden Yaswen, "Sunrise Hill Community: Post-Mortem," 2d ed., mimeographed essay, 1970, 7. Abridged versions of Yaswen's evocative account appeared in several other publications; see, for example, The Good Life, ed. Jerry Richard (New York: New American Library, 1973), 140–72; Communes: Creating and Managing the Collective Life, ed. Rosabeth Moss Kanter (New York: Harper and Row, 1973), 456–72.

40. Joyce Gardner, Cold Mountain Farm: An Attempt at Community (n.p., 1970), 23.

41. For details of several grisly conflicts in Taos see Jon Stewart, "Communes in Taos," Conversations with the New Reality (San Francisco: Canfield/Harper and Row, 1971), 210; William Hedgepeth and Dennis Stock, The Alternative: Communal Life in New America (New York: Macmillan, 1970), 72.

42. Glenn Lyons, 60s Communes Project interview, 20 March 1996.

43. Communities Directory: A Guide to Intentional Communities and Cooperative Living (Rutledge, Mo.: Fellowship for Intentional Community, 2000).

Thirteen

"Machines of Loving Grace"
Alternative Technology, Environment, and the Counterculture

Andrew Kirk

I like to think (and
the sooner the better!)
of a cybernetic meadow
where mammals and computers
live together in mutually
programming harmony
like pure water
touching clear sky

I like to think
    (right now, please!)
of a cybernetic forest
filled with pines and electronics
where deer stroll peacefully
past computers
as if they were flowers
with spinning blossoms

I like to think
    (it has to be!)

of a cybernetic ecology
where we are free of our labors
and joined back to nature,
returned to our mammal
brothers and sisters,
and all watched over
by machines of loving grace

—*Richard Brautigan, "All Watched Over by Machines of Loving Grace" (1967)*[1]

The counterculture is often remembered as a purple haze of sex, drugs, and rock and roll. Visions of back-to-nature, neo-Luddite communes complete with bearded wilderness advocates and naked children draped in flowers living off edible plants easily spring to mind. Many counterculturists did in fact reject the modern world of large-scale technological systems in favor of a simpler, more primitive, and environmentally-conscious lifestyle. Faced with the grim reality of mechanized death in Vietnam, rivers so polluted they caught fire, smog alerts that sent children and the elderly running for cover, the omnipresent threat of nuclear annihilation, and the cold dehumanization of the labor force by industry, many understandably technophobic younger Americans rejected industrial society outright and began experimenting with alternative lifestyles and communities that de-emphasized reliance on modern technology.

At the same time other counterculturists moved in an entirely different direction. Influenced by New Left politics, this faction turned their attention to a critical reevaluation of long-standing assumptions about the relationship between nature, technology, and society. In the 1960s and '70s technologically minded counterculturists helped reshape the American environmental movement, infusing it with a youthful energy and providing it with a new sense of purpose and direction. Unlike their predecessors in the conservation movement, and their technophobic counterculture cohorts who tended to focus on wilderness preservation and resource scarcity, these new counterculture environmentalists concentrated on alternative technologies as a response to contemporary concerns over pollution, overpopulation, and the realization that America was entering a new phase in its development.

This next phase was envisioned as a "post-scarcity" economy, in which advanced industrial societies theoretically possessed the means to provide abundance and freedom for all and reconcile nature and technology if only they chose to do so.[2] Led by social theorists such as Herbert Marcuse and Murray Bookchin, post-scarcity adherents shared the belief that "the poison is . . . its own antidote."[3] In other words, if technology deployed in an amoral and unecological fashion created the social and environmental problems of industrial capitalism, then perhaps technology used morally and ecologically could create a utopian future. These critics, who were especially influential within New Left circles, emphasized that social and environmental problems in America stemmed not from a lack of resources but from a misguided waste of the "technology of abundance."[4] If the American people could be convinced to abandon their bourgeois quest for consumer goods, these critics argued, then valuable resources could be redirected toward establishing social equity and ecological harmony instead of consumerism and waste. In the late 1960s post-scarcity assumptions fueled a brief period of technology-based utopian optimism that profoundly influenced a generation of environmentalists.

This thoughtful reevaluation of the possible beneficial ways that alternative technologies might be used by enlightened and empowered individuals is perhaps the most significant and lasting contribution of the counterculture to American culture. The trend manifested itself in many ways—from Buckminster Fuller designing affordable and environmentally sympathetic geodesic domes to Steve Jobs and Steve Wozniak developing "personal" computers to put the power of information in the hands of individuals.[5] Working toward similar goals, other counterculture environmentalists and sympathetic scientists and engineers focused on alternative energy, earth-friendly design, recycling, and creative waste management as the best ways to subvert the large industrial structures most damaging to the environment. Whether it involved building personal computers in one's garage or designing composting toilets, the idea that technology could be directed toward shaping a brighter future became a driving force in environmental advocacy after 1970.

The utopian optimism and revolutionary political program of the New Left, however, failed to become a part of the mainstream environmental movement. Consumed with the reactive fight against the Vietnam War and entrenched university bureaucracies, the predominantly campus-based New Left movement fragmented and disintegrated during the early 1970s. But the aftermath of the OPEC cartel's oil embargo of autumn 1973 helped confirm the urgency of environmental concerns while tempering utopian ambitions that were predicated on post-scarcity. The politicized counterculture environmental movement survived the New Left's demise and remained active in a multifaceted attempt to construct an alternative society.

The relationship between the counterculture, technology, and the environment is complex. While this essay uses terms like "counterculture environmental movement," it would be a mistake to assume that all of those who considered themselves both counterculturists and environmentalists thought or acted alike. Even among those who advocated the use of technology to solve environmental problems there was rarely a clear program of action or analysis. Often it seemed as if countercultural environmentalists occupied separate but parallel universes defined by whether they considered technology to be the problem or the solution. Thus the relationship between the counterculture and technology was always one of fundamental ambivalence. Just as in the counterculture in general, counterculture environmentalists never constructed a unified philosophy that united like-minded individuals and organizations under one banner. They were instead a diverse group with a wide variety of perspectives, often pursuing opposed or mutually exclusive projects. Nevertheless, what differentiated counterculture environmentalists from other environmental activists in the 1960s and 1970s was a shared desire to use environmental research, new technologies, ecological thinking, and environmental advocacy to shape a social revolution based on alternative lifestyles and communities, alternatives that would enable future generations to live in harmony with one another and the environment.

From Technophobia to Alternative Technology

The technology debate dates to the beginnings of the Industrial Revolution of the nineteenth century. While some Americans looked at advances in science and technology with a wary eye, others tended to view technology as beneficial and benign. This was particularly true for a generation of middle-class Progressive conservation advocates who believed that rational planning, expert management, and science were the keys to a sound environmental future. From amateur conservation advocacy groups to the utilitarian U.S. Forest Service of Gifford Pinchot, American conservation advocates looked to science for solutions to waste and wanton destruction of scarce natural resources. For the better part of the twentieth century most resource conservation advocacy was predicated on the notion that through science and the march of progress humans could tame and control all elements of the natural world, stopping waste and maximizing productivity. This type of thinking inspired massive reclamation and irrigation projects and experiments with chemicals to rid the world of unwanted pests and predators. Such steadfast faith in technology and the scientific worldview prevailed well into the 1950s.[6]

Despite this widespread faith in science, the rise of environmental advocacy in America was characterized by a split between utilitarian conservationists and holistic preservationists. In contrast to conservationists, preservationists consistently rejected the utilitarian and technologically based solutions of the conservation movement. In the early decades of the twentieth century preservationists like John Muir, Aldo Leopold, and Robert Marshall, among others, worked to develop more ecologically sound alternatives to what they perceived as the materialism and hubris of the conservationists. This perceptive minority looked closely at the impact of unchecked industrial development on the environment, including attempts to regulate and conserve. For them, the technological advances of the modern world seemed anything but benign.

These preservationists were joined in their distrust of modern industrial society and technological quick fixes for complex environmental problems by intellectuals from a variety of backgrounds and ideological perspectives. From the mid-nineteenth century on, a disparate collection of utopians, anarchists, back-to-the-landers, and antimodernists all contributed to a growing subcurrent in American culture aimed at rethinking the relationship between technology, society, and the environment. But through the Second World War, these voices of dissent remained a distinct minority.[7] The vast majority of Americans, including most conservation proponents, remained dedicated to the ideal of progress achieved through science and technology.

In the decades following World War II, attitudes toward technology gradually began to change. While never a mainstream trend, more Americans began questioning the dominant view of technology and progress. A catalyst for this reevaluation was the horrifying devastation caused by use of the atomic bomb in Japan. Once the patriotic fervor surrounding the end of the war subsided, many conservationists and public intellectuals started discussing what it now meant that humans had the power to destroy the world. Books like John Hersey's *Hiroshima*, published in 1946, graphically depicted the awesome destructive power of nuclear weapons and inspired a growing segment of society to recognize the far-reaching implications of such technology. Likewise, after years of turning out prowar propaganda films, Hollywood, along with a legion of science fiction writers in the 1950s, started producing a steady stream of books and films presenting horrifying visions of technology run amok. A generation of Americans born after World War II grew up watching giant nuclear ants or other such mutants of technology destroying humanity in movies like Gordon Douglas's *Them!* (1954). By the mid-1960s a growing segment of American society, particularly young Americans, exhibited an increasing ambivalence about technology. This new generation enjoyed an unprecedented level of material prosperity predicated on the traditional notion of progress through science and technology. At the same time there was a growing sense of genuine terror over the malign potential of science practiced without a social conscience.

During the late 1950s and early '60s, many older members of the conservation movement also found themselves increasingly alienated from the world of modern atomic science, massive land reclamation projects, and consumer technology. They were distressed particularly by the consequences of technocratic thinking for American society and culture. Fear shaped much of the conservationist alienation from the postwar world, fear that the prominence of the hard sciences, the expansion of the space race, and the explosion of consumer technology de-emphasized contact with the natural world. Fear in particular about the consequences of nuclear technology for American society led conservationists like John Eastlick to wonder if Americans had been "blinded by the fearful brightness of the atomic bomb," and were now stumbling through life with little awareness of the environmental and social degradation that surrounded them.[8] Eastlick was not alone.

Interestingly, despite their deep concerns about the state of the modern world, most conservationists continued to use modernist means to express and act upon their antimodernist revulsion. Even as their alienation from postwar technocracy grew, their Progressive faith in government agencies and protective federal laws continued to be a staple of the movement.[9] For most of its history, the conservation movement embraced organizational principles and actions based on the idea of linear progress through Progressive enlightenment. At the same time, its adherents tended to view the history of the twentieth century as a steady decline into chaos and environmental collapse, brought on by rampant population growth and unregulated technological expansion.[10] Although these two ideals seemed to be diametrically opposed, both shared the same roots as direct responses to concerns about the relationship between nature and technology in postindustrial America. By drawing on both traditions, whether consciously or not, postwar conservationists and critics of technology attempted to reconcile dreams for reform with competing fears that the system was beyond repair. They were simultaneously hopeful and fearful.

Other postwar social critics, including a growing contingent of more radical environmentalists and a group of prominent European and American intellectuals, were less inclined to search for compromise and more willing to propose far-reaching structural changes. The most stunning of these critiques came from the biologist Rachel Carson, whose explosive *Silent Spring*, published in 1962, explained in chilling detail the ecological consequences of humanity's attempt to control and regulate the environment.[11] Carson became the first of many to warn of an impending environmental "crisis." During the 1960s a series of widely discussed books predicted an apocalyptic future if the present course was not altered. Carson's fellow biologist Barry Commoner produced several best-sellers along these lines, including *The Closing Circle*, which warned of the dangers of sacrificing the planet's health for temporary material gain.[12]

Three other writers also provided inspiration for a new generation of Americans who were questioning technology's role in fostering social, economic, and environmental injustice. Jacques Ellul's *The Technological Society* asserted that "all embracing technological systems had swallowed up the capitalistic and socialistic economies" and were the greatest threat to freedom in the modern world.[13] Ellul argued that there was "something abominable in the modern artifice itself": the system was so corrupted that only a truly revolutionary reorientation could stop social and environmental decay.[14] Like Ellul, Herbert Marcuse, in his popular *One Dimensional Man*, described a vast and repressive world technological structure that overshadowed national borders and traditional political ideologies.[15] Marcuse popularized the insights of the Frankfurt school of Marxian philosophers and sociologists.[16] Together Marcuse and Ellul provided a critical intellectual framework for Americans looking to construct alternatives to the hegemonic scientific worldview.

Perhaps the most influential of the structural critics of the technological society was Lewis Mumford. Mumford began his career as a public intellectual as a strong proponent of science and technology. His 1934 classic *Technics and Civilization* strengthened the popular belief that technology was moving human civilization toward a new golden age.[17] Like most Progressive thinkers of the industrial period, Mumford envisioned a modern world where technology helped provide order to the chaos of nature and restore ecological balance. In *Technics*, Mumford extolled the virtues of the machine. He painted a positive picture of how technology could reshape the world to eliminate drudgery and usher in an unprecedented period in history where machines and nature worked together for human benefit. But this prophet of the machine age began to rethink his position in the 1960s. Like Marcuse and Ellul, Mumford became increasingly alarmed about the power of large technological systems. As he looked around at the world of the 1960s and '70s, Mumford worried that the ascendance of the "megamachine" boded ill for human society.[18] The "machine," once the symbol of progress, gradually began to be recast as a metaphor for describing a seemingly out-of-control capitalist system.[19]

The preoccupation with technology and its consequences became one of the central features of 1960s social and environmental movements, and of the counterculture in particular. In 1969, Theodore Roszak released his influential study of the youth movement, *The Making of a Counter Culture*.[20] Roszak maintained that the counterculture was a direct reaction to "technocracy," which he defined as a "society in which those who govern justify themselves by appeal to technical experts, who in turn justify themselves by appeals to scientific forms of knowledge."[21] The counterculture radicals of the 1960s, Roszak argued, were the only group in America capable of divorcing themselves from the stranglehold of 1950s technology and its insidious centralizing tendencies. Roszak's position on technocracy was similar to Ellul's and

Marcuse's. For Roszak the most appealing characteristic of the counterculture was its rejection of technology and the systems it spawned. Charles Reich, in his best-seller *The Greening of America* (1970), also highlighted the youth movement's rejection of technology as a fundamental component of the counterculture ideology.[22] For both Reich and Roszak what was evil about the technocracy was its bureaucratic organization and complexity. From the perspective of Roszak, Reich, and a growing number of the younger generation, the problem with America stemmed from the realization that there was nothing small, nothing simple, nothing remaining on a human scale.

This mind-boggling bigness and bureaucratization likewise concerned the British economist E. F. Schumacher, whose popular book *Small Is Beautiful* (1973) articulated a decentralized humanistic economics "as if people mattered." [23] Of all the structural critiques of technological systems, Schumacher's provided the best model for constructive action and was particularly important in shaping an emerging counterculture environmentalism. Unlike more pessimistic critics of the modern technocracy, Schumacher provided assurance that by striving to regain individual control of economics and environments, "our landscapes [could] become healthy and beautiful again and our people . . . regain the dignity of man, who knows himself as higher than the animal but never forgets that *noblesse oblige.*"[24] The key to Schumacher's vision was an enlightened adaptation of technology. In *Small Is Beautiful* he highlighted what he called "intermediate technologies," those technical advances that stand "halfway between traditional and modern technology," as the solution to the dissonance between nature and technology in the modern world.[25] These technologies could be as simple as using modern materials to construct better windmills or small water turbines for developing nations; the key was to apply advances in science to specific local communities and ecosystems. Schumacher's ideas were quickly picked up and expanded upon by a wide range of individuals and organizations, often with wildly different agendas, who came together under the banner of a loosely defined ideology that became known as "appropriate technology" (AT).

Appropriate technology emerged as a popular cause at a conference on technological needs for lesser-developed nations held in England in 1968.[26] For individuals and organizations concerned with the plight of developing nations, Schumacher's ideas about intermediate technologies seemed to provide a possible solution to the problem of how to promote a more equitable distribution of wealth while avoiding the inherent environmental and social problems of industrialization.[27] Appropriate technology quickly became a catch all for a wide spectrum of activities involving research into older technologies that had been lost after the Industrial Revolution and the development of new high- and low-tech small scale innovations. The most striking thing about the move toward appropriate technology, according to the historian Samuel Hays, was "not so much the mechanical devices themselves as the kinds of knowledge and management they implied." Alternative technology represented a move away from the Progressive faith in expertise and professionalization and toward an environmental philosophy predicated on self-education and individual experience.[28]

The AT movement was also bolstered by ideas emerging from the New Left. Particularly influential were the writings of the eco-anarchist Murray Bookchin. Bookchin provided a critical political framework for appropriate technology by situating the quest for alternative technologies within the framework of revolutionary politics. In books such as *Our Synthetic Environment* (1962) and *Post-Scarcity Anarchism* (1971) he argued that highly industrialized nations possessed the potential to create a utopian "ecological society, with new ecotechnologies, and ecocommunities."[29] Bookchin held that the notion of scarcity, a defining fear of the conservation movement, was a ruse perpetuated by "hierarchical society" in an attempt to keep the majority from understanding the revolutionary potentialities of advanced technology. More than most critics on the left, Bookchin also clearly linked revolutionary politics with environmentalism and technology. "Whether now or in the future," he wrote, "human relationships with nature are always mediated by science, technology and knowledge."[30] By explicitly fusing radical politics and ecology the New Left provided a model for a distinctly countercultural environmentalism. From this perspective pollution and environmental destruction were not simply a matter of avoidable waste, but a symptom of a corrupt economic system that consistently stripped the environment of its resources while diminishing the rights of the average citizen.[31]

Although the utopian program of Bookchin and the New Left ultimately failed to capture the hearts of most environmentalists, it did help establish a permanent relationship between environmental and social politics. This linking of the social, political, and environmental in the 1970s paved the way for new trends of the 1980s such as the ecojustice movement. For some of those who felt alienated from the predominantly white middle-class environmental groups like the Sierra Club or the Wilderness Society, the New Left vision of environmental politics provided inspiration. By connecting ecological thinking with a set of social politics the New Left introduced environmentalism to a new and more diverse group of urban Americans who had felt little connection to the wilderness and the recreation-based advocacy of the conservation movement.

At the same time, the New Left helped bolster the growing technological fascination of many counterculture environmentalists. The AT movement represented a different direction for radical politics in the late 1960s and into the '70s. By then the campus-based New Left was primarily a movement against the Vietnam War. New Left politics on the campus focused on striking back at the military-industrial complex and representatives of the technocratic power structure. Escalating violence, renewed scarcity fears, and a host of pressures both inside and outside the movement caused the New Left to fracture and ultimately collapse. Disillusioned by the failure of the revolution, many counterculturists began to move away from radical politics altogether. At the same time proponents of appropriate technology in Europe and America were taking New Left–inspired politics in some different and unconventional directions. Individuals like Stewart Brand, a former member of Ken Kesey's Merry Pranksters, and organizations like the New Alchemy Institute began working to create an alternative society from the ground up by adapting science and technology for the people.

By the early 1970s, the neo-Luddites in the American environmental movement had ceded ground to a growing number of appropriate technologists. This new group of counterculture radicals, environmentalists, scientists, and social activists looked to new modes of protest that recognized the liberating power of decentralized individualistic technology. The appropriate technology movement was varied and diffuse with much disagreement even among its adherents as to how to define their ideology. The term meant different things to different groups, but broadly most agreed that an "appropriate" technology had the following features: "low investment cost per work-place, low capital investment per unit of output, organizational simplicity, high adaptability to a particular social or cultural environment, sparing use of natural resources, low cost of final product or high potential for employment."[32] In other words, an appropriate technology was cheap, simple, and ecologically safe. The proponents of appropriate technology also agreed on the basic idea that alternative technologies could be used to create more self-sufficient lifestyles and new social structures based on democratic control of innovation and communitarian anarchism. For supporters of appropriate technology, the most radical action one could take against the status quo was not throwing bombs or staging sit-ins but fabricating wind generators to "unplug from the grid."

The move toward appropriate technology represented a significant break for the counterculture and the environmental movement. A new breed of young environmentalists built on the ideas of Schumacher, Bookchin, Marcuse, and others to craft a very different political agenda from their technophobic predecessors in the environmental movement. This new agenda found its best expression in the pages of a new publication, *The Whole Earth Catalog*.[33] *Whole*

Earth was run by young radicals who wanted to fight fire with fire; they wanted to resist technocracy and frightening nuclear and military technology by placing the power of small-scale, easily understood, appropriate technology in the hands of anyone willing to listen. A closer look at *Whole Earth* provides insights into the way changing perceptions of the use and abuse of technology influenced the counterculture and the environmental movement.

SOFT TECH AND HARD FACTS

No single institution or organization better represents the technological universe through which counterculturists defined themselves and the multiple responses and programs of the appropriate tech movement than the *Whole Earth Catalog* (*WEC*) and its successor *CoEvolution Quarterly*. This eclectic and iconoclastic publication became a nexus of radical environmentalism, appropriate technology research, alternative lifestyle information, and communitarian anarchism. First published in 1968, the same year appropriate technology burst onto the world scene, *WEC* brought together all of the divergent counterculture technology trends under one roof. Commune members, computer designers and hackers, psychedelic drug engineers, and environmentalists were but a few of the groups who could find something of interest in the pages of *Whole Earth*. The publication's founder, Stewart Brand, set out to create a survival manual for "citizens of planet Earth" and "hippie environmentalist spacemen."[34] According to Brand, *WEC* was a "movable education" for his counterculture friends "who were reconsidering the structure of modern life and building their own communes in the backwoods." Under Brand's direction, *Whole Earth* and its successors extolled the virtues of steam-powered bicycles, windmills, solar collectors, and wood stoves, alongside new "personal computers," satellite telephones, and the latest telecommunications hardware. Brand and his followers were convinced that access to innovative and potentially subversive information and energy technologies was a vital part of changing cultural perceptions that contributed to environmental decay.

Brand's creation perfectly captured the post-Vietnam counterculture movement of the mid-1970s with its emphasis on lifestyle and pragmatic activism over utopian idealism and politics. *WEC* marketed real products, not just ideas, and the focus was always on theoretically feasible, if not always reasonable, solutions to real-world problems. For Brand and his colleagues, *Stop the 5–Gallon Flush*, a guide to stopping water waste with simple household technological fixes, was just as revolutionary a book as *Das Capital*, maybe even more so.[35] Brand was appealing to the growing numbers of disenchanted New Left radicals who were tired of sitting in crowded meeting rooms and coffeehouses endlessly debating politics but still wanted to somehow subvert the system. The publishers of *WEC* inadvertently advanced the radical notion that by staying home from the protest demonstration and modifying your toilet, or building a geodesic dome or a solar collector, you could make a more immediate and significant contribution to the effort to create an alternative future than through more conventional expressive politics.

In contrast to the downbeat rhetoric of the late 1960s campus-based New Left, Brand and his enthusiastic collaborators remained optimistic about a coming revolution brought about by appropriate technology. Drawing on the optimism of utopian post-scarcity visions of the future, Brand and other AT proponents were representative of a new movement within the counterculture characterized by intellectual curiosity and a love for creative technical innovation. Inspired by the work of R. Buckminster Fuller, Brand wanted to expand the "outlaw area" of counterculture innovation away from music production and psychedelic drug research toward areas like alternative energy and information technology.[36] This is not to say that Brand was a pragmatist; he was a dreamer. *WEC* began with the working assumption that large numbers of Americans would prefer to live in self-sustaining, ecologically friendly communities. The first issues of the catalog were aimed at those individuals who were working to use the best of small-scale technology to literally disconnect themselves from the oppressive structures of mainstream society and relocate to rural or wilderness areas. At first, *WEC* promoted technologies that encouraged radically detached self-sufficiency as the key to a fulfilling life.

No one better captured the optimistic spirit of appropriate technology as presented in the pages of *WEC* than the iconoclastic self-taught designer and Harvard dropout Buckminster Fuller. Born in 1895, Fuller may have been an old man by the 1970s, but he was still full of radical perspectives that a younger generation found inspiring.[37] For more than four decades he had been on a personal quest to create a completely new way of viewing design, construction, and the environment. Fuller wanted to reform the "human environment by developing tools that deal more effectively and economically with evolutionary change."[38] Although a prolific designer, Fuller is best known for his revolutionary geodesic domes and the concept of "dymaxion" design. Fuller defined dymaxion as "doing the most with the least."[39] His geodesic dome epitomized the ideal of appropriate technology, using the most sophisticated design principles and the latest technologies to make more with less. Fuller was an acute observer of the natural world. Unlike most of his contemporaries, especially in the 1930s, Fuller saw the universe in terms of interconnected triangles and spheres instead of straight lines and boxes. As the ultimate example of his design ideal, the geodesic dome was fabricated out of a series of linked triangles forming a sphere that proved to be so strong it could be built with very lightweight materials yet remain structurally sound in virtually any size. Although the geodesic dome was based on complex mathematics and design principles, it was a structure so uncomplicated that almost anyone could build one from materials at hand. Domes consequently were adapted as the building style of choice for counterculture communes such as Colorado's Drop City because they were relatively cheap, easy to build, potentially portable, and environmentally friendly.[40] Fuller's practical design epitomized the ideal of using appropriate technologies to develop alternative communities. Through *WEC* Brand and his fellow staff members disseminated information on Fuller and others who were working to create alternative ways of living by means of design and technical innovation.

In its early years *WEC* articulated an appealing vision for those looking for a permanent retreat from the status quo. Individuals who planned their escape through the pages of *WEC* discovered a program of action where "choices about the right technology, both useful old gadgets and ingenious new tools, are crucial," but "choices about political matters are not."[41] For appropriate technology enthusiasts lifestyle became the most important form of political expression. In *WEC* Brand assembled an almost mind-boggling array of information on tools, science, products, services, and publications ranging from the mundane to the downright weird—but all somehow concerned with crafting alternative lifestyles that subverted traditional networks of political, spiritual, and physical energy. For those who encountered *WEC* the experience was often a revelation. According to Gereth Branwyn, subsequently a staff writer for *Wired Magazine*,

> I got my first *Whole Earth Catalog* in 1971. It was the same day I scored my first bag of pot. I went over to a friend's house to smoke a joint . . . he pulled out this unwieldy catalog his brother had brought home from college. I was instantly enthralled. I'd never seen anything like it. We lived in a small redneck town in Virginia—people didn't think about such things as "whole systems" and "nomadics" and "Zen Buddhism." I traded my friend the pot for the catalog.[42]

At a time when the New Left movement was dissipating, *WEC* and the AT movement provided hope that the quest to construct an alternative future was still possible. Even so, not all counterculturists or appropriate technology advocates agreed with the radical self-sufficiency message of *WEC*. The first *WEC* appealed to the dropout school of hippies and back-to-the-landers who took their political cues from the likes of Ken Kesey, who encouraged them to "Just . . . turn your back and say . . . 'Fuck It' and walk away."[43] Years later

Clard Svenson stands inside a half-finished geodesic dome designed as a "Theater for Psychedelics" at Drop City, Las Animas county, Colorado, 6 August 1967. He holds a painting by members of the commune entitled *The Ultimate*. When Drop City was organized by a group of artists the previous year, it became one of the earliest rural hippie communes in the country. It was also the very first one to embrace R. Buckminster Fuller's geodesic dome as their signature style of architecture. The "Droppers" utilized salvaged automobile tops as a medium for enclosing these domes. Courtesy of the Western History/Genealogy Department, Denver Public Library.

Brand realized that *WEC*'s uncritical enthusiasm for self-sufficiency and dropout politics in those early years may have caused more harm than good. In *Soft Tech*, an anthology he co-edited in 1978, Brand wrote with some regret, "Anyone who has actually tried to live in total self-sufficiency . . . knows the mind-numbing labor and loneliness and frustration and real marginless hazard that goes with the attempt. It is a kind of hysteria."[44] Despite his concerns about an overemphasis on self-sufficiency and escapism, most readers of the *Catalog* never took the message literally. The vast majority of the almost two million people who purchased copies of *WEC* in its first three years never left the city, never dropped out of mainstream society for a lonely exile. The message that most readers were apt to have gotten from the *Whole Earth Catalog* was unbridled technological optimism, the idea that innovation and invention guided by a conscience could overcome even the worst social and environmental problems. It was this message, so profoundly different from the technophobia expressed by a previous generation of environmentalists and critics like Roszak, that made *Whole Earth* such a significant phenomenon. Brand and other proponents of the appropriate technology movement understood something about "technocracy's children" that Roszak did not: the youth culture of the 1960s and '70s was, in the words of the appropriate tech pioneer and historian Witold Rybczynski, "immensely attracted to technology."[45]

From the beginning *WEC*, and the appropriate technology movement as a whole, directed that attraction in two distinct directions: the "outlaw edges" of alternative energy technology, and information and communications technology. Thus, over the years, readers of the *Catalog* could find careful descriptions of the Vermont Castings "Defiant" wood stove closely followed by the latest information on Apple computers. This seemingly incongruous juxtaposition made perfect sense to Brand. "The Vermont Castings tool manipulated heat, the Apple tool manipulated information." "Both cost a few hundred dollars, both were made by and for revolutionaries who wanted to de-institutionalize society and empower the individual, both embodied clever design ideas," all characteristics of appropriate technology. According to Brand, the ability to manipulate energy and information were the basic skills required to change the system.[46] In other words, the only way one could hope to cast off the chains of the industrial world was to steal the keys to the kingdom. Acquiring the knowledge to manipulate energy in particular was viewed by supporters of appropriate technology and a growing faction of the environmental movement as a crucial step in freeing oneself from existing structures of oppression and environmental degradation and enabling self-sufficiency.

With this broadened agenda in mind, the energy focus at *Whole Earth* and then *CoEvolution Quarterly* shifted from low-tech basic tools, like the wood stove or individually crafted hand saws, to much more sophisticated alternative energy solutions like solar, geothermal, biogas and biofuels, and high-tech wind-harnessing devices like the ever-popular "Gemini Synchronous Inverter." Brand and crew drew inspiration from groups like the New Alchemists who were pushing the edges of appropriate technology and putting the latest alternative energy technologies into active use in their laboratories on Prince Edward Island and Cape Cod.[47] Other organizations sprung up elsewhere to explore appropriate technology from a variety of perspectives such as the Faralones Institute of San Francisco, the Intermediate Technology Group, and the California Office of Appropriate Technology, to name only a few. These organizations researched new household technologies such as composting toilets, affordable greenhouses, and organic gardening techniques along with alternative energy technologies. While the research of individuals and organizations working in the area of AT varied greatly, all of those involved shared the common goal of using technical research to enable simpler, more ecologically-sensitive lives and economies of a human scale.

The focus on alternative renewable energy at *WEC*, the New Alchemy Institute, and similar organizations reflected a larger shift in direction in the American environmental movement as a whole. The energy crisis of the early 1970s caused environmentalists to realize that many of the ecological problems of the postwar era were linked to the acquisition and distribution of energy. Long lines at gas stations and soaring fuel prices brought home the reality of finite energy resources. This renewed awareness that scarcity was once again a real and long-term problem forced counterculture environmentalists to reevaluate the aspects of their technological enthusiasm that had been predicated on notions of a postscarcity world. By the mid-1970s it was clear the earlier presumption that postscarcity conditions had arrived was at best premature. The move away from a postscarcity politics and toward an appropriate technology philosophy that recognized scarcity and reformulated utopian radicalism paved the way for AT to move into the mainstream. The energy crisis forced millions of Americans to reevaluate their environmental positions and helped the environmental movement expand its support base dramatically. Organizations working in the area of AT were poised to provide a new vision of environmental activism to this broadened audience of concerned Americans. The community of individuals and organizations working on alternative energy solutions became particularly influential during the 1970s.

All of the new and renewable energy technologies featured in the pages of *WEC* became components of what the British physicist Amory Lovins referred to as the "soft path." Lovins popularized the soft path to energy solutions in a widely read and highly controversial 1976 article in the prestigious journal *Foreign Affairs*.[48] For Lovins and his supporters the soft path was the moral alternative to an American "federal policy . . . [that] relies on rapid expansion of centralized high technologies to increase supplies of energy."[49] Instead of increasing centralization soft path proponents supported decentralized appropriate technologies and urged Western nations, and particularly the United States, to direct their research toward renewable alternatives and explore the possibility of establishing a more equitable relationship with developing nations. The benefits of appropriate soft technologies like passive solar, which combined new technologies with traditional building materials to heat buildings with energy from the sun, were available immediately to all who wished to pursue them. Lovins emphasized that the advantages of soft tech design were easily transferable to developing nations. Simple passive solar techniques, like painting a wall black behind south-facing windows so as to better absorb the sun's radiant energy, could appreciably decrease the dependence on fossil fuels in the Northern Hemisphere.[50] Soft path proponents could point to several significant energy technologies with long and productive histories that perfectly fit with the ideal of easily accessible renewable energy for a modern world. In fact, most of the soft path solutions to modern energy problems were not new, but retooled versions of existing technologies. None of these older technologies better captures the spirit of the soft path energy movement than the venerable windmill.

The use of wind as a source of power dates to antiquity when humans first harnessed the wind to power ships and soon after as an efficient means for the mechanization of food production and irrigation. For thousands of years cultures all over the globe relied on wind power to mill their grains, drain their lowlands, draw water from aquifers, and saw their lumber.[51] In America the windmill became an emblem for self-sufficiency as farmers and ranchers moved into the arid plains of the West and mastered the technology of the windmill in order to survive far from established services and energy sources. Americans quickly discovered that windmills could be fabricated out of a wide variety of locally available materials and constructed cheaply from mail-order plans. As early as 1885 windmills were used to generate electrical power. Early researchers learned that windmills were an excellent source of electrical power on a small scale, and even small windmills could easily provide enough electricity for a home or small business. Existing windmills could be retrofitted with electrical generators and provide power to a remote farm or mill while retaining the capacity to pump water or grind wheat.[52] Although many adopted the wind generator as a permanent source of power, for most of the twentieth century the harnessing of wind energy never became as widespread as its early proponents had expected.

The energy crisis of the 1970s renewed a popular interest in wind energy. One of the reasons that wind power had failed to be more widely adopted was a fundamental inability to regulate the wind. The power from wind generators ebbed and flowed according to the fickleness of the wind. This made it a poor substitute for hydroelectric or coal turbines that could sustain a constant and manageable flow of energy for large systems and power grids. Soft path supporters, however, were unconcerned about wind power's unsuitability for large systems, since by definition they were looking for sources of power that were better suited to decentralized systems.

Like E. F. Schumacher, Lovins and other soft tech proponents believed that the ability to construct small-scale, self-sufficient systems provided individuals and communities with a closer connection to the earth and a greater degree of control over their lives. The windmill was the type of technology that could enable one to use the latest research in electric power generators and new materials like fiberglass to build machines that produced few if any pollutants while providing inexpensive, renewable energy. For soft path proponents the potential of the wind generator was both practical and political. Disconnecting yourself from the power grid was the first step toward a cleaner environment and a move toward reevaluating all of the large systems that dominated the economy and daily life of developed nations. The key to the politics behind soft path and AT science was the notion that real change came not from protest but from constructing viable alternatives to the status quo starting with the basic elements of human life: food, energy, and shelter. Lovins's credentials as a professionally trained scientist lent credibility to the appropriate technology movement and prompted both opponents and supporters to more carefully articulate their energy positions. Brand approved not only of Lovins's ideas but his terminology as well: "'Soft' signifies that something is alive, resilient, adaptive," Brand mused in 1978, "maybe even lovable."[53] By the mid-1970s soft path energy research into solar power, wind, geothermal heat, biogas conversion, and recycled fuels moved to the forefront of the environmental and AT movements.

At the same time that environmentalists were exploring different paths toward decentralization through renewable energy development, others were working within the second area of the "outlaw edge": information technology. For Brand, alternative energy was important, but information technology was where the real action was. As he later expressed it, "Information technology is a self-accelerating fine-grained global industry that sprints ahead of laws and diffuses beyond them."[54] Brand was intrigued by what he called the "subversive possibilities" of technologies as diverse as recording devices, desktop publishing, individual telecommunications, and especially

BY THE EDITORS OF "RAIN"

RAINBOOK

RESOURCES FOR APPROPRIATE TECHNOLOGY

with Hundreds of Illustrations

The front cover of a 1977 publication entitled *RAINBOOK: Resources for Appropriate Technology*. It features an illustration by Diane Schatz that is a portion of a poster she produced called "Visions of Ecotopia" (itself inspired by Ernest Callenbach's 1975 bestselling novel *Ecotopia*). The drawing depicts an intricately detailed cityscape which represents the counterculture's post-Oil embargo 1970s blueprint for an alternative society that had fully integrated renewable sources of energy and adopted a "small is beautiful" approach to appropriate technology. Plainly visible are wind generators; a geodesic dome; an "Urban farming" school's rooftop greenhouses; and a parking ramp in the process of being converted into a multipurpose facility to house a solar power manufacturing establishment, a food co-op, and a bike shop. Also visible are a community-owned credit union, public bath house, and a recycling center. Courtesy of Michael William Doyle.

personal computers. As such, he was among a growing group of countercul-
turists who had a deep respect for innovators like Steve Jobs and Steve
Wozniak, who were designing and then using their computers to push what
Brand referred to as "the edges of the possible and permissible."[55] As with
Lovins and the soft path proponents, alternative information technology was
viewed, perhaps somewhat naively, by people like Steve Jobs and Stewart
Brand as a means of personal empowerment. The mandate at Apple was to
"build the coolest machine you could imagine," something so different that
people would rethink the role of the machine in modern life.[56] The naming
of their products suggested that these machines were somehow more natural
than their predecessors. Where older mainframe computers were identified
by acronyms and numbers, the new personal computers were named Apple
and were operated by a pointing device called a "mouse." This was friendly
technology, designed to be unthreatening and easy to use. The specifics of
how information and communications technology could become weapons in
the war against the status quo were never clearly articulated by AT proponents. There was a general sense among optimistic counterculturists that the
personal computer and other new technologies were intrinsically radical and
could somehow change the world for the better simply by existing. The
details would be worked out later. In the meantime the contagious enthusiasm and inventive genius touched off by these new machines produced a
technological revolution that ultimately transformed the American economy
in unanticipated ways and created some ironic ideological paradoxes for the
AT pioneers who helped spawn that revolution.

For many in the counterculture of the early 1960s, computers had represented the epitome of all that was wrong with technology in the service of
technocracy. During that era computers were giant humming machines that
were immensely expensive and required a high level of technical expertise to
operate. They were the heartless mechanized brains of oppression, used by
IBM and the Pentagon to design weapons of destruction and quantify the
body counts in Vietnam. Neo-Luddites dismissed the computer as a malevo-
lent machine of centralization and dehumanization. Critics, such as Theodore
Roszak, argued that computers were nothing more than "low-grade mechanical counterfeits" of the human mind, devices propagated by the "most morally
questionable" elements of society.[57] Many of the first readers of *WEC* would
have agreed with these critiques. They would have had a hard time conceiv-
ing a role for computers in their utopian back-to-nature communes. But other
counterculturists, including Brand, were quick to recognize the potential of
the new wave of microcomputers and personal information technology to link
individuals and organizations who were working to humanize American soci-

ety. The widespread dissemination of information was essential to the project of constructing alternative institutions and transforming society root and branch. Long before most, Brand and others involved in the AT movement realized that computers had the potential to help build a new cybercommunity. What, these pioneers wondered, could be more alternative than an electronic utopia, an alternative universe where individuals separated by huge distances could share ideas, images, and thoughts with thousands of other like-minded people all over the world? AT enthusiasts were some of the first Americans to go online, and the Whole Earth 'Lectronic Link (WELL) became one of the early attempts to create a "virtual community."[58] By the mid-1970s, *WEC*'s successor, *CoEvolution Quarterly*, was dedicating more space to information technology than any other subject, and it was not alone.

By the end of the 1970s, organizations like *WEC*, the New Alchemy Institute, and others had brought together some of the best and the brightest members of the counterculture to attempt to reconcile nature and the machine. For Stewart Brand and his fellow appropriate technology enthusiasts the research they promoted, in both alternative energy and alternative information systems, succeeded in substantially altering the way Americans thought about the power of technology as a benevolent force for environmental protection, ecological living, and personal liberation. In many ways the reconciliation of ecology and technology popularized by *WEC* provided a much more integrated and realistic model for environmentalism. By demonstrating that there were possibilities for a middle ground between modern technology and environmental consciousness, the appropriate technology movement contributed to acceptance of environmentalism in mainstream American culture.

Despite this success the AT movement was not without its ironic consequences. The liberal idealism that drove AT often failed to account for the degree to which even small-scale and individualistic ideas, like the personal computer, could very rapidly be incorporated into, and even strengthen, the very systems they were designed to subvert. In 1980, Alvin Toffler argued in his hugely popular book, *The Third Wave*, that the world was on the brink of a third industrial revolution. [59] According to Toffler this third revolution would grow out of the transformation of information technologies and would have profound consequences for industry and society. In many ways Toffler has been proved right. Information technology in particular has reshaped the American economy and society at an incredible pace. One of the most profound ironies of the counterculture technology movement is that it helped prepare the way for this revolution and the new industrial giants it spawned. Corporations like Apple, Intel, and Microsoft, founded by young counterculture or counterculture-inspired entrepreneurs who started their careers pushing the "outlaw edges" of the "possible and permissible," now dominate the American economy. Many of the radicals of yesterday have become the capitalist elite of today.

We live in an age of technological systems of a level of complexity that makes the systems of the 1960s look positively antiquated. One of the central notions of the alternative technology movement was the belief that access to innovative information and energy technologies was a vital part of changing cultural perceptions and social conditions that contributed to environmental decay. Today the "outlaw edge" of technology that inspired the counterculture is more often occupied by new industrial behemoths like Intel. Corporations whose factories drain millions of gallons of water a day out of ancient desert aquifers to wash the silicon chips that power personal computers exhibit little concern for the effect on the environment.[60] Examples like this lend credence to declensionist readings of the counterculture. But the story of the counterculture, technology, and the environmental movement is far more complex than has been previously acknowledged. The relationship between counterculture environmentalists and technology was always ambivalent. Therefore, it should come as no surprise that the legacy of their technological revolution is similarly ambivalent. But the majority of the AT initiatives have had an overwhelmingly positive impact on American culture and American environmentalism. The promotion of renewable energy resources and energy conservation through technological invention is one example of success. Energy-efficient houses, thermal windows, solar power, and high-efficiency electrical devices have become widely accepted as standard features of American consumer culture. Curbside recycling and the proliferation of post-consumer waste recycling have also become a part of daily life. Many of these technologies and services that seem so obvious and sensible that they go unnoticed today resulted from the radical innovation of counterculture environmentalists. Whether they went back to the land or into the laboratory, they infused environmentalism with an optimistic hope that with a little creativity and a lot of ingenuity Americans could fashion an alternative future based on harmony between humans, nature, and the machine.

ACKNOWLEDGMENTS
I would like to thank my mentor, Virginia Scharff, for advice on this essay and for pointing me toward alternative technology as a research topic. I would also like to thank the editors of this volume for invaluable comments on several drafts. William Rorabaugh, who commented on this essay as part of a panel at the 1998 annual meeting of the Western Historical Association, also pointed out some important weaknesses to my argument and gave me excellent suggestions on how to revise this essay for publication.

NOTES

1. Richard Brautigan, *The Pill versus the Spring Hill Mine Disaster* (San Francisco: Four Seasons, 1968), 1. This poem was distributed as a free broadside by the Communications Company in the Haight-Ashbury, June 1967.

2. Murray Bookchin, *Post-Scarcity Anarchism* (Berkeley: Ramparts Press, 1971).

3. Ibid., 12.

4. Ibid., 11.

5. Steven Levy, *Hackers: Heroes of the Computer Revolution* (New York: Penguin Books, 1994).

6. The classic study of the conservation movement is, Samuel P. Hays, *Conservation and the Gospel of Efficiency: The Progressive Conservation Movement, 1890–1920* (Cambridge: Harvard University Press, 1959). Hays refined his take on conservation and environmentalism in *Environmental Politics in the United States, 1955–1985* (Cambridge: Cambridge University Press, 1987) and *Explorations In Environmental History* (Pittsburgh: University of Pittsburgh Press, 1998). Many others have explored the history of conservation and environmentalism. The following were particularly useful for this essay: Stephen Fox, *The American Conservation Movement: John Muir and His Legacy* (Madison: University of Wisconsin Press, 1981). Roderick Nash, *Wilderness and the American Mind* (New Haven: Yale University Press, 1974). Samuel Hays, *Beauty, Health, and Permanence: Environmental Politics in the United States, 1955–1985* (Cambridge: Cambridge University Press, 1987). Donald Worster. *Nature's Economy: A History of Ecological Ideals* (Cambridge: Cambridge University Press, 1977). See also, Michael P. Cohen *The Pathless Way: John Muir and the American Wilderness* (Madison: University of Wisconsin Press, 1984); Robert C. Paehlke, *Environmentalism and the Future of Progressive Politics* (New Haven: Yale University Press, 1989); Michael Fromme, *Battle for the Wilderness* (New York: Praeger, 1974); Richard Lamm and Michael McCarthy, *The Angry West: A Vulnerable Land and Its Future* (Boston: Houghton Mifflin, 1982); Kirkpatrick Sale, *The Green Revolution: The American Environmental Movement, 1962–1992* (New York: Hill and Wang, 1993); Philip Shabekoff, *A Fierce Green Fire* (New York: Hill and Wang, 1993); Hal Rothman, *The Greening of a Nation? : Environmentalism in the United States since 1945* (New York: Harbrace, 1997), and *Saving the Planet: The American Response to the Environment in the Twentieth Century* (Chicago: Ivan R. Dee, 2000); Bob Pepperman Taylor, *Our Limits Transgressed: Environmental Political Thought in America* (Lawrence: University Press of Kansas, 1992).

7. Lewis Mumford, *Technics and Civilization* (New York: Harcourt, Brace & World, 1962).

8. John Eastlick, "Proposed Collection of Conservation of Natural Resources," FF-51, box 4, Conservation Library Collection archive.

9. Fox, *The American Conservation Movement*. Fox highlights Muir's antimodernist rhetoric as evidence that the conservation movement had, from the beginning, two distinct strains of thought: one, progressive and modern, focused on efficiency and reform; and the other, anti-modernist, focused on the esthetic and spiritual values of wilderness. The best discussion of these ideas can be found in Max Oelschlaeger, *The Idea of Wilderness: From Prehistory to the Age of Ecology* (New Haven: Yale University Press, 1991).

10. Oelschlaeger, *The Idea of Wilderness*, 2.

11. Rachel Carson, *Silent Spring* (Fawcett, 1962).

12. Barry Commoner, *The Closing Circle: Nature, Man, and Technology* (New York: Knopf, 1971).

13. Jacques Ellul, *The Technological Society*, trans. Joachim Neugroschel (New York: Continuum, 1980), first published in French in 1954 and in English in 1964. Quote is from Thomas P. Hughes, *American Genesis: A Century of Invention and Technological Enthusiasm* (New York: Penguin Books, 1989), 450.

14. Quote is from Langdon Winner, "Building a Better Mousetrap: Appropriate Technology as a Social Movement," in *Appropriate Technology and Social Values: A Critical Appraisal,* Franklin A. Long and Alexandra Oleson, eds. (Cambridge, Mass: Ballinger, 1980), 33.

15. Herbert Marcuse, *One Dimensional Man: Studies in the Ideology of Advanced Industrial Society* (Boston: Beacon Press, 1964).

16. Hughes, *American Genesis*, 445.

17. Mumford, *Technics and Civilization*.

18. Hughes, *American Genesis*, 446–50. Lewis Mumford, *The Myth of the Machine: The Pentagon of Power* (New York: Harcourt Brace Jovanovich, 1970).

19. For an in-depth look at the "machine" in American culture, see Leo Marx, *The Machine and the Garden: Technology and the Pastoral Ideal in America* (New York: Oxford University Press, 1964). This classic study remains the best source on the strange relationship between technology and nature in American culture. Also see Richard White, *The Organic Machine* (New York: Hill & Wang, 1995).

20. Theodore Roszak, *The Making of a Counter Culture: Reflections on the Technocratic Society and Its Youthful Opposition* (Berkeley: University of California Press, 1995).

21. Ibid., 8.

22. Charles A. Reich, *The Greening of America: How the Youth Revolution Is Trying to Make America Livable* (New York: Random House, 1970).

23. E. F. Schumacher, *Small Is Beautiful: Economics As If People Mattered* (New York: Harper & Row, 1973).

24. Ibid., 124.

25. A useful taxonomy of technologies can be found in Marilyn Carr, ed., *The AT Reader: Theory and Practice in Appropriate Technology* (New York: Intermediate Technology Development Group of North America, 1985), 6–11.

26. Witold Rybczynski, *Paper Heroes: A Review of Appropriate Technology* (Garden City, N.Y.: Anchor Books, 1980), 1–4.

27. David Dickson, *Alternative Technology and the Politics of Technical Change* (Glasgow: Fontana/Collins, 1974), 148–73.

28. Hays, *Beauty, Health, and Permanence*, 262.

29. Lewis Herber (Murray Bookchin), *Our Synthetic Environment* (New York: Knopf, 1962). Murray Bookchin, *Post-Scarcity Anarchism* (Berkeley: Ramparts Press, 1971). Quote is from *Post-Scarcity*, 22. Also see Ulrike Heider, *Anarchism: Left, Right, and Green* (San Francisco: City Lights Books, 1994); and Arthur Lothstein, ed., *"All We Are Saying . . . ": The Philosophy of the New Left* (New York: Capricorn Books, 1970).

30. Bookchin, *Post-Scarcity*, 21.

31. The best overview of the New Left, the counterculture, and environmentalism can be found in Robert Gottlieb's excellent *Forcing the Spring: The Transformation of the American Environmental Movement* (Washington, D.C.: Island Press, 1993), 81–114. For a very different point of view from Gottlieb's and from that in this essay, see Hays, *Beauty, Health, and Permanence*, 259–65. Hays argues that there were only superficial similarities between the "negative" counterculture and the "positive" environmental alternative lifestyle movement.

32. Gottlieb, *Forcing the Spring*, 9. There are many fine sources on the development of appropriate technology; see, for example: David Dickson, *Alternative Technology*; Nicholas Jéquier, ed., *Appropriate Technology: Problems and Promises* (Paris: Organization for Economic Co-operation and Development, 1976); Franklin A. Long and Alexandra Oleson, eds., *Appropriate Technology and Social Values*; Witold Rybczynski, *Taming the Tiger: The Struggle to Control Technology* (New York: Penguin, 1985); Mathew J. Betz, Pat McGowan, and Rolf T. Wigand, eds., *Appropriate Technology: Choice and Development* (Durham: Duke Press Policy Studies, 1984); Ron Westrum, *Technologies and Society: The Shaping of People and Things* (Belmont, Calif.: Wadsworth Publishing, 1991); and Theodore Roszak, *Where the Wasteland Ends: Politics and Transcendence in Postindustrial Society* (Garden City, N.Y.: Anchor Books, 1973). Two recent works shed new light on the history of alternative technology: Martin W. Lewis, *Green Delusions: An Environmentalist Critique of Radical Environmentalism* (Durham:

Duke University Press, 1992), and Charles T. Rubin, ed., *Conservation Reconsidered: Nature, Virtue, and American Liberal Democracy* (Lanham, Md.: Rowman and Littlefield, 2000).

33. *The Whole Earth Catalog* has had many incarnations. Because of the editor's iconoclastic style and alternative publishing methodology, *Whole Earth* is maddeningly difficult to properly cite. The first addition was published in 1968 as *The Whole Earth Catalog: Access to Tools*, edited by Stewart Brand and published by the Portola Institute with distribution provided by Random House. Several new versions followed between 1969 and 1971 (all with Brand as the lead editor), when *The Last Whole Earth Catalog* (Portola & Random House, 1971) appeared. *The Last Whole Earth* won the prestigious National Book Award in 1972. All of the *Whole Earth*s were reprinted many times, and often there were seasonal editions. Between 1972 and 1999 there were several notable editions. See, especially, Stewart Brand, ed. *The Next Whole Earth Catalog: Access to Tools* (Point Foundation with distribution by Rand McNally in the United States and Random House in Canada, 1980). This particular edition is notable for sheer size, 608 over-sized pages, and breadth of coverage. There were also several *Whole Earth*–type companion volumes, such as J. Baldwin and Stewart Brand, eds., *Soft-Tech* (New York: Penguin Books, 1978), and Kevin Kelly, ed., *Signal: Communication Tools for the Information Age, A Whole Earth Catalog* (New York: Harmony Books, 1988), that focused on particular issues. Brand relinquished the editorship in the 1980s and several editors have since shepherded the perennially popular publication through several more editions. Most notable among these are: Howard Rheingold, ed., *The Millennium Whole Earth Catalog* (San Francisco: Harper San Francisco, 1994), and Peter Warshall, ed., *30th Anniversary Celebration: Whole Earth Catalog* (San Rafael, Calif.: Point Foundation, 1999). The 30th anniversary edition includes a wonderful collection of alternative technology and counterculture essays by leaders from the 1960s to the 1990s.

34. Winner, "Building a Better Mousetrap," 31.

35. Witold Rybczynski, *Stop the 5-Gallon Flush* (Montreal: Minimum Cost Housing Group, 1975).

36. Kelly, ed., *Signal: Communications Tools*, 3.

37. Robert Marks, ed., *Buckminster Fuller: Ideas and Integrities* (Englewood Cliffs, N.J.: Prentice Hall, 1963). Robert Snyder, ed., *Buckminster Fuller: Autobiographical Monologue/Scenario* (New York: St. Martin's Press, 1980).

38. Snyder, ed., *Buckminster Fuller: Autobiographical*, 38.

39. Ibid., 54–55.

40. Clark Secrest, "'No Right to be Poor': Colorado's Drop City," *Colorado Heritage* (winter 1998): 14–21.

41. Winner, "Building a Better Mousetrap," 32. Quote is Winner's.

42. Gareth Branwyn, "Whole Earth Review." Streettech home site. http://www.streettech.com/bcp/BCPgraf/CyberCulture/WholeEarthReview.html. 21 September 1998.

43. Tom Wolfe, *The Electric Kool-Aid Acid Test* (New York: Bantam Books, 1997), 191–200.

44. Baldwin and Brand, eds., *Soft-Tech*, 5.

45. Witold Rybczynski, *Paper Heroes*, 94.

46. Kelly, ed. *Signal: Communication Tools*, 3.

47. John Todd, "The New Alchemists." in *Soft-Tech*, ed., Baldwin and Brand, 149–65.

48. Amory Lovins, "Energy Strategy: The Road Not Taken," *Foreign Affairs* 55 (October 1976), 65–96. Hugh Nash, ed., *The Energy Controversy: Soft Path Questions and Answers* (San Francisco: Friends of the Earth, 1979). Jim Harding, ed., *Tools for the Soft Path* (San Francisco: Friends of the Earth, 1979).

49. Lovins, "Energy Strategy," 65.

50. Ibid., 82–83.

51. Robert W. Righter, *Wind Energy in America: A History* (Norman: University of Oklahoma Press, 1996). David Rittenhouse Inglis, *Wind Power and Other Energy Options* (Ann Arbor: University of Michigan Press, 1978). Michael Hackleman, *The Homebuilt, Wind-*

Generated Electricity Handbook (Culver City, Calif.: Peace Press, 1975). Richard L. Hills, *Power From Wind: A History of Windmill Technology* (Cambridge: Cambridge University Press, 1994). See also Nicholas P. Chermisnoff, *Fundamentals of Wind Energy* (Ann Arbor: Ann Arbor Science, 1978); Douglas R. Coonley, *Wind: Making It Work for You* (Philadelphia: Franklin Institute Press, 1979).

52. Hills, *Power from Wind*, 265–81.

53. Baldwin and Brand, eds., *Soft-Tech*, 5.

54. Kelly, eds., *Signal: Communication Tools*, 3.

55. Ibid. For more on Jobs, Wozniak, and Apple, see Steven Levy, *Insanely Great: The Life and Times of Macintosh, The Computer That Changed Everything* (New York: Penguin Books, 1995); Steven Levy, *Hackers: Heroes of the Computer Revolution* (New York: Penguin Books, 1994); and Jeff Goodell, "The Rise and Fall of Apple Inc.," *Rolling Stone*, 4 April 1996, 51–73 and 18 April 1996, 59–88.

56. Goodell, "The Rise and Fall of Apple Inc.," 52.

57. Theodore Roszak, *The Cult of Information: A Neo-Luddite Treatise on High-Tech, Artificial Intelligence, and the True Art of Thinking* (Berkeley: University of California Press, 1994), xiii–xv.

58. The WELL website. http://www.well.com. 21 September 1998.

59. Alvin Toffler, *The Third Wave* (New York: Bantam Books, 1982).

60. Bruce Selcraig, "Albuquerque Learns It Really Is a Desert Town," *High Country News* 26 (26 December 1994): 1–6.

Contributors

Beth Bailey is associate professor of American Studies and Regents Lecturer at the University of New Mexico. She earned her doctorate in history at the University of Chicago in 1986. Her published works include *The Columbia Guide to America in the 1960s* (co-editor) (Columbia University Press), *Sex in the Heartland* (Harvard University Press, 1999), and *From Front Porch to Back Seat: Courtship in Twentieth-Century America* (Johns Hopkins University Press, 1988).

Peter Braunstein is a journalist and cultural historian based in New York City. He writes about fashion, film, celebrity, the 1960s, music, technology, and pop culture for such publications as the *Village Voice, Forbes' American Heritage*, the *Chronicle of Higher Education, Women's Wear Daily, W,* and *culturefront.* He received his M.A. from New York University in 1992, having written a thesis on the Haight-Ashbury counterculture.

Philip Deloria is associate professor of history at the University of Michigan, Ann Arbor. He is the author of *Playing Indian* (Yale University Press, 1998), for which he was welcomed into the Outstanding Book Winner's Circle by the Gustavus Myers Center for the Study of Bigotry and Human Rights in North America. He earned a Bachelor's in Music Education (1982) and an

M.A. in Journalism and Mass Communications (1988) from the University of Colorado; his doctorate in American Studies at Yale University was awarded in 1994.

Michael William Doyle worked in the new-wave food co-op movement during the 1970s while living communally on an organic farm he helped found in Wisconsin. He went on to earn a B.A. at the University of Wisconsin-Madison (1989) and a Ph.D. at Cornell University (1997); he currently is assistant professor of history at Ball State University in Muncie, Indiana. His revised dissertation, *Free Radicals: The Haight-Ashbury Diggers and the American Counterculture of the 1960s*, will be published as part of the CultureAmerica series by the University Press of Kansas.

David Farber is professor of history at the University of New Mexico. He earned his doctorate from the University of Chicago in 1985. His books include *The Columbia Guide to America in the 1960s* (co-editor) (Columbia University Press), *The Sixties: From Memory to History* (editor) (University of North Carolina Press, 1994), *The Age of Great Dreams: America in the 1960s* (Hill and Wang, 1994), and *Chicago '68* (University of Chicago Press, 1988). His current project is titled *The Conservative Sixties*.

Jeff A. Hale is director of Development at the University of New Mexico's College of Education in Albuquerque. He holds a B.A. from the University of Southern Maine (1984), an M.A. (1985) and a Ph.D. (1995) in history from Louisiana State University. His dissertation is titled "Wiretapping and National Security: Nixon, the Mitchell Doctrine, and the White Panthers."

David E. James teaches critical studies at the University of Southern California School of Cinema-Television. His books include *The Hidden Foundation: Cinema and the Question of Class* (University of Minnesota Press, 1996), *Power Misses: Essays across (Un)Popular Culture* (co-editor) (Verso, 1996), *To Free the Cinema: Jonas Mekas and the New York Underground* (editor) (Princeton University Press, 1992), and *Allegories of Cinema: American Film in the Sixties* (Princeton University Press, 1989).

Andrew Kirk is assistant professor and director of the Public History Program at University of Nevada-Las Vegas. He earned his Ph.D. in history from the University of New Mexico in 1998. He is the author of *Collecting Nature: The American Environmental Movement and the Conservation Library* (University Press of Kansas, [forthcoming, October 2001]), a cultural history of the environmental movement told through a case study of one of America's most unusual libraries, and *Human/Nature: Biology, Culture and Environmental History* (co-editor)(University of New Mexico Press, 1999).

Robert McRuer is assistant professor of English at the George Washington University. After earning his Ph.D. at the University of Illinois at Urbana-Champaign (1995), he authored *The Queer Renaissance: Contemporary American Literature and the Reinvention of Lesbian and Gay Identities* (New York University Press, 1997), and guest edited, with Abby Wilkerson, a forthcoming special issue of *GLQ: A Journal of Lesbian and Gay Studies* on the intersections of queer theory and disability studies. He is currently completing a book project titled *De-Composing Bodies: Cultural Signs of Queerness and Disability.*

Debra Michals is a doctoral candidate in American history at New York University, where she specializes in comparative women's history. Her dissertation, "Beyond Pin Money: The Rise of Women's Small Business Ownership, 1945–1980," looks at the intersection of personal choices with the economic, political, and cultural climate of the various decades. She has also worked as a journalist for over fifteen years with articles appearing in *Ms., Working Woman, Harper's Bazaar,* and *Self.* She spent two years as the acting associate director of the undergraduate program in women's studies at New York University. Her long-term research interests, reflected in her essay here, center on the history and culture of the women's movement in the twentieth century.

Timothy Miller is professor of religious studies at the University of Kansas from where he earned his doctoral degree in 1973. His published works include *The 60s Communes: Hippies and Beyond* (Syracuse University Press, 1999), *The Quest for Utopia in Twentieth-Century America* (Syracuse University Press, 1998), *America's Alternative Religions* (editor) (State University of New York Press, 1995), and *The Hippies and American Values* (University of Tennessee Press, 1991).

Lauren Onkey is associate professor of English at Ball State University, Muncie, Indiana, where she teaches postcolonial literature and cultural studies. She earned her B.A. at the College of William and Mary (1985) and her Ph.D. from the University of Illinois at Urbana-Champaign (1994). She has published essays on contemporary Irish theater, fiction, and rock and roll, and is currently working on a book on the discourse of race in Irish culture.

Doug Rossinow is assistant professor and chair of the history department at Metropolitan State University, Minneapolis. He earned his Ph.D. at Johns Hopkins University in 1994. The author of *The Politics of Authenticity: Liberalism, Christianity, and the New Left in America* (Columbia University Press, 1998), as well as numerous articles, his current book project is entitled *The Vital Margin: Interpreting 'Progressive' Politics in Modern America*.

Marilyn B. Young is professor of history at New York University. A veteran of the antiwar and feminist movements of the 1960s and '70s, she is the author of *The Vietnam Wars, 1945–1990* (HarperPerennial, 1991), and editor or co-editor of several books including most recently *Human Rights and Revolutions* (Rowman & Littlefield, 2000). Her current project is a book about the Korean War.

Index

abortion, 59, 337
acid. *See* LSD
African Americans
   hippies resented, 12
   and Jimi Hendrix, 191, 193, 195, 204–8,
      213n59 (*see also* Hendrix, Jimi)
   in London, 196–98
   in police forces, 152n13
   radical heroes, 217
   and SFMT's *A Minstrel Show*, 75–76
   whites and black culture, 126–27, 169,
      301–2n13
   See also Black Panther Party; *and specific*
      individuals
AIDS, 234, 235, 237, 340
Albion College, 126
alcohol, 20
alienation, New Left's construction of, 110
Allen, Arthur, 191, 195
Allen, Lewis, 279
Allen, Pam, 52–54
"All Watched Over by Machines of Loving
   Grace" (Brautigan), 353–54
Alpert, Richard (Ram Dass), 22–24, 254,
   258, 336
alternative technology, 353–74
   appropriate technology (AT), 360–68
   energy technologies, 332, 362, 368–70
   information technology, 355, 363, 367,
      370–73

and postscarcity thinking, 354–55
   RAINBOOK illustration, **371**
   soft path, 368–69
   and the *Whole Earth Catalog*, 36, 362–68,
      372–73, 377n33
"Amateur versus Professional" (Deren),
   278–79
American Civil Liberties Union (ACLU), 71
Ananda World Brotherhood Village, 339
Anderson, Chester, 95n28
Anderson, Terry H., 217
Anderson, Wallace ("Mad Bear"), 168
Andrews, Lynn, 178
androgyny, 211–12n30
Ann Arbor, Michigan, 136, 138–39, 146–47.
   See also Trans-Love Energies
Anticipation of the Night (1958 film), 283, **284**
antiwar movement
   Anti-Military Balls, 73, 92–93n6
   antiwar skit in *A Minstrel Show*, 76
   and communal living, 340
   and the Festival of Life/Democratic
      Convention (1968), 44, 89–91 (*see also*
      Festival of Life)
   "Flipped Out Week," 113, **115**
   increasing numbers of, 251
   and Indianness, 164–66
   Kesey at 1965 Berkeley demonstration, 50,
      106
   media coverage, 291, 302n27

musical style, 194–95, 201, 204–5, 207–8, 211n24
on musicians, 254
racial distinctions rejected, 195, 204–5, 211n21
recordings, 199, 201, 202, 204, 207–8, 212n39, 213n50
stage antics, 197–200, 204
"Star-Spangled Banner," 190, 191, 209n3
violence rejected, 207
"Voodoo Child (Slight Return)," 191, 201, 207, 208
and whites, 191–93, 197–202, 212n41
at Woodstock, 189–90, 207
Higgins, John, 338
hippies
Be-Ins and Happenings, 44, **165**, 217, 250–51, 255–56
childlikeness aspired to, 253–54, 260
and communal living (*see* communes)
and the co-op movement, 118
"Death of Hippie," 36, 83, **84**, 261
and the Diggers, 81
dress, 166, 169, 251
drug use, 35 (*see also* drugs; LSD; marijuana)
feminists not usually hippies, 45
"flower child" phase (love ethic), 251–53, 261
goals, 217
Houseboat Summit, 258–60
vs. the New Left, 50, 100–101, 107–8, 218, 252
postscarcity orientation, 11–12
presentism, 255–58, 260
Reagan's definition, 6
sexuality and homophobia, 217–18 (*see also* sex)
as term, 11
and the underground press, 307–8
victimization of, 261
white hippies' privilege, 12, 17–18
Hoffman, Abbie, 35, 85–90, 96n35, 140–41, 169–70. *See also* Yippies
Hoffman, Dustin, 166, 298
Hofmann, Albert, 7, 20, 22
Holleran, Andrew, 233
Hollinger, David, 177
Hollingshead, Michael, 22, 49
Hollywood. *See* film
homophobia, 217–18
homosexuality. *See* gay/lesbian movement
Hoover, J. Edgar, 147
Hopper, Dennis, 1–2, 286

House Un-American Activities Committee, 9, 269
Howe, Irving, 102, 122n9
Hubbard, Alfred M., 49
Hughes, Walter, 231, 232–33
Hundred Flowers (underground paper), 309, 316
Huxley, Aldous, 7, 22, 49, 253

identity
charades (changing identity), 246, **247**, 251, 261, 269
gay identity, 222–23, 232–34, 237, 238n21
Indianness and American identity, 166–68, 176
lesbian identity, 226–27, 234
racial identity (*see* Hendrix, Jimi)
IMF. *See* International Monetary Fund
independent film. *See* underground film
Indian Country Today (journal), 181, 182
Indianness, 159–84
and American identity, 166–68, 176
and the antiwar movement, 164–66
attractions of, 162, 164, 183–84
and Chief Seattle's speech, 171–72
contradictory meanings, 163–64, 170–72, 179
as countercultural symbol, 164–71, **165**
and drug use, 164, 173
"Indian" communes, 159–61, 163–64, 183–84, **335**, 335–36, 346
Little Big Man (1970 film), 166
and the New Age, 174–82
and politics, 164–70
San Francisco "Pow-Wow," **165**
and spirituality, 172–79, 187n33, 188n46, 346
symbols of, 166, 169, 170, 180
See also Native Americans
individualism, 2, 231–32
Industrial Workers of the World (IWW), 118–19
information technology, 355, 363, 367, 370–73
International Monetary Fund (IMF), 237
Internet, 63–64, 373
intoxication, legal vs. illegal, 18, 19–20, 34, 38n13. *See also* alcohol; drugs; LSD; marijuana
Israel Family, 339–40

Jacobs, Paul, 76
Jameson, Fredric, 162
Jay, Karla, 218, 220–21, 236, 240n57. *See also* Out of the Closets

World Even if You Never Thought You Could, A Step-by-Step Guide to Social Action (Sommers), 61

NOW. *See* National Organization of Women

Noyes, John Humphrey, 329, 330

nudism, 329, 345–46

Nurriddin, Jalal, 207–8, 213–14n64

O'Jay, Eddie, 213n59

Old Left, 103–4

Olivia Records, 224

One Dimensional Man (Marcuse), 359

Oneida Community, 329, 330

Ono, Yoko, 169

oppression, as term, 64n3

Oracle (underground paper), 29

orphan myth, 267, **268**

Otis, Sheldon, 135

Oughton, Diana, 136

Out of the Closets: Voices of Gay Liberation (Jay and Young), 218, 220–23, 233, 236, 240n57

pacifism, 331. *See also* antiwar movement

Packer Corner Farm, 336

The Paper (underground paper), 309

Pardun, Robert, 108–9

Parker, Bonnie. *See Bonnie and Clyde*

Parker, Genie. *See* Plamondon, Genie (Parker)

parks, 73, 92n5, 136, **167**. *See also* guerrilla (street) theater

Parsons, Talcott, 7, 13n8

Peck, Abe, 96n39, 97n41

Penn, Arthur. *See Bonnie and Clyde*

Perez, Judy Schiffer, 108, 109, 115

personal, as political, 48, 99–100

"The Phonus Balonus Blues" (Crumb comic), 313–14

Pipkin, Paul, 115

Plamondon, Genie (Parker), 132, **141**, 148, 154n44

Plamondon, Lawrence Robert ("Pun"), 132, 138–39, **141**, 142–43, 145, 147–48, 150, 154n44

play

Bonnie and Clyde charade, 261–65

dance as, 247–48

hard play, 249–50

revolutionary play, 265–70

police

Austin police, 107

Detroit police force, 129–30, 134–36, 152n13, 153n16

and the Diggers, 84–85

increasing confrontations with, 144–45

racial makeup, 152n13

vs. Sinclair and the WPP/TLE, 130, 134–36, 138–39, 153n16

See also Federal Bureau of Investigation

politics

fusion with culture, 69

gay politics, 227–31, 235

Indianness and, 164–70, **167**

Leary and Kesey's antipolitical stance, 50, 106, 365

personal as political, 48, 99–100

political vs. apolitical movements, 69

protest film and, 290–98, **292**

See also Left; New Left; *specific parties and individuals*

pornzines, 312–13

postmodernism, 161–62, 164. *See also* multiculturalism

postscarcity society

and alternative technology, 354–55, 364

and communal living, 332, 334, 347

and the Diggers, 81–82

and the energy crisis, 368

New Left's view of, 111–12

and play, 249–50

postscarcity orientation, 11–12

Potter, Paul, 74

prescription drugs, 19–20

presentism, 255–58

Presley, Elvis, 192

Presmont, Jud, 340

Pridgeon, Faye, 205–6

Pueblos, 164

Pull My Daisy (1959 film), 279

"Pun." *See* Plamondon, Lawrence Robert

puppets, 83, 95n29

Quarry Hill, 330

Quashie, Mike, 195

Quayle, Marilyn, 234, 239n51

queer culture, 234–37. *See also* gay/lesbian movement

race

hybridity, 193, 210–11n17, 211n19 (*see also* Hendrix, Jimi)

in London, 196–98

and music, 192–93, 204–7, 210n14, 210n16, 213n59 (*see also* Hendrix, Jimi)

race riots, 8, 135–36, 251

transcendence of, 193, 212n41

See also African Americans; Indianness; Native Americans